THE
INSIDERS' GUIDE
TO
North Carolina's
CENTRAL COAST
& NEW BERN

THE INSIDERS' GUIDE® TO
North Carolina's
CENTRAL COAST
& NEW BERN

by
Tabbie Nance
and
Janis Williams

By The Sea
Publications
Inc.

Published and distributed by:
By The Sea Publications Inc.
Hanover Center P.O. Box 5386
Wilmington, NC 28403
1 (800) 955-1860

•

FIFTH EDITION
1st printing
Copyright ©1996
by By The Sea Publications Inc.
Jay Tervo, Publisher
Printed in the United States of America

•

This book is produced under a license granted by:
The Insiders' Guides Inc.
P.O. Box 2057
Manteo, NC 27954
(919) 473-6100

•

Special Thanks to Peter S. Vinal, an International Photographer
Top left, top right photos: NC Division of Tourism
bottom photo: Peter S. Vinal

•

•

ISBN 0-912367-95-4

Preface

Welcome to *The Insiders' Guide®* to *North Carolina's Central Coast and New Bern*. This book is designed to give you an Insider's perspective on this beautiful coastal area. Use it like a road map and keep it handy. If you are a newcomer, you'll learn about each area in our Area Overviews chapter. You'll discover favorite spots and special events. If you've been around awhile, you're sure to enjoy our sidebars and learn about a place or two you didn't know existed. Keep this guide handy for all your visiting relatives and friends.

This book is divided into two major parts. The first section deals with the beautiful Crystal Coast, which includes all of Carteret County and Swansboro. The nickname Crystal Coast was given to the Carteret County beach area several years ago by the Carteret County Chamber of Commerce. It was hoped the name would attract visitors to the county's crystal waters and brilliant beaches and it has. The second section of this book addresses the historic city of New Bern. Best known as the site of Tryon Palace, the city offers so much to visitors and guests. New Bern is the second-oldest town in North Carolina and is rich with history.

Besides the Crystal Coast and New Bern, you'll also discover information about our neighboring city of Havelock, home to Marine Corps Air Station Cherry Point and the associated Naval Aviation Depot. Have-lock is the largest city in Craven County and is continually growing.

We've packed this book with chapters that deal with just about every topic you can imagine, including History, Restaurants, Accommodations, Vacation Rentals, Shopping, Nightlife, Annual Events and Festivals, Camping and more. We even suggest places to launch and store your boat, have a picnic, get a surf report, rent a boat, go for a hike and play a round of golf. There are also chapters on schools, churches, relocation services, industry, sports and parks. The service directory offers a wealth of information including libraries, town halls, tax rates, emergency services and bus and taxi services. You'll also find information about buying or building a home.

Please be assured that the businesses featured in this guide are chosen from the many as being the best in the area. We decide which businesses to include based on their quality, their uniqueness or their popularity.

We've provided some general maps to help you see the overall picture. These are site detailed and should be used in conjunction with your regular road map. We also offer the following general hints. U.S. Highway 70 takes on a different name in each town it passes through: Main Street in Havelock; Arendell Street in Morehead City; and Cedar and Live Oak streets in Beaufort. N.C. Highway

58 takes on a new name in each of the beach towns it passes through: Fort Macon Road east or west in Atlantic Beach; Salter Path Road between Atlantic Beach and Indian Beach; and Emerald Drive in Emerald Isle.

The Crystal Coast, New Bern and Havelock are within the 919 telephone area code. A recent change brought a new area code, 910, to the area. The dividing line is at the Carteret County-Onslow County line, which is marked by the White Oak River. Phones on the Carteret County side remained in the 919 area code, and phones on the other side changed to 910. Because of this change, dial 910 to reach Swansboro and Wilmington. All telephone numbers in this book are in the 919 area code unless otherwise noted. Milepost numbers are given to help locate places on Bogue Banks.

We even offer daytrip itineraries to a few favorite getaway spots including Ocracoke, the Outer Banks, Wilmington, Oriental and Belhaven.

From a map, the entire area might seem to be little more than a highway. However, North Carolina's Crystal Coast and New Bern have much to offer visitors and residents. If you are visiting the area, don't expect to see it all in one trip. If you have relocated to the area, we urge you to spend a weekend now and then exploring the many treasures that surround you.

This is the fifth edition of *The Insiders' Guide® to the North Carolina's Central Coast and New Bern*. We've tried to include as many as the wonderful sights, sounds and tastes of the area as possible. We've done our best to ensure that all the information is accurate, however, we know there is always room for improvement. Let us know what you think so that future editions can accommodate your ideas and suggestions. Write to us in care of By The Sea Publications Inc., Hanover Center, Box 5386, Wilmington, North Carolina 28403.

Our hope is that the coast's lure and its varied pleasures will suit you as well as they do us and other Insiders. We trust this book will be a helpful guide to the area and that you will enjoy exploring, revisiting or living along North Carolina's Central Coast and in New Bern.

— Tabbie and Janis

Those of you familiar with this guide may be a bit surprised to note the name change on the front cover this year since our four previous editions were known as *The Insiders' Guide® to North Carolina's Crystal Coast and New Bern*. While the moniker Crystal Coast is familiar to locals, many of our prospective visitors don't recognize the name. We chose the name *The Insiders' Guide® to North Carolina's Central Coast and New Bern* in hopes that everyone who wants to find information about our seaside towns and crystal waters will be able to.

About the Authors

Tabbie Nance moved to Carteret County 14 years ago to work as a reporter/photographer for the local newspaper. A North Carolina native, she was reared on a small farm in Guilford County and graduated from High Point College with degrees in media communications and human relations. Tabbie's travels throughout the United States, New Zealand and Europe have given her a special insight into the kind of information travelers and newcomers want and need.

Tabbie is the director of school-community relations for the Carteret County School System. She is involved in various community volunteer activities, including serving on the Core Sound Waterfowl Museum board and as a child advocate through the court's guardian ad litem program. She also works as a freelance writer, and this is her fifth year as co-author of *The Insiders' Guide to North Carolina's Central Coast and New Bern*.

Tabbie lives in an old house in Beaufort that is slowly being fixed up. She enjoys running, biking, swimming and has completed an Ironman triathlon (2.4-mile swim, 112-mile cycle and 26.2-mile run) and hopes to do it again.

Janis Williams moved to Carteret County 16 years ago to publish an entertainment magazine, *The Maritimes*, with a friend. To their surprise, it worked, and they eventually learned how to do it. She worked as managing editor for eight years, sold it, and went into the retail clothing business. For six years she learned how that was done and, realizing that it wasn't the 1980s anymore, she closed the store and returned to editing. She is employed by *Coaster Magazine* where she keeps up with the Crystal Coast all year.

Winters Janis works with her husband managing the galley aboard their charter sailboat, *Good Fortune*, in the Florida Keys and Bahamas. She's also aboard whenever possible in the summers in Beaufort.

Photo: NC Travel and Tourism

Walking hand in hand along the beach is a great way to end a day along the Crystal Coast.

Acknowledgments

My part of this book couldn't have been completed without the help of many, many people. I am grateful to all those who shared with me and took time to lend a hand. My special thanks go to Havelock's Mary Kurek for her help with the Havelock section, to Jay for yet another edition and to Molly for her great patience. Thanks also to my parents — Buddy and Tabbie Nance, my sister — Miriam Lewis, and my best friend — Ralph Merrill, for always supporting and loving me. My continued gratitude goes to Rodney Kemp, a Moreheader with a contagious love for Carteret County, who taught me that this truly is the best place on earth.

— Tabbie

I would like to list the names of all the kind people who returned my calls and helped take the chase out of updating this year's book. Your names are numerous, and I will find you in 1996 to personally thank you face to face. The most enjoyable thing about updating this book is the face-to-face encounters in the winters which are always warm visits, and I really enjoyed that warmth this winter. I never thought I'd thank the telephone company for anything, but this year, the extended service from Morehead City to New Bern was a gift that deserves thanks. I really appreciate that, telephone company. It has kept me intimately in touch with New Bern. And thank you Ron, Mama and Jennifer for excusing my absences.

— Janis

One to one.
Person to person.
Face to face.
Welcome to
Personal Banking.

Welcome
to Wachovia.

Main Office	Main Office
New Bern	Morehead City
401 Tryon Palace Drive	800 Arendell Street
New Bern, NC 28563	Morehead City, NC
(919) 638-6121	(919) 726-7181

Table of Contents

Directory of Maps

Photo: Scott Taylor

A young bird stands sentinel, waiting on breakfast.

Beaufort is a favorite stop for boaters on the north-south Intracoastal Waterway run.

Crystal Coast
Getting Around

Whether by land, sea or air, more and more people are coming year round to visit or relocate to the Crystal Coast and historic New Bern. Getting to the area is half the fun by sea or air, but 95 percent of the millions who visit our shores annually arrive on land.

By Land

If you're coming to the area from the north or south, Interstate 95 or U.S. Highway 17 will take you to either U.S. Highway 70 and on to Morehead City or to N.C. Highway 58 which leads straight to Emerald Isle. From the west, Interstate 40 will also take you to Highway 70, which leads directly to Morehead City. From the east, travelers who will persevere to see the last of North Carolina's Outer Banks after Ocracoke must reserve space for the 2¼-hour ferry ride to Cedar Island. At the ferry landing, N.C. Highway 12 continues a short distance to intersect with Highway 70 W. at the town of Atlantic, the highway's point of origin. (Interestingly enough, it ends in Los Angeles.) From here, it's an astonishing ride through lowland fields of junkus and spartina marsh grasses and Down East fishing villages to Beaufort and the Crystal Coast or on to Havelock and New Bern.

Between Morehead City and Emerald Isle or Swansboro, the main thoroughfare is N.C. Highway 24. This partially four-lane highway offers lovely views of Bogue Sound as you cross its bridges at Broad Creek and Gales Creek. Work is now in progress to complete the four-laning of Highway 24.

On the island of Bogue Banks, Highway 58 runs parallel to the beach for more than 20 miles from Atlantic Beach west to Emerald Isle. Milepost markers along the way make it easy to locate anything. Mile 1 (MP 1) begins at Fort Macon State Park on the east end of the island.

Daily bus service by Carolina Trailways, 726-3029, arrives in Morehead City at 105 N. 13th Street. Connections to Morehead City from all directions are made in Raleigh.

By Air

Passenger airline service is available at several airports convenient to the coastal area. You can reach New Bern by commercial carrier, or you can fly into New Bern or Beaufort by private plane. Flights directly to the Crystal Coast are accommodated at the area's only airport in Beaufort.

Beaufort's **Michael J. Smith Airport**, N.C. Highway 101, Beaufort, 728-1777, has no landing fee but charges for overnight storage of aircraft. Rental cars, an airport courtesy car and taxi service are available. Charter service is also available. Beaufort Aviation is the fixed-base operator and handles all fueling, rentals, flight instruction, charters and sightseeing flights. The airport was named for Capt. Michael J. Smith, a Beaufort native who died aboard the space shuttle *Challenger*.

The **Craven County Regional Airport**, Highway 70 in New Bern, 638-8591, is the closest airport to Morehead City. Daily flights by USAir Express take passengers to the large hub airport of Charlotte. Charter services are available with Carolina Air, 633-1400. For information about car rental agencies based at the airport, see the New Bern Service Directory chapter of this book.

The **Albert Ellis Airport** in Jacksonville, (910) 324-1100, is 20 miles west of Jacksonville toward the town of Richlands. It is the closest airport to Camp Lejeune, the U.S. Marine Corps Base at Jacksonville. The airport offers commuter service of USAir, Henson and ASA Delta to the hubs of Charlotte and Atlanta.

The **Raleigh-Durham International Airport** in the Triangle Area, 840-2123, is the major international airport in the middle part of the state and is about a 3-hour drive from the Crystal Coast. The airport is a major hub for domestic and international travelers and is served by all major and several feeder carriers.

By Sea

The Intracoastal Waterway (ICW) provides access by water to the Crystal Coast via Morehead City, Beaufort, Swansboro and Emerald Isle. To reach New Bern by water, slip into Pamlico Sound and head up the Neuse River. Beaufort is a favorite stop for boaters on the north-south ICW run. Transient dockage at either the Beaufort Town Docks or Town Creek Marina is hospitable, and anchorage is plentiful in the town's harbor of refuge north of the Grayden Paul drawbridge or in the designated anchorage off the town's waterfront. See our Marinas chapter for details.

Once You're Here

When you get to either New Bern or the Crystal Coast, you'll find that a car is almost essential. There isn't a public transportation service in either place, and a look at the map will show you that most communities are far enough apart to make a car a must. Each of the major towns has one or more cab companies to supplement transportation, but a car of your own is the best way to get around.

If you've brought your bicycle, there are some marked bike routes, but remember you're in a tourist area, and vehicle traffic is often heavy. Beaufort has a marked bike route; a routing guide is available at the Welcome Center on Turner Street. Biking in residential developments on Bogue Banks and in Morehead City neighborhoods is safe and pleasant. Improvements on the Atlantic Beach Causeway that will be completed by summer 1996 include biking and walking paths to link Atlantic Beach with Morehead City in relative safety.

Now, about the roads within the area.

Highway 70 is generally very easy to drive from New Bern through Havelock

Insiders' Tips

Crystal Coast beaches face south rather than east from the southern point of Core Banks at Cape Lookout to the west end of Bogue Banks. Therefore, the sun rises and sets on the ocean here, and the north wind calms the sea close to the beaches.

and on to Morehead City, Beaufort and Down East. From Beaufort east, however, Highway 70 is a two-lane highway that winds through marshes and between canals, but the road is adequately wide and always in excellent repair. An important detail to remember about Highway 70 is that it has many names as it traverses Carteret County. In Morehead City, it's Arendell Street, the main street through town. It's also the Morehead-Beaufort Causeway. In Beaufort, it's called Cedar Street until it takes a left turn and becomes Live Oak Street. And by any name, it's always heavily trafficked.

Upon arrival in the Crystal Coast area, stop at one of the Carteret County Tourism Development Bureau's visitors centers: in Morehead City at 3409 Arendell Street next to North Carolina's Institute of Marine Sciences; in Cape Carteret on Highway 58 at the bridge to Emerald Isle; and at the North Carolina Ferry Division's visitors center at the Cedar Island terminal. The friendly staff at all locations will offer you maps and brochures and will answer your immediate questions. As you will find, there is much to see and do on the Crystal Coast. It's also a beautiful destination for doing nothing at all. Whatever you choose, you have an enviable exploration ahead.

We support the community with no strings attached. (Or wires, for that matter.)

Whether we're running ads in a publication like this one, sponsoring

local events, or providing cellular phones for emergencies,

360° Communications is proud to support the communities it serves.

Call 1-800-409-4343 for details.

360° Communications

Crystal Coast
Area Overviews

North Carolina's Central Coast, or as we call it, the Crystal Coast, is such a diverse and dynamic place that just one introduction to the entire area wouldn't do it justice. So, we have divided the county into geographic sections in hopes of helping you easily find your way. Each chapter of this book features information in the following order: Bogue Banks, Beaufort, Morehead City, Swansboro, Down East and western Carteret County. If you are looking for a restaurant on the beach, go to the Restaurants chapter and look for the Bogue Banks section. If you're looking for accommodations in Beaufort, go to that chapter and flip to the Beaufort section.

We're starting the Crystal Coast section of the book with a brief introduction to each geographic area. The chapters that follow focus on specific subjects such as shopping, restaurants, attractions, marinas, fishing and watersports, neighborhoods and schools. There is also a service directory complete with all types of information ranging from emergency numbers to libraries to tax rates to utilities.

You're sure to find the information in this book helpful, and you'll learn a little bit more about the area as you go through this book. There is a lot to enjoy on the Crystal Coast, so take your time. We'll still be here!

As N.C. Highway 58 passes through the different communities, it often takes on a new name. In Atlantic Beach, it is called Fort Macon Road. East Fort Macon Road is the strip between the old fort and the main intersection in town. West Fort Macon Road is the strip between that intersection and the western edge of town. The longest stretch of the highway is called Salter Path Road: It stretches from Atlantic Beach, through Pine Knoll Shores, Indian Beach and Salter Path. In Emerald Isle, the highway is called Emerald Drive. It really isn't as confusing as it sounds — it's just one road with lots of names.

Bogue Banks

Bogue Banks is the narrow island almost parallel to Morehead City and N.C. Highway 24. It begins at Fort Macon in Atlantic Beach on the east and stretches to Emerald Isle on the west. The 30-mile-long island is connected to the mainland by a high-rise bridge at each end. Because the island continues to attract visitors and summer residents, there are many second homes, condominiums and hotels on the island.

N.C. Highway 58 extends the length of the island. Along the way it is marked with mileposts (MP). The MP series begins with mile 1 at the east end of the island and continues along the road to mile 21 on the west end. Throughout this book, we have given the MP as part of the address for places on Bogue Banks.

The great majority of Bogue Banks development, both business and residential, is along Highway 58. A ride from one end of the island to the other on Highway 58 and down a few of the side streets can give you a quick overview of the island communities and what is offered. From several points along the road you can see the sound and the ocean at the same time.

There are basically five townships on the island, although they tend to blend together. Atlantic Beach is at the far east end of the island and borders the town of Pine Knoll Shores. Indian Beach surrounds the small unincorporated community of Salter Path, and Emerald Isle is at the far west end of the island. Each town has its own personality and points of interest. Glancing at the maps in this chapter might help you get an overall picture of how these towns combine into Bogue Banks.

Atlantic Beach

A pavilion built on the beach in 1887 seemed to give birth to Atlantic Beach. That one-story building had a refreshment stand and areas for changing clothes. The popularity of surf bathing was growing, and guests at the Atlantic Hotel in Morehead City (which stood at the site of today's Jefferson Motor Lodge) were taken to the sound side of Atlantic Beach by sailboat. The guests then walked across the island to the pavilion, which faced the ocean.

Later, a large two-story pavilion was built on the island, and a boardwalk was built from the dock to the pavilion. Supplies were carted over the sand dunes by ox cart. In 1916, the first pavilion and 100 acres were bought by Von Bedsworth and the 100-room Atlantic View Beach Hotel was built. The hotel later burned. By 1928, a group of county citizens developed a plan, built a toll bridge from Morehead City to today's Atlantic Beach, and constructed a beach resort complete with a dining area, bathhouses and a pavilion. Just a short year later, the entire complex was destroyed by fire. A New York bank took possession of the property, and a new hotel was built. In 1936 the bridge was sold to the state, and the toll charges were dropped. In 1945 Morehead City resident Alfred Cooper bought the property, and in 1953 a drawbridge replaced the old bridge. In the late 1980s, the drawbridge was replaced by the high-rise bridge.

Today, Atlantic Beach has a year-round population of about 3,000 that swells to about 35,000 during the summer. The current town board and residents are working to improve the waterfront area known as The Circle, found at the southernmost end of the Atlantic Beach Causeway, which will also be getting a facelift in 1996.

Pine Knoll Shores

Incorporated in 1973, Pine Knoll Shores is in the center of Bogue Banks. This planned community was developed by heirs of Theodore Roosevelt and is called one of the state's most ecologically

Wave Away The World

At Atlantic Beach you can hide away on beaches that are intimate and peaceful... leave the hurried world behind and spend your vacation days stretching endlessly in time.

A Place At The Beach, Sands Villa Resort and SeaSpray offer oceanfront condominiums with full amenities. Relax in our indoor/outdoor pools and whirlpools or perfect your tennis game on our lighted courts. We'll be happy to arrange tee-times for golfers on any of our 12 nearby courses or arrange charter boats for off-shore angling.

For a day off the beach, our surrounding historic town offers quaint and inviting shopping and antique treasures.

The Sands Kids Club keeps kids busy flying kites, treasure hunting, building sand castles and trips to the Aquarium. We even have a summer baby sitting service for kids aged 2-10 when parents want their own fun.

Visit us soon. We promise you'll leave with some sand in your shoes and plenty of memories that will make you want to return for more. For reservations, brochures and information on our condominium sales call **1-800-334-2667** ext. 34.

**Sands
Oceanfront
Resorts**

Local: **919-247-2636** Ft. Macon Rd. Atlantic Beach, N.C. 28512 Fax: 919-247-1067

sensitive communities. The town's 1,400 residents share their community with the N.C. Aquarium, Theodore Roosevelt Natural Area and the Bogue Banks Public Library.

The N.C. Aquarium is one of the state's three aquariums. It offers educational exhibits, displays and a meeting area for civic and special-interest groups (see the Attractions chapter). Theodore Roosevelt Natural Area is a 265-acre maritime forest owned and protected by the state (see the Attractions chapter). The natural area lies around the N.C. Aquarium and is one of the few remaining maritime forests on North Carolina's barrier islands.

Pine Knoll Shores officials stress the importance of protecting existing maritime forests in town and enforce regulations that restrict the amount of maritime for-

est acreage that can be cleared for development. The town itself owns significant forest tracts.

A historic marker stands at the corner of Highway 58 and Roosevelt Boulevard noting the area of the first landing of Europeans on the North Carolina coast. Giovanni da Verrazzano, a Florentine navigator in the service of France, explored the state's coast from Cape Fear north to Kitty Hawk in 1524. His voyage along the coast marked the first recorded European contact with what is now North Carolina.

Indian Beach

Indian Beach is a resort and residential town near the center of Bogue Banks. Incorporated in 1973, the town offers residents and visitors a fishing pier and wide, beautiful beaches for sunbathing, surf fishing and watersports. Quite a few condominiums, camping areas and restaurants are in this area and are profiled in various chapters within the Crystal Coast section.

The town surrounds the unincorporated community of Salter Path creating an east Indian Beach and a west Indian Beach.

Salter Path

Much of the quaintness of Salter Path was lost when modern development began moving in. Now, the community's modest homes seem crowded together. But the character of the community can still be seen in the close family ties, the fishing boats beside the homes and the fish nets being mended in the yards.

In the late 1890s the first families to settle in Salter Path came over from Diamond City, which at the time was the largest community on Shackleford Banks, a 9-mile-long island that is now part of Cape Lookout National Seashore. Diamond City was a whaling community, and a large hill in the center of town was used as a lookout. Once a whale was spotted, the men would jump into boats and row after the whale and, if successful, harpoon and kill the creature.

By 1897, about 500 people lived in Diamond City and had erected stores, a school, a post office and church buildings. Two hard storms in the late 1890s convinced many Diamond City residents it was time to leave the island. Houses were cut into sections, tied to skiffs and floated or sailed across the water. Once at the new homesites, the houses were reconstructed. Many settled on Harkers Island, in the Shackleford Street area of Morehead City or in Salter Path.

Legend has it that the name Salter Path originated with Joshua Salter, a Broad Creek area resident who often came by boat from the mainland to the beach area to fish and hunt. He made a path from the sound area where he anchored his boat to the oceanfront. Folks called the walkway Salter's Path, and the name stuck.

Many locals credit the early residents of Salter Path with bringing shrimp into the culinary limelight. These plentiful creatures were once considered only a menace by fishermen. After local residents began to eat them, the seafood soon became a marketable item throughout the county and all coastal areas.

Emerald Isle

Stories say this end of the island was originally home to nomadic Indians and whalers. It is also said that about 15 families, perhaps from Diamond City, came here in 1893 and settled at Middletown, a small section of the island that is now part of Emerald Isle.

Other than those small groups, Emerald Isle was largely unsettled until the 1950s. Several years after Atlantic Beach was developed as a seashore resort, a Philadelphia man named Henry K. Fort

When you're in doubt about directions, stop and ask a local. Chances are you'll meet a friendly person and learn a lot about the area.

Insiders' Tips

bought the land that now makes up most of Emerald Isle and about 500 more acres on the mainland in what is today the town of Cape Carteret. Fort planned to tie the two areas together with a bridge and develop a large resort. When support for constructing a bridge could not be raised from the state or county, he abandoned the project. A ferry was later operated in the area where he had hoped to put a bridge. The ferry carried motorists and pedestrians between the beach and mainland and landed on the beach near Bogue Inlet Pier, which was the first recreational spot at the island's west end.

Today, a modern high-rise bridge provides guests access from the mainland to Emerald Isle and the western end of Bogue Banks. The Cameron Langston Bridge spans the Atlantic Intracoastal Waterway and from the top provides a great view of area land formations, the waterway and Bogue Banks.

Emerald Isle has a year-round population of 2,434 and a seasonal population of 16,000. The town's $1.4 million municipal complex and community center offers large meeting rooms, a full basketball court and a gym area (see the Sports, Fitness and Parks chapter). The town's

residential and business sections line Emerald Drive (Highway 58). Several new housing areas have been developed west of the high-rise bridge in the area surrounding the Coast Guard Station.

Last summer *Business North Carolina* magazine placed Emerald Isle as number seven in the "Top Ten Tarheel Towns Overall."

Beaufort

Beaufort is a small seaport brimming with charm and history. Once you walk along the wooden boardwalk and quiet tree-lined streets, hear the tolling church bells and smell the salt air, you will come to understand the special feeling Beaufort gives.

Beaufort is the third-oldest town in North Carolina and was named for Henry Somerset, the Duke of Beaufort. The town was surveyed in 1713, nearly 20 years before George Washington's birth. Beaufort was incorporated in 1722 and has been the seat of Carteret County since that time. The English influence is apparent in the architecture and, more noticeably, in the street names: Ann and Queen, for Queen Anne; Craven, for the Earl of Craven; Orange, for William the Prince of Orange; Moore, for Col. Maurice Moore; and Pollock, for the governor at the time of the survey.

Beaufort offers a glimpse at a relatively unspoiled part of North Carolina's coastal history. The town has made great strides in the restoration of many of its oldest structures. Much of that can be credited to the Beaufort Historical Association, which was organized in 1960 to celebrate the town's 250th anniversary. The first home "plaqued" was the Duncan House, c. 1790, at 105 Front Street. To be plaqued, a home must be at least 80 years old and have retained its historic and architectural integrity. Through the years, the Beaufort Historical Association has moved old structures threatened with demolition to an area on Turner Street. For more information about the Beaufort Historic Site see the Attractions chapter.

The town's designated historic district is between Gallant's Channel and the east side of Pollock Street and between Taylor's Creek and the south side of Broad Street. (Gallant's Channel flows under the drawbridge and Taylor's Creek is the body of water faced by the boardwalk.) The one-block area of the county courthouse is also included in the historic district.

Beaufort's historic houses and sites each have their own story to tell. Many structures and areas are listed on the National Register of Historic Places. The house with the most lively history is the Hammock House of 1698, which is considered Beaufort's oldest standing house. It once stood so close to the water that visitors could tie a skiff to the front porch. Through the years, dredging changed the creek's course, and now the house stands one block back from the creek. The house later served as an inn or "ordinary" and Blackbeard, the fiercest of all pirates, was a regular guest. Legend has it that Blackbeard hung one of his wives from a live oak in the front yard, and neighbors can still hear her screams on moonlit nights. Now privately owned, the house was used as accommodations by the Union Army during the Civil War.

The Old Burying Ground on Ann Street is an interesting place to wander and look at grave markers and the messages they bear. Deeded to the town in 1731, the Old Burying Ground was declared full in 1825, and the General Assembly said no more burials would be allowed. The town was ordered to lay out a new graveyard, but the townspeople did not support the act and

Beaufort
DOWNTOWN

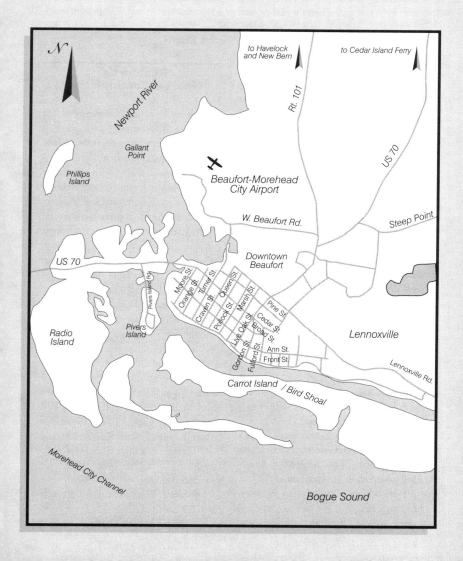

N

to Havelock
and New Bern

to Cedar Island Ferry

Rt. 101

Newport River

Gallant
Point

US 70

Phillips
Island

Beaufort-Morehead
City Airport

W. Beaufort Rd.

Steep Point

US 70

Downtown
Beaufort

Pivers Island Rd.

Moore St.

Orange St.

Turner St.

Craven St.

Queen St.

Pollock St.

Marsh St.

Live Oak St.

Cedar St.

Pine St.

Broad St.

Gordon St.

Fulford St.

Ann St.

Front St.

Radio
Island

Pivers
Island

Lennoxville

Lennoxville Rd.

Carrot Island / Bird Shoal

Morehead City Channel

Bogue Sound

continued to bury their loved ones in the Old Burying Ground until the early 1900s. The north corner of the graveyard is the oldest section.

There are many interesting graves in the grounds, and tours are often given by the Beaufort Historical Association. Those buried here include Capt. Josiah Pender, whose men took Fort Macon in 1861; James W. Hunt, who had the distinction of marrying, making his will and dying the same day; Esther Cooke, mother of Capt. James W. Cooke, who once commanded the Ironclad *Albemarle*; the Dill child, who was buried in a glass-top casket; the common grave of the *Crissie Wright* crew, who froze to death when the ship wrecked on Shackleford Banks in 1886; and the child who died aboard a ship and was brought to Beaufort in a keg of rum for burial — keg and all.

With the town's waterfront revitalization project in the late 1970s, Beaufort took a new direction. The renovation involved tearing down many old waterfront structures not considered salvageable and building the existing wooden boardwalk, docks and facilities. With this, businesses were encouraged to stay or move to the downtown waterfront. Soon word of the "new" old town spread, and it hasn't been the same since. What was once a coastal hideaway is now a favorite spot for visitors traveling by car or boat.

As you enter Beaufort from the west, you will cross the Grayden M. Paul Bridge. The bridge's namesake was a lively 96-year-old historian, best known for his songs, poems and tales about Beaufort and Carteret County. He lived on Front Street with his wife, Mary Clark, until his death in the summer of 1994.

Drawbridges in coastal areas are slowly becoming things of the past as more and more towns are choosing to replace these romantic bridges with concrete high-rises. And that's the case for this old landmark. Because of the increased traffic, plans are in the works to replace the drawbridge in the next few years. The only sticking point is where to locate the new high-rise bridge.

Beaufort is home to a number of attractions, including the North Carolina Maritime Museum and Watercraft Center and the Rachel Carson Component of the North Carolina National Estuarine Research Reserve.

Beaufort's Nearby Communities

Lennoxville is the community closest to Beaufort. The area begins at the east end of Front Street and continues to the east end of Lennoxville Road. This is primarily a residential area with the exception of Beaufort Fisheries and Atlantic Veneer (see the Commerce and Industry chapter). At one time, there were several tomato canneries in the community. Lennoxville is surrounded by water: Taylor's Creek on the south and North River on the north. New developments continue to spring up along the forested waterfront areas of Lennoxville.

North River is a small community that lies to the north of Beaufort on Merrimon Road. The community can be reached by traveling east on U.S. Highway 70 out of Beaufort and continuing straight at East Carteret High School. (A right turn at the school would take you to the Down East area.) Baseball pitcher Brien Taylor put the community of North River on the map in 1991 when, as a high school senior, he signed a $1.55 million contract with the New York Yankees.

The **South River** community actually lies to the north of the North River community. Named for the body of water it nestles beside, South River is primarily a fishing-based community. Many of this community's early residents came from Lukens. Today, much of the land is owned by recreational hunters and businesses, and there are several private airstrips in the area. Many artifacts and Indian pottery pieces have been found in the South River area throughout the years.

The community of **Merrimon** lies to the west of South River. This rural area borders the Neuse River and Adams Creek, which is a stretch of the scenic Intracoastal Waterway. The seaport of Oriental is just across the Neuse River and, on most days, is visible.

In recent years, a few neighborhood developments have sprung up around South River, Merrimon and the Intracoastal Waterway. Sportsman's Village, Jonaquin's Landing and Indian Summer Estates offer waterfront and mainland lots.

Harlowe is the community that lies off N.C. Highway 101 between Beaufort and Havelock. Part of the community is in Carteret County and part is in Craven County. Harlowe is, and always has been, primarily a farming area.

Morehead City

Morehead City is the county's largest city. A look into the history of the city starts with an early land prospector from Virginia by the name of John Shackleford. In 1714, Shackleford saw a future for the area and purchased 170 acres at the mouth of the Newport River, stretching from Bogue Sound on the south to Calico Creek on the north.

The land became known as Shepard's Point after it was purchased in 1723 by David Shepard. The community grew but was not incorporated until 1861.

In 1852 the state decided to extend a railroad line to connect Raleigh with the coast; several towns vied for the location since it would bring growth to their communities. For a while, it was considered inevitable that it would end in Beaufort. To make a bid for the rail business, a new town named Carolina City was formed by the Carolina City Company. The company purchased 1,000 acres at the western end of the Shepard's Point land, and Carolina City lots went on sale in 1855.

John Motley Morehead, who was elected governor of the state in 1840 and again in 1842, came to the coast in 1856 when he was put in charge of extending the railroad to the coast. He began to buy land in what is now, appropriately, Morehead City. In 1857, he began selling lots at public auction. (Gov. Morehead also established the planetarium in Chapel Hill, a state school for the blind and the school of business at the University of North Carolina at Chapel Hill.)

In May 1858, Gov. Morehead described the area: "The City of Morehead is situated on a beautiful neck of land or dry plain, almost entirely surrounded by salt water; its climate salubrious; its sea breezes and sea bathing delightful; its drinking water good and its fine chalybeate spring, strongly impregnated with sulfur, will make it a pleasant watering place . . . ."

The sale of the land was successful, Gov. Morehead was successful in his bid for the end of the railroad, and Morehead City was incorporated. When the N.C. Legislature authorized the incorporation of the town, surveyors laid out the streets and named the primary ones after men who had been influential in the settlement of the area — Fisher, Arendell, Bridges, Evans, Shackleford and Shepard.

At that time, the only roads entering the county were sandy, narrow lanes, so most of the influential visitors arrived by rail, steamer or sailboat.

One of the first commercial buildings in Morehead City was the Macon Hotel at the corner of Arendell and Ninth streets. Constructed in 1860, this three-story building was a landmark for 80-some years.

The town was started just in time to be taken over by the Union forces when they attacked Fort Macon on April 26, 1862, thus ending for a time any significant development. Even after the end of the War Between the States, Morehead City was not able to get its commercial life active again until about 1880 when the shipping industry began to bring business to town. In the early 1880s, a new Atlantic Hotel was built in Morehead City, replacing the old Atlantic Hotel that had been destroyed by a hurricane. Located where the Jefferson Motor Lodge now stands, the Atlantic Hotel had 233 rooms and claimed to have the largest ballroom in the South. It drew the cream of the state's society to the coast until it was destroyed by fire in 1933.

In 1911, the city began a road improvement program to alternately "pave the way" and keep up with the town's slow but steady growth.

Crab Point is one area that grew as a result of road improvement. Crab Point is what Moreheaders call that part of the city that is east of Country Club Road and north of the 20th Street Bridge over Calico Creek. The area got its name because when tides came in crabs got trapped on the shoreline, making them an easy catch. In the early days, Crab Point served as a port and had windmills for grinding grain and generating power for lumber companies. A private cemetery in the area has graves dating back to the early 1700s.

Today, Morehead City continues to grow and to offer many services to residents and visitors. The town has recently

incorporated several areas along its western border and the North Carolina Department of Transportation is planning to make major road improvements along Highway 70/Arendell Street within the next five to six years.

The most visible changes taking place in town are along the waterfront. Morehead City's leaders have provided for a major facelift of the downtown waterfront area that includes wide sidewalks, new docks, bathroom facilities and parks. This project should be substantially completed in June or July 1996, although phases of the project will continue to be handled throughout the summer.

Swansboro

From its origins as the site of an Algonquian Indian village at the mouth of the White Oak River to its current status as the "Friendly City by the Sea," Swansboro is a lovely place to visit, because of its relatively mild climate and its warm and friendly residents.

The history of the town of Swansboro began about 1730, when Jonathan and Grace Green moved from Falmouth, Massachusetts, to the mouth of the White Oak River. With them, and owning half of their property, was Jonathan Green's brother, Isaac. They lived there about five years until Jonathan Green died at the early age of 35. His widow married Theophilus Weeks, who had moved with his family from Falmouth to settle on Hadnot Creek a few miles up the White Oak River.

After their marriage, the Weekses moved into the Green family home on the Onslow County side of the White Oak River. Theophilus soon purchased the interest of Isaac Green to become sole owner of the large plantation. Weeks first farmed, then opened a tavern and was appointed inspector of exports at the thriving port. In 1771, he started a town on that portion of his plantation called Weeks Wharf, selling 48 numbered lots recorded as being "in the plan of a town laid out by Theophilus Weeks," thus earning him the title of founder of the town.

Originally called Week's Point, the New-Town-upon-Bogue was established by law in 1783. The General Assembly named the town Swannsborough, in honor of Samuel Swann, former speaker of the N.C. House of Representatives and longtime Onslow County representative.

Another name that became well-known in Swansboro (the later version of

Down East

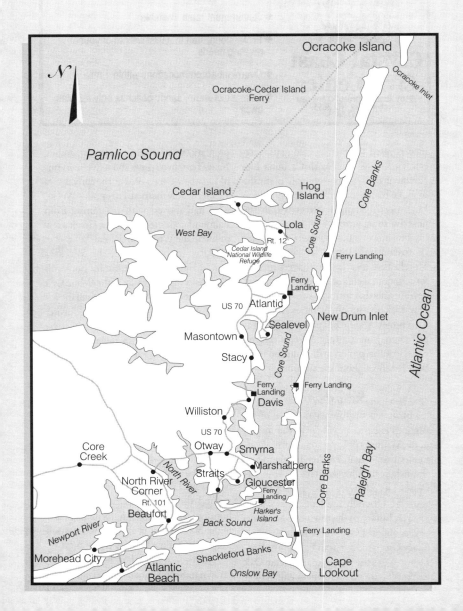

the town's name) was that of Otway Burns. During the War of 1812, this native son became a privateer with his schooner, the *Snapdragon*. His participation during this "Second War of Independence" was acclaimed as an act of bravery and patriotism. After the war, he returned to the trade of ship building and was later appointed keeper of the lighthouse at Portsmouth where he died in 1850. He is buried in Beaufort's Old Burying Ground.

Swansboro's port continued to prosper, particularly because of the nearby pine forests that produced the lumber, tar, pitch and other naval items shipped through the port. It continued to prosper until the end of the War Between the States. Then, gradually, the town came to support itself with farming and fishing.

The town is water-oriented, situated on the Intracoastal Waterway and along the mouth of the White Oak River, with the Atlantic Ocean easily accessible through Bogue Inlet. A good many fishing boats call Swansboro home port, and many residents keep sportfishing boats at marinas in Swansboro or Cedar Point.

The town's historic commission supervises the restoration of many of the town's oldest structures. Several of these fine structures now house businesses, while others remain private residences.

Down East

The term "Down East" refers to the area that stretches from the North River on the east side of Beaufort to Cedar Island. This is a beautiful area that includes marshes, canals and undisturbed areas, particularly as you get closer to Cedar Island.

In the past, the livelihood of the Down East people depended on the water. Today, some still rely on the water, but many work in Beaufort or Morehead City or travel to Air Station Cherry Point in Havelock. Still, that tie and love for the water is obvious by the number of boats, fish houses and seafood businesses.

There are no incorporated towns in the Down East area, so it is governed by the county. Activities center around the schools, churches, volunteer fire and rescue squads, post offices and local stores. Most of the communities lie along Highway 70, which is the main road in the Down East area. The history of this area is rich and could fill volumes. We'll just give you a very brief overview of the area, and invite you to explore it on your own.

Bettie is the first Down East community you reach after leaving Beaufort on Highway 70. It lies between the North River Bridge and the Ward's Creek Bridge. The next community is **Otway**, named for famous privateer Otway Burns, who is buried in Beaufort's Old Burying Ground.

Straits is the name of the community that surrounds the road going to Harkers Island. It is also the name of the body of water that lies between the Straits community and the island. The spelling of Straits is shown on early maps as "Straights." Later, cartographers probably noticed the name was not applicable to a water course, so they changed the spelling to Straits, meaning narrows. Years ago, Straits was a farm community, and a substantial amount of cotton was grown here. Straits United Methodist Church, c. 1778, was the first Methodist Church built east of Beaufort.

Originally called Craney Island, **Harkers Island** was once the home of a thriving band of Tuscarora Indians. By the turn of the 20th century, all that remained of the native Indian settlement was a huge mound of sea shells at the east end of the island, now called Shell Point. Folks say the Indians were attempting to build a shell walkway through the water to Core Banks. Standing at Shell Point today, you can see the Cape Lookout Lighthouse and nearby islands.

In 1730, George Pollock sold the island to Ebenezer Harker of Boston, Massachusetts, who began living on the island. Later he divided the island among his three sons, and the divisions he used, "eastard," "westard" and "center," have remained unofficial dividers ever since. The Harker heirs did not part with their land for years, so the island population remained sparse. By 1895 there were still fewer than 30 families living on the island. The population grew when folks from the Shackleford Banks community of Diamond City left because of the devastation of hurricanes. Some loaded homes on boats and brought them to this safer ground. With this new surge in population, schools, churches and businesses sprang up. Still, the island was isolated. Ferry operations to the mainland began in 1926, with the ferry leaving from the west end of the island and docking in the Gloucester community. A bridge to the island was built in 1941. The island is home to the Core Sound Waterfowl Museum and the Cape Lookout National Park Service Office.

Average Annual Air and Water Temperatures along North Carolina's Crystal Coast:

	Low	High	Water
January	32	53	50
April	48	75	59
July	69	88	78
October	51	75	70

INSIDERS' GUIDE
SHOWCASE

Photo: NC Travel & Tourism

Now, where did I leave that shovel?

The **Smyrna** community was named in 1785 from a deed that conveyed 100 acres from Joseph Davis to Seth Williston. The land was on Smunar Creek, and the spelling was later changed to Smyrna.

Deep Hole Point was the first name for **Marshallberg**. Folks say that clay was dug from the area and used to fill ramparts and cover easements at Fort Macon, leaving a large hole, thus the name. It was later named for Matt Marshall, who ran the mailboat from Beaufort.

Marshallberg lies on a peninsula formed by Sleepy Creek and Core Sound.

Graham Academy was established in Marshallberg by W.Q.A. Graham in 1880 at the head of Sleepy Creek. Curriculum prepared students for college, and students who did not live in town stayed in the school's dormitories. Monthly board was about $5.50 per student, and the school's attendance in 1892 was 126. The Academy was destroyed by fire in 1910.

Gloucester was named in the early 1900s by Capt. Joseph Pigott for the Massachusetts town that he loved. A ferry once ran between Gloucester and Harkers Island.

Williston was named for John Williston who was one of the area's first settlers. The community has long been nicknamed "Beantown," though why is still a point of confusion. Some say it was because of the large amount of beans that were grown in the community, and others say it was because residents had a reputation for loving beans. Williston United Methodist Church was built in 1883.

Davis was settled by William T. Davis in the 1700s and was a farming village. People worked the water and the land to make a living. Farm crops, such as cotton and sweet potatoes, were taken by sailboat to Virginia to be sold or traded for

needed items (flour, sugar, cloth). Davis residents were known as "Onion Eaters," either because of the number of green onions grown in the community or because Davis Shore people simply liked onions. An Army camp was opened in Davis during World War II, and some of the old camp buildings remain along the water's edge.

Stacy is really made up of two even smaller communities: Masontown and Piney Point. The post office was opened in 1885. Stacy Freewill Baptist Church is more than 100 years old.

Originally called Wit, **Sea Level** is still the fishing community it has always been. In 1706, Capt. John Nelson was granted about 650 acres by the King of England, and that land is today's Sea Level. Sailors' Snug Harbor, the oldest charitable trust in America, opened a fa-

Menhaden Industry

Jule Wheatly remembers when Beaufort merchants used their sense of smell as an economic indicator. They could judge the winter business season by the smell in the air. When merchants and residents awoke to the smell of fish cooking at the town's menhaden plants, they knew things were going well and money was coming into the town.

When the 46-year-old president and general manager of Beaufort Fisheries was growing up, Beaufort was home to three menhaden plants, and there were just as many in Morehead City. Now, his is the only plant left in the county.

"The town of Beaufort's first name was Fishtowne," Wheatly said. "I remember when there were so many menhaden boats stacked along the Beaufort waterfront that they had to get a court order to get the owners to move them so other boat traffic could get through the creek."

Menhaden is an oily, high-protein fish that is processed into fish meal, oil and soubles (see the Commerce and Industry chapter). Menhaden, often called fatbacks or shad, are a restless fish that move in huge schools up and down the coast.

Wheatly's grandfather, the late Claude Wheatly Sr., joined the late Will Potter in partnership to buy the plant in about 1934. Jule Wheatly began working at the plant in 1973 and became president-general manager in 1983.

"Fishing is so much different now than it was back then," Mr. Wheatly said. "Now, we depend on speed, and it is strictly business." Planes are used to spot menhaden schools and direct the boats to them. The factory is capable of processing 4 million fish every 24 hours. Annual production at Beaufort Fisheries varies from 80 to 160 million fish.

"There are more menhaden out there now than ever," Mr. Wheatly said. "If we quit fishing, you would see large fish kills on the beaches." He noted large menhaden kills within the last few years in Maine, Massachusetts and elsewhere. The growing menhaden population is attributed to the closure of fish meal plants along the coast — many being forced out of business by environmental groups and other lobbying organizations.

Continually, there are proposals and regulations being applied to the menhaden fishing business, including the restriction of fishing within 3 miles of the shoreline. Beaufort Fisheries catches the majority of its fish within one-eighth of a mile of shore.

"It takes a lot of coast to do fishing," Mr. Wheatly said. "We survived through bad prices, through low catches and through bad weather, but we'll have trouble surviving all these regulations."

Beaufort Fisheries employs between 70 and 90 workers and has three boats. With the ability to carry 2.5 million fish, *Coastal Mariner* is the plant's newest vessel. The *Gregory Poole* can carry 1.5 million fish, and the smaller *Taylor's Creek* can handle about 600,000.

Men leave these larger boats in small purse boats to surround the fish. A purse net is used to surround the fish and is so called because it is drawn shut like a handbag. In early years, workers pulled the fish-ladened nets up from the

The Menhaden Chanteymen often perform locally.

water by hand. In order to synchronize the pulling and lifting, the men sang songs, or chanteys as they were called. Today, the nets are pulled up with hydraulic lifts.

John Henry Pritchett was one of those men who did the work by hand. Like many African Americans from Beaufort, Mr. Pritchett, who was 74 years old when he died last April, worked in the menhaden business.

"Singin' was the way we got those fish up," Mr. Pritchett once said. "It made us pull together — kept us in rhythm. You'd sing before you'd bend down to pull. There weren't any engines to raise those fish. You had to do it by hand. After they got this hydraulic stuff, you didn't have to sing chanteys."

With the introduction of hydraulic equipment, he knew the old work songs the crew sang would be forgotten. To keep these work songs alive, he and fellow former fishermen formed The Menhaden Chanteymen in 1988.

"We're trying to keep these chanteys alive," Mr. Pritchett said in an interview months before his death. "Those songs are old. Folks were singin' them before we were old enough to go on the boats."

Mr. Pritchett retired from the menhaden business in 1986 after working 46 years, most of that time as an engineer. "I first stopped around 1980, but every year they wanted me to go back. They needed an engineer, so I went."

The Menhaden Chanteymen often perform locally at the N.C. Maritime Museum in Beaufort and have performed at Carnegie Hall in New York. The group has appeared on CBS's "Sunday Morning" with Charles Kuralt. They have also given performances for the North Carolina State Legislature and many other groups.

Mr. Pritchett's favorite chantey was "Going Back to Weldon." One man would sing the opening and the crew would respond. The response is noted in all capital letters.

Going Back to Weldon
I'm going back to WELDON, WELDON, WELDON.
I'm going back to WEL-DON,
To get a JOB IN THE WELDON YARD.
Chorus:
Oh, I'm going back to WELDON, WELDON, WELDON.
Oh, I'm going back to WEL-DON,
To get a JOB IN THE WELDON YARD.
Oh, Captain, if you FIRE ME, FIRE ME, FIRE ME.
Captain, if you FIRE ME,
You've got to FIRE MY BUDDY TOO.
Chorus:
Oh, the captain's got a LUGER, LUGER, LUGER.
Oh, the captain's got a LU-GER,
And the MATE'S GOT AN OWL'S HEAD.
Chorus:
I don't want no WOMAN, WOMAN, WOMAN.
I don't want no WO-MAN,
Who's got HAIR LIKE A HORSE'S MANE.
Oh, I don't want no WOMAN, WOMAN, WOMAN.
I don't want no WO-MAN,
Who's got HAIR LIKE A HORSE'S MANE.
Chorus:
Oh, the house is on FIRE, FIRE, FIRE.
Oh, the house is on FI-RE,
And it's ALMOST BURNING DOWN.
Oh, the house is on FIRE, FIRE, FIRE.
Oh, the house is on FI-RE,
And it's ALMOST BURNING DOWN.

cility for retired merchant marines there in 1976. The original facility of its type opened in 1833 on Staten Island. Sea Level Extended Care Facility is a nursing home on Nelson's Bay. A satellite clinic of Carteret General Hospital now operates alongside the nursing home.

Atlantic was settled in the 1740s and was originally called Hunting Quarters. The first post office opened in 1880, and the name was changed to Atlantic. The community's nickname is Per, and old timers refer to their home as Per Atlantic. In the 1930s progress arrived in the form of paved roads. A ferry once operated between Atlantic and Ocracoke. Atlantic is home to two of the East Coast's largest seafood dealers, Luther Smith & Son Seafood Company and Clayton Fulcher Seafood Company.

Cedar Island was known by that name until two post offices were established in the early 1900s. Then the east end of the island became known as Lola and the west end as Roe, each with its own post office and school. In the 1960s, the two post offices closed and a new one was opened. The whole island became known as Cedar Island again. Locals still use the old names, and some homes on the is-

Photo: NC Travel & Tourism

Mending nets is a regular part of the work day for many Down East residents.

land date back to the 1880s. Many locals believe that Cedar Island is the site of the so-called "Lost Colony" (see the Lost Colony sidebar in the Attractions chapter).

Newport/ Western Carteret County

Newport is known as "the town with old-fashioned courtesy." When traveling from New Bern to Carteret County, it is the first incorporated town you pass. *Business North Carolina* magazine ranked Newport as number ten in the "Top Tarheel Towns Overall."

The town continues to grow along with Marine Corps Air Station Cherry Point in Havelock. That growth resulted in last year's hiring of the town's first manager, who works with the town commissioners and residents to handle town affairs. The last census showed a popu-

lation of 2,569, meaning the town grew by 1,000 people in the past 10 years.

Chartered in 1866, Newport was first supported by logging, farming and fishing. Today, many residents work at Cherry Point. Newport is home to a development park on Highway 70 and the National Oceanic and Atmospheric Administration Weather Forecast Office that offers state-of-the-art weather tracking and forecasting. Operated as part of the National Weather Service, this facility includes a Doppler weather radar system with advanced weather capabilities.

Newport offers many quiet residential areas, a school, stores, a town hall and a public library. Newport is home to the popular Newport Pig Cooking Contest each April. The town has a strong volunteer fire department and rescue squad.

Northeast of Newport is the community of **Mill Creek**. This is mainly a farm-

Photo: Scott Taylor

The rock jetty at Fort Macon State Park is a great fishing spot.

CRYSTAL COAST AREA OVERVIEWS

ing community, including a large blueberry farm, that can be reached from Newport or Highway 101 out of Beaufort.

Highway 24 traces the waterfront west along Bogue Sound from Morehead City to Onslow County. The highway passes through several communities, then across the White Oak River into Onslow County and the town of Swansboro.

From Cape Carteret, Highway 58 goes west through the Croatan National Forest through several old settlements including Peletier, the Hadnot Creek community and Kuhn's Corner and then into Jones County. If you turn east on Highway 58 from Cape Carteret, you'll cross a high-rise bridge and enter the beach town of Emerald Isle.

Cedar Point is the westernmost incorporated town in Carteret County and the westernmost point of the county. The town was established in 1713 but not incorporated until 1988.

Cape Carteret is one of the few "planned" communities in Carteret County. It was chartered in 1959, and the late W.B. McLean began the development of the town. The first homes were built on the Bogue Sound waterfront near the foot of what is now the B. Cameron Langston Bridge, the high-rise bridge

built in 1971 to replace the ferry. The town grew slowly and today is complete with stores, a town hall, fire and rescue departments and a school.

Bogue is the newest town in the county. It was incorporated in a special election held in September 1995. With about 200 registered voters, the town's new commissioners and mayor are now busy putting together policies and regulations. Bogue is home to the U.S. Marine Corps Auxiliary Landing Field.

Several communities dot the western part of the county. **Ocean** is an old community and was once a small thriving village with one of the county's first post offices. **Broad Creek** is another old-timer, once made up almost exclusively of commercial fishermen and their families. Some of these fishermen came to the area as much as 100 years ago; others came from Diamond City on Shackleford Banks after the horrible hurricanes forced them to vacate. Today, there is a school and lots of new residential developments.

Kuhn's Corner marks the intersection of Highway 24 that leads to **Stella**, which was once a thriving community with stores, a couple of mills, a good many farmhouses and even a couple of huge plantation houses.

Locals consider soft-shell crabs a delicacy and favorite ways to prepare them include battering and lightly frying or sauteing in butter and wine.

Crystal Coast
Restaurants

Seafood is the featured entree in most Crystal Coast restaurants. In all coastal Carolina areas, deep fried used to be the most common preparation of seafood, but today restaurant-goers have a choice of steamed, broiled, baked, grilled, blackened or fried seafood in addition to many creative entrees exclusive to individual restaurants.

Fried hush puppies continue to be a local favorite and are often used as a means of rating restaurants. Hush puppies are made with cornmeal, flour, eggs and sugar. Some folks add some chopped onion, others add sweet milk. Once blended, the mixture is dropped by the spoonful into hot fat and fried to a golden brown. Old-timers say the name derived from cooks, who while preparing meals, tossed bits of fried batter to yapping dogs in an effort to quiet them.

Most natives were raised on conch and clam chowders, and now newcomers are discovering these treats. Local conch chowder is made with whelk. To easily remove the meat from whelks and clams, locals recommend freezing the shell; once thawed, the meat is easily pulled out. Traditional chowder is made with chopped meat, water, butter, salt, pepper and diced potatoes. For a different flavor, you might also add squash, onions and spices.

Collards have long been a mainstay in the diet of most locals, especially those living Down East. A "mess" of collards cooking in the kitchen creates an unforgettable aroma that you either love or hate. Collards are leafy green vegetables that grow almost year round in this area. Most locals say the best way to cook collards is with a streak-of-lean salt pork or some fatback added to the pot and topped off with a few new red potatoes and some cornmeal dumplings. Cornmeal dumplings are unique to eastern North Carolina and are basically cornmeal, water and salt shaped into small patties and dropped into the collard pot for about 15 minutes.

There is nothing like a traditional Down East clam bake — you won't find eating like this on any restaurant menu. But, you can luck out and catch a school or fire department holding a fund-raising clam bake. If that happens, drop all your plans and head on over for some real good food. It is said that the idea for the clam bake came from the Native Americans who taught early residents to cook clams, fish and corn in the steam of hot stones. Today, there are businesses that have large steamers for hire. Modern-day clam bakes offer clams, chicken, sweet potatoes, white potatoes, onions, carrots, corn and sometimes a few shrimp. They are all steamed together in a net bag or cheesecloth and served with melted butter. This is not the time for table manners, so use your fingers!

Peelers, pickers, jimmies, white bellies,

hens, steamers, paper shells or soft-shells — no matter what you call them, they're still crabs. Learning the difference between the names and the stages of a crab's life is the hard part. Knowing when crabs are ready to shed and are marketable as soft-shells is important to the livelihood of many Crystal Coast fishermen. Understanding the process a crab goes through to become a soft-shell is an art as well as a science.

A peeler is a crab that will, if all goes well, become a soft crab within 72 hours. They are carefully handled and put in vats where they can go through this molting process. Jimmies are the large crabs that measure 6 inches from upper shell tip to tip, and steamers or pickers are just regular crabs. The sure way to tell if a crab is a peeler is by the pinkish-red ring on the outer tip of the flipper or back fin. Those that complete the molting process are sold live or dressed. Many are packed with damp sea grass, refrigerated and shipped live to restaurants as far away as New York. Most are sold dressed because live soft-shells are delicate to handle and have a life of only about three days. Locals consider soft-shell crabs a delicacy, and favorite ways to prepare them include battering and lightly frying or sauteing in butter and wine.

Shrimp burgers, another very popular local seafood treat, are little more than fried shrimp on a hamburger bun with slaw and special sauce. Each restaurant has its own sauce, which is the secret to a great shrimp burger. Some places have come up with variations (oyster burgers, clam burgers), but it's all basically put together the same way. And, oh, what a wonderful lunch it makes.

There are increasing numbers of fast food and chain restaurants finding their way to the Crystal Coast. Most of these places seem to concentrate on U.S. Highway 70, which is the main artery through

the area. You'll find Burger King, Hardee's, McDonald's, Bojangles, Pizza Inn, Shoney's, Taco Bell, KFC, Wendy's and many more. These places balance out the number of seafood spots and provide diners with a greater variety of restaurants from which to choose. This guide does not review chain restaurants, under the assumption that you are probably already familiar with their fare.

Planning and Pricing

When planning your lunch or dinner outing, we recommend you call ahead to verify the information offered in the following restaurant profiles and to check the hours or seating availability. Although most of the restaurants in the area are locally owned and have been in business for years, a few will change hands during the off-season. While we seek to be as accurate as possible, these changes often mean a modification of menu items. Some area restaurants traditionally close in the winter, and some that remain open limit menu items to ensure freshness.

Mixed drinks are available in restaurants and lounges in all towns throughout the Crystal Coast except Newport. Mixed drinks are not served in the Down East area or any other unincorporated area except in the Bogue Banks' community of Salter Path. Most restaurants do serve wine and domestic and imported beer, and some allow brown-bagging.

Some restaurants in the area offer special discounts to early diners, and many have discounts for senior citizens and children's dinner menu items.

Because of the large number of restaurants on the Crystal Coast and the limited space in this chapter, we have referred you to restaurants that continue to be favorites. There are certainly more restaurants than this; check the local phone book and

The Trawl Door
Restaurant and Lounge

Nationally awarded and recognized restaurant celebrated for our excellence in food, service, and atmosphere.

Located in an original 1915 brick hardware and grocery store, The Trawl Door is situated in the quaint sailing and fishing village of Oriental - just a short drive from New Bern on Hwy. 55 or take the Minnesott/Cherry Branch Ferry from Havelock.

Open at 5:00 nightly / All ABC Permits
Foot of Bridge / 249-1232

newspaper advertisements for other suggestions. We have designed these brief reviews in hopes of making your selection easier, but we know you will want to try several of the establishments in town to get a full taste of local favorites. Restaurants are arranged alphabetically according to their location. We have given the milepost (MP) number for those on N.C. Highway 58 on Bogue Banks to help you find them more easily.

We have also arranged a price code to give you a general idea of the cost of a dinner for two, including appetizers, entrees, desserts and coffee. Because entrees come in a wide range of prices, the code we used reflects an average meal — not the most expensive item or the least expensive item. For those restaurants that do not serve dinner, the price code reflects the cost of lunch fare. These codes do not reflect gra-

tuity or the state's six percent sales tax. Most of the dinner establishments listed honor major credit cards and take reservations.

The price code is as follows:

Less than $20	*$*
$21 to $35	*$$*
$36 to $50	*$$$*
More than $51	*$$$$*

Bogue Banks

Atlantic Beach

BISTRO BY THE SEA
401 Money Island Dr., MP 1¼   247-2777
$$

Bistro By The Sea is a locals' favorite for dinner. This small restaurant beside Sportsman's Pier offers a casual atmosphere and fine food. A favorite appetizer is the roasted peppers and Italian sausage. Salad favorites include the Caesar with char-grilled tuna and the leafy spinach with shrimp. Seafood entrees vary nightly according to freshness and availability. We recommend the char-grilled filet mignon or rib eye, liver in orange liqueur or stir-fried chicken with rice and wontons. Pasta creations include seafood-and-cheese-filled pasta shells, eggplant Parmesan and capellini with pesto, vegetables and scallops. Sandwiches are also available, along with a tempting selection of desserts. Bistro By The Sea has a bar area and serves mixed drinks, beer and wine.

CHANNEL MARKER
RESTAURANT & LOUNGE

Atlantic Beach Causeway   247-2344
$$-$$$

Channel Marker specializes in grilled fish and aged beef. Overlooking Bogue Sound, the restaurant offers waterfront dining and has all ABC permits. House specialties include grilled fish, land and sea combinations, seafood platters, steak-and-shrimp kebabs and broiled lobster tails. A grilled or broiled fish is offered each night, and the chef also prepares cold-plate entrees, grilled chicken breasts and stuffed flounder. Desserts include French silk, lime and lemon pies and Bananas Foster. The dock in front of the restaurant is available for those arriving

by boat, and the adjoining lounge (see the Nightlife chapter) has all ABC permits and a good selection of wines and beers. The restaurant can accommodate groups of up to 100.

NO NAME AT THE BEACH

MP 3   240-2224
$$$

No Name At The Beach offers the same great menu as its sister restaurant in Beaufort, plus a few extras, including breakfast. Guests will find great pizza, all kinds of subs, Greek entrees and authentic gyros, great burgers, pasta dishes, kabobs and stir fries. The Greek salad is loaded with feta cheese and served with a loaf of garlic bread. The chef's salad is piled high with meats and cheeses. No Name also serves sandwiches, steaks and chicken and offers desserts, including baklava. No Name At The Beach serves a weekend breakfast and dinner buffet, and, for a perfect fast solution for any meal, there's drive-through service.

DJ SHOOTERS
RESTAURANT AND LOUNGE

MP 4¾   240-1188
$$

DJ Shooters serves a country breakfast with farm-fresh eggs, a variety of meats, omelettes, cream chipped beef, homemade corned-beef hash and fruit waffles until

Insiders' Tips

If you come across a school or fire department holding a fund-raising clam bake, drop all your plans and head on over for some real good food. Clam bakes offer clams, chicken, sweet potatoes, white potatoes, onions, carrots, corn and sometimes a few shrimp — all steamed together in a net bag or cheesecloth and served with melted butter. This is not the time for table manners, so use your fingers!

★ ★ ★ ★ ★

Award Winning

- *Seafood*
- *Famous Baby Back Ribs*
- *Black Angus Steaks & Prime Ribs*

- Seniors' Menu
- Children' s Menu
- Take Out
- All ABC Permits
- VISA, MC, AMEX, DISCOVER

Restaurant 240-1188
Night Club 247-7468

Located across from the
Sheraton, Atlantic Beach

The Freshest Fish In Town

You won't find his sculptures in any art gallery; he's just not that kind of artist. And although they're not edible, you will find Craig Gurganus' Ping-Pong-eyed flounder, triggerfish, crabs, clown fish and barracuda at some of the best restaurants in the Crystal Coast, the Outer Banks, Wilmington and Chapel Hill. Craig's puffy works of art are called Fish Bouffant.

Art took this surfer by surprise, and the startled looks that characterize his personable fish and sea creatures are very much an exclamation point of *artiste remarque*. Craig, a handy and personable Rocky Mount boy compelled by the surf, spent one winter painting houses — when the surf was contrary — but knew he had undeniable art genes. His family has produced a bestselling novelist and screenwriter, a psychologist, a landscape designer and primitive artist, and Craig. It was inevitable.

He found the perfect fodder for his art while watching a friend's surf shop that winter in Rodanthe on Hatteras Island. In the forms of broken surfboards Craig saw Fish Bouffant. ("They're in there. I don't make them," said Craig.)

Craig Gurganus creates a Shark Bouffant in his studio.

He carves the fish out of the broken polyurethane foam of the boards, applies spray paint and resin, then trims them out with fins of structured wooden skewers, fiberglass cloth and resin. The finished product, with an appropriately protruding eye, is a Fish Bouffant.

After a show at the N.C. Aquarium in Manteo a little more than 10 years ago and then shows in specialty coffee shops and at Crook's Corner in Chapel Hill, Craig finally learned the value of making himself known. "Someone wanted to buy all of them, but nobody knew how to find me," he said. "A close friend advised, 'Craig, it's got to be either house-painting or art.'"

He chose art. After all, an artist whose work sells without being in a gallery, and for whom the main factor navigating any day is the surf conditions, is an artist who will take a chance.

Craig's designs are named things such as "Yikes" (his signature surprised flounder), "Rickles" (the clown fish), "Elvis" (the star-quality seahorse) or "Buster" (a blue crab, of course).

The home of Fish Bouffant is in Beaufort in a perfect house for their creation. A former neighborhood grocery surrounded by collards and tropical plants bordered with bowling balls, Craig Gurganus' studio is in the garage. Inside, in the Board Room — where the director is Craig's own surfboard — broken boards quietly wait to be relieved of the Fish Bouffant inside.

"Great Food without an Attitude"

Lunch & Dinner
All Day - Everyday - Year Round
11:00 am - 10:00 pm

Emerald Plantation Shopping Center
Emerald Isle, NC / (919) 354-2413

early afternoon. The lunch and dinner menu is filled with selections of fresh local seafood, juicy steaks and tender baby back ribs. Steamed shrimp, crab legs and fillet of flounder or trout are offered along with plentiful combination platters, surf and turf specials and live Maine lobsters. Other menu items include pork chops, chicken and prime rib. DJ Shooters has a good repeat business among locals and visitors who also enjoy Shooters Nightclub. (See our Nightlife chapter.) They offer specials to senior citizens and children. The restaurant serves wine, beer and mixed drinks, and a late-night menu is available.

HARPER'S OCEANFRONT
AT THE JOLLY KNAVE

Oceanfront, Atlantic Beach Circle   726-8222
$-$$

The Jolly Knave offers casual indoor and outdoor oceanfront dining. Voted by locals as providing the "Best Oceanview on the Island," the outside second-floor deck is a great place to dine and enjoy the view of the Atlantic Ocean and beach. Appetizers include potato skins, wings, shrimp, beef ribs and oyster cocktails. They offer all kinds of sandwiches (club, barbecue, chicken breast), burgers and salads. Dinner entrees include seafood (try the combination platter broiled or fried), steak, pasta, barbecued beef ribs and daily specials that are often fresh fish caught by the owner. The chef also makes pizza, fajitas, soups and cold plates, and a children's menu is offered. This establishment has all ABC permits. For information about the lounge, see our Nightlife chapter.

KELLI'S

Atlantic Beach Causeway   247-1094
$$$

Kelli's has become known for its Angus beef and great seafood. Appetizers include crab-stuffed mushrooms and chicken fingers. Entrees feature rib eye, prime rib, stuffed flounder and shrimp, lobster, chicken and all kinds of seafood, broiled, grilled, fried or panned in butter. There is a variety of land and sea combination platters available. Entrees include a garden or spinach salad, baked potato, fries or wild rice and rolls. There is a fresh fish special each day. Guests can park cars in front or dock boats at the lounge deck. Patrons often enjoy a drink in the lounge or on the deck before or after dinner (see the Nightlife chapter).

MAN CHUN HOUSE RESTAURANT
MP 1½   *726-8162*
$$

Man Chun House has been serving wonderful Chinese food for many years and has an excellent reputation. The restaurant features a complete Chinese menu and has a few American menu items. The egg-drop and wonton soups are tasty, and the hot-and-sour soup is wonderful. Marinated barbecued ribs and egg rolls are favorite appetizers. So is the famous flaming pu-pu platter that has a selection of several appetizers. Favorite entrees include marinated beef with snow peas and vegetables, shrimp and peas, chicken and broccoli, scallops with vegetables, sesame chicken, duck, lobster and sweet and sour shrimp and chicken. The restaurant has all ABC permits and serves beer and wine. Man Chun offers a takeout service too.

NEW YORK DELI
Crow's Nest Shopping Center   *726-0111*
Atlantic Beach Causeway
$

This is the place for authentic deli food, and it is wonderful. We recommend a Manhattan cheesesteak — heck, order two cheesesteaks and we'll join you. They serve overstuffed sandwiches, subs, great kraut, chili dogs, homemade soups and salads. They also have one of the area's best supplies of imported beers and wines. Deli meats and cheeses are also available for you to take home and create your own feast. New York Deli offers takeout or eat-in service, catering, party trays, gift baskets and a retail wine shop.

SKIPPER'S COVE
RESTAURANT AND LOUNGE
MP 2   *726-3023*
$$-$$$

Skipper's Cove is a popular restaurant that offers an extensive buffet and live entertainment. The restaurant's famous all-you-can-eat buffet is served every day from 4 to 10 PM. It features all types of seafood — shrimp, fish, clams, crabs, scallops, oysters and more — along with beef, chicken, ham, pasta, barbecue, soups, salads, vegetables and breads. Homemade salad dressing and tempting desserts round out the delicious menu. Skipper's Cove offers banquet facilities. Entertainment varies and includes the house six-piece band who play beach, country and Top 40 music for dining and dancing.

Pine Knoll Shores

CLAMDIGGER RESTAURANT
Ramada Inn, MP 8¼   *247-4155*
$-$$

Open for breakfast, lunch and dinner, the Clamdigger in the Ramada Inn prides itself on serving made-from-scratch items. You'll find fluffy omelettes for breakfast and prime rib sandwiches for lunch. Dinner entrees include steaks and all kinds of seafood. The Clamdigger features authentic Mexican cuisine every Friday at lunch. There is a special every evening — oysters on Monday, rib eye on Tuesday, seafood combination on Wednesday, shrimp on Thursday, flounder on Friday, lobster and shrimp on Saturday and steak and shrimp on Sunday.

PARADISE RESTAURANT
Sheraton Resort, MP 4¾   240-1155
$$-$$$

Overlooking the ocean on Atlantic Beach at the Sheraton Resort, the restaurant serves breakfast, lunch and dinner daily. It spreads a gorgeous seafood buffet on Friday evenings and a prime rib buffet on Saturday. À la carte dinner selections are varied among the seafood, poultry, beef and veal specialties served with salad, baked potato or rice. They include tempting selections such as shrimp Rockefeller or crabmeat-stuffed flounder served with a fresh dill sauce, lemon-pepper chicken and veal Saltimboca, which involves shaved ham and provolone over veal medallions finished with a Marsala wine sauce. The Sunday brunch buffet includes carved top round roast, ham, omelettes or eggs to order, salads, cheeses, soup, chicken and seafood entrees, pasta and an array of desserts. Paradise Restaurant has all ABC permits.

TRADEWINDS
Royal Pavillion Resort, MP 5½   726-5188
$$-$$$

Tradewinds is in the newly renovated Royal Pavillion Resort. The restaurant features a wonderful Sunday brunch with a large selection of entrees, breads, fruits and desserts. Dinner entrees include seafood, aged prime beef, pasta and chicken along with soups and salads. Try the Jack Daniels rib eye or one of the other house specialities. Tradewinds often features live entertainment and offers banquet and meeting facilities. The Passport Lounge is at the resort. Late fall and winter bring dinner-theater productions that are a full evening's treat.

Indian Beach/Salter Path

BIG OAK DRIVE IN
Heart of Salter Path, MP 10½   247-2588
$

Turn on the blinker and stop the car. Big Oak has the Best Shrimp Burger on the Crystal Coast — that's the vote of an Insiders' poll. While others serve a good shrimp burger, Big Oak serves a great one. They've been at it for 19 years. Other goodies you'll find include barbecue sandwiches, burgers, hot dogs, chicken sandwiches, pizza and even BLTs. Big Oak has plates of barbecue, fried chicken, chicken salad and shrimp as well as mighty good french fries, onion rings and slaw. But it's that shrimp burger that will keep you coming back!

CRAB SHACK
On Bogue Sound, MP 10½   247-3444
$$

Tucked back off the main road, The Crab Shack offers excellent seafood and a wonderful view of Bogue Sound — the restaurant actually hangs over the water. This is one of the our favorite places for steamed crabs in addition to shrimp, crab cakes and crab legs. Yum! The restaurant has an extensive seafood menu and will fry, grill, pan in butter or broil your choice. For the landlubber, there is rib eye, chicken and hamburger steak. The Crab Shack serves wine, beer and has setups for those wishing to brown-bag their favorite beverage. The outside deck is a great place to relax.

FRANK AND CLARA'S
RESTAURANT & LOUNGE
MP 11   247-2788
$$-$$$

Frank and Clara's is a locals' favorite and is very popular with visitors too. The restaurant serves a variety of dinner choices that include seafood and steaks.

Insider favorites are the crab cakes, cut-to-order char-grilled steaks and flounder stuffed with your choice of crabmeat, shrimp, scallops or oysters. Each meal is prepared to order. Dinner entrees come with cheese and crackers, a salad with homemade dressings, a cup of clam chowder, hush puppies or rolls, and a potato, french fries or rice. There are special entrees for senior citizens and children. Beside the Salter Path Post Office, the restaurant has all ABC permits. Come early — Frank and Clara's has a lot of repeat business so there might be a short wait. There is also an upstairs lounge.

FROST SEAFOOD HOUSE AND OYSTER BAR

MP 10¾   247-3202
$$

In the heart of Salter Path, Frost's serves all kinds of seafood and has an oyster bar. The restaurant serves dinner every day and all three meals in the summer, including all-you-can-eat breakfast specials. Frost's serves seafood, steak, chicken, barbecue, lobster and fresh vegetables. Favorites include shrimp scampi, popcorn shrimp and snow crab legs. Frost's prepares seafood Salter Path-style from old family recipes and has the best hush puppies around. The restaurant has facilities to accommodate private parties and offers a takeout service. During the summer, a line of hungry people forms, so we suggest you go early. Frost Seafood Market is also the place to get fresh local seafood to prepare at home.

SQUATTER'S SEAFOOD RESTAURANT

MP 11   247-3464
$$-$$$

This is the place to go if you are really hungry for seafood. The all-you-can-eat dinner buffet includes a salad, seafood and dessert bar. There you will find pop-

corn shrimp, fish, snow crab legs, crab cakes, clam strips, deviled crabs, shrimp Creole, seafood casserole, lasagna, meatballs, game fish, vegetables and chef's specials. If none of this suits your fancy, try any of the seafood, steak or chicken entrees from the full menu. Squatter's offers a breakfast buffet, early bird specials and special menus for senior citizens and children.

Emerald Isle

BUSHWACKERS RESTAURANT

100 Bogue Inlet Dr.   354-6300
$$

Bushwackers, at Bogue Inlet Pier, is known for its fun wait staff, spectacular oceanfront view and adventurous decor. It is a favorite dinner spot for fresh seafood prepared in a variety of ways, although broiled and steamed are the specialties, along with steaks, inventive pastas and other entrees. Their appetizer menu is extensive, including gator bites and calamari. We love the blooming onion and the stuffed clams. Entrees feature fresh seafood — often just caught off the neighboring pier — char-grilled Angus steaks, prime rib and more. Try the rock 'n' roll cheesecake for dessert. The Safari Lounge is a great place to meet friends and make new ones. Bushwackers has all ABC permits and serves beer and wine. Come enjoy an island dining adventure.

CAFE 58

8802-5 Reed St.   354-4058
$$-$$$

If you'd like to impress someone with your knowledge of good food, take them for lunch or dinner to Cafe 58 across from Emerald Plantation. There are no disappointments here. The chef is a pro, the ownership is the same as Westside Cafe

in Morehead City and the harmony works for the discerning diner. With the light decor, pleasant patio for drinks, modern jazz and food to match, you may just want to move in. Don't hesitate to try a gourmet pizza for lunch. Fresh fish dinner entrees are prepared grilled, sauteed, poached or steamed with a selection of perfect sauces. All menu items are available for takeout convenience in case you'd like to move your feast to the beach.

RUCKERJOHNS
A RESTAURANT & MORE
140 Fairview Dr., MP 19½   354-2413
$$

RuckerJohns offers great food and fun for the entire family. The restaurant is just off the main road behind NationsBank and is one of our favorites. Entrees, prepared to order, include fresh seafood, pasta, barbecued shrimp, beef ribs, steaks, chicken and pork chops. Favorite appetizers include the fried calamari, shrimp cooked in beer, hot crab dip and chicken wings. For lunch, try the grilled Cajun chicken salad, the spinach salad with hot bacon, coastal pasta salad, any of the juicy burgers or a creative sandwich. Dinners feature seafood, steaks and ribs. RuckerJohns has all ABC permits and also has a location in Wilmington. The "More" in their name refers to the lounge (see our Nightlife chapter).

Beaufort

BEAUFORT GROCERY CO.
117 Queen St.   728-3899
$$-$$$

Beaufort Grocery Co. is a favorite of locals and visitors. In a relaxed atmosphere, chef Charles Park offers fine cuisine in a restored town grocery store. The lunch menu consists of creative salads (try the smoked-fish salad), soups and sandwiches. Favorites are the gougeres (herb pastries stuffed with crab, shrimp, chicken or egg salads), smoked turkey, country ham and cheese sandwich on sourdough or chicken salad with apples on a croissant. Dinner starts with such creative appetizers as Oriental pork ribs marinated in dried fruit, fabulous Carolina crab cakes, or the fisherman's soup filled with shrimp, scallops, clams, fish and vegetables. For your entree, we suggest fresh grouper encrusted with crabmeat and asparagus, grilled turkey steak served with corn salsa or the filet mignon. The dinner menu features fresh seafood, choice steaks, chicken, duck and lamb. Early diner's specials are also offered. Top your meal off with raspberry cheesecake or any other dessert. Entrees are served with a salad, fresh vegetables and bread. Beaufort Grocery Co. offers a wonderful Sunday brunch, a takeout menu and a full delicatessen with meats, cheeses, homemade salads and breads. There is also a small bar area; the restaurant has all ABC permits.

115 QUEEN STREET
115 Queen St. 728-3899
$$$$

This is the perfect restaurant for a special dinner or if you just want to travel a little bit without leaving Beaufort — 115 Queen offers the ultimate in international cuisine. Chef Charles Park takes you away with his culinary creations. Each week the menu changes to feature a different cuisine from around the world. It might be German, African, Thai, Hungarian, Chinese, French — whatever direction Chef Park wants to go. His inspiration for menus comes from books, travels and friends. Each menu is arranged with sev-

eral selections in each of the four or five courses. Reservations are recommended and can be made next door at Beaufort Grocery Co. 115 Queen is open for catering and special parties.

BEAUFORT HOUSE RESTAURANT
502 Front St. 728-7541
$$

With a beautiful view of Taylors Creek and the Beaufort waterfront, lunch and dinner is served offering local seafood selections including blackened fish, prime rib and pasta selections. A kid's menu is also available. The Sunday brunch buffet features carved roast beef, fried shrimp and clams, bacon, eggs, cheese grits, fruits, salad and soups.

CLAWSON'S 1905 RESTAURANT
429 Front St. 728-2133

Clawson's 1905 is a wonderful mix of old and new. An architectural focal point in the middle of downtown, the newly remodeled restaurant expanded during the winter of 1996 to comfortably accommodate its appreciative clientele. Clawson's 1905 is housed in what was Clawson's General Store back in the early 1900s and is decorated with what may have been some of the wares available. But the menu items are new creations. Two lunch favorites are the Dirigible, a hearty baked potato stuffed with seafood, vegetables or meats, and the French dip, roast beef on a toasted roll with au jus for dipping. Other lunch items include overstuffed sandwiches, burgers, salads, soups and seafood plates. Dinner entrees offered always include fresh seafood prepared with style, zesty ribs, steaks, chicken and pasta. Clawson's serves mixed drinks, wines and the greatest selection of domestic and imported beers in town. This place gets crowded during the summer months, so

Made To Order

"Hi, Darlin'. What can I get for you?" asks Louise, the waitress at Morehead City's legendary El's Drive-In.

The answer from people in about 400 cars a day is, most frequently, a burger — shrimp burger, oyster burger or El's Superburger. And no one forgets to order the fries. Nouvelle cuisine be damned. There are too many times in Carteret County when only an El's burger will do.

This is one of those times. Sitting in her truck with a sea gull waiting on the hood for any leftovers, one customer says, "I've been coming here since before I was born, and (of course) my family did before me." And why? "The FOOD," answers the man with the burger in the passenger seat. "This," says the woman, indicating her shrimp burger, "tastes the same as it did 20 years ago!"

And El's it isn't just the locals' fancy.

"My uncle came from Germany with his wife who'd never been here," the woman behind the wheel continues, "and after all the seafood they caught, and ate while they were here, their favorite thing was the burgers at El's."

"We just recently had some people from Seattle, Washington, order take-out shrimp burgers and ask us to wrap each ingredient separately so they could take get them back home and put them together themselves," says Thursday's cook Robin Paul who has assembled burgers at El's for four years.

". . . California, Florida . . ." Louise adds. "We had a man land in a private plane in Beaufort and take a cab here for nine or 10 shrimp burgers to take to friends in Fort Lauderdale."

Photo: Janis Williams

El's Drive-In is a Morehead City favorite for burgers, shrimp burgers and oyster sandwiches.

So, what is it that keeps them coming to El's from childhood and Fort Lauderdale?

"We start every day with 120 to 150 pounds of fresh ground beef, then press the burgers. The oysters and shrimp are from Beaufort. We make the slaw. . ." says Robin. "We make everything. That's how they've always done it."

And they assemble it their way or yours. Their way starts with the basic burger, fried shrimp or oysters depending on your choice of burger. Add slaw and you're holding the building block on which El's reputation is built. No special sauces here. Just flavors you can trust like real hamburger, ketchup, that sort of thing. Continuous customer satisfaction also comes from the custom features that distinguish each individual burger. If you want shrimp on your cheeseburger, so be it. Onions? Mustard? Oysters? It's your burger.

"This is the second grill in the history of the business," says Robin indicating the shiny stainless centerpiece of the short-order kitchen. "From this 32- by 16-foot building, we serve about 800 burgers a day."

Some changes have happened over the nearly 50 years of El's Drive-In history. The location has changed, small Coke bottles have been replaced by soft-drink cans, and the soft-serve ice cream window was ditched because it became a hassle. When high school students began to collect the window trays they had to be replaced with bags. No one minds the few modernizing changes — customers wait up to 45 minutes for an El's burger in summer. But no one minds that either — El's is worth the wait.

go a little early. To save time, lunch orders can be faxed to 728-2692.

FINZ GRILL & EATERY

330 Front St.   728-7459
$

Finz is the perfect place to relax, enjoy good food and visit with friends in a casual atmosphere. Guests can sit inside at a table or at the bar or on the back porch over Taylor's Creek. Lunch and dinner menus focus on sandwiches, subs, burgers, soups (try the wonderful gumbo or black-bean) and baskets that might include grilled, blackened or fried seafood and steaks and pasta dishes. Finz prides itself on offering seafood caught by local fishermen, many of whom are their friends and customers. Items vary depending on the catch and could include fresh Spanish, king, flounder or grouper. Finz has great desserts, all ABC permits and a popular bar.

FRONT STREET GRILL

419 Front St.   728-3118
$$-$$$

This new American bistro focuses on seafood, grilled meats, pasta and other creative entrees for lunch and dinner. The lunch menu includes soups, creative salads with grilled tuna, hot fried chicken or shrimp, overstuffed sandwiches with grilled chicken, turkey and smoked cheese or fish, crab cakes and pasta. Dinner appetizers include hot crab dip, pepper-fried calamari and black-bean and goat-cheese quesadillas. Try the herb-encrusted tequila grilled shrimp, seared tuna and grilled beef with tomato chutney. Nightly chalkboard specials are also featured. The chocolate raspberry truffle cheesecake and Key lime cheesecake are favorites for dessert. Front Street Grill has all ABC permits plus an extensive beer and wine selection. Espresso and cappuccino are also available. Reservations are suggested.

HARPOON WILLIE'S RESTAURANT & PUB

300 Front St.   728-5247
$$

Why not relax and dine overlooking Taylor's Creek and an island that is home to roaming ponies? That's what Harpoon Willie's offers, so come on in. The restaurant operates on two menus — a dinner menu and a bar menu. Dinner appetizers include crab cakes, steamed clams, seafood gumbo and stuffed shrimp. Entrees focus on fresh local seafood and certified

The Net House

STEAM RESTAURANT AND OYSTER BAR

Call for Serving Hours

- As featured in Newsweek magazine's articles entitled "The Glories of American Cooking"

- A creative blend of a unique New England atmosphere and the finest of traditional Southern coastal cooking

- Featured entrees nightly

133 Turner Street / Historic Beaufort, NC 28516
(919) 728-2002

Angus beef. Diners can enjoy the daily catch broiled, baked, blackened, fried, steamed or sauteed. Favorites include shrimp Alfredo, savory scallops, baby back ribs, rib eyes and seafood platters. The bar menu features soups, salads, burgers and seafood. The restaurant has all ABC permits and offers wine and domestic and imported beers. Harpoon Willie's pub is next door. A ferry to Shackleford Banks and Carrot Island leaves the restaurant dock several times each day during the summer.

MARIO'S PIZZERIA & RISTORANTE
Beaufort Square Shopping Ctr.
Hwy. 70E.   728-6602
$$

Mario's offers a brick-cooked pizza that is turning a lot of heads. Fresh vegetables as toppings include spinach, broccoli and tomatoes, and garlic lovers find complete satisfaction in the fresh-garlic pizza. Subs, calzones and strombolis also have fresh vegetable awareness. Mario's keeps a steady stream of return diners with very reasonable prices and delicious selections such as cavetelli pasta with broccoli sauteed with garlic, fettucini Alfredo and chicken Marsala.

NET HOUSE
STEAM RESTAURANT & OYSTER BAR
133 Turner St.   728-2002
$$-$$$

The Net House specializes in steamed seafood, has a raw bar and is a favorite among locals and visitors. Guests can enjoy an atmosphere of weathered pine and nautical antiques in this family-owned-and-operated business. Try the creamy clam chowder, conch chowder, crab soup or seafood bisque for lunch or as a dinner appetizer. Sandwiches, salads and seafood are also offered for lunch, which is served during every season except summer. Dinners are wonderful, whether you like seafood steamed, broiled, panned in butter or lightly fried. Favorites include steamed crabs, clams, oysters and shrimp or the broiled platter that includes flounder stuffed with crabmeat, scallops, oysters and shrimp. The Net House is known for its famous Key lime pie, and it has all ABC permits

NO NAME PIZZA AND SUBS
408 Live Oak St.   728-4978, 728-4982
$

This is the best place for pizza, according to our own personal survey. It is also a great place for subs (everything from meatball to vegetarian), burgers and spaghetti with meatballs. The Greek salad is loaded with feta cheese and is served with a loaf of garlic bread. No Name also serves pasta dishes, Greek dishes, sandwiches and chicken. The baklava is wonderful. The menu is the same for lunch and dinner, and you'll leave satisfied and feeling like you got your money's worth. No Name offers dine-in or drive-through service.

PURPLE PELICAN

Town Creek Marina   728-2224
$$-$$$

Owner Martha Bourne offers Beaufort diners a wonderful treat at Purple Pelican. Above Town Creek Marina, this restaurant is a local favorite, offering lunch, dinner and a bar menu. Enjoy the spectacular view of Gallant's Channel and the Intracoastal Waterway while dining inside or on the deck. Lunch features grilled fish, a variety of seafood, chicken sandwiches, soups, salads and burgers. The dinner menu emphasizes fresh local seafood and offers chicken, beef and pasta entrees and nightly specials. Top off your meal with one of the delicious homemade desserts. You can be sure of a creatively prepared meal and good service here. The bar menu features lighter fare and finger foods. The Purple Pelican has all ABC permits, wines and domestic and imported beers. Reservations are suggested, and off-season hours vary, so call ahead. An elevator is available. Martha also operates Bogue's Pocket on the Morehead City waterfront. She can arrange on- and off-site catering, and the Purple Pelican is available for private parties.

THE SPOUTER INN

218 Front St.   728-5190
$$$

A maroon awning marks the Front Street entrance to this intimate restaurant over the water with a wonderful view of Beaufort Inlet and Taylor's Creek. Summer diners can be served at shaded tables on the outside dock. Lunch favorites are the Spouter's soups, salads and legendary sandwiches named for legendary characters or local haunts. Our favorite is the Out Island, a delightful assembly of shrimp, mushrooms, onions, provolone, tomatoes and sprouts on rye. Also legendary is the Spouter's banana cream crepe dessert. Announced dinner entrees take advantage of fresh seafood availability. From the menu, appetizers and entrees are spectacular. We suggest starting with cajun oysters served with a bourbon-spiked remoulade. Fire-roasted beef entrees, such as tenderloin served with wild mushroom sauce, get a big thumbs up. Another delicious taste combination is pecan chicken with hot pear compote. Entrees are served with a choice of smoked gouda mashed potatoes or wild rice and seasonal vegetables. Wednesday nights offer accompanying live jazz. The Spouter Inn serves lunch and dinner Tuesday through Saturday, Sunday lunch and has all ABC permits.

Morehead City

ANCHOR INN
RESTAURANT & LOUNGE

2806 Arendell St.   726-2156
$$-$$$

The Anchor Inn Restaurant is well-known by locals and visitors for fine food and quality service. For 26 years, the restaurant has offered creative entrees and opened for breakfast and dinner. A variety of omelettes, waffles, fruits, pancakes, quiches, biscuits and muffins are served at the hearty breakfast. Dinners are served by candlelight and include Black Angus beef and prime rib, fresh local seafood,

fresh pasta and chicken dishes. Seafood is blackened, grilled, broiled or fried. A special diet menu is offered, and there are daily breakfast and dinner specials. Desserts are unsurpassed and include their famous tollhouse pie and chess pie. Private banquet and meeting rooms are available, and the restaurant has all ABC permits. The adjoining lounge often features a live piano bar.

CALYPSO CAFE
506 Arendell St.   240-3380
$$$

Calypso Cafe offers tropical cuisine in a nonchalant atmosphere for dinner. Each dish is carefully prepared, and the results are fabulous. Selections vary depending on availability and freshness. Start with an appetizer: black bean torta, baked stuffed jalapenos or curried potato bisque. Entrees focus on local seafood presented with is-

land fruits and spices. Favorites include the shrimp curry with tropical salsa, grilled fish with ginger salsa and New York strip with caramelized onions. You'll also find pork loin, pasta, seafood fajitas and blackened or grilled seafood. Desserts, such as paradise pie (a brownie and ice cream covered with strawberry puree) are sure to tempt. Guests can dine at table, at the bar or on the patio. The cafe serves mixed drinks, wine and beer, but is well-known for its creative cocktails.

CAPT. BILL'S
WATERFRONT RESTAURANT
701 Evans St.   726-2166
$$-$$$

This family-style restaurant has been serving lunch and dinner on the Morehead City waterfront for 51 years. John and Diane Poag own Capt. Bill's today, and the tradition of good food continues. The menu features fresh local seafood and homemade items, including sauces, dressings, soups and hush puppies. Daily lunch specials include an entree (baked chicken, pepper or ham steak, chicken and pastry, shrimp or beef stew), two vegetables and hush puppies for $3.95. Monday is all-you-can-eat fish day, and Friday is all-you-can-eat fish and popcorn shrimp day. Wednesdays and Saturdays are conch stew days. Capt. Bill's also offers cold plates, salads, seafood casseroles, seafood combination plates, Cajun-style catfish, steaks, chicken and sandwiches. Items approved by USA Weight Loss Center and the Diet Center are available along with an extensive children's menu. Desserts are made from family recipes and include the original Down East Lemon Pie. Come by boat or by car, but don't leave without sampling one of the 13 flavors of fudge made at the restaurant or without stopping by the gift shop. Capt. Bill's Catering Service can take care of any event.

CHARTER RESTAURANT
405 Evans St.   726-9036
$$-$$$

On the Morehead City waterfront, the Charter specializes in fresh local seafood and is open for lunch and dinner. Diners have a good view of the Morehead City waterfront, the state port and the surrounding water because the dining area is actually over the water. Lunches offer all kinds of seafood, along with ribs, hamburger steak, soups and salads. Our favorite is Crabby Dan, hot crabmeat heaped on an English muffin and topped with a tomato slice and cheese. There are always lunch specials along with a full menu. Dinner appetizers may include oyster supreme, clam chowder,

seafood bisque and wonderful marinated grilled shark bites. Entrees include homemade crab cakes, shrimp and flounder stuffed daily. Seafood is steamed, fried or broiled. Chicken, charbroiled steaks and barbecue ribs are also offered. The restaurant's salad bar includes vegetables, breads, pasta and cheese. Our recommendations for dessert: Granny's apple-caramel pie or homemade tollhouse pie. The Charter offers menus for senior citizens and children and has all ABC permits.

EL'S DRIVE-IN
3600 Arendell St.   726-3002
$

El's has been a Carteret County tradition since 1959. This is an old-fashioned drive-in — that means you are waited on by a carhop and sit in your car and eat. El's has great burgers, hot dogs, fries and milk shakes. The superburger is a Carteret County tradition and is a rare burger, indeed, assembled with slaw and chili. Try a shrimp or oyster burger, a BLT, a fish or steak sandwich, a shrimp or oyster tray or fried chicken. This is a favorite lunch and dinner spot for locals, so go early to get a parking place. And don't forget to lob a french fry or two out the window to the waiting sea gulls.

JASON'S
403 Arendell St.   240-1040
$$-$$$

Chef/owner Jason Veasey has quite a following, which means reservations are a good idea. The reason is the Jason's-only specialties. Salmon en croute is a case in point. A salmon fillet is topped with fresh crab meat and asparagus, enclosed in puff pastry and topped with a Dijon hollandaise sauce. The blackened grouper always gets rave reviews, and it's

Photo: Tabbie Nance

Seafood lovers savor the steamed oysters offered at many fall festivals on the Crystal Coast.

hard to steer away from the prime rib served either grilled, roasted or blackened and topped with fresh Béarnaise sauce. In season, the steamed oyster bar is a great natural resource. Jason's has a delightful porch for dining overlooking Bogue Sound on the Morehead City waterfront. It's one of the best places to enjoy a sunset.

MAGNOLIA TREE CAFE

105 S. 11th St.   *726-2225*
$$

Lunch or dinner at the Magnolia Tree Cafe is a Southern hospitality experience. A flock of followers gather for the warmth of proprietor Ruthie King, but her preparations charm all appetites. Try the shrimp and grits with black-eyed pea salsa or filet mignon with Ruthie's famous bourbon sauce. Whatever's fresh in seafood often inspires specials. For lunch, the sandwiches, omelettes and hot specials are tempting but if you haven't tried her chicken salad, the decision's made. The setting is a restored 18th-century house with private dining rooms and comfortable porches cooled by Bogue Sound breezes. The Magnolia Tree is hard to beat.

NIKOLA'S

Fourth and Bridges sts.   *726-6060*
$$-$$$

Nikola's serves Northern Italian cuisine with a warm, Old World charm. This is the perfect place to take someone special or to gather with a group of close friends. The 1920s two-story Victorian house provides eight separate dining rooms, and guests can enjoy five course meals as well as à la carte selections. Meals include a choice of appetizers, homemade soups or pasta, tossed green salads, two vegetables, an entree, dessert and beverage. Creative entrees could be fresh seafood, red snapper, veal Marsala, filet mignon, steak pizzaiola or fettuccine Alfredo. Favorites include the spinach soup, any of the made-from-scratch pastas, broiled rack of lamb, flounder sauteed in almondine sauce and shrimp scampi. Nikola's has all ABC permits.

OTTIS' WATERFRONT RESTAURANT

711 Shepard St.   *247-3474*
$$-$$$

Here you'll enjoy a variety of cooking — blackened, Cajun, pan-fried, sauteed, grilled and broiled. Appetizer selections include calamari served with sweet and sour sauce, crab-stuffed mushrooms and blackened shrimp served spicy. Enjoy steamed oysters, clams, shrimp and snow crab legs in season. Menu entrees vary and feature fresh grilled seafood, steaks, pasta, chicken and local specialties. Try the baked orange roughy in a champagne-dijon mustard, roasted salmon topped with basil butter, the blackened shark fillet topped with salsa or the Cajun spiced tuna. Other favorites are choice rib eye, New York strip steaks, pasta primavera and chicken Marsala. Ottis' features an extensive selection of California wines, and the restaurant has all ABC permits and a good selection of beers. Ottis' Restaurant can also cater any affair.

RAPSCALLIONS

715 Arendell St.   *240-1213*
$$

Raps is a favorite for lunch, dinner or drinks served in a casual 1890s family atmosphere. House specialties include steamed clams and crabs, a true Philly cheesesteak, the original Raps Burger and seafood Alfredo. You'll also find ribs, crab legs, soups and steaks. Raps has a wonderful taco salad and dressed-up hamburgers, seafood gumbo and overstuffed sandwiches. Lunches feature a light and lively special that could be shrimp salad one day and a delicious fruit plate the next. The bar at Raps is a popular gathering place on weeknights and weekends. Bar patrons are served hot popcorn and can watch the wide-screen television.

REX RESTAURANT

U.S. Hwy. 70 W.   *726-5561*
$$-$$$

Rex is a true Italian restaurant that has been pleasing locals and visitors since 1947. A family business now in its fourth generation, Rex is a popular lunch and dinner spot. The restaurant focuses on Italian foods, fresh local seafood and choice steaks. Favorite appetizers are the clams casino and the hot seafood antipasta. Entrees are creative and include veal and eggplant Parmigiana, manicotti, lasagna, linguine with red clam sauce and more. We recommend the evening Italian buffet. Rex is also famous for pizzas and fresh breads. Dessert favorites include Italian rum cake, homemade cheesecakes and homemade pastries. Rex has all ABC permits, an extensive line of wines and beers and a small bar area, where live entertainment is often provided. Contact the Rex with your catering needs, and let them design a cake for any occasion. The bread comes out of the oven late each morning and lots of folks stop by to take a loaf home for a real treat.

RIVERWALK DELI & CAFE

714 Shepard St.
Morehead City Waterfront   *808-2166*
$

Riverwalk offers a casual soup, salad and sandwich menu all day in casual surroundings. Try the antipasta, chef's salad or shrimp, chicken or tuna salads garnished with veggies, cheeses and fruits. There is always a soup and daily lunch

Insiders' Tips

The Crystal Coast offers great "secret" fishing spots, like the back side of Shackleford Banks and the jetty at Fort Macon.

and dessert special. Sandwich selections include turkey with provolone cheese, roast beef with Swiss, shrimp in pita bread and the popular Salty Dog, a quarter-pound beef frank anyway you like. They also present a legendary Reuben. The deli offers imported meats and cheeses along with side dishes such as creamy potato salad, cole slaw and pasta salad. Recent remodeling promises grilled specialties and a raw bar. Riverwalk has all ABC permits and makes a great Bloody Mary.

SANITARY FISH
MARKET & RESTAURANT
501 Evans St.
Morehead City Waterfront   *247-3111*
$$

Sanitary has been a landmark on the Morehead City waterfront for 55 years. In 1938 Ted Garner and Tony Seamon, both now deceased, opened a waterfront seafood market in a building rented for $5.50 per week with the agreement that no beer or wine would be sold and that the premises would be kept clean and neat. The name Sanitary Fish Market was chosen by the partners to project their compliance. When 12 stools were set up at the counter, the first seafood restaurant on the city's waterfront was in business. Today, son Ted Garner Jr. operates the family-oriented business. Customers will find old favorite menu items plus many new additions. Best known for fresh seafood, the restaurant also offers steaks, poultry, pork and pasta entrees. Seafood is served broiled, steamed, grilled or fried. Lunch features always include a good selection of vegetables. Appetizers vary and include shrimp and clam cocktails, shrimp salad, clams on the half shell and homemade chowders and soups. Dinner favorites include seafood combination platters, char-broiled Angus beef, grilled chicken and steamed Maine lobster along with cold plates of shrimp, shrimp salad and crabmeat, fried shrimp and fish and rib eye. Sanitary Fish Market sells fresh local seafood for those who prefer to cook it themselves.

SUMMER PALACE
CHINESE RESTAURANT
3402 Arendell St.   *726-6000*
$

Summer Palace offers Mandarin, Szechuan and Cantonese cuisine. The lunch and dinner buffets and full menu offer a huge variety. The lunch menu offers a wide selection served with soup, salad and dessert. Lunch includes such favorites as beef with broccoli or vegetables, shrimp chow mein, sweet and sour pork and chicken Cantonese. Dinner appetizers include the popular pu-pu tray with a variety of items, fantail shrimp, steamed or fried dumplings and a good selection of soups. Entrees feature chicken, duck, beef, seafood and pork. Two favorites are the Peking duck served with scallions and Chinese pancakes and the orange beef. Hot and spicy items are noted. Summer Palace offers a children's menu and an American menu including chicken. Takeout service is available.

TEXAS STEAKHOUSE & SALOON
U.S. Hwy. 70 at N.C. Hwy. 24   *240-2633*
$-$$

Morehead City has been beefed up with a new place to hitch your ride and pull up a chair for a hand-cut steak to your specifications. Texas Steakhouse & Saloon opened in October 1995, offering a selection of 27 longneck beers to get off the road dust while you wait for that steak to be seared. Have some roasted peanuts and go ahead and toss the shells on the floor. It really is a lot of fun, and the aged beef is excellent. Seafood and pasta alternatives are also offered, but it's best to stick with the program. There's constant country music in the air just in case you think you're not in Texas.

THE WATERFRONT SEAFOOD DELI & CAFE
Jib of Shepard and Evans sts.   *247-3933*
$

This small cafe is in the jib, or triangle, between Shepard and Evans streets and across from Ottis' Waterfront Restaurant. The lunch and dinner menu features seafood platters, crab cake sandwiches, shrimp burgers, hamburgers, hot dogs, soups, salads and more. Dinner specials are fresh fish, grilled or blackened, and may be tuna, trigger fish, mahi mahi, wahoo or grouper, whatever's fresh on the waterfront. You'll also find shrimp and oyster plates, along with a good selection of beer and wine. Takeout lunches are convenient for boaters or anyone on the go. Patrons can either eat in the cafe, outside in a grassy park in front of the cafe or take their meals with them.

WEST SIDE CAFE
4370-A Arendell St.   *240-0588*
$$-$$$

West Side Cafe is a favorite among locals and regulars. This upscale cafe offers creative lunches and gourmet dinners. The lunch menu offers soups (try the almost famous tomato soup), specialty sandwiches, burgers, hot dogs, subs and salads. Favorites include the pastrami, knockwurst and Swiss grilled on rye with Russian dressing; the stadium dog with slaw, kraut and chili; the grilled shrimp salad; and the smoked turkey sandwich.

While lunch is wonderful, dinner is when the West Side Cafe shines. Favorite appetizers are glazed shrimp, seafood

Insiders' Tips

The best place to find sand dollars or to rake clams is on the sand bars behind Carrott Island, which is part of the Rachel Carson Research Reserve in Beaufort.

Photo: Scott Taylor

Straight from the water to your plate. There's no better way.

potstickers with Oriental dipping sauce and soups. Entrees include shrimp and sun-dried tomatoes in a cream sauce over linguine, grilled beef in a cognac cream sauce and sauteed breast of chicken in a raspberry glaze. Each week a "temptations" menu is prepared to accompany the regular dinner menu. West Side Cafe has all ABC permits and serves beer, wine, select coffees and wonderful juices. There is a full deli offering homemade salads, meats, cheeses and fresh baked goods, and live jazz is a house special twice a week.

MRS. WILLIS' RESTAURANT
3004 Bridges St.   726-3741
$-$$

Mrs. Willis and her family have been serving home-cooked meals since 1949. The restaurant actually began in the home of "Ma Willis" as a barbecue and chicken takeout specializing in mini-lemon pies. Customers ate right in the kitchen, which is now Capt. Russell's lounge. In 1956, the restaurant moved into the garage, which is the front of today's restaurant, and additions were made through the years. The restaurant is a favorite of locals and visitors

who want a meal made from family recipes without going to the trouble themselves. Specialties include fresh pork barbecue, local seafood, char-grilled steaks and fresh vegetables. We recommend the Down East conch chowder for starters and then the prime rib — it is truly the best around for the value. Other entree suggestions include the seafood combination plate, chicken livers, pork chops, stuffed crab, rib eye or roast beef. There is a special every day and night. Mrs. Willis' can accommodate groups of any size and has all ABC permits.

Swansboro

CAPT. CHARLIE'S RESTAURANT
N.C. Hwy. 24 at Front St.   (910) 326-4303
$$

Capt. Charlie's restaurant specializes in fresh seafood, prime rib and steaks. Fried seafood is still popular, although there are plenty of other choices. Try the stuffed flounder or broiled shrimp and scallops. The steaks have developed a following too. Well-cooked food served in ample amounts brings people back to Capt. Charlie's again and again. With all ABC permits, you can have a drink while you wait for your dinner or with it if the mood strikes you.

THE FLYING BRIDGE

N.C. Hwy. 24E.   (910) 393-2416
$-$$

The Flying Bridge has a location advantage overlooking the Intracoastal Waterway and a neighboring sandy island. The restaurant has three delightful components: a restaurant serving lunch and dinner and featuring fresh grilled seafood, pasta, chicken, veal and steaks; a steam and raw bar offering oysters, clams, crabs and shrimp; and a ship's store deli, bakery and seafood market offering subs, bagels, and seafood. The restaurant and bar have all ABC permits. The restaurant offers daily specials and wonderful desserts.

WHITE OAK RIVER BISTRO

206 Corbett St.   (910) 326-1696
$$$

Just after the bridge in the familiar white building with inviting porches, White Oak River Bistro offers European cuisine for lunch and dinner. Among the lunch entrees, one may choose from a number of pastas and a selection of sauces or specialty Italian sandwiches. Dinner entrees include pastas with veal, chicken and seafood. White Oak River has all ABC permits and seating inside or out on the expansive porch.

YANA'S YE OLDE DRUGSTORE RESTAURANT

Front St.   (910) 326-5501
$

Just about everybody in Swansboro eats at Yana's at some time during the day. Whether it is the food or the company that attracts you, once you've been in, you'll come again and again. Breakfast specialties are many and all are cooked to order. Lunch can include a variety of sandwiches or soups, but the Bradburger, an all-beef hamburger with egg, cheese and bacon, lettuce and tomato, is worth a sample. And the desserts, well, see for yourself! The milk shakes are real, made with real ice cream and milk.

Down East

DRIFTWOOD RESTAURANT

Cedar Island   225-4861
$$

On the banks of Core Sound, the Driftwood includes a motel, a restaurant, a campground, a gift shop, a convenience store and a hunting guide service, but locals refer to everything at the complex by simply saying, "the Driftwood." The restaurant is known far and wide for the Friday night prime rib special and Saturday seafood buffet. Other entrees feature all types of seafood, including fresh crabmeat, shrimp salads, five-seafood combination plates and soft-shell crabs. You'll also enjoy ham, pork chops, chicken, barbecue and a children's menu. The restaurant is beside the Cedar Island-Ocracoke Ferry Terminal. This is a very popular restaurant year round, and we suggest you call for the off-season schedule. For information about the motel, see

the Crystal Coast Accommodations chapter, and for information about the campground, see the Camping chapter.

ISLAND RESTAURANT

Harkers Island   728-2214, 728-2247
$-$$

Liston and Carolyn Lawrence have been serving island residents and guests for 14 years from the same location. Open for breakfast, lunch and dinner, Island Restaurant offers everything from pizza and sandwiches to seafood platters and prime rib. Shrimp and eggs, along with all the traditional dishes, are served for breakfast. The lunch menu includes hamburgers, subs, pizza and spaghetti. Sandwiches range from oyster and shrimp burgers to flounder and crab sandwiches, and there is a takeout service. The restaurant's prime rib special and weekend seafood buffet just can't be beat and are well worth the drive no matter where you are. There is a full menu that includes shrimp and fish dinners, roast pork and cold seafood platters. You can have your meal prepared as you like it — fried, broiled, steamed or charbroiled. The "little mates menu" offers selections for children.

SEA LEVEL INN RESTAURANT

Sea Level   225-3651
$$

Twelve miles from the Cedar Island ferry terminal, Sea Level Inn Restaurant offers casual waterfront dining on Nelson's Bay off Core Sound. The inn is being converted to condominiums, but the restaurant is still open to the public. It serves lunch and dinner most weekdays, dinner on Friday and Saturday and breakfast and a lunch buffet on Sunday. The breakfast menu offers traditional Southern items. There is usually a hot lunch special, along with salads, seafood plates and sandwiches. Fresh local seafood and beef are favorites on the dinner menu, and everything is cooked to order.

Western Carteret County

BUTCHER BLOCK CAFE
Chatham St., Newport   223-5336
$

This cafe has a reputation for serving ample portions of well-prepared, home-style food. Breakfast is a time for pancakes, steak and eggs, omelettes and homemade biscuits. For lunch or dinner, guests will enjoy steak, seafood, roast turkey, chicken and pastry and more. Of course, there are sandwiches, soups and salads and daily lunch and dinner specials. Butcher Block Cafe is in downtown Newport.

GRANNY'S DINER
U.S. Hwy. 70, Newport   223-6106
$

Granny's Diner is country cooking in a family atmosphere. Open at 5:30 AM every day, Granny's serves a hearty breakfast that can't be beat. You'll find pork tenderloin, hamburger gravy on toast, eggs and all your favorites. For lunch and dinner, the menu features such entrees as barbecued ribs, steak, chicken and fish. Each Friday and Saturday night features prime rib and seafood, which draw quite a crowd, but it's the homemade banana pudding that keeps folks coming back. Granny's serves three meals a day Monday through Saturday. On Sunday, it's open for breakfast and lunch only.

FAIRWAY RESTAURANT
N.C. Hwy. 58, Cape Carteret   393-6444
$-$$

The Fairway Restaurant is a popular lunch spot for golfers, construction workers, business people, tourists and locals. Guests will find salads, quiche, specialty sandwiches, homemade soups and creative burgers. Dinner turns to steak and local seafood, and one of the specialties of the house is the prime rib. Done to perfection, exactly the way you request, it's moist and delicious. Fairway is closed on Sunday.

McCALL'S BAR-B-QUE & SEAFOOD
N.C. Hwy. 58, Cape Carteret   393-2929
$

This eastern North Carolina favorite opened in Cape Carteret during the fall of 1995, offering the barbecue and chicken that eastern North Carolina was raised on plus all the country vegetables that Grandma fixed. Add fresh fried fish, beef ribs and steaks and you've pretty much viewed the menu, but most folks go for the buffet. A seniors menu and takeout are offered, which makes beach arrivals very easy.

MAZZELLA'S ITALIAN RESTAURANT
N.C. Hwy. 58, Cape Carteret   393-8787
$$

About 2 miles north of Cape Carteret is Mazzella's. This is an authentic Italian restaurant with excellent dinners. The family-owned-and-operated business provides only the finest Italian cuisine and keeps diners coming back again and again. A number of creative entrees along with fresh pastas, homemade sauces, seafood and more, even sandwiches and pizzas are available.

T & W OYSTER BAR AND RESTAURANT
N.C. Hwy. 58, near Cape Carteret 393-8838
$-$$

T & W, since 1972, has had customers coming from any distance for steamed oysters served in rustic surroundings with a roaring fire when the weather is right. Try the combination of two or more seafood items, steak, chicken or a hamburger.

Guests will also find sandwiches and burgers made with fried shrimp, oysters, scallops or fish. T&W serves beer or wine and has an ABC license for brown-bagging. Don't let the line fool you. The restaurant can accommodate parties of close to 400, and the bar can handle plenty who stop by to feast on steamed oysters.

Crystal Coast
Nightlife

Most folks don't come to the Crystal Coast just for the nightlife. Many residents and visitors consider an after-dinner drink, a walk on the beach or a stroll along the boardwalk about all the nightlife they want after a full day of watersports or exploring the sites. Still, others want to dance and socialize in clubs.

The nightlife here can be divided into two categories: outside or inside. For those who prefer to be outside (the area's mild climate allows that most of the year), there are harbor cruises, the beach and deck bars. Some nightspots offer both, with lounges inside and out.

You won't find the number of rockin' and rollin' places other beach areas offer, but there are a few dance spots and watering holes for those who want to mingle.

Shagging to beach music is very popular here, and many clubs on the beach cater to shaggers. The shag is a type of dance that was probably a derivative of the beach bop, although it is smoother and done to rhythm and blues or North Carolina's own beach music. The dance is basically an eight-step, alternate-step that has a definite rhythm and distinct appearance. A few local beach clubs offer shagging lessons on certain weeknights.

Most coastal nightlife takes place on or around the water. In addition to the many waterfront bars, several local boats offer sunset trips or dinner cruises. Check our

Fishing, Watersports and Beach Access chapter for more information about cruises.

We have listed the spots that cater primarily to nightlife seekers. Some of these nightspots close during the winter so calling ahead is a good idea in the off-season. If the business is on Bogue Banks, we have used the milepost (MP) number for easy location. Many restaurants are considered nightspots because they feature live entertainment or have a bar, so check our Restaurants chapter for more information too. The local newspapers or any one of the weekly vacation guides might also help you in selecting a nightspot.

At the end of this section, we have included information about movie theaters, and about area liquor laws and ABC stores, which are the only places allowed to sell bottles of liquor.

Atlantic Beach

Atlantic Beach is home to a number of reputable nightspots that have stood the test of time and continue to offer quality entertainment. There are a few other spots that have been around for awhile, but we don't feel comfortable recommending them. New spots often open each spring. If you see a nightspot and we haven't listed it below, there may be several reasons for its omission — it may not be one we would recommend to a friend, it may have just opened in the spring or we may have unintentionally overlooked it. Check a place out with another Insider before you venture out if you have any doubts. Here are a few suggestions.

BEACH TAVERN
MP 2½   247-4466

Beach Tavern has been around since 1972 and continues to attract a very diverse group of people who aren't looking for anything fancy. There are pool tables, darts, a jukebox and a wide-screen television. The grill serves burgers, hot dogs and good pizza. Beach Tavern is open year round, seven days a week.

CAPT. STACY
Atlantic Beach Cswy.   247-7501
           (800) 533-9417

The Capt. Stacy fleet is well-known for its deep-sea fishing charters, but it also offers moonlight cruises and harbor tours during the summer. Private party and dinner cruises can also be arranged. For more information about the Capt. Stacy fleet, see the Crystal Coast Fishing, Watersports and Beach Access chapter.

CHANNEL MARKER
Atlantic Beach Cswy.   247-2344

The Channel Marker offers a fun bar and waterfront atrium lounge. An outside deck overlooks Bogue Sound, and dock space is available for those arriving by boat. The bar has all ABC permits and is a popular nightspot for all ages.

NO NAME
GRILL AND LOUNGE
MP 3   240-2224

The lounge and bar area are separated from the dining area, and there is usually a crowd in the summer. Cold domestic and imported beer, wine and mixed drinks will quench the thirst you work up dancing.

COURTNEY'S BEACH AND SHAG CLUB
Atlantic Beach Cswy.   247-7766

Courtney's caters to shaggers and beach music fans of all ages. The club is open to members and guests and has all ABC permits. Courtney's also offers weekly shag lessons to anyone interested, and they are sure to get you moving.

KELLI'S
Atlantic Beach Cswy.   247-1094

The professional crowd frequents Kelli's on weeknights, but on the weekends, a more diverse crowd of all ages fills the bar. The lounge has all ABC permits. Patrons can sit at the bar, at inside tables or on the outside deck. Dock space is available for those arriving by boat. For information about meals, see the Restaurants chapter.

JOLLY KNAVE
RESTAURANT AND LOUNGE
Oceanfront, Atlantic Beach Circle   726-8222

The Jolly Knave, also called Harpers, is right on the beach and offers a great view of the ocean and happenings on the beach. Kim's Upstairs Lounge provides a relaxed atmosphere for mingling. Down-

stairs, summertime guests will find a restaurant offering indoor or outdoor dining. The lounge and restaurant have all ABC permits and serve beer and wine.

MARY LOU'S BEACH CLUB
MP 2   240-7424

Mary Lou's is another nightspot for those interested in beach music and shagging. The DJ spins lots of beach music along with a little Top 40, and takes requests.

THE REEF RESTAURANT AND LOUNGE
Atlantic Beach Cswy.   726-3500

The Reef's upstairs lounge is a very popular place after work and on the weekends. At indoor tables, on the deck or at the bar, creative appetizers and island-style drinks are served along with beers, wines and mixed drinks. Live entertainment is provided during the summer.

SHA-BOOM
Atlantic Beach Cswy.   726-7000

Sha-Boom definitely caters to the younger, or those who consider themselves younger, crowd. The club DJ spins Top-40 tunes and the dance floor is usually packed. If you're a fan of events such as bikini contests, lingerie shows and male burlesque shows, you'll find them here. Sha-Boom has all ABC permits.

SKIPPER'S COVE RESTAURANT AND NIGHTCLUB
MP 2   726-3023

Skipper's Cove is a popular nightspot for those seeking a dinner club or just some entertainment and dancing. The club's popular house band plays beach, country and Top 40. Live entertainment is included with your dinner, and the restaurant is well-known for its extensive all-you-can-eat buf-

Photo: N.C. Travel and Tourism

The North Carolina Seafood Festival, held the first weekend in October in Morehead City, features arts and crafts, a street dance, fireworks, seafood sampling and a variety of water and beach sports.

fet. For those who would like to stop by later for a drink, some music and dancing, there is a small cover charge.

Pine Knoll Shores

CUTTY SARK LOUNGE
Ramada Inn, MP 8¼   247-4155

This lounge is in the Ramada Inn and is very popular. A disc jockey entertains on various nights, and the lounge is open weekdays and weekends.

MOLLY'S BAR & GRILL
Sheraton Resort, MP 4¾   240-1155

Offering beach nightlife at its best,

Molly's is an open-air bar and grill directly on the ocean. Molly's is just the spot to enjoy drinks with grilled seafood or chicken while you relax by the pool and the ocean.

WOODY'S ON THE BEACH
Sheraton Resort, MP 4¾   240-1155

Woody's is an oceanfront club with all ABC permits, and featuring a DJ and Top-40 music. This is a comfortable place to go with a crowd or to slip away with a special friend. The nightclub opens around 8 PM.

Indian Beach/Salter Path

FRANK AND CLARA'S
RESTAURANT & LOUNGE
MP 11   247-2788

The upstairs lounge offers a variety of music from beach and shag to country and rock. There is no cover charge and no membership required, so this is the perfect spot if you are visiting the area. The downstairs restaurant is excellent.

Emerald Isle

RUCKER JOHN'S
RESTAURANT AND MORE
143 Fairview Dr., MP 19½   354-2413

This relaxing, upbeat nightspot is very popular with the younger and middle-age sets. You'll find a nice bar area separate from the dining area. Rucker John's has all ABC permits and is just the right place to meet friends.

Beaufort

BACK STREET PUB
429 Front St.   728-7108

This laid-back place is in an alley be-hind Clawson's Restaurant and is called Back Bar by the regulars. In this small, out-of-the-way, yet popular spot, there is usually standing room only. An outdoor courtyard can offer some respite from the crowds. Beer, wine and wine coolers are served at the huge wooden bar. Upstairs is a "sailors' library" where folks can bring a book to swap or to read. Often there is live entertainment.

CRYSTAL QUEEN
600 Front St.   728-2527

This 82-foot coastal riverboat replica operates from the Beaufort waterfront and offers a variety of services. Guests can board for a sunset/moonlight cruise or a narrated daytime scenic tour. Private charters and catered events can also be accommodated. The vessel is licensed for 150 passengers.

DOCK HOUSE
500 Front St.   728-4506

Dock House has long been the traditional gathering place for locals and for those traveling along the Intracoastal Waterway. In spring, summer and fall, patrons sit on the boardwalk or on the upstairs deck and watch the boardwalk and

• 63

the Taylor's Creek boating activity. Live music is featured during the season. Dock House offers a great selection of beers, mixed drinks, wines and wine coolers, and it serves lunch and dinner.

MYSTERY TOUR
Beaufort Waterfront   728-7827

Docked in Beaufort's Taylor's Creek, the 65-foot double-decked *Mystery* tour boat cruises 18 miles of area waterways. See the writeup in our Attractions chapter for a complete description.

ROYAL JAMES CAFE
117 Turner St.   728-4573

Some consider the Royal James the best place in eastern North Carolina to shoot pool, and it is somewhat of a Beaufort tradition. You're likely to find players there whose fathers also frequented the place. The jukebox belts out country and rock. Ice-cold beer, wine, wine coolers, soft drinks and bar food are available.

Morehead City

ANCHOR INN
RESTAURANT & LOUNGE
2806 Arendell St.   726-2156

The Anchor Inn is beside Best Western Buccaneer Motor Inn (see our Accommodations chapter). Patrons can sit at the bar or cozy up in comfortable chairs. This is a great place to go to wind down after work or to wind up for weekend nightlife.

CAPT. RUSSELL'S LOUNGE
3004 Bridges St.   726-3205

Beside Mrs. Willis' Restaurant (see our Restaurants chapter), Capt. Russell's serves munchies, sandwiches and your favorite beverages every day. The lounge opens at 5 PM and has all ABC permits. Inside, you can relax at the bar or at tables. A game area has darts and six pool tables.

CAROLINA PRINCESS
Eighth St.   726-5479, (800) 682-3456

After unloading the anglers and their catches from a day of deep-sea fishing, the Carolina Princess is cleaned and prepared for a night of activity. The vessel offers cruises and is available for private charter.

CONTINENTAL SHELF
513 Evans St.   726-7454, (800) 426-7966

The Continental Shelf offers spring and summer evening cruises and a chance to see the surrounding area and wildlife by night. This 100-foot vessel is also available for private charter year round.

RAPSCALLIONS
715 Arendell St.   240-1213

Raps is a favorite gathering place among locals and is often packed during the summer. The downstairs bar area surrounds a huge oak bar and has tables and plenty of floor space. Upstairs are two levels of dining areas.

Swansboro

In the past, if you were looking for nightlife in the Swansboro area, you could check out one of the roadside pubs or lin-

Insiders' Tips

Sitting on the boardwalk in Beaufort is a great place to watch the sunsets.

ger over your dinner at a restaurant. Things have improved in recent years, and there are a few more options now for folks who don't want to go straight home. **The Flying Bridge Restaurant** in Cedar Point and several restaurants on the Swansboro waterfront have lounges that offer pleasant surroundings and mixed drinks.

Blowfish Grill, Front Street, (910) 326-3709, is a new bar and restaurant on the waterfront in downtown Swansboro. The bar offers a separate menu and a big-screen television. **K.W. McKenzie's**, 108 Corbett Avenue, (910) 326-2100, is a new bar that offers all ABC permits and plenty of hot hors d'oeuvres. **Swansboro Yacht Club**, Highway 24 between the bridges between Cape Carteret and Swansboro, (910) 326-6054, offers memberships for $5 per year. The club has a full bar and features live entertainment on weekends.

Movie Theaters

Atlantic Station Cinema 4, MP 3, at the west end of the Atlantic Station shopping center in Atlantic Beach, 247-7016

Emerald Plantation Cinema 4, MP 20 ¼, Emerald Isle, 354-5012

Cinema Triple, Morehead Plaza Shopping Center, Bridges Street in Morehead City, 726-2081

Morehead Twin, 1400 Arendell Street in Morehead City, 726-4710

Liquor Laws and ABC Stores

Mixed drinks, beer and wine are available in establishments in every incorporated town on the Crystal Coast except Newport. The community of Salter Path also has liquor by the drink. Mixed drinks are not allowed to be served in restaurants in the other unincorporated areas of Carteret County, which includes the Down East area. Most area restaurants offer a good selection of domestic and imported beers and wines. According to North Carolina law, a restaurant serving mixed drinks can not allow patrons to brown bag, or bring their own alcohol.

Grocery stores, convenience stores and specialty food shops throughout the area carry a variety of beers and wines. Liquor is only available through the county-operated Alcohol Beverage Control (ABC) package stores, that are found throughout the state. Local ABC stores are open Monday through Saturday. Hours vary depending on the season. Summer hours are generally from 10 AM to 9 PM, and winter hours, which usually begin in November and end around Easter, are from 10 AM to 7 PM.

Purchases at all of these ABC stores must be made with cash, MasterCard or VISA. No personal checks are accepted, and North Carolina law prohibits anyone younger than 21 years of age from entering the store or purchasing liquor.

There are six packages stores on the Crystal Coast:

Beaufort ABC Store, just north of the Highway 70/Live Oak Street intersection, 728-7924

Morehead City ABC Store, A & P Shopping Center, Highway 70, 726-2160

Atlantic Beach ABC Store, MP 2½, 726-3221

Emerald Isle ABC Store, MP 20¼, 354-6000

Cape Carteret ABC Store, Highway 24 beside the police department, 393-2631

Newport ABC Store, just east of the Highway 70/Howard Boulevard intersection, 223-4136

Swansboro ABC Store, Highway 24 between the bridges, 326-4810

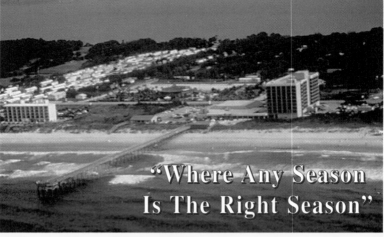

"Where Any Season Is The Right Season"

- Great Beachfront Location
- Indoor and Outdoor Pools
- Whirlpool and Fitness Center
- In-Room Refrigerator, Microwave, Coffee Maker, Hair Dryer, Iron & Ironing Board
- MOLLY'S BEACH SIDE BAR & GRILL—(seasonal) Casual fare and beverages poolside
- HARRY'S ISLAND BAR—The ideal place to relax, with comedy every Friday & Saturday nights
- WOODY'S II ON THE BEACH—The Island's Hottest Night Club
- PARADISE RESTAURANT—A popular place to dine with a Friday Seafood Buffet and Sunday Brunch
- 600' fishing pier

 **RESORT PACKAGES AVAILABLE**

- Seven Nights Make A Week
- Romance and Honeymoon
- Golf and Tennis
- Super Fall & Winter Getaways
- Special Holidays
- Winter Temperature 50° Average

1996 RATES

DATE	Oceanfront Suite	Oceanfront Guestroom	Oceanview Guestroom
March 29-May 23			
Sun.-Thurs.	$145	$115	$95
Fri. & Sat.	$145	$125	$115
May 24-Sept. 2			
Sun.-Thurs.	$210	$165	$135
Fri. & Sat.	$210	$165	$135
Sept. 3-Nov. 16			
Sun.-Thurs.	$145	$115	$95
Fri. & Sat.	$145	$125	$115
Nov. 17-Feb. 27, '97			
Sun.-Thurs.	$99	$69	$49-$59
Fri. & Sat.	$99	$79	$69

P.O. Box 3040
2717 W. Fort Macon Rd.
Atlantic Beach, NC 28512
(919) 240-1155

800-624-8875

FAX (919) 240-1452

Sheraton Atlantic Beach
RESORT

ITT Sheraton

Crystal Coast
Accommodations

The Crystal Coast is a diverse resort area with plentiful accommodations near natural and historic attractions. There are many attractive lodging choices, some rich with history and all full of our special Southern hospitality. Choose from luxurious oceanfront or soundside hotels and resorts, family-style motels and efficiency suites or cozy bed and breakfast inns.

On the beach, as in all resort areas, rates vary according to the season and the lodgings' proximity to water. If, for economy's sake, you are considering a location away from the water, you may want to ask about access either to the ocean or sound and if it is within easy walking distance.

The Crystal Coast is, more and more, becoming a year-round resort. There is little "off-season" anymore when visitors aren't here in some abundance, so it is always wise to make reservations in advance no matter what time of year. However, during the early spring and late fall shoulder seasons and in the winter, many establishments offer attractive weekend getaways, golf packages and special rates. The area is a popular site for meetings and conventions throughout the year, and many facilities offer meeting rooms and convention services. The Crystal Coast Civic Center (see Attractions) in Morehead City accommodates sizeable shows and gatherings with hotels and other lodgings conveniently nearby.

Each establishment has a different deposit and refund policy. While some require a deposit equal to one night's stay in advance, others will simply hold your reservation on your credit card. Often, a 24-hour notice is sufficient for a full refund, but some require as much as a three-day notice. Because of the area's popularity, extending your stay can be difficult but not impossible. Some places require up to 72-hours' notice for extensions past your originally scheduled departure date.

Many of the area's lodgings offer non-smoking rooms by request. The older inns restrict smoking to certain areas and often do not offer facilities to accommodate small children. North Carolina law prohibits pets in hotels and motels, although some lodgings make provisions for them.

This guide doesn't attempt to list all the accommodations available on the Crystal Coast. Rather, we've provided a sampling of some of our favorites. For more information about lodging, contact the Carteret County Tourism Development Bureau, P.O. Box 1406, Morehead City, NC 28557, (800) SUNNY NC or 726-8148. The bureau operates visitors centers at 3409 Arendell Street (U.S. Highway 70) in Morehead City and on N.C. Highway 58, just south of the intersection of highways 58 and 24.

For the purpose of comparing prices, we have placed each accommodation in a price category based on the rate for a double-occupancy room per night during the summer season. Winter rates can be substantially lower. Rates shown do not include state and local taxes. We've tried to be accurate, but amenities and rates are subject to change. It's best to verify information important to you, including credit cards accepted, when making your reservations.

$25 to $52	$
$53 to $75	$$
$76 to $99	$$$
More than $100	$$$$

Bogue Banks

Accommodations we'd recommend on the beach are just too numerous to list. Here, we offer a sample range of accommodations from full-service resorts to more rustic family and angler favorites. We also suggest you contact condominium developments on the beach (see the Crystal Coast Vacation Rentals chapter) because most offer attractive vacation rates.

Atlantic Beach

SHOW BOAT MOTEL

Atlantic Beach Causeway	726-6163
$-$$$	(800)SHO-BOAT

With easy access to Bogue Sound, this familiar motel with a stern paddlewheel offers lodging as well as water sports at affordable rates. Guests can fish from the motel wharf, complete with a fish-cleaning table, or take a dip in the pool. All rooms have refrigerators, and guests can enjoy picnic areas, grills and continental breakfasts. The motel offers family, corporate and AARP rates and is open all year. Also on site is Wreckreational Divers, 240-2244, a full-service dive shop for those who like to go "down under."

The Quiet Place
At Island Mile Post 5

The Atlantis is a special place created from a beautifully wooded, oceanfront site, unlike any other on the coast.

Most of our units are suites with efficiency kitchens, dining, living and sleeping areas. All have patios or decks facing the surf, cable TV with remote, HBO and all expected amenities, and pets are welcome in most units.

Our extraordinary outdoor pool is not the usual little concrete hole, but an environment created within a maritime woods; usually a quiet place for reading, swimming or merely floating.

You see, we are not an ordinary motel in an ordinary place. We are a very special place on the "Crystal Coast." Others have written. . ."*We have found our hotel*". . ."*one of the first, the Atlantis may still be the best.*"

Come let us show you.

Morehead City, NC - On the Ocean in Pine Knoll Shores
(919) 726-5168 - In U.S. TOLL FREE 800-682-7057

SUNDOWNER MOTEL

Atlantic Beach Causeway   726-2191
$-$$$

This older hotel offers quiet, clean waterfront accommodations to anglers and families. Kitchenettes are available, and patrons are given free boat-launching access and a wet slip during their stays. Complete with a pool, the motel has picnic tables, barbecue grills, brewed coffee and storage spaces. There is even a cozy wood stove for those chilly evenings.

BROWNSHIELDS BED & BREAKFAST

407 E. Atlantic Blvd.   726-5634
$$

Hosts James and Linda Brownshield offer casual, comfortable bed and breakfast hospitality in their fully renovated house that is a block from the beach. The inn has a first floor suite with a private entrance and two upstairs rooms with a shared bath.

Either choice will accommodate families with children or groups of friends. A full breakfast is served each morning in the dining room, and guests are encouraged to enjoy a second cup of coffee along with the ocean breeze on the front porches.

OCEANANA FAMILY RESORT MOTEL AND PIER

E. Fort Macon Rd. MP 1½   726-4111
$$-$$$

This comfortable, no-frills motel on the ocean provides guests with lots of extras. It offers a pool, children's play area, fishing pier, picnic tables and grills, free patio breakfasts in the warm season, beach chairs and a patrolled beach. Guests choose from standard rooms, oceanfront rooms or suites, all of which include refrigerators. The Oceanana closes for the season in mid-November and reopens the week before Easter.

HOLLOWELL'S MOTEL

E. Fort Macon Rd. MP 1¾   726-5227
$-$$$

Hollowell's is a family-oriented motel operated by Don Hollowell. It is three blocks from the ocean, and an easy walk to restaurants and shopping. Guests are offered quiet rooms with kitchenettes or refrigerators, a bridal suite or private cottages. All rooms have telephones, cable TV and HBO. A swimming pool with a slide is popular with children.

BUDGET INN

221 W. Fort Macon Rd. MP 2½   726-3780
$-$$$ (800) 636-3780

This clean, comfortable motel was recently remodeled and offers family and commercial rates by the day, week or month. All rooms have HBO, telephones and access to the pool. Kitchenette efficiencies are also available. The motel is an easy three-block walk from the ocean and is close to restaurants, shopping areas and the main beach amusement circle.

DAYS INN SUITES

Salter Path Rd. MP 2½   247-6400
$$-$$$$ (800) 972-3297

Days Inn Suites offer 90 attractive units. All rooms are on the main floor and two steps down will take you to a sunken sitting area and onto a private porch with a wonderful view of Bogue Sound. Suites offer either one king-size or two double beds, microwaves, refrigerators and coffeemakers. Guests have use of the outdoor pool, the boat ramp and the dock, and boat slips are available by reservation. Golf and dive trip packages are available. Days Inn Suites is within walking distance of the beach, shopping areas and restaurants.

SHERATON ATLANTIC BEACH RESORT

Salter Path Rd. MP 4½   240-1155
$$$$ (800) 624-8875

Sheraton is a full-service beachfront resort. All rooms include a refrigerator, a microwave, a coffee maker, a hairdryer, an iron and ironing board, and a private balcony. Suites with one bedroom, a living room and a whirlpool tub are available. The staff will arrange anything from same-day dry cleaning to golf and tennis. Fine dining is available in the resort's Paradise Restaurant (see our Restaurants chapter) and, in season, an oceanfront grill serves casual fare and beverages. Lafftrax offers live weekend comedy shows, and Woody's nightclub (see our Nightlife chapter) is a local's favorite for dance music and drinks. The resort has its own fishing pier for anglers. Catering and full banquet services are available for small or large meetings. Guests enjoy the indoor pool and spa, the outdoor pool, the fitness room, the game room and the gift shop.

Pine Knoll Shores

WINDJAMMER INN

Salter Path Rd. MP 4½   247-7123
$$$-$$$$ (800) 233-6466

All of the rooms at the attractive Windjammer Inn are oversized and oceanfront with private balconies, refrigerators, cable TV and two telephones. The

A Brogue All Their Own

Down East is the area in Carteret County that begins at the North River Bridge just east of Beaufort and continues to Cedar Island. Natives of the Down East area have a brogue all their own that combines Old English sayings and pronunciations with terms coined and used by elders. As modern ways encroach on these communities and more people leave the area to take jobs elsewhere, the unique Down East brogue seems destined to lose its purity.

Even North Carolina natives don't always understand Down Easters terms. A few of the terms you might need to know before you wander off are offered below. Listen carefully.

Addle/Addled: dazed or confused. He was addled by all the new fishin' laws.

Blow: wind or windy conditions. There's going to be a blow tonight.

Cam (calm): There are several degrees of cam. "Cam" indicates no wind but possibly some motion in the water. "Slick cam" means a stillness in the air and the water.

Catawampus: out of line or crooked. She turned the whole thing catawampus.

Common: not in good taste; to act below oneself. What he did was common.

Cut: a small body of water that cuts away from the main body and leads to land.

Ding batter or **Dit Dot**: someone from out of the area, or from "off."

Off: somewhere out of the Down East area. He married a girl from off.

He ain't ugly: he is handsome.

I think: used in agreement, in place of yes.

Ill: irritable or angry. Mom's ill with sister for not behaving.

Jot: to write.

Landin': the shore. I'm going down to the landin'.

Merkle bush: a type of myrtle bush; said to keep bugs away.

Mommick: to bother, harass or aggravate. I have been mommicked by that son of mine.

Nary: none. I haven't heard nary a word.

Purty: pronunciation of pretty, but often used to mean unattractive. He sure is purty with that black eye and dirty hair.

Run a'ground: to finish, end anything; unable to move. I've eaten so much I've run a'ground.

Scrape: a bad or undesirable situation. My car's not running so I'm in a scrape now.

Skiff: a small, usually cabinless, boat. There will be a few skiffs in the creek today.

Slam: an intensifier usually meaning completely. He loaded the pot slam full of hard crabs.

glass-enclosed elevator is an unexpected surprise and offers a great view of the ocean. Guests enjoy the oceanfront pool, private beach area with beach services and complimentary coffee each morning. There is a two-night minimum during summer weekends and a three-night minimum on holiday weekends. We recommend you get a room on the top floor and relax.

SEA HAWK MOTOR LODGE
Salter Path Rd. MP 4¾   726-4146
$$$ (800) 682-6898

This comfortable and newly remodeled lodge offers 36 oceanfront rooms with balconies or patios, phones, cable TV and refrigerators. Connecting double rooms, a cottage and villas are also available. The coffee shop is open in season, and a pool is situated in the middle of a large, grassy lawn facing the ocean. Guests especially enjoy lazing on the lawn in the late evening.

HOLIDAY INN OCEANFRONT
Salter Path Rd. MP 4¾   726-2544
$$$-$$$$ (800)733-7888

The dependable Holiday Inn services and accommodations are further enhanced by the oceanfront location. Open year-round, the hotel offers 114 rooms with refrigerators. Guests enjoy the pool, pool bar, 800 feet of private beach, a picnic area and special golf privileges. The hotel is home to the Palms Restaurant and Oasis Lounge and can accommodate small or large groups for vacations or meetings.

ATLANTIS LODGE
Salter Path Rd. MP 5   726-5168
$$$-$$$$ (800) 682-7057

Set among the beautiful live oaks on the oceanside, the Atlantis Lodge was among the first hotels built on Bogue Banks. Its patrons are faithful and never disappointed. Most units are arranged as suites, offering efficiency kitchens, dining, living and sleeping areas. All have patios or decks facing the surf, cable TV and other expected amenities. Recreation areas, equipment, golf packages and complimentary beach furniture and lifeguard services are extended to guests. The outdoor pool is a quiet place for sunning and swimming and the third-floor lounge has an adjoining library. Unlike most hotels, the Atlantis makes provisions for pets. In August the lodge hosts a popular sand-sculpture contest (see the Crystal Coast Annual Events chapter).

ROYAL PAVILION RESORT
Salter Path Rd. MP 5½   726-5188
$$-$$$$ (800) 533-3700

This is the newest oceanfront resort and conference center on Bogue Banks. Many remember it as the former John Yancey Motor Hotel; however it has been extensively renovated, and the new resort offers 115 light, airy guest rooms. Many rooms are equipped with special amenities, including complete efficiency kitchens. An outdoor pool, 1,500 feet of private beach, cable TV service and local activities arrangements, including golf packages, provide guests with an abundance of leisure-time choices. The resort offers four conference

Insiders' Tips

The deep roots of sea oats help anchor the sand dunes. The plant is protected by law, so don't even think of harvesting a few, even if they're dead.

rooms for meetings or private events and the Tradewinds Restaurant (see the Crystal Coast Restaurants chapter) and lounge.

IRON STEAMER RESORT

Salter Path Rd. MP 6¾   *247-4221*
$$-$$$ *(800) 332-4221*

On its quiet stretch of the island, the Iron Steamer got its name because the remains of a sunken Civil War blockade runner are visible from the resort's pier at low tide. Favored by families and anglers, it has 49 oceanfront rooms and an 800-foot lighted pier complete with tackle shop, fishing gear rentals and a 24-hour snack bar. Rooms are available with refrigerators and private balconies. Guests have access to the beach, pool and pier. Its operating season is from Easter to Thanksgiving.

RAMADA INN OCEANFRONT

Salter Path Rd. MP 8¼   *247-4155*
$$$-$$$$ *(800) 338-1533*

On the oceanside in a quiet mid-island residential area, this seven-floor inn offers all oceanfront rooms with double or king-size beds. Each room has a small private balcony, and guests have access to the beach, the pool, golf and tennis courts, the Cutty Sark Lounge and the Clamdigger Restaurant, a favorite of locals who know all about the weeknight specials. Meeting and banquet facilities are available. Open year round, the Ramada Inn offers attractive weekend packages from November through March.

Salter Path

WILLIAM-GARLAND MOTEL

Salter Path MP 10½   *247-3733*
$-$$

This small family-owned motel has eight rooms and three mobile units. Nine are efficiencies, and two provide only simple sleeping accommodations. Don't expect anything fancy, but do expect a family atmosphere and clean, comfortable surroundings. Guests have access to the ocean via a nature trail walkway (about 200 yards) and access to the 20-acre Salter Path Dunes Natural Area, perfect for walking, sunning and picnicking. William-Garland Motel is beside the Big Oak Drive-In, home of the famous shrimpburger.

Photo: Scott Taylor

Vacations are for floating around.

Oak Grove Motel

Salter Path MP 10½   247-3533
$-$$

This motel has impressed us because it's so tidy, and in the shade of live oaks, it always looks cool, even on the hottest days. It has one- and two-story stone-sided units with standard rooms and efficiency apartments with porch rockers for enjoying the shade. The motel is a family facility and has lots of repeat business. It does not take one-night reservations on weekends.

Emerald Isle/Cape Carteret

Islander Motor Inn

Islander Dr.   354-3464
$$-$$$ (800) 354-3464

Islander is on the ocean in Emerald Isle, and although the rooms do not directly face the water, most offer a wonderful east-west view of the sea and beach. The two-story brick motel offers guests easy beach access, a pool, a luxurious lawn area, a restaurant, room refrigerators and large meeting rooms for conferences or gatherings.

Parkerton Inn

N.C. Hwy 58 N.   393-9000
$-$$ (800)393-9909

Opened two years ago, the Parkerton Inn is just north of the intersection of highways 58 and 24. It is especially convenient for guests overnighting for the summer outdoor drama, *Worthy Is The Lamb*. Guests may choose any of several room arrangements including kitchenette efficiencies and rooms equipped for the handicapped. Golf

packages are offered, and a complimentary continental breakfast is included.

Emerald Isle Inn and Bed and Breakfast

502 Ocean Dr.   354-3222
$$$

A.K. and Marilyn Detwiller accommodate their island guests in two-bedroom suites with private baths and patios or in double rooms with a shared bath. Guests enjoy views of the ocean and sound from porches with comfortable swings, nearby beach access and the use of beach chairs and umbrellas. A full breakfast is served each morning in the dining room. The Detwillers also offer apartments that accommodate eight guests, but they do not provide linens or breakfast in these apartments.

Harborlight Guest House

332 Live Oak Dr.   393-6868
$$$-$$$$ (800) 624-VIEW

Situated on a spectacular peninsula on Bogue Sound off Highway 24, the Harborlight Guest House offers bed and breakfast accommodations in its seven suite or room arrangements. The rambling three-story inn, once a restaurant used by the ferry service, is particularly graced with views, 530 feet of shoreline and a quiet setting close to Emerald Isle beaches and attractions. Gourmet breakfasts are served in the dining room, on the waterfront terrace or privately for guests in the luxury upstairs suites. Open year round, the inn offers its 20-person capacity conference room for seminars, weddings and other group gatherings.

Beaufort

The majority of accommodations in Beaufort are historic bed and breakfast inns that offer charming surroundings, memorable views and warm hospitality. All are in the historic district and within walking distance of the waterfront, boardwalk, shopping areas, restaurants, N.C. Maritime Museum and historic sites.

Room arrangements and breakfast specialties vary in each inn. Most do not have facilities for young children or pets, and many limit smoking to certain areas of the house. There are two large hotel-like inns, Beaufort Inn and Inlet Inn. Both were constructed in the old Beaufort style, as required by the Beaufort Historic Preservation Commission.

BEAUFORT INN

101 Ann St.   728-2600
$$$-$$$$ (800) 726-0321

On Gallant's Channel, Beaufort Inn offers 44 rooms, all with private porches and rocking chairs for viewing the activity in the waterway. Rooms are furnished in

early American decor incorporating local arts and crafts.

Owned and operated by Bruce and Katie Ethridge, the inn opened in 1987 and has become well-known for its complimentary breakfasts. A typical breakfast, served in a cozy dining room with a fireplace, includes Katie's breakfast pie, croissants, cereal, Danish pastries, fresh-squeezed juice and coffee. The inn has one large meeting room and two smaller meeting rooms, which accommodate 18 to 20 people. An exercise room, spa and boat slips are available, and Katie can loan you a bike or help you with area information.

CAPTAIN'S QUARTERS BED & BISCUIT

315 Ann St.   728-7711
$$$-$$$$

This two-story white home with its luxurious wraparound porch offers guests the quiet elegance of a Victorian summer at the shore. You'll find Ms. Ruby, Capt. Dick Collins and daughter Polly to be delightful hosts.

The three upstairs bedrooms feature private powder rooms and baths. House traditions include a fresh biscuit continental breakfast and a toast to the sunset each

evening, which is celebrated with wines and fresh fruit juices. The Collins family assists guests with area information, reservations and services, including use of a PC, modem and fax machine. Payment by personal check is preferred.

THE CEDAR'S INN AT BEAUFORT
305 Front St.   728-7036
$$$-$$$$

Standing at the corner of Front and Orange streets, the two stately homes that make up the inn are surrounded by gardens whose flowers and herbs color each room and flavor the specialties served by the inn's restaurant. Both houses, c. 1768 and 1851, have been completely restored and furnished with period pieces. Linda and Sam Dark extend their hospitality in every detail. There are 15 rooms and suites with private baths and second-floor porches with rocking chairs. Some rooms are designed with separate sitting rooms; one has a whirlpool tub and others have fireplaces. The inn is open all year, and a full breakfast is included in the price.

COUSINS BED AND BREAKFAST
303 Turner St.   504-3478
$$$

Hosts Martha and Elmo Barnes extend their hospitality in Beaufort at the Ward-Adair House, c. 1855, across the street from the county courthouse. Accommodations include four private rooms with baths, breakfast prepared by Elmo, who has authored his own cookbook, and use of the house and private garden for customized occasions. The dining room will comfortably seat 20 for small meetings, parties or wedding receptions, which the Barnes are happy to cater. Cousins welcomes guests year round and offers winter weekend cooking packages featuring Elmo's guidance and instruction.

DELAMAR INN BED AND BREAKFAST
217 Turner St.   728-4300
$$$ (800)349-5823

Delamar Inn, c. 1866, is restored to its original charm and accommodates guests in three antique-furnished guest rooms with private baths. The Scottish charm and hospitality of hosts Mabel and Tom Steepy begin with a breakfast of homemade breads, muffins, jams, cereals and fruits and extends to helpful arrangement of their guests' plans to enjoy the beaches, explore the town by bicycle, golf, tennis or whatever suits the moment. Cookies and refreshments await at the day's end. The Steepys welcome guests year round.

INLET INN
601 Front St.   728-3600
$$$-$$$$

The 35-room Inlet Inn opened in 1985 in the same block of Front Street occupied by the original Inlet Inn of the 19th century. Today's inn offers harborfront rooms with a sitting area, bar, refrigerator and ice maker. Many rooms open onto private porches. Others offer cozy fireplaces or window seats for viewing the Cape Lookout Lighthouse, Beaufort Inlet and Beaufort waterfront from the best vantage available. Guests are served a continental breakfast of homemade pastries, fruits, coffee and tea in the lounge, where they are also invited to come between 5 and 7 PM for complimentary wine and cheese. Boat slips, a courtyard garden, the rooftop Widow's Walk Lounge and an on-site meeting room are also available for guests' use year round.

LANGDON HOUSE
135 Craven St.   728-5499
$$$-$$$$

Innkeeper and restorer of the Langdon

PECAN TREE INN
Bed & Breakfast
Innkeepers: Susan and Joe Johnson

"A magnificent Victorian home located in the heart of the Beaufort Historic District, one half block from the waterfront."

(919) 728-6733
116 Queen Street • Beaufort, NC 28516

House (c. 1733), Jimm Prest extends the hospitality of a good friend and provides all the extras that give his guests a personalized experience of Beaufort. He'll arrange for boating to the best getaway beaches and send you there with a beach basket of comforts. He can tell you where and how to catch sea trout, take care of an ache or pain, help with a restaurant selection or reservation and take care of needs you didn't know you had. Each of the four guest rooms has a queen-size bed, a private bath and is furnished with antiques in keeping with the old Colonial/Federal home. Go there to relax: Sleeping late is considered a compliment to the innkeeper. The hallmark of Jimm's hospitality is the full breakfast, served until 11 AM. A hearty helping of fresh fruits is followed by one of the house specialties such as stuffed French toast or Belgian waffles. With a word in advance,

he's happy to cater to special diets and preferences. Just ask. There are no problems unless you plan to pay with a credit card, none of which are accepted, but personal checks are just fine as long as you promise there's money in your account. Bring a change of clothes and a good attitude, and Jimm will take care of the rest.

PECAN TREE INN
116 Queen St.   728-6733
$$$-$$$$

This 1860s two-story Victorian home, complete with gingerbread trim and turrets, is a charming seven-guestroom bed and breakfast remodeled by hosts Sue and Joe Johnson. Each spacious room has special character and a private bath, and two romantic suites have king-size canopied beds and Jacuzzis. A stay at the inn includes an expanded continental breakfast served in the formal dining room or on the

inviting wraparound front porch. You will enjoy Susan's fresh-baked homemade muffins, cakes and breads, fruit, cereal and specially ground coffee. The Johnsons are glad to assist with daytrip plans or arrange for box lunches, beach chairs or bicycles. They encourage simple relaxation on the cool porches overlooking the inn's ever-expanding herb and flower gardens.

Morehead City

BEST WESTERN
BUCCANEER INN

2806 Arendell St.   726-3115
$$-$$$ (800) 682-4982

The Buccaneer Motor Lodge has 91 attractive rooms with refrigerators, some with a king-size bed and Jacuzzi. Guests are offered complimentary full, hot breakfasts, newspapers, free local calls and cable TV. Meeting and banquet facilities are available. Special rates apply for corporate, commercial and military guests, and golf packages are available. The lodge is beside Morehead Plaza for shopping and is a short driving distance from Atlantic Beach. The Anchor Inn Restaurant and Lounge (see the Restaurants chapter) is beside the motel.

COMFORT INN

3012 Arendell St.   247-3434
$-$$$ (800) 422-5404

The Comfort Inn, like others in the national hotel chain, offers reliably comfortable rooms, a pool and complimentary continental breakfast each morning. Convenient to the Crystal Coast Civic Center and all beach and historic attractions, the Comfort Inn has 100 rooms and additional meeting facilities to accommodate any gathering. Local phone calls are free, fax service is available and each room has cable TV. Golf, diving and fishing packages are also available. The inn is near Shoney's, Hardee's and the Morehead Plaza. Corporate, AARP and AAA discounts are offered.

ECONO LODGE CRYSTAL COAST

3410 Bridges St.   247-2940
$-$$$ (800) 533-7556

The Econo Lodge is two blocks from the Crystal Coast Civic Center and offers 56 rooms at very attractive rates. Amenities include cable TV, free local calls, a pool and complimentary continental breakfasts. Special packages for golf, deep-sea fishing, scuba diving and other area activities offer real values. A restaurant and a lounge are nearby.

HAMPTON INN

4015 Arendell St.   240-2300
$$-$$$ (800) 538-6338

Hampton Inn, overlooking Bogue Sound, offers beautiful views of the waterway and the island of Bogue Banks. The 120-room inn has a fresh nautical decor. Guests enjoy an outside pool and deck area, free continental breakfasts served in a sunroom, free accommodations for children and an exercise room. Meeting rooms, plenty of parking and golf, tennis and fishing packages are available. Restaurants and shopping areas are nearby.

Down East

There are a few motels in the Down East area and we've listed them here. For information about Down East campgrounds, see the Camping chapter.

MORRIS MARINA KABIN KAMPS

1000 Morris Marina Rd.
Atlantic   225-4261
$

Rustic cabins that vary in size to accommodate four to 12 people are rented

on North Core Banks by the day. The price indicated here is a per-person rate based on a full cabin. "Rustic" means mattresses or bunks, gas cooking stoves, a sink and a toilet. Most cabins have hot water and showers; some have lights. Although water is potable, most visitors bring their own. Pack as you would for a camping trip and you'll be most comfortable. Long a guarded secret of anglers, this cabin settlement is also the choice getaway for shellers in the spring and birdwatchers in the fall. Three ferries a day (until December) run from Atlantic to the cabins. Making reservations well in advance is recommended. Take your four-wheel drive vehicle and drive the 22 miles of beach to historic Portsmouth Village at Ocracoke Inlet. See the Ferries chapter for more information.

ALGER G. WILLIS FISHING CAMPS
Hwy. 70E., Davis   729-2791
$

Twenty-five rustic cabins are available on South Core Banks at Shingle Point. Cabins accommodate four to 12 people and are rented on a per-night basis for about $11 per person if full. All that is provided is mattresses, a gas stove, potable water (but don't forget to bring your own), sinks, toilets, a roof, a floor and walls. Bring your own of everything else, but expect a beautiful getaway. A caretaker is available when you run out of kerosene, ice, bread or whatever. He'll get supplies you need on the next ferry from the mainland. Four ferries arrive daily between early April and late October. It's not just

for anglers anymore, so plan ahead and reserve early. See the ferries chapter for more information.

DRIFTWOOD MOTEL
Cedar Island   225-4861
$

This remodeled motel at the Cedar Island-Ocracoke Ferry Terminal consists of 37 rooms, each with two double beds and a television. There are no phones in the rooms, so this is a good place to get away from it all. The motel complex also has a restaurant known for fresh local seafood and prime rib, a campground (see the Camping chapter), a gift shop, a grocery store and a guide service for hunting and fishing. The motel closes from mid-January to mid-March.

CALICO JACK'S INN AND MARINA
Harkers Island   728-3575
$

During summer and fishing seasons, this 24-room motel offers comfortable accommodations with two double beds and a restaurant. The marina accommodates boats up to 50 feet and offers gas and diesel fuel, supplies, refreshments and a complete tackle shop. Charter boats and ferry and water-taxi service to Cape Lookout are also available.

FISHERMAN'S INN
Harkers Island   728-5780
$

This six-room motel faces the water and is owned and operated by Don and Linda Flood. The Floods also have a cot-

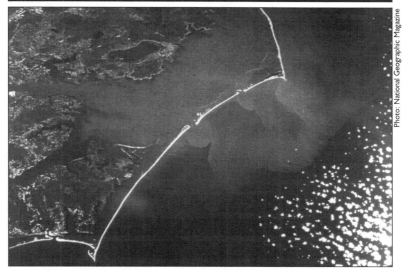

Photo: National Geographic Magazine

The Crystal Coast forms the southern part of North Carolina's Outer Banks.

tage with a full kitchen and bath available. The inn offers a marina, campground, boat slips, tackle and bait shop and charters.

HARKERS ISLAND FISHING CENTER
Harkers Island   728-3907
$-$$

Harkers Island Fishing Center has a 20-room motel that sits back off the road and offers standard, no-frills accommodations. Ten efficiencies containing two double beds, a refrigerator and a stove are available. Guests have easy access to the marina, boat ramp, charter boats and ferry service to Cape Lookout.

SEA LEVEL
EXTENDED CARE FACILITY
Sea Level   225-4611
Cost determined by amount of care required

Sea Level Extended Care Facility provides long-term care as well as day-to-day care for those in need of attention. The facility has a guest program that allows vacationers to bring a family member requiring special care along. The program is used by many people who want a vacation but find it difficult to leave someone behind. Contact the facility for more information about this program.

Resort To A Simpler Lifestyle.

Vacations for Thousands . . . that's what Emerald Isle Realty is all about. With over 30 years of experience in sales and rentals, vacationers have become owners who now relax in their very own beach home.

Happy families who return year after year have made us one of the most successful sales and property management real estate companies on the East Coast.

While vacationing with us, stop by and discuss owning your own place at the beach. Our experienced sales staff will assist you in finding "just the right" property for you.

Emerald Isle Realty

A Tradition On The Carolina Coast Since 1962

SALES: (919) 354-4060 • (800) 304-4060
RENTALS: (919) 354-3315 • (800) 849-3315

7501 Emerald Drive, Emerald Isle, NC 28594

Crystal Coast
Vacation Rentals

The Crystal Coast is the perfect place to vacation. If this is your first visit, you are about to discover why so many people come back year after year. The climate is moderate year round, the scenery is spectacular and the people are friendly and welcoming.

Now, let's make your stay on the coast as easy as possible. There are about 10,000 beds for rent on the Crystal Coast. That's the figure the Tourism Development Bureau, 726-8148 or (800) SUNNY NC, uses, and those options range from small fishing units near the pier — perfect if you spend all your time surf casting or pier fishing — to plush condos. All you need to do is make a few simple decisions, starting with when to visit the coast.

The Rate Season

Rental rates change according to the season and that's sometimes confusing. To add to the confusion, not all rental agencies on the Crystal Coast use the same season schedule. It's always best to check with each company for specific season/rate changes.

Generally, most rental agencies on the east end of Bogue Banks use two seasons: in-season (Memorial Day through Labor Day) and off-season (any other time). On the west end of Bogue Banks, many rental agencies use these descriptions: prime season (mid-June through mid-August), mid-season (May through mid-June and mid-August through September), off-season (September through November and March through April) and winter (December through February).

Vacation rentals can vary from $275 a week to more than $1,500. Costs can be as much as 25 to 30 percent less in off-season than in-season. For that reason, and because the weather is relatively warm year round, many people decide to vacation here in the "shoulder seasons" of spring, fall and winter. Decide what you need, and call rental agencies listed in the following pages or others listed in the phone directory to see what is offered.

Most visitors to the Crystal Coast come in the months of June, July and August. Tourism plays a big part in the county's economy. The average visitor stays 4.2 nights, and all together, visitors have an estimated $242,342,321 annual impact on the Crystal Coast.

Locations and Types of Accommodations

Rental agencies can help you find the perfect place, whether that's the angler's cottage close by the pier, the family cottage within walking distance of the beach or the oceanfront condo with all the amenities of home. Rental costs vary with the type of accommodation and the location. Always check rental brochures or

The**Prudential**
Sun-Surf Realty

We manage over 250 vacation homes and condos on North Carolina's Crystal Coast

RESERVATION HOTLINE
800-553-7873
(919) 354-2658

The**Prudential**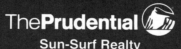

Sun-Surf Realty
7701 Emerald Drive
Emerald Isle, NC 28594

800-849-2958   919-354-2958

with an agent about the location. This is very important if you are planning to walk to the beach. Carrying chairs, coolers and an umbrella while watching out for your children can make a short trip seem a lot longer if you are several rows back from the water. Of course, generally speaking, the farther away from the water, the less expensive the rental rate.

Here's the general idea of what location descriptions mean. Oceanfront means facing the ocean with no physical barrier, road or property lines between you and the beach. Oceanside means you can walk to the beach without crossing a major road, but there might be other rows of houses between your cottage and the ocean. Soundfront means the cottage fronts the sound and you have easy access to the water. Soundside means you are on the sound side of the road and in walking distance of the sound. Often, soundside cottages and developments offer guests access to the

ocean and beach by means of a walking path.

Pets

If you plan to bring a pet, tell the agent. Some places allow them but charge an additional fee, and others don't allow them at all. Vacationers who choose to violate this rule are subject to eviction and the loss of their deposit. Boarding kennels are available in the area. Check the Animal Services section of the Service Directory in this book.

Furnishings and Equipment Rentals

If you are renting an apartment or condo, it will likely be fully furnished. Most rental brochures list the furnishings (small appliances, TVs, VCRs, stereos, toasters, microwaves) and other items that are provided, such as beach chairs and umbrel-

Spring and fall at the Crystal Coast offer visitors a more relaxed atmosphere with fewer vehicles on the roads and fewer people on the beaches or at restaurants.

Insiders' Tips

las, hammocks and grills. You might only need to bring your sheets and towels, or you can rent those from the rental company. If not, there are a few independent agencies that rent linens along with other extras, such as baby furniture and extra folding beds. Check our Service Directory. In many of the units, a telephone is available for local calls and for credit card or collect long-distance calls. Some do not have phones, so if that's important check ahead.

Occupancy

Most vacation rentals are offered on a weekly basis, particularly in the summer. If you would like just a few days at the beach, check with an agency and see what can be arranged. Everything is more flexible in the off-season. Each rental unit is governed by rules and regulations spelled out in rental brochures and contracts.

Other Tips

Renting vacation accommodations is a business on the coast, so approach it that way. Be sure to read the rental agreement carefully, and ask questions if there is anything you don't understand. By getting all your questions answered, you can often reduce the number of items you bring and make it an enjoyable vacation for everyone. If you are a smoker, check to see if smoking is permitted. If you are planning a house party, let the agent know in advance. If large parties are prohibited and you ignore this rule, you could be evicted and lose your money.

Most visitors who arrange rentals on the Crystal Coast are family-oriented people who prefer a quiet, relaxed beach vacation.

Rental Companies

The Crystal Coast offers numerous cottages and condos to choose from, but you need to shop early. Many places are booked early in the year. Below is a listing of just a few of the many Crystal Coast companies that handle rentals. If you spot a particular place you would like to rent, just jot down the location and contact one of these rental companies. Or, simply tell the company representative what you want in the way of size and location and let them guide you. Most can send a picture-illustrated brochure featuring the available cottages and condos to help you make your choice. We have alphabetically arranged these companies and given their telephone numbers for your convenience.

Bogue Banks

Alan Shelor Rentals, 240-7368, (800) 786-7368, offers condo and cottage rentals in Atlantic Beach and Pine Knoll Shores, as well as some rentals in the Morehead City area.

Photo: Scott Taylor

The famous wild ponies can be spied from Beaufort's Front Street as they graze on Carrot Island.

Bluewater Associates Better Homes and Gardens, 354-2323, (800) 326-3826, handles 118 cottages and condominiums in the Emerald Isle area. Let Carol or Faye handle your special rental needs.

Century 21 Coastal Properties, 726-2718, (800) 849-1995, can suit your every vacation desire. Whether you are seeking a cottage, an efficiency or a condo — oceanfront, soundfront or something in between — Coastal Properties can help.

Century 21- Coastland Realty, 354-2060, (800) 822-2121, handles rentals of cottages and condos in a variety of styles and prices in Emerald Isle.

Coldwell Banker Spectrum Properties, Atlantic Beach, 247-5366 or (800) 334-6390; and Emerald Isle, 354-3040 or (800) 367-3381. Both offices offer condo and cottage rentals along Bogue Banks from Atlantic Beach to Emerald Isle, in Cape Carteret and in Morehead City.

Colony By the Sea, 247-7707, has oceanfront and ocean view one- and two-bedroom condo units.

Emerald Isle Realty Inc., 354-3315, 354-2355, (800) 849-3315, offers about

Family Vacations

Only the sun outshines us.
26 miles of sun, sand & surf.

Golf,
Fishing,
Historic
Sites.
The
Perfect Spot.

Call Today For a Free Brochure

Atlantic Beach Office
919-247-3096
1-800-334-2727

Bogue Shores Suites
919-726-7071
1-800-238-5339

SUMMER WINDS

Exclusive On-site Rental Agent
Summer Winds Office
919-247-1000
1-800-334-6866
Conference/Retreat Facilities
Fishing/Golf Packages

Tetterton Management Group

Full Service Sales Division in Each Location

650 vacation properties in Emerald Isle, Atlantic Beach and Pine Knoll Shores.

ERA Carteret Properties Rental, 354-3005, (800) 448-2951, continues to offer a large selection of cottages and condos in Emerald Isle, and will provide extra attention to meet your every vacation need.

Gull Isle Realty, 726-7679, (800) 682-6863, handles vacation rentals of cottages and condos from Atlantic Beach west to Salter Path.

Ketterer Realty, 354-2704, (800) 849-2704, offers a wide variety of vacation rentals — everything from oceanfront homes to beach cottages and condos — in Emerald Isle.

LOOK Realty, 354-4444, (800) 849-0033, offers a wonderful selection of rental cottages and condo units in Emerald Isle.

National Sound 'n Sea Real Estate, 247-7368, (800) 682-RENT, has vacation houses and condos rentals in Atlantic Beach and Pine Knoll Shores.

Ocean Resorts Inc. - Condo Rentals, 247-3600, (800) 682-3702, handles the vacation rentals for the condo subdivisions of Dunescape Villas, Island Beach & Racquet Club, Bogue Shores and Beachwalk Villas at Pine Knoll Shores.

Realty World-Johnson Realty, 247-5150, (800) 972-8899, features seasonal rentals of all types including oceanfront rentals and first- or second-row rentals.

Sands Oceanfront Resorts, 247-2636, (800) 334-2667, handles vacation rentals for Sands Villa Resort, A Place At the Beach and Sea Spray, all in Atlantic Beach. For information about timeshare

units at A Place at the Beach, see the Timeshare section below.

Sun-Surf Realty, 354-2658, (800) 553-SURF, handles the rental of more than 200 homes, cottages and condos from Emerald Isle to Pine Knoll Shores.

Tetterton Management Group, Atlantic Beach, 247-3096, (800) 334-2727; Indian Beach 247-1000, (800) 334-6866, offers a variety of vacation cottages and condo rentals from Atlantic Beach to Emerald Isle south to Topsail Beach.

Whaler Inn Beach Club, 247-4169, (800) 525-1768, features attractive oceanfront one- and two-bedroom condominiums for rent for the two night minimum or for a week.

Sunny Shores, 247-2665, 247-7347, (800) 626-3113, handles many vacation rentals of condos and cottages in Atlantic Beach, Pine Knoll Shores and Emerald Isle.

Windward Dunes, 247-7545, (800) 659-7545, is an eight-story condo development in Indian Beach that offers 50 direct oceanfront one- and two-bedroom units.

Information about timeshare or interval ownership follows at the end of this chapter.

Beaufort

Beaufort offers no condos to vacationers, but there are a few rental apartments and houses available. Rates vary for one night, a week or longer.

While a few people advertise their own rentals with a sign out front, many list them with local agents. If you are looking for a rental in Beaufort, we recommend you contact a Beaufort real estate company, look in the *Carteret County News-Times* or ask another Insider.

Down East

A drive Down East, particularly on Harkers Island and Cedar Island, will turn up several nice rental cottages/ houses. Many of these are not handled by a real estate agency; they simply have the owner's name and a phone number posted out front. Most rental places are booked year after year by the same people, so we suggest you find the one you are interested in and make arrangements early.

Timeshare, Interval Ownership

There are several developments on the Crystal Coast set up for interval ownership or timesharing. Billed as a way to have a lifetime of affordable vacations, the plan is set up so you actually purchase a block of time, one or more weeks in length, for a specific unit. Each year, the time you purchased is yours at that unit. Of course, your plans may change one year. With almost all of the companies you can exchange your week on the Crystal Coast for another location, some around the nation or world. Check on this before you purchase.

Before you arrange to buy into an interval ownership condo, there is a maintenance fee to consider. Once you pay off the note, you receive the deed to your week in your specific unit. Some organizations do put restrictions on resale, even after you own the time in that unit, so check on that before you put your name on the dotted line.

The unit will be completely furnished, down to the linens, dishes and pans, so you just stop by the supermarket to pick up food, bring in your suitcases, unload the sporting equipment, and you'll be set for the duration. Each of these interval-ownership facilities is loaded with amenities, and each one is different.

If you are seriously considering purchasing into a timeshare or interval ownership property, give the resort a call and arrange a tour. A few of the facilities on the Crystal Coast that offer interval or fractional ownership are listed here.

Coldwell Banker-Spectrum Resort Properties Inc., 354-3070, offers fractional ownership of resort properties. This concept involves 10 individuals owning a 10th

Photo: Scott Taylor

A full moon can light the way for a romantic beach walk or nighttime swim.

of a deeded interest in resort property. For this, each individual gets five weeks occupancy of the condos; weeks and holidays rotate each year. Two weeks are left for maintenance.

Peppertree, 247-2092, offers one-, two- and three-bedroom units, many with an ocean and sound view. Owners also can use the facility property year round. This allows owners who might live nearby to come to the beach and park and use shower facilities as well as all the other amenities. The facility offers something to non-property owners as well — a daily club membership that you might want to use if you move to the area but live somewhere other than on the beach. For a fee, you can park at the resort and use its private beach house for your visits to the shore. Peppertree has four pools, three outdoor and one indoor, and a security guard. New units are under construction.

Sands Oceanfront Villas, 247-2636,

offers 98 units for timeshare purchase at A Place at the Beach. Designed as one-, two- and three-bedroom units, each provides all the luxuries of home and then some. Each unit is fully furnished, and linens, towels and a fully-equipped kitchen are provided. A laundry facility is on site. Additionally, the two- and three-bedroom units feature washers and dryers. A Place at the Beach has an indoor heated pool and outdoor pool with a waterslide. For information about rentals at A Place at the Beach, see the rental section above.

Whaler Inn Beach Club, 247-4169, features attractive oceanfront one- and two-bedroom condominiums. Completely furnished, the units offer fully equipped kitchens complete with dishwashers and all the kitchenware and utensils vacationers need. Units also offer balconies for relaxing and washers/dryers for cleaning up. Owners have immediate and full access to the ocean and sandy beaches in front of the club as well as to the club's heated pool and Jacuzzi. Ownership also allows those living or visiting nearby to continue to use the facility for parking, beach access, showers, swimming and other amenities. Whaler Inn is part of Interval International, allowing owners access to more than 11,000 resorts worldwide. Whaler Inn's helpful staff can offer more information about the beach club.

To really get away from it all, try camping at Cape Lookout National Seashore or Bear Island, both of which are accessible only by private boat or ferry.

Crystal Coast
Camping

Camping is one of the best ways to relax and enjoy the surrounding beauty, but it is not for everyone. North Carolina's Crystal Coast offers a variety of camping opportunities, from rent-a-space RV camping with all the conveniences of home to tent camping with no conveniences at all. Primitive camping is offered at Cape Lookout National Seashore, Bear Island and in the Croatan National Forest (see the Attractions chapter).

Camping along the coast is popular almost year round because of the mild winter climate. Summer campers may need to create shade with tarps or overhangs to protect themselves from the sun's blistering rays. Campers will find beach camping a little different from mainland camping. Longer tent stakes may be needed in the sandy soil to hold things down in the strong ocean breezes. Netting is almost a must, except in the dead of winter, to protect against the late-afternoon and early-morning mosquitoes and no-see-ums, those barely visible flying insects. A roaring fire and a good insect repellent help also. If you aren't fond of plastering yourself with pesticides, try mixing Avon's Skin So Soft with water and spraying it on. This mixture will fend off most insects and it smells good too. It also works to protect dogs.

To really get away from it all, try camping at Cape Lookout or Bear Island, both of which are only accessible by boat or ferry. There are no designated camping sites on Cape Lookout National Seashore and camping is allowed everywhere except on a small amount of well-marked, privately owned land. Bear Island has quiet, secluded campsites. Croatan National Forest, which includes land in Carteret and Craven counties, offers two options: Stay in one of the two planned campgrounds or pitch a tent anywhere on National Forest land that isn't marked for private use.

Overnight fees vary from campground to campground and usually depend on the location (whether oceanfront or off the beaten path) and the facilities offered. Fees for commercial campgrounds generally range from $12 to $35 a night and reservations are suggested. There is no charge to camp at Cape Lookout National Seashore or at some sites in Croatan National Forest.

Most piers along Bogue Banks also offer RV and tent spaces (see our Fishing, Watersports and Beach Access chapter).

ARROWHEAD CAMPSITE
MP, 11½, Hwy. 5
Indian Beach   247-3838

On Bogue Sound in the middle of Bogue Banks, Arrowhead Campsite offers 12 acres with full hookup, tent sites and clean restroom/shower facilities. Most types of water activities, such as sailing, shelling, fishing and clamming, are enjoyed in the sound. The campsite has a boat ramp, a pier and a protected-swimming area, and ocean access is just 600 feet away. Popular restaurants, shops and a grocery store are within walking distance. The campground has a lot of regulars who return every year, so reservations are a good idea. Arrowhead usually closes in late November and opens before Easter.

SALTER PATH FAMILY CAMPGROUND
MP 11¾, N.C. Hwy. 58
Salter Path 247-3525

This campground offers sites on the ocean or the sound in the middle of Bogue Banks. It has been owned by the Lindsay family for 27 years. All sites have electrical outlets, water taps and picnic tables, and most sites have sewer and cable hookups. Shower facilities, volleyball, basketball, fishing, wind surfing, a laundry room, a camp store, a boat ramp, a pond and a dump station are available. This campground is within easy walking distance of a grocery store, restaurants and shops. It is open mid-March through early November. Reservations are suggested, and it might save you a few bucks to check out the spring and fall weekly and monthly rates. Clam rakes are rented at the office for 15¢ per hour and users are asked to contribute one clam to the campground saltwater aquarium. They also provide instructions for preparing your catch.

WATERSPORTS RENTALS AND RV CAMPGROUND
MP 12, Indian Beach 247-7303

This camp spot is on Bogue Sound right across the road from the Indian Beach Pier. The watersports equipment rental business offers spaces for RV full-hookup camping and tents. The business rents sailboats, motor boats, Jet Skis and gives lessons on how to use the equipment and how to water- ski (see our Fishing, Watersports and Beach Access chapter).

BEACHFRONT RV PARK
MP 19¼, N.C. Hwy. 58
Emerald Isle 354-6400

On the oceanfront with about 158 full-hookup and tent camping sites, Beachfront RV Park is beside Bogue Inlet Fishing Pier. The park owners pride themselves in offering pleasant surroundings and clean bathhouses. A camp store with RV supplies, a dump station, a pier, surf fishing and a game room are available. Seafood restaurants are within walking distance. The campground is closed from early December to early March.

HOLIDAY TRAV-L-PARK RESORT
MP 21, N.C. Hwy. 58
Emerald Isle 354-2250

This oceanfront camping resort offers 365 grass sites with full-hookups along with a host of amenities, including paved streets, shower facilities, shaded tent sites, a complete grocery store with RV supplies and LP Gas, a yogurt shop, a recreation hall, a dump station and an outdoor swimming pool. Mopeds and bicycles can be rented and there are basketball and tennis courts, a shuffleboard area and a go-cart track. A summer activities director lines up live entertainment, so there is always something

Insiders' Tips

If you are planning to take a vehicle to Cape Lookout, schedule your trip well in advance to ensure room on the ferry from Davis or Atlantic.

Photo: Curtis Krueger

A careful look in area lakes and streams can sometimes reveal surprising finds.

going on for those who want to stay active. But there is also plenty of peace and quiet. In business since 1976, Holiday Trav-L-Park enjoys a large following of repeat customers. The park is the site of the huge Emerald Isle Beach Music Festival in mid-May. Storage facilities are available for campers, boats and motor homes. The park is within walking distance of grocery stores, restaurants, movie theaters and shops and is open all year, except two or three weeks in late December and early January.

BRIDGEVIEW FAMILY CAMPGROUND
MP 21, N.C. Hwy. 58
Emerald Isle 354-4242

Bridgeview is near the foot of the highrise bridge connecting Bogue Banks with the mainland. The campground sits off the highway and fronts Bogue Sound. About 113 RV sites are available for rent, usually for 9- to 12-month periods of time. About five tent sites are offered. Bridgeview has a boat ramp, a swimming pool and a fishing pier. Several lots are

wooded, and picnic tables and a playground area are featured.

WHISPERING PINES CAMPGROUND
N.C. Hwy. 24
12 miles west of Morehead City 726-4902

Situated on Bogue Sound, Whispering Pines has 140 full-hookup sites, a swimming pool, paddleboats, a miniature golf course, a freshwater pond and fishing. The camp store and the park are open all year. The park offers mail and phone message services. Whispering Pines offers special off-season monthly rates. On-site and off-site storage is available for boats and campers.

TOMMY'S FAMILY CAMPGROUND
N.C. Hwy. 24, Cedar Point 393-8715

On the Intracoastal Waterway between Cape Carteret and Swansboro, Tommy's offers 42 full-hookup sites and about 10 tent sites amid shady weeping willows. A favorite among fishermen and their families, the campground provides a boat ramp

Photo: Irv Hooper

This young one keeps a watchful eye on area waters.

and basin as well as a storage area for campers and boats. Tommy's is open all year.

BEAR ISLAND
Hammock's Beach Rd.
west of Swansboro Ranger Station   326-4881

Access to Bear Island is provided from Hammock's Beach State Park (see the Attractions and the Ferries chapters) or by private boat. The 3.5-mile island offers primitive, private camping at designated spots for a small fee. Campers must register with the park office on the mainland before going over to Bear Island. There is a bathhouse in the center of the island, but it is a good distance from the camping areas. Campsites for boaters are also offered, but some sites are tricky to get to because of shallow water. Campers traveling by ferry are advised to travel light because it is close to a mile walk from the ferry landing to some sites. To minimize human disturbance of nesting loggerhead sea turtles, Bear Island is closed to camping during the full-moon phases of the months of June, July and August.

GOOSE CREEK RESORT
N.C. Hwy. 24
7 miles east of Swansboro   393-2628

Goose Creek Resort offers facilities for family camping on Bogue Sound. Campers will find a boat ramp, a pool, a waterslide, a game room, a heated/air conditioned bathhouse, a camp store, tent sites, a 250-foot fishing pier, basketball, skiing, clamming and crabbing and a dump station. The resort is open year round, and all 300 sites offer full-hookup services. Special long-term rates are offered, and on-site boat and RV storage is available.

COASTAL RIVERSIDE CAMPGROUND
216 Clark Ln., Otway   728-5155

Otway is a small Down East community just east of Beaufort. This campground has all the extras you would expect, plus a security gate to ensure privacy, 57 sites with hookups and additional tent sites. This shady campground is on North River and has a pier, a pool, a boat ramp, a bathhouse, a store, a game room, cable hookups and a dump station. They also offer RV and boat storage and seasonal rates. The campground is open all year.

CEDAR CREEK
CAMPGROUND AND MARINA
U.S. Hwy. 70, Sea Level   225-9571

Cedar Creek caters to family camping with shady sites and easy access to Core Sound and Drum Inlet. Guests will find a swimming pool, flush toilets, hot-water showers, a dump station, boating, fishing, horseshoes and basketball, along with 20 sites with full hookups and 35 additional sites for RVs and tents. Parts of the campground and marina are open all year, although the facilities are only fully operational between April 1 and November 30. About 12 miles from the Cedar Island-Ocracoke ferry terminal, Cedar Creek also offers an RV storage area.

DRIFTWOOD CAMPGROUND
N.C. Hwy. 12, Cedar Island   225-4861

This waterfront campground is beside the Cedar Island-Ocracoke ferry terminal and has 65 sites. Swimming, fishing, volleyball, horseshoes and video games are offered along with a bathhouse, a store and a dump station. The campground is open March 1 through December 15. It is part of the Driftwood complex, which includes a restaurant and a convenience store and grill. Driftwood is well-known for its hunting and fishing guide service and its great food. (See our Crystal Coast Restaurants and Accommodations chapters for more information.)

CAPE LOOKOUT NATIONAL SEASHORE
Ranger Station, Harkers Island   728-2250

Cape Lookout National Seashore (see the Attractions chapter) offers waterfront camping at its best. This is the place to go if you want privacy. You might see a ranger and a few anglers around the cabins or folks around the lighthouse keeper's quarters; otherwise, you are on your own. Imagine sitting around the fire at dusk, listening to the waves roll on the beach and watching the sweeping light of the Cape Lookout lighthouse as it cautions boaters of shallow water — water as far as you can see, with the Atlantic Ocean to one side and Core Sound to the other. There are no developed campsites, no bathhouses (there is a toilet at the lighthouse), no fees and no access without a boat. There are two primitive cabin complexes with flush toilets and showers (see our Accommodations chap-

ter). So how do you get to this wonderland? By boat or by ferry. Ferry service is provided by several concessionaires permitted by the National Park Service (see our Ferries chapter) and numerous charter boats. Like all National Parks, some restrictions apply, so talk to a ranger before scheduling your trip.

CEDAR POINT TIDELAND TRAIL
1 mile north of Cape Carteret
Ranger Station   638-5628

This is one of the two planned camping sites in Croatan National Forest. On the banks of the White Oak River, the area offers 50 camping spaces, drinking water, toilets and an unpaved boat ramp. Cedar Point can be reached by following the signs from Highway 58 about a mile north of Cape Carteret. Reservations are not required. The Cedar Point Tideland Trail, an interpretive nature trail, is here and offers a short loop, a one-hour walk and a two-hour walk (see our Attractions chapter).

CROATAN NATIONAL FOREST
U.S. Hwy. 70, Ranger Station   638-5628

Croatan National Forest is made up of 157,000 acres spread between Morehead City and New Bern. Recreational areas are available for a day's outing or for overnight camping. The forest has two planned campsites, Cedar Point and Neuse River, where you will find drinking water, bathhouse facilities and trailer space. Primitive camping is permitted all year and campfires are allowed. Much of the park is closed November through March, except the Cedar Point and primitive camping sites that are open year round. For more information on the Croatan National Forest, see our Attractions chapter.

Swansboro's
Front Street and
the associated
side streets are
home to several
antiques stores.

Crystal Coast
Shopping

Shopping is a favorite recreation for many vacationers, and the Crystal Coast accommodates that activity with plenty of unique stores and boutiques.

Initially, a newcomer or visitor in the area may find it difficult to locate what he or she needs because there are no single, all-inclusive large shopping centers or malls. However, the shops do exist. There are mini-malls, strips of shops and several good-size shopping centers. The combination is enough to allow you plenty of places to find what you need and want.

Because the Crystal Coast is considered a resort area, you'll find plenty of shops that cater to the beachgoer or surfer. If you're looking for a beach souvenir, a gift for someone back home, the perfect-fitting swimsuit, a special T-shirt or a beach wrap, you can find them. If you need clothing or equipment for your favorite summer sport, you will find many brands of goods including everything from surf boards to tennis togs. Because this is a resort area, some of the shops close in the winter, particularly those shops on Bogue Banks.

Grocery shoppers on the Crystal Coast have several large chain stores and seafood shops to choose from as well as seafood markets and roadside fruit and vegetable stands.

We have designed this section to offer you a brief look at a few of the shops in each Crystal Coast community. Antiques shops, decoy shops and flea markets are listed separately at the end of this section. There is no way we could mention every shop that warrants your attention, so explore on your own and ask around. Other Insiders will be delighted to share information with you.

Bogue Banks

Most Bogue Banks' shopping is focused on the active lifestyle of beachgoers — both residents and visitors. Shops offer swimwear, watersport accessories, casual wear, seashells and souvenirs. Here is a sampling of some of the shops you'll find on Bogue Banks, beginning in Atlantic Beach and wandering west to Emerald Isle. We have given the milepost (MP) number for the shops on N.C. Highway 58 (the main road on the island).

Atlantic Beach

Bert's Surf Shop, MP 2½, stocks swimwear, activewear, beach T-shirts, a large variety of sports equipment and sunglasses. Bert's also has a shop in Emerald Isle. **Marsh's Surf Shop** on the Atlantic Beach Causeway offers everything from dresses and shorts to T-shirts and jackets for men, women and children. There are plenty of beach items too — sunglasses, surfboards, swimsuits, beach bikes and all the accessories. Marsh's also carries a wonderful selection of leather clogs and active footwear.

Sandi's Beachwear, MP 2½, offers a variety of swimwear and activewear. You are sure to find the perfect suit and accessories at this store. **Atlantic Beach Surf Shop**, MP 2¾, offers quality beachwear, casual clothes and officewear. Footwear, jewelry, sunglasses, surfboards, beach bikes and all the accessories are for sale. **Davis Beachwear Shop**, on the Circle, has been in business for years and carries a complete line of sportswear and swimwear for ladies, men and children.

Presents, Atlantic Beach Causeway, is the place to shop for unique gifts, gourmet foods, toys, decorator and garden items, stationery and gift baskets. **Catco**, Atlantic Beach Causeway, offers distinctive handcrafted nautical jewelry. **Wings**, MP 2¼, has two beach-oriented retail stores within the same block carrying lots of T-shirts, bathing suits and casual apparel along with shells and jewelry.

Hi-Lites, MP 2¼, specializes in discounted clothing in juniors, misses and plus sizes with an emphasis on sporty separates with nothing over $15. You'll also find swimsuits, belts, earrings, bags and hats. **Tony's Beach Shop**, MP 4¾, is across from the Sheraton. The store offers everything from ice cream and yogurt to swimwear and boogie boards. Tony's also offers gifts, souvenirs, hermit crabs and the largest selection of seashells in the area.

Christmas By The Sea, MP 5, is a shop that is filled with holiday decorations, ornaments and more. There are plenty of wonderful gift ideas for Christmas, or for any occasion.

The **Atlantic Station Shopping Center**, MP 3, offers a variety of shops. The center is anchored by **Atlantic Station Cinemas** and **Pak-A-Sak** Food Store. **Outer Banks Outfitters** is just the store for anglers. This is a marine electronics store that, along with radios, stereos and spotlights, carries fishing tackle, clothing, jewelry and much more. **Beach Book Mart** offers a great selection of paper and hardback books at reduced prices. Beach Book Mart also offers a good selection of local books along with bestsellers, cookbooks and much more. **Kites Unlimited** offers hundreds of wind-borne treasures in designs and sizes and for all ability levels. Inside you will find quality kites, windsocks, flags, unique games and puzzles. Other shops include **Atlantic Photo**, providing film processing services; and **Video City**, offering a wide selection of movies for rent. **Coastal Crafts Plus** features the work of more than 30 crafters — pottery, jewelry, paintings, and wood crafts. The **Bake Shoppe Bakery** tempts shoppers with donuts, bagels, fresh breads, pies and some health food items. **Great Mistake**s features savings on brand-name clothing for women and men. They also have a store in Beaufort. **Special Moments** arranges anything for any occasion — gift baskets, balloons, cards, stationery, gourmet candy, coffee, mugs, stuffed animals, T-shirts, souvenirs and more. Let them create a fabulous gift arrangement for that special moment. **Sunsplash** sells beach and rock 'n' roll souvenirs, posters and blacklights, and they even rent boogie boards.

Across Highway 58 from Atlantic Station Shopping Center is **Coral Bay Shopping Center**, MP 3. This small center includes **Eckerd Drug Store** and **Food Lion** supermarket.

Pine Knoll Shores

There are no outright shopping areas in Pine Knoll Shores. This residential town does offer a convenience store and several hotels and piers with gift shops or tackle shops.

Salter Path and Indian Beach

There are a few places to shop in Salter Path and Indian Beach. **Village Gift Shop & Beach Wear**, MP 11, offers beachwear, T-shirts, shell items, gifts, jewelry, hats, suncatchers and lots more. **Fishin' Fever**, MP 11½, is a seafood market and tackle shop. Someone around the store can always tell you where to go to wet a line, what bait to use that day and how to prepare your catch. For unlucky anglers, the fresh seafood market will save the day.

Old Island Store, MP 11½, offers nautical beachwear, gifts, shells, beach supplies, art, lamps, flags, windsocks and more. **Dog Island Outfitters**, MP 10½, is on the sound a block off the highway. Here you will find outdoor apparel and watersport rentals.

Island Rigs, MP 12, is a watersport rental business (see the Fishing, Watersports and Beach Access chapter) that also offers watersport accessories,

sportswear and beachwear. **Food Dock**, MP 11¼, is the local grocery store.

Emerald Isle

Shops line Emerald Drive (Highway 58) and are in Emerald Plantation (see below). Here, we have included a sampling of the shops you'll find in town.

Fran's Beachwear, MP 19½, is celebrating its 22nd year in business. The shop carries an excellent selection of swimwear for everyone from the daring to the shy, along with sporty and dressy separates and a wide range of shoes, accessories and souvenirs. **Fran's Gifts** (same location) offers such collectibles as Tom Clark Gnomes, Dept. 56 Snow Village and Precious Moments. You'll also find gifts, jewelry and accessories.

Especially for You, MP 19¼, offers clothing and accessories for the fuller-figured woman. This shop is very popular and enjoys much repeat business. **BeachMart**, MP 20, is filled with T-shirts, souvenirs, bathing suits, beachwear, sunglasses and more.

Bert's Surf Shop, MP 19½, was the town's first surf shop. The shop stocks beach clothing for all ages, skateboards, windsurfing equipment and surfboards. Bert's always has activewear, sunglasses, hats and beach T-shirts. **Wing's**, MP 19½, offers T-shirts, bathing suits, casual apparel, shells and jewelry. **Great Mistakes**, MP 20¼, features discount brand-name clothing for women and men. There are sister stores in Beaufort and Atlantic Beach.

The **Emerald Plantation Shopping Center**, MP 20¼, offers stores in a courtyard-type setting. The center is anchored by **Food Lion**, **Revco Drug Store**, **Sound Ace Hardware** and **Emerald Plantation Cinema 4**. **Tom Togs Factory Outlet** sells a large selection of well-known clothing brands at drastically reduced prices. Inside you will find items for women, men and children along with accessories. Be sure to check Tom Togs before you pay full price elsewhere. **J.R. Dunn Jewelers** features distinctive jewelry for women, men and children, along with many nautical creations. J.R. Dunn also has a shop in Cypress Bay Plaza, Morehead City. **Elly's Personal Touch** is packed with children's clothes, games, books and all kinds of gifts including stained glass, pottery, decoys and wreaths. **Emerald Isle Books & Toys** has books and magazines for all ages. **Country Store** offers baskets, windsocks, flags, cards, wreaths, brass, clocks, frames and Christmas items.

Beaufort

The specialty shops in Beaufort are sure to suit anyone's taste. Although there are others, most shops are along the downtown waterfront area. Because our generally mild climate attracts visitors year round, only a few of Beaufort's shops close in the winter.

Beaufort's many attractions — the waterfront, the museum, historic sites and pubs — provide respite for those who find themselves in Beaufort with a born shopper. We couldn't possibly list all the shops, so we hope you will do some exploring on your own.

Downtown/Waterfront

Fabricate Apparel specializes in clothes of natural fibers. The shop offers trendy, expressive clothes as well as conservative outfits for women, men and children. You'll find jewelry, belts, bags, a small selection of shoes, T-shirts and sweatshirts that feature Beaufort scenes, environmental messages and drawings by M.C. Escher.

Scuttlebutt specializes in "nautical books and bounty." An outstanding selection of nautical books and charts, clocks, music, games, toys, models and galleyware are available.

Mary Elizabeth's caters to women seeking the career look in traditional clothing, shoes and all types of accessories. Mary Elizabeth's also offers sportswear. **The Ladies' Shop** has been in business on Front Street for 23 years. The shop offers traditional apparel, sportswear and accessories.

Stamper's Gift Shop sells fine china, all kinds of gifts and novelty items as well as an extensive line of collectibles by Gorman, Lee Middleton, Susan Wakeen, M.I. Hummels and Tom Clark Gnomes. Stamper's also offers a variety of throw rugs and blankets, including those featuring scenes from Beaufort. Next door, **Stamper's Jewelers** offers a full line of jewelry items as well as engraving and excellent repair services.

For great ice cream or a few more souvenirs, stop by **The General Store** where you'll find all kinds of memorabilia to take home — hats, T-shirts, shells, saltwater taffy and jewelry. **Top Deck** is one of the best places in town for name brand clothing, shoes, T-shirts, casual wear, Ray Bans and things labeled "Beaufort." **The Harbor Shop** offers all kinds of things — baskets, rugs, stained glass, art, jewelry and so much more. Owner Rob Davis carries some cards, drawings and jewelry created by local artists. **La Vaughn's Pottery** has plenty of gourmet coffees and wines, some from North Carolina vineyards. As the name reflects, the store has pottery items along with furniture, collectibles and jewelry.

Local artist Alan Cheek displays his work at **Down East Gallery**. Alan's artwork will serve as a lovely reminder of time spent in the Beaufort seaport. Down East Gallery does custom framing. On the Beau-

fort Historic Site, the **Mattie King Davis Art Gallery** features paintings, sketches, note cards, carvings, photographs, weavings and gifts created by local artists. **Chachkas** has creative gifts of handpainted furniture, murals and accents along with jewelry and florals.

Chadwick House is a retail interior design store offering lamps, prints, paintings, furniture, upholstery, wallpaper and window treatments. The shop's lovely accessories include glass vases, picture frames, baskets, garden ornaments and kitchen accents. **For Nature's Sake** offers art, clothing, gifts and products, all aimed at passing on the messages of conservation, preservation and peace. **Great Mistakes** offers brand-name clothing for women and men at discount prices. The store features first-quality overruns, closeouts, samples and imperfects.

Bell's has been serving the people of Beaufort and visitors since 1918 and continues that same friendly, professional service today. Along with drugstore items, Bell's Drug Store has fountain drinks, film, personal care items, gifts and cards.

Somerset Square houses a number of shops. This two-story building is on Front Street at the south end of Turner Street. **Handscapes Gallery** specializes in works by North Carolina artists and craftspeople and is the perfect place to find special gifts and treasures. Owner Alison Brooks fills the shop with pottery, jewelry, paintings, glass and wood items. The **Rocking Chair Book Store** is celebrating its 16th year of offering books for adults and children. Be sure to check the selection of regional books, sailing books and helpful book lights. Owners Neva Bridges and Josephine Davis are full of information, and they will order any

North Carolina Yacht Racing Association's annual race series occurs each Memorial Day weekend.

Photo: Scott Taylor

book for you. The **Fudge Factory** makes creamy, sinful fudge from natural ingredients on marble-top tables right in front of you. **Containing Ideas** carries an extensive line of Patagonia apparel (jackets, pants, hats and accessories) and lots of T-shirts, bags and hats with environmental messages.

Just outside the downtown area is **Gaskill's True Value Farm & Garden Center** on Highway 70. One step inside will take you back in time. Bo Sullivan and his helpful crew stock this country seed store with everything you need to get the garden going, the lawn tamed, the house and boat fixed or the animals fed.

Holland's Shoes in Beaufort Square Shopping Center, carries an excellent selection of shoes for the entire family with great prices to match. You'll find major brand-name shoes, including Reebok, Nike, Rockport and Sperry, along with handbags, socks, laces and shoe-cleaning items.

A number of grocery stores, drug stores and variety shops are on Highway 70 east of downtown Beaufort.

Morehead City

Morehead City offers the largest selection of shops on the Crystal Coast. Shopping opportunities are spread from one end of the city to the other and range from clothing boutiques and craft shops to book shops and marine hardware suppliers. Here we have tried to describe a few of the shops in the city and have arranged them by area.

Downtown/Waterfront

In the last few years the downtown/waterfront sections of Morehead City have seen quite a bit of revitalization. Projects provided for sidewalks, trees and benches along the waterfront, and work continues to be done. Here is a small sampling of the businesses you will find.

Dee Gee's Gifts and Books is a tradition on the waterfront and continues to offer a huge selection of books, cards and novelties. Dee Gee's features special sections of local and regional books, children's educational books, games and nautical charts. Let owners Doug and Jane Wolfe help you with your special book request.

Carving Their Own Niche

Traditionally, decoy carvers are thought of as older men sitting on a front porch; men who have hunted and fished all their lives and know the species like the backs of their hands. While the faces of carvers are changing — more young men and women are beginning to carve — the art is still predominantly practiced by males.

Each year since 1987, many men, and a few women, have gathered to exhibit and sell their work at the Core Sound Decoy Festival on Harkers Island. The event takes place the first weekend in December at the island's elementary school. And for each of the festivals, a man has been named the Featured Carver.

But a little bit of a change took place at the 1995 festival. It was the first time that a man and a woman jointly received the Featured Carver honor in the art form that has traditionally been dominated by men. Gail and Bernie Corwin were selected as the festival's Featured Carvers.

Working as a team, the Corwins have gained quite a reputation as decoy carvers and artists. They are well known for their attention to detail, their creativeness and their open door to friends.

Perhaps best known for their half-size decoys and baby puddle ducks, the Corwins own and operate Lucky Duck's in the Down East community of Bettie. The shop features original and old decoys and wildlife art.

Decoys became a part of Bernie's life in 1971 when he met the late Vernon Berg. Bernie's first job with him was stripping decoys so they could be repainted. Berg ran a guide service in Dare County and Bernie also worked as a professional hunting guide. Later, Bernie and Gail married and they worked together in the construction business. With their only child on the

Gail and Bernie Corwin give some finer points in decoy painting
to their daughter, Caroline.

way, Gail decided it was time to stop climbing ladders, roofing houses and hauling lumber. Knowing they had a market for the decoys with Vernon Berg, Bernie taught Gail to carve in 1983.

"I really took to it and felt like it was what I was meant to do," Gail said. "I never thought I had any artistic talent, and then suddenly I found my niche."

Gail gets her kicks out of using the *trompe l'oeil* ("to fool the eye") technique to make a slick surface appear textured. She enjoys knowing that someone will come up to one of her decoys, touch it to feel the feathers and find out it is slick. Bernie enjoys creating stylish working decoys. All the Corwins' creations are jointly signed.

The Corwins have participated in decoy-carving shows up and down the East Coast since 1984 and are charter members of the Core Sound Decoy Carvers Guild, having joined in the first month it was created in 1987.

They are also regular participants in the Core Sound Decoy Festival, and believe it is one of the best all around decoy shows they attend.

"You get a good mixture of the tremendous amount of local talent and quality carvers from all over, plus there are all kinds of decoy-related exhibits, activities and competitions," Bernie noted. "The Core Sound Decoy Festival is a showcase of the carving tradition of this area."

And the Corwins are doing their part to keep the tradition alive, not only in their own work but also in the work of their daughter, Caroline. Admittedly a "Daddy's girl," Caroline started carving when she was 8 years old. Now 12 years old, she has ribbons from junior competitions in four states. She is very interested in duck species and identification, and often goes hunting with her father although, as yet, she does not shoot.

The Corwins strive to educate young people about decoy carving. One way they do this is through the children's decoy painting event at the Core Sound Decoy Festival, where children are invited to paint decoys at set times on Saturday and Sunday.

"Children need a lot of encouragement in their artistic endeavors and they should be encouraged to try different types of art," Gail said. "Decoy carving and painting are different types of art. They are not like finger painting or drawing.

"Anyone can be artistic even if they are convinced they cannot be," she continued. "Art can be taught and you can learn to carve or paint. I learned."

Waterfront Junction is the place to stop for craft supplies, needlework, prints, crewel embroidery and nautical gifts. The shop is well-known for its custom framing and its stock of ready-made frames. **Taste Makers** offers a wonderful selection of gourmet food items, coffees, baked goods, wines and more. The staff creates custom gift baskets and also offers cooking classes. **Windward Gallery** offers oils, watercolors and pastels by acclaimed local artist Alexander Kaszas and many others. Inside you will also find jewelry, pottery, scrimshaw and glass pieces. For clothing for women, **Lee's "Of Course"** has it — and they specialize in one-of-a-kind fashions for all sizes.

Branch's is a traditional office supply

shop with lots of extras. Gifts, home accessories, cards and supplies for drafting, art and school. **Kennedy's Office Supply** has a complete line of office supplies and paper products along with calendars, art supplies, pens and office furniture.

Mary's Flowers and Pastries offers gorgeous flower arrangements, one-of-a-kind gift items and local creations. European pastries and gourmet coffees are extra incentives to visit this shop. The shop offers a European-type breakfast and soups, salads and sandwiches for lunch. Tempting desserts and coffees are served throughout the day.

Through the Looking Glass creates distinctive floral arrangements for every occasion and offers crystal, exclusive gifts for that very special person and a Christmas shop. **Morehead City Floral Expressions** offers potted plants and flower arrangements.

City News Stand offers an endless number of magazines, greeting cards and books and many major newspapers. **Fannie's Attic** showcases antiques, collectibles, pottery, afghans, holiday items, art-to-wear, dolls, pottery, dried flowers, wind chimes, dolls and more.

Carolina City Smoked Seafood has delicious varieties of smoked seafood, spreads and delicacies. Our favorites are the smoked salmon and bluefish in lemon pepper. They offer party trays and have a mail-order service. **Ottis' Fish Market and Carolina Atlantic** has been in business on the Morehead City waterfront for 45 years. If you don't catch it yourself, this is the place to go for all kinds of fresh, local seafood. Stop by and take some seafood home to enjoy later. Ottis' will even pack the cooler for you.

Sew It Seams has sewing patterns and notions, fabrics, books, craft supplies and quilting items. Classes are often taught here. **Parsons' General Store** has a wonderful collection of gifts, local crafts, books, home accessories, seasonal decorations and sweets. Stop by **Crystal Coast Crafters** if you are looking for craft and art supplies of any kind, including stained-glass supplies. **Ginny Gordon's Gifts And Gadgets** offers a wonderful collection of cookware, cookbooks from near and far, every cooking utensil imaginable and lots of special things — sauces, coffees and more.

Around Morehead City

Here we have listed shops that are in the city but not clustered in a particular area or shopping center. The street address should make them easy to find.

Recreation enthusiasts should stop by **EJW Outdoors**, 2204 Arendell Street, for new fishing gear and outdoor clothing or to have a bike tuned up. **Teacher's Pet** and **A Sea of Learning**, 2408 Arendell Street, are two of the most wonderful shops in the area. Whether you are a teacher, a parent or learning yourself, you are sure to enjoy these two stores. Teacher's Pet focuses on all types of learning aides, everything from charts and artwork to books and equipment. A Sea of

Learning features educational games and toys for children of all ages.

Morehead Plaza is between Arendell and Bridges streets and is anchored by **Belk**, a full-line department store; **Roses Stores**, a discount retail store; **Byrd's Food Store**, a grocery store with a good deli section; and **Eckerd Drugs**, a drugstore and pharmacy. **The Light Within**, with items that will help you focus on your overall health and healing, is a wonderful store to explore. Natural herbs, essential oils, mineral salts, books and tapes are sold. The Light Within also offers a complete yoga school with day and evening classes for all levels. **Maurice's** carries trendy clothing for women and men. **Crystal Sports** offers sporting goods equipment, clothing, training shoes and plaques and trophies ready to be personalized.

Dubbed a '60s shop, **Yesterdaze Closet** offers vintage clothing, music and jewelry along with incense, books and memorabilia.

At the back of Morehead Plaza, facing Bridges Street, is **Williams Hardware**, one of the best-supplied hardware stores in the area. It has a helpful staff that won't keep you waiting. **Anderson Audio** is the perfect place to look for that home or car stereo system or other electronic sound ma-

Photo: Scott Taylor

Kite flying is a great oceanside sport but can be a challenge for even the most die-hard enthusiast.

chine. **Crystal Coast Brass** cleans brass, silver and copper and sells items ranging from vases and cups to decorative pieces.

Morehead Plaza West is a strip of shops behind Morehead Plaza that can be reached from Bridges Street. The largest store in the plaza is **Western Auto** where you can find everything you need for do-it-yourself auto repairs or have one of their mechanics do it for you. They have tires, batteries, accessories, cleanup kits and bicycles. **Jewelers' Workbench** is our favorite place to go for custom-made jewelry — everything from wedding rings to earrings. They will place special pieces in just the right setting. Owner Laurie Stinson professionally handles any jewelry creation, repair or cleaning and offers her own designs for sale. Laurie can bring new life to any old jewelry.

Twin Book Stores, 3805 Arendell Street, is the place to find thousands of new and used hardbacks, paperbacks, comic books, cookbooks and North Carolina books.

Diamond Shoal Jewelers, 4637 Arendell Street, offers a wonderful selection of jewelry and watches for men and women. Diamond Shoal's specialists also make repairs. **The Painted Pelican**, 4645 Arendell Street, features the work of local artists and craftspeople in the form of prints, pottery, shorebirds, jewelry, scrimshaw and much more. You'll also find a frame shop offering custom work and readymades. **Wind Creations**, 4109 Arendell Street, offers all kinds of special flags and banners. A number of their own creations are on hand, and the shop will design special orders.

Howard's Furniture Showrooms, 4024 Arendell Street, offers a full line of home furnishings, bedding, accessories and window treatments. Howard's staff also offers a complete home design service. Sharing the same building is **Superior Carpet and Appliance**, who offer top-of-the-line carpets and vinyl floorings, GE appliances and all types of outdoor furniture. Superior installs and services carpet and appliances. **Creative Lighting** recently moved next door and is filled with fixtures for kitchens and baths along with cabinets and countertops of all types. You'll love the many unique chandeliers.

The **Gourmet Galley**, 4050 Arendell Street, offers gourmet cheeses, pastas, domestic and imported wines, some gourmet candies, spices and plenty of coffees. The shop is where Carolina Swamp Sauces were created and are offered for sale.

Auto Brite, 4303 Arendell Street, is the best place in town to pamper your car with a professional cleaning job and to get a car-related gift. While your car is being cleaned, you can browse among car coffee mugs, tapes and CDs, shirts, cards or any number of small items for the maintenance and upkeep of your car.

Pelletier Harbor Shops, 4428 Arendell Street, includes a number of specialty shops. For women's clothes, visit **The Golden Gull**, featuring the latest fashions and accessories for ladies. The **Jewelry Nest** offers custom-designed nautical jewelry created with 14K gold and sterling silver. **Lynette's** carries distinctive fashions for women. The shop offers lovely jewelry, handbags and all the right accessories. **Knowledge of Christ Books & Gifts** is a wonderful store filled with books, gifts, stained glass, collectibles, dolls, prints and paintings. The store also offers Bibles for adults and children. **Over The Rainbow** is a great place to shop for distinctive clothing, footwear and accessories for that favorite little person and maternity wear for a special mom. **Cameo Boutique** offers all types of lingerie for women plus a few items for men. There are also accessories, adult games, lotions, stockings and gifts. **ETC** sells everything from denim to sequins. **Crystal Palate** features gourmet food items such as coffees and teas, cheeses and crackers, domestic and imported beers and wines and scads of those one-of-a-kind kitchen gadgets that are perfect as gifts — or better yet, for your own kitchen. **McQueen's Furniture and Interiors** has lovely home and office decorations, furniture, lamps, prints and accessories. **Consider the Lilies Florist** delivers and wires flowers and create wedding flowers. If you are shopping for clothes and accessories for that favorite gentleman or lady, stop by **Graff's Fashions**. **Shoe Splash** can provide just the right shoes to go with any ensemble, and **Sun Photo** offers a reliable one-hour color photo service. **J. Alden Limited for Women** and **J. Alden Limited for Men** offer dress and adventure wear.

The **Marketplace** is at 4900 Arendell Street at the junction of Highway 70 and Country Club Road. **Rack Room Shoes** carries a wide selection of women's, men's and children's name-brand shoes — everything from casual to dressy to athletic, plus lots of handbags. The **Dress Barn** sells women's clothes at discount prices. **14K Jewelers** features lovely jewelry for women, men and children. **Paper Plus** offers a variety of paper products for the office or the home. This is the place to go when planning your next party. If you want to stay home and watch a movie, pick from a wide selection at **Blockbuster Video**.

Cypress Bay Plaza is between highways 70 and 24, and **Wal-Mart** is the plaza's largest store. **Sears Roebuck And Co.** features appliances, hardware, clothing, shoes and an auto shop. **J.R. Dunn Jewelers** features distinctive jewelry for men, women and children, along with many nautical creations. **Carolina Linen** has a large inventory of bed and bath accessories. Other stores in the center include **Food Lion** supermarket, **Revco Drug Store**, and **Gloria's Hallmark**. Shoppers will also find a **Baskin-Robbins Ice Cream & Yogurt Shop**, a couple of small take-out food shops, a video rental store, clothing stores and more.

Truckers Toy Store, Highway 70 W., handles a full line of truck, sport utility and van accessories, and has a full installation department. The staff's goal here is to help people personalize their vehicles,

Photo: Scott Taylor

Feral horses roam Shackleford Banks, which is part of the Cape Lookout National Seashore.

whether that means truck caps, hitches, step bumpers, running boards or toolboxes. They stock hundreds of accessories and can order those hard-to-find items. You'll even find things for your car such as sun roofs and window tinting.

William's Floor Covering and Interiors, Highway 70 W., offers a full line of floor coverings — everything from carpet to ceramic to hardwood to vinyl. Customers will also find a large selection of wallpapers, blinds, fabric, drapes and more. Let the consultants at William's work with you on your new construction or remodeling project for a home or an office.

Pine Ridge Arts & Crafts, 5901 Arendell Street, offers art and needlework supplies, crafts, gifts and classes.

Inside **Colonial Carolina Pottery,** off Highway 70 W., you'll find china, crystal, glassware, brass, gifts, bird feeders, rugs, baskets, cookware, furniture, linens, candles, housewares and silk flowers. A separate department offers a huge selection of bath and bed linens and lamps. **Sunshine Garden Center** is next door and offers potted plants, silk flowers and arrangements, baskets, home decorations and every lawn and garden item imaginable.

Swansboro

Shops in Swansboro are basically in two areas — along the waterfront and its adjoining side streets, and along the highway. We suggest you take some time, walk along the White Oak River, shop a bit, enjoy lunch at one of the restaurants and relax in Bicentennial Park.

The waterfront shops are clustered along Front Street. Inside **Russell's Olde Tyme Shoppe** you'll find country crafts, jewelry, handcrafted clothing, pottery, furniture, baskets, silk and dried flowers and kitchen and cooking items. Each purchase in Maxine Russell's store is placed in a handpainted shopping bag, a gift in itself. **Noah's Ark** offers novel gifts for adults or children. The shop carries women's and children's clothing, plenty of accessories, some toys, books and cassette tapes.

Keepsake Originals is on the second floor of the 1839 William Farrand Store. The shop features cards, rubber stamps, handmade alpine lace, beautifully crafted gift boxes, and soothing music on tape and CD.

Through the Looking Glass offers memorable floral arrangements for any occasion along with candles, greeting cards, wines, and porcelain and crystal sculptures. The **Christmas House** is packed with all the seasonal items you can imagine and more. **Sunshine and Silks** features baskets, silk flowers, wreaths, ribbons, knickknacks, gifts and wood art.

Down East

There are only a few Down East shops, but each is uncommon and special and well worth the trip. Because hours vary, we suggest you call ahead.

Lucky Duck's in Bettie is a wonderful shop filled with antique decoys, waterfowl carvings by local artists, wildlife art, gifts and accessories. Artists Gail and Bernie Corwin also carry a complete line of supplies at the store. (See our sidebar on the Corwins in this chapter.)

The **Core Sound Waterfowl Museum Gift Shop** on Harkers Island is filled with unique Down East gifts, most of which have waterfowl and environmental themes. There are decoys, wildlife art, books, cards, house flags, windsocks, clothing, bird houses, bird feeders and much more. The shop also features decoy and local history exhibits.

Somethin' Special in Smyrna sells handmade baskets, decoys, stained-glass items, furniture, pillows, afghans, lamp shades, craft supplies, cross-stitch patterns, thread and a good selection of fabric.

Newport

Newport offers a number of shops in the downtown area and a few along Highway 70, just outside the town.

In the downtown area you'll find **C.M. Hill Hardware**. This traditional hardware store carries everything from guns and fan belts to mowers and Westinghouse appliances. **Newport Garden Center** offers everything for the lawn and garden and also sells and services equipment. The center's greenhouse provides fresh, locally grown plants.

Cape Carteret

The town's shopping center features **Piggly Wiggly**, a chain food store; **Kerr Drug Store**, a drug store and pharmacy; **Max-Way**, a discount clothing and supply store; and **Village Cleaners & Laun-**

Photo: Scott Taylor

The waters in the coastal counties provide for peaceful getaways for quiet fishing and wildlife-watching.

dry, a dry cleaners offering alterations and shoe repair. **West Carteret Medical Center**, operated by Carteret General Hospital, is in the town's shopping center.

Western Carteret County

There are a number of good stores scattered throughout the western part of the county. Most communities have a convenience/gas store, a beauty salon and tanning booth, or maybe a craft and flower shop. We have listed a few of the stores you will find there.

Carolina Home and Garden (formerly Russell's Hardware), Highway 24 in Bogue, offers a variety of hardware, gardening and lawn-care supplies at reasonable prices. The shop is also home to Yardworks, a quality landscaping and lawn-care company. **Walston True Value Home Center**, Cedar Point, is an extremely well-equipped store with hard-

ware and building products along with plants and gardening supplies. **Redfearn's Nursery** in Cedar Point has landscaping and potted plants, planters, garden seeds, fertilizers, herbicides or pesticides.

Wild Birds Unlimited, Cedar Point, is a fascinating shop offering special blends of bird seeds, unique feeders for a variety of animals and books and videos on bird types and how to attract birds to your feeder. Wild Birds also has educational items for children, clothing and gifts.

Winberry Farm Produce, Highway 24, Cedar Point, and **Smith's Produce**, Highway 24, Ocean, are two well-known roadside stands that offer seasonal local vegetables, Bogue Sound watermelons and cantaloupes.

Antiques

Antiques shops are plentiful along the Crystal Coast. If you are looking for antique decoys, check the next section in this chapter.

Beaufort offers several antiques shops, and we will just highlight a few. **The Flea Market**, 131 Turner Street, has old furniture, toys, jewelry, kitchen items and hardware. A good number of old nautical items are usually around.

Also in Beaufort is **Waterfront Antiques & Collectibles**, 121 Turner Street, a cozy shop that has several rooms of items, including a large selection of brass and lots of plates, kitchen gadgets, old furniture, trunks, jewelry, toys, advertising collectibles and children's clothing. **Craven Street Antiques & Collectibles**, 121 Craven Street, buys items and sells antiques, collectibles and furniture. Often you'll find some wonderful items from old Beaufort homes.

Morehead City is also home to a number of antiques shops. **Cheek's Antiques**, 727 Arendell Street, is a good place to start your search. Long established, this shop has a variety of antiques certain to keep you busy browsing. The shop's specialty is matching old sterling. **What Not Shop**, 1015 Arendell Street, is an antiques and collectibles shop that features lots of old Pepsi and Coke memorabilia. **Seaport Antique Market**, 509 Arendell Street, offers more than a dozen vendors' booths set up in an attractive manner to give you an opportunity to see more than one collector's wares at a time. You'll find furniture, books, glassware, knickknacks, jewelry and even some clothing and accessories.

Swansboro's Front Street and the associated side streets are home to several antiques stores. A sampling of those shops is given here. **Lighthouse Antiques**, Front Street, fills a two-story historic house with antiques of almost every sort — miniatures, furniture, clocks, dishes, old decoys and

jewelry. One room features pottery, another Chinese antiques and another children's furniture and toys. Shoppers will also find a few decoys, some rugs and jewelry. The **Barber Shop Antiques and Collectibles**, Front Street, features quilts, collectibles, dishes and furniture.

Cedar Point is dotted with antiques shops. The town's 5-mile stretch of Highway 24 between Cape Carteret and Swansboro is a great place for stopping and browsing. **Swansboro Antique Mall**, offers a conglomeration of booths representing many dealers showing their wares in a 12,500-square-foot building. You'll find kitchen collections, decoys, hunting and fishing equipment, furniture, quilts, paintings, toys, books, old radios and cameras, political memorabilia, clothing, tobacco and medical products and original stained glass. **Calico Village Antiques and Carpentry Shop** offers oak furniture, bric-a-brac, toys and collectibles. Next door is **The Grapevine**, a rustic old house with antiques, baskets and furniture. **Lazy Lyon's Auction Service** is behind Calico Village and is the site of frequent estate sales. Lazy Lyon's also has a shop on Front Street in Swansboro.

Decoys

Old working decoys and new handcarved ones are plentiful in the area, and collecting these art forms is becoming very popular. Many shops along the Crystal Coast offer a few decoys, but the majority available, old or new, are sold by the collectors or from the crafter's home.

If you are looking for a decoy or two, keep your eyes open for yard signs and stop by the Core Sound Waterfowl Museum on Harkers Island for a flyer listing area decoy shops. The museum also sells decoys and has hundreds on display.

Most of the area's decoy shops are east of Beaufort and in the Down East area. Not all the "shops" are really shops. You might be browsing in someone's living room or garage and discover a real treasure. They advertise using signs along the road. But don't let that fool you. These guys aren't just messing around with some wood — they are creating works of art. One stop will prove that to you. Whether you are looking for carved ducks, geese or shorebirds, you are sure to find them here.

Well-known for its excellent hunting grounds, the Carteret County area has been hunted by locals and sportsmen from near and far for hundreds of years. Catering to the many hunting visitors, locals took to the task of chopping the forms of ducks and geese from blocks of wood to use to lure waterfowl to within firing range. As the sport became more popular, plastic and lightweight decoys were used in place of the carved decoys.

Core Sound Decoy Carvers Guild was formed about nine years ago to bring back the art of carving and to support those locals who had never quit chopping at blocks of wood. Of course, the ducks, geese and other waterfowl these men and women now craft are not all used in the water. Instead, many are collected, bought, sold and displayed. The Guild's membership is made up of handcarvers of working, decorative and realistic waterfowl, collectors, painters, taxidermists, photographers and breeders.

Each December the Guild hosts a large and impressive festival at Harkers Island Elementary School. Scheduled for the first weekend each December, the Core Sound Decoy Festival attracts local and nationally known carvers, goose callers and other artists. Decoys are judged, sold, displayed, made and auctioned. There are booths set up to display artifacts, promote conservation and preservation efforts and focus on wildlife clubs. But most of all, there are decoys, lots and lots of decoys. This is one educational festival not to be missed — even if you're not a collector. The 9th Annual Core Sound Decoy Festival is scheduled for early December on Harkers Island. For more information about Core Sound Decoy Carvers Guild, Core Sound Waterfowl Museum or area carvers and shops, contact the museum at P.O. Box 556, Harkers Island, North Carolina 28531, or call 728-1500.

Flea Markets

There are two large flea markets in the area — one between Newport and Morehead City and the other outside Cape Carteret. Both are very active in the summer and have varying winter hours.

Newport-Morehead Flea Mall, Highway 70, is actually several large open-air buildings joined together. Dozens and dozens of vendors gather here to sell all kinds of items — crafts, appliances, clothing, food, books, antiques, artwork, vegetables, plants and hardware. **Cedar Point Open Air Flea Market**, junction of highways 24 and 58, offers a tremendous variety with booths rented to dealers who sell everything from baseball cards to original paintings. You'll also find handmade wooden items, plants, uniforms, clothing, cosmetics, produce and jewelry.

A popular exhibit at the North Carolina Aquarium at Pine Knoll Shores is the loggerhead nursery, where turtle hatchlings that have been injured, abandoned or for some reason were unable to reach the sea are monitored until they can be safely released into the ocean.

Crystal Coast
Attractions

Ocean-related activities and coastal parks are much of what make the Crystal Coast so attractive to tourists and so protected by residents. Cape Lookout National Seashore, Fort Macon State Park, Hammocks Beach State Park, Theodore Roosevelt Natural Area, Rachel Carson Research Reserve, Croatan National Forest and Cedar Island National Wildlife Refuge offer a wide variety of pristine beaches, maritime forests and waterways to enjoy and explore.

The unique cultural and natural histories of the area, our aquarium and museums enhance the visit of every tourist and the daily lives of every resident.

Among the attractions we've included in this chapter are a few of the interesting islands that surround the Crystal Coast. We've described county and local parks, along with sporting activities and annual events in the Sports and Fitness and Annual Events chapters. For attractions the whole family will enjoy, especially the kids, see our Kidstuff chapter.

General Attractions

NORTH CAROLINA AQUARIUM AT PINE KNOLL SHORES
Salter Path Rd., Hwy. 58, MP 7   247-4003

The North Carolina Aquarium at Pine Knoll Shores celebrates its 20th anniversary in 1996. In recognition of the occasion, special events and programs have been added to the aquarium's ongoing visitor activities, a new salt-marsh exhibit has been developed, building expansion plans are under way and a new pontoon field excursion is set to begin in late summer.

The aquarium is one of the most popular attractions on the Crystal Coast and one visit will tell you why. Visitors enjoy films, talks, programs and workshops on coastal topics and sign up for outdoor field trips and other fun and educational activities.

Tucked away in the maritime forest of the Theodore Roosevelt Natural Area, the aquarium is open year round and bustles with activity from spring to fall. The Pine Knoll Shores Aquarium is one of the state's three aquariums. Another is on Roanoke Island near Manteo and one is at Fort Fisher near Wilmington.

Each aquarium conducts a variety of activities and displays numerous exhibits and showtanks that are home to colorful fish and other marine life native to North Carolina waters. The aquariums educate the public about our state's fragile aquatic and marine resources. In fact, the aquariums were first called Marine Resources Centers. They were renamed in 1986 as part of their 10-year anniversary.

While all the programs and exhibits are designed to educate, there is a lot of fun involved too. The popular hands-on touch tanks allow everyone to get a feel for and a close-up look at common marine animals. At the Pine Knoll Shores Aquarium, visitors find a collection of freshwater and saltwater plants and animals. The Precious Waters exhibit features a 2,000-gallon salt-marsh tank and a riverbank display with live alligators. Its accompanying video presentation explains conservation issues such as loss of habitat and coastal water quality.

A popular exhibit is the loggerhead nursery, where turtle hatchlings that have been injured, abandoned or for some reason were unable to reach the sea are monitored until they can be safely released into the ocean. Each year, usually in May, the aquarium stages a Turtle Release trip (one of the aquarium's most popular events), at which time these sea turtles are returned to the open sea.

Other popular programs include onboard collecting cruises, canoe trips, snorkeling instruction, interpretive beach walks and excursions to remote barrier islands. The aquarium's surf-fishing weekend workshop held each fall is a favorite for anglers of all ages.

The aquarium publishes a calendar of events four times a year that lists all programs and activities. Some field trips, classes and workshops require a nominal fee and all require advance registration. To register or to find out about programs call 247-4004.

The Alice Hoffman Nature Trail is on the aquarium grounds and leads visitors on a short, loop-trail hike through a maritime forest. An interpretive trail brochure is available at the visitor service desk. In spring 1996, the aquarium opened its new outdoor Salt Marsh Safari exhibit along Bogue Sound. The soundside walkway features overlooks, bird scopes and informational signs that discuss the importance of the salt marsh and the plants and animals living there.

Back inside, the aquarium gift shop offers an inviting selection of educational and environmentally aware items ranging from pens, pencils and puzzles to T-shirts, CDs and pottery. For gift shop information call 247-3599.

Admission fees are: adults, $3; senior citizens and active military $2; children (6 to 17 years old), $1; registered school groups, Aquarium Society members and children younger than age 6, free of charge. Admission fees have created a special fund to be used for renovations, improvements and expansion of the three existing aquarium facilities. Membership in the Aquarium Society entitles participants to newsletters, calendars, special functions and discounts on programs and gift-shop purchases. Aquarium society members are also entitle to free admission to the state's three aquariums and to more than 120 other zoos and aquariums across the country.

Aquarium hours are 9 AM to 5 PM Monday through Saturday and 1 to 5 PM on Sunday from September 1 to May 31. From June 1 through August 31, hours are 9 AM to 7 PM daily.

BEAUFORT HISTORIC SITE

100 Block of Turner St.
Beaufort   728-5225

The Beaufort Historic Site is a large area in the center of town that is the home of a number of restored houses and buildings. Cared for by the Beaufort Historical Association, the site is available for tours as well as classes, workshops and events throughout the year.

Most of the restored buildings were moved to the site from other locations in town. These moves were necessitated in many cases by property owners who were ready to tear down an old structure to

The 10th Annual North Carolina Seafood Festival

October 4-6, 1996

Morehead City Waterfront

- ◆ Live Entertainment
- ◆ Games
- ◆ Activities
- ◆ Seafood, Seafood, Seafood

P.O. Box 1812
Morehead City, NC 28557
(919)726-6273(NCSF)

build a new one. Among the restored buildings on the site are those described below.

Josiah Bell House, c. 1825, is the large yellow house used as the welcome center for the Beaufort Historic Site. Its Victorian furnishings reflect the typical customs of its original era. **Samuel Leffers Cottage**, c. 1778, was once the schoolmaster's house. It is furnished in a primitive style and features a Beaufort-type roof line.

Carteret County Courthouse of 1796 was the county's third courthouse and is the oldest public building remaining in Beaufort. It has been restored with authentic furnishings. **Old County Jail**, c. 1829, is in excellent condition. Its three cells and jailkeeper's quarters were in use until 1954. There is a museum room in one of the cells. The **Apothecary Shop and Doctor's Office**, c. 1859, features a wonderful collection of medical instruments and memorabilia from the first county doctors and dentists.

R. Rustell House, c. 1732, is home to the Mattie King Davis Art Gallery. In its time, it was a typical Beaufort cottage and was owned by prominent early citizen Richard Rustell Jr.

Guided tours begin at the Josiah Bell House Monday through Saturday, 9:30 AM until 4:30 PM April through October.

After a tour of the historic site, hop on the old English double-decker bus and listen to a guide as you pass through the town's historic district. Bus tours depart the historic site on Monday, Wednesday and Saturday. Architectural walking tours of Beaufort's historic district are narrated on Tuesday and Thursday, and guided tours of the Old Burying Grounds are scheduled on Monday and Wednesday. In addition, the Beaufort Historical Association conducts its annual Beaufort Old Homes Tour during the last weekend in June (see the Annual Events chapter). Activities include tours of private and association-owned homes, musical performances, an antique show and sale, military re-enactments and more.

The **Robert W. and Elva Faison Safrit Historical Center** will be newly opened for summer 1996 at the south end of the historic site. Visitors will be treated to pictorial, video and artifact displays as well artist demonstrations and exhibits. The center will orient visitors to the historic site before they begin touring the buildings. A new gift shop will also be connected.

For information about the Beaufort Historic Site or any of its activities, stop by the yellow house on the first block of Turner Street. We guarantee you'll wish you had a few more days in town.

N.C. MARITIME MUSEUM
315 Front St.
Beaufort 728-7317

The N.C. Maritime Museum interprets North Carolina's historical alliances with the sea. The museum's theme, "Down to the Sea," celebrates the state's coastal heritage, maritime and natural history and natural resources.

The 18,000-square-foot building is constructed of wood, resembling facilities used in the 19th century by the U.S. Lifesaving Service, the forerunner of the U.S. Coast Guard. The museum's interior is designed to impart the feeling of being in the hold of a large ship. On the ground floor are exhibit areas, offices, an auditorium, a classroom, a library and a bookshop.

The museum houses an impressive collection of ship models, ranging from sailing skiffs to full-rigged ships, including a model of the *Snapdragon*, once captained by the privateer Otway Burns of Swansboro. Burns sailed the North Carolina coastal waters during the War

of 1812. Other museum exhibits include native coastal birds, fish and mammal specimens, marine fossils, marine artifacts, decoys, small watercraft and salt water aquariums. The museum also houses a huge collection of sea shells, the Brantley and Maxine Watson collection, from international and local waters. The museum's library offers the best references and periodicals collection you'll find in maritime topics, and you're welcome to use it while you're there.

Museum programming reflects maritime history. Films, talks and lectures are conducted for the public in the large auditorium, and if you are looking for a special book on natural or maritime history or a navigational or topographical map, chances are the museum bookstore will have it.

The **Cape Lookout Studies Program** is a special educational program that be-

gan operating through the museum in 1989. It has been a smashing success. The program is actually an intense short course of study designed to meet the needs of any particular group. Groups of eight to 15 people stay at the old Coast Guard Station on Cape Lookout to learn about and experience coastal ecology. Courses of study have included dolphin behavior, tern and turtle nesting, barrier island ecology and other marine-related subjects.

Each year, the museum hosts its **Traditional Wooden Boat Show**, which features beautiful handcrafted boats, music, boat races, talks, entertainment and displays (see our Annual Events chapter).

The N.C. Maritime Museum is open year round and targets its programs and activities to interest visitors of all ages. Its **Junior Sailing Program** offers sailing skills instruction in classes scheduled from

June through August, and **Summer Science School** for youngsters (see Kidstuff) addresses such subjects as sea shells, marine archaeology, pirates, fishing and salt marsh habitats. Field trips and programs for both adults and children range from how to harvest, clean and cook clams to hands-on trawl and dredge trips aboard a research vessel. A trained naturalist might take adventurers on a hike through the marshes, on a trek to look for waterfowl or on a boat ride to explore one of the area's many surrounding undeveloped islands. Whatever the topic, a unique coastal experience is sure to follow.

There is no admission fee; museum hours are from 9 AM to 5 PM Monday through Friday, 10 AM to 5 PM Saturday and 2 to 5 PM Sunday.

HARVEY W. SMITH WATERCRAFT CENTER
Front St.
Beaufort   728-7317

The beautiful watercraft center is an extension of the N.C. Maritime Museum and is just across the street from it on Front Street. The watercraft center is the hub of the museum's Small Craft Program, which researches and preserves boat styles traditional to area uses. It is a busy, bustling arena of activity, where the sounds of hammers, saws and drills and the smells of wood chips and salt air bring images of traditional boatbuilding and early seafarers. The center's viewing platform above the boatshop floor allows visitors to observe the process of making boats. In addition to boatbuilding and restoration projects, the center offers classes in boatbuilding carpentry, oar making, lofting, tool making and halfmodeling. It also houses the **John S. MacCormack Model Shop**, where model builders construct scale models of a variety of vessels, including the colonial

merchantmen, small craft and other historical ships. There is no admission charge. Hours are 9 AM to 5 PM Monday through Friday; 10 AM to 5 PM, Saturday; 1 PM to 5 PM, Sunday.

CARTERET COUNTY MUSEUM OF HISTORY AND ART
100 Wallace Dr.
Morehead City   247-7533

In 1985, the Carteret County Historical Society was given the old Camp Glenn School building, c. 1907, which had served the community first as a school and later as a church, a flea market and a print shop. The society moved the building from its previous location to Wallace Drive, facing the parking lots of Carteret Community College and the Crystal Coast Civic Center, just off Arendell Street in Morehead City. The members renovated the building and created a museum to show visitors and residents how life used to be in Carteret County. There are rotating exhibits with emphasis on the area's Native American heritage, schools, businesses and homes. The museum houses the society's research library, available to those interested in genealogy and history, and it conducts occasional genealogy workshops. Monthly exhibits feature area artists, and there is a gift shop. The museum is open Tuesday through Saturday from 1 until 4 PM. There is no admission charge.

CORE SOUND WATERFOWL MUSEUM
SR 1335, just east of the school
Harkers Island   728-1500

Established in 1988 as an outgrowth of efforts by the Decoy Carvers Guild, the museum is funded by its own membership, which numbers nearly 2000. Each December, it hosts the Core Sound Decoy Festival (see the Annual Events chapter), a

The Lost Colony

The Lost Colony was not lost at all — just misplaced. Or that's what some Crystal Coast locals believe.

The term Lost Colony refers to the English colony established in the New World in 1587. Led by John White, three ships from Plymouth, England, carrying 120 men, women and children, established a colony, history tells us, at Roanoke Island, on the Outer Banks of North Carolina. According to most historic accounts, White returned to England and left the colony on Roanoke Island. When he returned in 1590, the colony had been evacuated and the colonists had vanished, never to be found.

Locally, there is a strong belief that John White's colony was not established on Roanoke Island at all, but on Cedar Island, which his colonists had never occupied. But the settlers weren't lost. They were just further south on Cedar Island. It was White and the returning crew who were lost.

That theory and facts to document it are offered by Melvin Robinson in a book, *The Riddle of the Lost Colony*, published in 1946. A copy of the book is housed in the North Carolina Collection at the Carteret County Public Library on Turner Street in Beaufort and is available for in-house reading.

Robinson supports his argument that Cedar Island was the site of the original settlement by using census reports and maps of land formations, inlets and surrounding islands.

One of the many interesting points Robinson makes is that the logs form John White's original voyage indicate the settlers were left at an island seven leagues, about 20 miles, from the harbor they entered. Roanoke is about 40 miles from the nearest possible point of entry at that time. On the other hand, Cedar Island is just about 20 miles from Ocracoke Inlet.

According to Robinson's research, there was a strong belief in the 1940s that the descendants of these colonists continued to live in Carteret County. The first official census in the United States, completed in 1790, reported a white population of 3,019 in Carteret County. Sixty people bore surnames of the original colonists.

Regardless of what you believe now about the so-called Lost Colony, a short review of Robinson's book will leave you considering new possibilities. Who knows? You might join some of the locals and be convinced the Lost Colony wasn't lost at all — just misplaced.

weekend-long gathering of waterfowl artists and decoy carvers held at the Harkers Island Elementary School. Truly a grassroots effort, the museum houses decoys from the collections of such renowned local carvers as the late Homer Fulcher, Eldon Willis and Julian Hamilton. It has pieces by Jack Dudley, author of *Core Sound Waterfowl Heritage*, and a Dixon reproduction decoy. Also exhibited are the blue-ribbon pieces from all past Core Sound Decoy Festival competitions in the decoy painting, gunning shore birds and best in show categories. The museum gift shop carries books, stationery, shirts, canvas geese and decorative decoys.

Plans are progressing to build a permanent museum building at the end of the road in Harkers Island next to the Cape Lookout National Seashore Park Service headquarters. The land has been acquired, and fund-raising efforts for the planned $2 million facility, which will be completely financed by membership contributions, began at the 1994 Core Sound Decoy Festival. Membership categories range from $25 for individuals to various statuses of contribution support.

CRYSTAL COAST CIVIC CENTER
3505 Arendell St.
Morehead City   *247-3883*

On the campus of Carteret Community College overlooking Bogue Sound, the Crystal Coast Civic Center is the largest facility of its kind on the North Carolina coast. A multiple-use facility with a 12,000-square-foot exhibition hall, the civic center can accommodate meetings of 1,000 people or dinners for 800, or its space can be divided into smaller areas. Each year, the Crystal Coast Civic Center hosts events that are major attractions to the resort area from the North Carolina Commercial Fishing Show to the Festival of Trees. Exhibitions and trade

shows are frequent throughout the year as are peripheral events such as awards dinners for the Big Rock and the Hardee's Atlantic Beach King Mackerel fishing tournaments and the Taste and Sound of N.C. dance during the North Carolina Seafood Festival weekend. Many private businesses and families schedule use of the Crystal Coast Civic Center for events involving a large number of people. Accommodations include a snack bar, full-service catering kitchen, public address system, portable stage and a 5,600-square-foot outdoor plaza over the beautiful Bogue Sound.

CRYSTAL COAST AMPHITHEATER/ WORTHY IS THE LAMB
N.C. Hwy. 58   *393-8373*
Pelletier   *(800) 662-5960*

This 2,100-seat amphitheater overlooks the White Oak River in the little community of Pelletier, just north of Cape Carteret. The amphitheater is home to *Worthy is the Lamb*, the only fully orchestrated musical passion play in production. The spectacular presentation is a sensitive, moving composition of art, spoken word and music with insightful, spiritual reflections that reveal a compelling

Photo: Kenny Barnes

Worthy is the Lamb *is an outdoor passion play depicting the life of Christ. Performances are at the Crystal Coast Amphitheater.*

portrait of the life and times of Christ. The amphitheater was awarded the Nisbet Award in 1995 by the Travel Council of North Carolina based on its positive impact on state tourism.

The production features costumes, ships, horses and chariots that reflect the pageantry of the period when Christ was alive. Sets have been carefully constructed to create a lifelike replica of the city of Jerusalem. State-of-the-art technology in computer-coordinated sound, lighting and special effects provide consistently outstanding performance quality. The soundtrack was recorded in London at the same historic English cathedral where the soundtracks for such movies as *Greystoke:The Legend of Tarzan* and *Yentl* were produced.

Worthy is the Lamb performances are staged at 8:30 PM Thursday through Saturday from mid-June through August. In September, performances begin at 7:30 PM on Friday and Saturday only. Adult tickets are $11; senior citizens, $9; children ages 6 through 12, $6. Discounts are offered to groups of 15 or more and active military.

Tours

N.C. COASTAL FEDERATION
3609 Hwy. 24, Ocean   393-8185

The North Carolina Coastal Federation is an active organization focused on protection of the coastal environment and culture through its activities in education, information and legislative accountability. It conducts fascinating tours from May through October as part of its education effort. On Mondays, a Croatan National Forest Safari takes explorers into the land of carnivorous plants — Venus's-flytraps, sundews, butterworts and four varieties of pitcher plants proliferate in the Croatan. A one or two-hour trail exploration of longleaf pines and the Patsy Pond natural area departs by appointment on Monday and is free of charge. On Tuesdays, an Open Beach and Inlet Investigation is offered to observe the changes effected on Bogue Inlet and nearby beaches by modern and historic development. The small-boat trip explores a salt-marsh habitat and allows for shell-collecting at Hammocks Beach State Park. Each Wednesday, a Barrier

WORTHY IS THE LAMB

NORTH CAROLINA'S THIRD LARGEST OUTDOOR DRAMA
JUNE 28, 1996 THRU SEPTEMBER 21, 1996

Island and Sound Adventure is a boating trip to sample marine life from sound water and islands. The importance of the sound as a food source and critical habitat is discussed as are the conflicting demands within this ecosystem. Thursday's boating venture is into the estuaries of Bogue Sound on a Trawl and Seine Expedition. Samples of marine life are collected in shallow waters for a look at their dependence on water quality. All trips are scheduled through the coastal federation office, and all but the trail tour require a small, but well-spent fee.

MYSTERY TOURS
Front St.
Beaufort   728-7827

Docked in Taylor's Creek in front of the Beaufort House Restaurant, the 65-foot double-decked *Mystery* tour boat takes cruises along 18 miles of area waterways. Complete with a covered cabin and snack bar, the boat provides visitors with a water view of Beaufort's historic homes, island ponies, salt marshes, bird rookeries, Morehead City State Port, Fort Macon, Shackleford Banks and other islands along the Intracoastal Waterway. Tours last 1½ hours and are conducted daily at 2, 4:30 and 7 PM, April through October. Costs are $8 for adults, $5 for children ages 6 through 12, and free for youngsters younger than 6. The *Mystery* also charters half-day fishing trips from 8 AM to noon and can make arrangements for dinner cruises. The boat is available for special-occasion charters

such as birthdays, weddings and anniversaries. Special-interest trips can be arranged for birders, shell collectors and other groups.

CRYSTAL QUEEN
600 Front St.
Beaufort   728-2527

Docked in Taylor's Creek on the Beaufort waterfront, the red, white and blue 82-foot paddle wheeler *Crystal Queen* is available for a variety of scenic tours. Licensed for 150 passengers, the *Crystal Queen* includes a snack bar with soft drinks, beer and wine on its enclosed, heated and air-conditioned lower deck. It also has a canopy and sundeck (complete with foul weather curtains) on its upper deck.

The tour boat offers several daily 1½-hour narrated sightseeing cruises in season. Two-hour evening dinner cruises are scheduled by reservation and usually have live musical entertainment aboard. Departure times for tours and dinner cruises are generally fixed during the summer months and change according to demand; call for departure times.

Tours take sightseers along the Morehead and Beaufort waterfronts, Shackleford Banks and surrounding waterways. The *Crystal Queen* also accepts private charters so you can choose your own route. Help is available with food planning, and the boat has all ABC permits.

Group rates, active military and senior discounts are available; children ages 6 to 12 ride at a reduced rate; children 5

Insiders' Tips

A trip to Cape Lookout requires that you take all your necessities with you, especially drinking water and sunscreen.

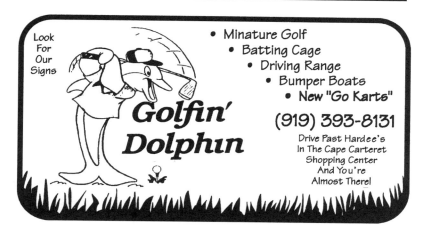
and younger ride free. Call for rates, departure times and reservations or fax to 728-1644.

WHITE SAND TRAIL RIDES

N.C. Hwy 12., Cedar Island   729-0911

There are beach trails to explore on horseback about as far Down East as you can go before getting wet. Lots of packages are available, but owner Wayland Cato also offers a half-hour ride just for kids. The 45-minute drive from Beaufort through Down East is a great exploration trip, too. Stop along the way at Harkers Island to visit the Core Sound Waterfowl Museum or at the Cedar Island Wildlife Refuge. In fact, this trip could pretty much devour a whole day.

State and National Parks

The Crystal Coast is fortunate to have national, state and local parks scattered from one border to the other. Here, we offer a look at national and state parks. Local parks are described in the Sports and Fitness chapter. Our coastal area parks are dazzling with historic interest and natural beauty, so get out there and enjoy them.

FORT MACON STATE PARK

E. Fort Macon Rd., N.C. Hwy 58, MP 0
Atlantic Beach   726-3775

Fort Macon State Park, at the east end of Bogue Banks, is North Carolina's most-visited state park and, with around 1.4 million visitors each year, the Crystal Coast's most-visited attraction. Initially, the fort served to protect the channel and Beaufort harbor against attacks from the sea. Today, the danger of naval attack is remote, but during the 18th and 19th centuries this region was very vulnerable. The need for defense was clearly illustrated in 1747 when Spanish raiders captured Beaufort and again in 1782 when the British took over the port town.

Construction of Fort Dobbs, named for Governor Arthur Dobbs, began here in 1756, but it was never completed. In 1808-09, Fort Hampton, a small masonry fort, was built to guard the inlet. The fort was abandoned shortly after the War of 1812 and by 1825 had been swept into the inlet.

Designed by Brig. Gen. Simon Bernard and built by the U.S. Army Corps of Engineers, Fort Macon was completed in 1834 at a cost of $463,790. The fort was named for Nathaniel Macon who was speaker of the House of Representatives and U.S. Senator from North Carolina. The five-sided structure was built of brick and stone with outer walls 4.5 feet thick. The fort was deactivated after 1877 and then regarrisoned by state troops in 1898 for the Spanish-American War. It was abandoned again in 1903, was not used in World War I and was offered for sale in 1923. A Congressional Act in 1924 gave the fort and the surrounding land to the state of North Carolina to be used as a public park. The park, which is more than 400 acres, opened in 1936 and was North Carolina's first functioning state park.

At the outbreak of World War II, the Army leased the park from the state and, once again, manned the fort to protect a number of important nearby facilities. In 1944, the fort was returned to the state, and the park reopened the following year.

Today, Fort Macon State Park offers the best of two worlds — beautiful, easily accessible beaches for recreation and a historic fort for exploration. Visitors enjoy the sandy beaches, a seaside bathhouse and restrooms, a refreshment stand, designated fishing and swimming areas and picnic facilities with outdoor grills. A short nature trail winds through dense shrub and over low sand dunes. There is abundant wildlife in the park, including herons, egrets, warblers, sparrows and other animals.

The fort itself is a wonderful place to explore with a self-guided tour map or with a tour guide. A museum and bookshop offer exhibits to acquaint you with the fort and its history. The fort is open year round, and the museum is open daily June through Labor Day and on weekends throughout the year. Re-enactments of fort activities are scheduled periodically. Talks on Civil War and natural history and a variety of nature walks are conducted year round. The fort is open daily

from 9 AM to 5:30 PM. The fort office is open from 8:30 AM to 12:30 PM.

Beside the park is Fort Macon Coast Guard Base, home port of four large cutters and several smaller vessels. The base is charged with patrolling the area from Drum Inlet on Core Banks south to the North Carolina-South Carolina border (see our Military chapter).

THEODORE ROOSEVELT NATURAL AREA
Roosevelt Dr., MP 7
Pine Knoll Shores 726-3775

This little gem of a nature trail is alongside the N.C. Aquarium on Roosevelt Drive in Pine Knoll Shores. Maintained and operated by Fort Macon State Park, the 265 acres have extensive maritime forests and freshwater ponds. The land was donated to the state by the family of Theodore Roosevelt, the country's 26th president. The forest attracts naturalists, birdwatchers and photographers. The nearby aquarium offers a nature trail guide that is available in the aquarium gift shop.

This soundside trail is a good place to see land birds. The marshes along this section of Bogue Banks are not extensive, so there are few marsh or water birds. The best birding along the trail is from mid-April through May or in late fall and winter. Mosquitoes take over the trail from late spring through early fall, so come prepared.

RACHEL CARSON COMPONENT OF THE NORTH CAROLINA NATIONAL ESTUARINE RESEARCH RESERVE
430-B W. Beaufort Rd.
Beaufort 728-2170

Just across Taylor's Creek from the Beaufort waterfront is a series of islands that make up the Rachel Carson Component of the North Carolina National Estuarine Research Reserve. Most locals refer to the entire chain of islands as Bird

Shoal or Carrot Island, the names the islands were known by prior to the state's acquisition of the land.

These islands are roughly 3.5 miles long and have an interesting recent history. Through the years, the land was privately owned by individuals or groups. In 1977, when the owner of 178.5 acres announced plans to divide the land and sell it in tracts, locals formed The Beaufort Land Conservancy Council and began collecting money and support for preserving the island chain. They sought the aid of the Nature Conservancy, a national nonprofit organization dedicated to the protection of natural areas, and together the groups raised $250,000 from individuals and businesses for the purchase of the islands. Now, the state of North Carolina manages the island reserve.

In the late 1960s, Congress recognized the need to protect coastal resources from pollution and the pressures of development. In particular danger were the nation's estuaries, those valuable, fragile areas where rivers meet the sea. So, the National Research Reserve was established. Now administered by the North Carolina Division of Coastal Management, the reserves are sites for walking, exploring, researching and educating about the natural and human processes that affect the coast.

Estuary waters make up the bays, sounds, inlets and sloughs along the coast and are among the most biologically productive systems on earth. More than two-thirds of the fish and shellfish commercially harvested in coastal waters spend part or all of their lives in estuaries. So, the economy of many coastal areas depends heavily on the health of these environments. North Carolina is fortunate to have four protected sites: Zeke's Island, Currituck Banks, Masonboro Island and Rachel Carson.

This site was named in honor of the late scientist and author, Rachel Carson, who did research on the islands in the 1940s and, through her research and writing, made people aware of the importance of coastal ecosystems. The Rachel Carson site is made up of salt marshes, tidal flats, ellgrass beds, sand flats and artificially created dredge spoil islands. It is a favorite spot for beachcombing, swimming, sunbathing and clamming, but camping is not allowed. Visitors are encouraged to leave everything — the animals, plants and research equipment — undisturbed. You'll need a boat to get there, and there are a few that can be hired to take you (see Ferries). You can volunteer to pick up litter while you visit, and the site specialists will make arrangements to transport you to and from the island.

The Rachel Carson site is home to a number of feral ponies descended from domesticated ponies that were taken to the islands to graze. They now roam the sandy expanse, living in small bands called harems, each consisting of one stallion, several mares and the year's foals. Bachelor males roam the island alone or in pairs. These are either older stallions who have lost their harem to a younger, stronger male or young stallions who have not yet challenged the dominant males. The ponies paw watering holes in the sand and often fight over the limited supply of water. As a result of the damage to the marsh caused by grazing and the seasonal food shortages that affect the ponies, reserve managers are considering different ways to protect the herd. The site is also home to about 160 species of birds.

Site education coordinators conduct free tours of the reserve twice a month from May through August, but boat transportation arrangements must be made to get there (see Ferries). A self-guided trail brochure is available at the N.C. Maritime Museum, the reserve office or at ferry service offices. An information sign about the reserve is displayed on Front Street in Beaufort across from the Inlet Inn.

HAMMOCKS BEACH STATE PARK
1572 Hammocks Beach Rd.
Swansboro   *(910) 326-4881*

Venture to Hammocks Beach State Park on Bear Island and be rewarded with one of the most beautiful and unspoiled beaches in the area. The park consists of a barrier island off the southernmost point of Bogue Banks and a small area off Highway 24 just south of the residential area of Swansboro where the park office and ferry landing are located (watch for state directional signs). Loggerhead turtles come ashore at night during nesting season to nest above the tide line. Explorers can discover marine life in tidal creeks and mudflats. The island is accessible only by ferry (see our Ferries chapter), and camping is allowed (see our Crystal Coast Camping chapter).

A bathhouse and snack bar provide the only shade and comfort facilities on the island, so go prepared. There's something about the access, the bathhouse architecture and the walk from the ferry landing to the beach (about a half-mile) that feel like Sunday beach trips must have felt in the 1920s. The trip is always a lot of fun.

CAPE LOOKOUT NATIONAL SEASHORE
131 Charles St.
Harkers Island   *728-2250*

Cape Lookout National Seashore is

North Carolina Maritime Museum

Preserving North Carolina's
♦ Coastal Heritage ♦

- **Annual Wooden Boat Show** *[first weekend in May]*
- **Summer Science School for Children**
- **Traditional Seafood Exhibition**
- **Fall Cultural Heritage Event**
- **Wooden Boat Preservation and Construction**
  [Workshops and courses]
- **Natural History Lectures, Tours, and Field Trips** *[monthly]*
- **In-House Research Library**
- **Museum Bookstore** *[Large selection of navigational charts]*
- **Interpretive Exhibits**

Hours:	
M – F	9–5
Sat.	10–5
Sun.	1–5

315 Front Street ♦ Beaufort, NC 28516 ♦ (919) 728-7317
A Division of the NC Department of Agriculture, James A. Graham, Commissioner

one of America's few remaining undeveloped coastal barrier island systems. It includes about 28,500 acres of barrier island environment bounded on the north by Ocracoke Inlet and on the south by Beaufort Inlet. Three islands make up the 56-mile seashore: North Core Banks, also known as Portsmouth Island; South Core Banks, or Cape Lookout; and Shackleford Banks. Each island is distinctive in history and characteristics.

Cape Lookout National Seashore was authorized by the United States Congress to be included in the National Park System in 1966. The National Park Service maintains authority over the seashore.

The seashore's pristine ocean beaches offer surfcasters, sunbathers, surfers, snorklers and shell collectors a wonderful escape. Other recreational pursuits in the park include picnicking, primitive camping, migratory waterfowl watching and hunting. The area is noted for its natural resources. Birds and animals are the only permanent residents. The endangered loggerhead sea turtle nests on the beaches each summer and seldom nests any farther north. The park is an inviting habitat for the plentiful resident and migrant birds. Raccoons, rabbits, nutria, a variety of insects, snakes and lizards are also among the park's permanent residents. Ghost crabs, mole crabs and coquina clams populate the beaches.

Cape Lookout National Seashore is surrounded by water and can only be reached by private or commercial boat. For some sites, limited ground transportation can be arranged with the ferry operator prior to departure, as can accommodations (see our Ferry chapter). Camping is permitted anywhere in the park (see our Camping chapter) except in posted areas.

One objective of the National Park System in preserving the banks was to return them to their natural state, and the acquisition of privately owned cabins, which are visible from the Cape Lookout light caused some ruffles. Some owners proved their points and were granted lifetime or 25-year leases on property that eventually will revert to the National Park Service. No further development on the islands is allowed.

The Cape Lookout Lighthouse is still an active aid to navigation. The first lighthouse was built on Core Banks in 1811-12 and was painted with red and white stripes. The current lighthouse was completed in 1859 as the prototype for other North Carolina lighthouses and wears a distinctive black and white diamond pattern. Visitors are welcome in the restored lighthouse keeper's quarters that houses a small natural history collection. Other associated structures (coal shed, etc.) are also preserved, and a new boardwalk takes visitors from the lighthouse area, over the dunes, to the ocean beach.

PORTSMOUTH VILLAGE

At the northernmost end of Core Banks at the Ocracoke Inlet is Portsmouth Village. The village was established in 1753 to serve as the main port of entry to several coastal communities. Named for Portsmouth, England, the port village was busy with lightering incoming vessels, an unloading and reloading process that allowed vessels passage through the shallow Ocracoke Inlet. During its heyday in the 1860s, the village had a population of about 600. After Hatteras Inlet opened, the village became less important in its port services.

From 1894 to 1934, the population of Portsmouth was mainly concerned with its lifesaving station. After a severe hurricane in 1935, the village population de-

clined, and by the early 1970s, no year-round residents remained.

Today, the village looks much like it did in the early 1900s. The remaining homes, cemeteries, church and pathways are used by former residents and their descendants. Structures that are not privately owned are maintained by the Park Service. Portsmouth Village was placed on the National Register of Historic Places in 1979 and is guided by policies of the National Historic Preservation Act.

SHACKLEFORD BANKS

Looking east from Fort Macon, Shackleford Banks is the island across the Beaufort Inlet. It stretches 9 miles east to Cape Lookout, bordered by the Atlantic Ocean on the south and Back Sound on the north. The island's sound side has long been a favorite weekend destination for residents escaping the crowded mainland beaches. The rock jetty is a favorite spot for anglers.

Shackleford Banks officially became part of Cape Lookout National Seashore on the first day of 1986. Until then, the island was dotted with cabins, or camps, that former banks residents and their de-scendants continued to use as getaway shelters. The acquisition of Shackleford Banks meant removing the structures and livestock that had been left to roam the island. Before 1986, the island was home to hearty herds of wild cattle, sheep, goats, pigs and horses. Today, only the horses have been allowed to remain, and management plans for them are currently in the discussion stage.

The island was named for Francis Shackleford who was granted the land in 1705. Permanent residents once populated communities on Shackleford. The largest community was Diamond City at the east end. By 1897, about 500 people populated Diamond City in a community complete with church buildings, stores, a post office and a school. According to information provided in *Island Born and Bred*, a history/cookbook compiled by Harkers Island Methodist Women, the most growth occurred in the 1850s because of a boom in the local whaling industry.

New England whaling vessels visited the area as early as 1726. By 1880, six crews of 18 men from Diamond City were whaling off the banks' shores. The whalers were a hearty people and included families of

Davises, Moores, Guthries, Royals and Roses — names still common in Carteret County. When a lookout spotted a whale, crews would launch their small rowing boats to harpoon the creature. If successful, a crewman would signal villagers on shore by holding an oar in the air. When the boats came ashore, pots of boiling water would be ready to process the blubber into valuable oil. Merchants in Beaufort and Morehead City sold the oil as lamp oil and lubricating oil or used it to make soap. Whale bone was valuable in making corset stays, ribs for umbrellas and other items. They sold the rest of the whale as fertilizer.

East of Diamond City, across what is now Barden's Inlet, was the community of Cape Lookout. West of Diamond City was Bell's Island, a settlement known for bountiful persimmon trees. The western part of Shackleford Banks was known as Wade's Shore. Two hurricanes that followed each other closely in 1896 and 1899

Annie Dixon Salter served for 30 years as postmaster of Portsmouth Island.

Photo: National Park Service

convinced most island inhabitants to move to the mainland. Many moved their homes by boat to Harkers Island or Morehead City. Others resettled in Salter Path on Bogue Banks.

CEDAR ISLAND NATIONAL WILDLIFE REFUGE

Lola Rd.
Cedar Island 225-2511

This 12,500-acre wildlife refuge on the southern end of Cedar Island is maintained by the U.S. Fish and Wildlife Service, which provides areas for hiking, bird-watching, launching boats, picnicking and hunting. No ranger services are available.

Waterfowl abundant during the year include mallards, black ducks, redheads, pintails and green-winged teals. Other wildlife at home in the refuge include raccoons, deer, bears, woodpeckers and river otters. In the spring and fall, this is a delightful picnicking and bird-watching destination.

The Cedar Island Wildlife Refuge was formed in 1964 to build waterfowl impoundments, primarily to help the black duck. All the planned impoundments have not been created and will require additional government funding. There are some restrictions for hunting on the impoundment.

The access is well-marked on Cedar Island. Turn on Lola Road and follow it to the refuge office. One boat ramp is across from the office, and another is just west of the new Monroe Gaskill Memorial high-rise bridge.

CROATAN NATIONAL FOREST

141 E. Fisher Ave.
New Bern 638-5628

Croatan National Forest is made up of 157,000 acres spread in a triangle between Morehead City, Cape Carteret and New Bern. Forest headquarters are on Fisher Avenue, approximately 9 miles east

of New Bern off Highway 70. Well-placed road signs make the office easy to find.

The name Croatan comes from the Algonquian Indians' name for "Council Town," which was once located in the area. Because of the forest's coastal location, you'll find many unusual features here. Some of the components of the ecosystem are pocosins, longleaf and loblolly pine, bottomland and upland hardwoods.

Sprinkled throughout the Croatan are 40 miles of streams and 4,300 acres of wild lakes, some fairly large such as Great Lake, Catfish Lake and Long Lake. Miles of unpaved roads lace through the woodland providing easy, if sometimes roundabout, access to its wilderness.

The forest offers excellent hiking, swimming, boating, camping, picnicking, hunting and fresh and saltwater fishing. Boat access is provided at several loca-

tions. Rangers advise that lake fishing is generally poor because of the acidity of the water. All fishing, hunting and trapping activities are regulated by the N.C. Wildlife Resources Commission. The forest has several planned camping sites (see our Camping chapter), and primitive camping is permitted all year. Some areas of the forest close seasonally, and fees can vary, so call headquarters for current rates and availability.

As with all national forests, the Croatan's natural resources are actively managed to provide goods and services for the public. Pine timber is harvested and replanted each year, and wildlife habitat for a wide range of animals is maintained on thousands of acres. Endangered and sensitive animal and plant species are protected. The red-cockaded woodpecker is among the endangered animals that find safety here. More common animals that abound include the southern bald eagle, alligators, squirrels, otters, white-tail deer, black bears, snakes and wild turkeys.

The area is known for its beautiful wildflowers, including five genera of insectivorous plants, a combination rarely seen elsewhere. The insectivorous plants include pitcher-plants, round-leaved sundew, butterworts, Venus's flytraps and bladderworts, all of which die if removed from their natural habitat; it is against the law to disturb them. Pamphlets about the wildflowers and insect-eating plants are available at the park headquarters.

Because the Croatan is so expansive and undeveloped, it is best to pick up a forest map from the headquarters if you plan to explore extensively. For short daytrips or hiking excursions, site brochures are sufficient.

Summer fires, whether spontaneous in nature or controlled for forest nurturance, are common. The insect-eating plants that proliferate in pocosin habitat are actually fire dependent, another reason not to try to take one home. They're well nurtured after a good burning and hungry for bugs. Nature is stranger than fiction.

Crystal Coast Islands

The Crystal Coast is a composition of many islands, some bridged to the mainland and some accessible only by boat. Many have been discussed earlier in this chapter, but there are others that are too interesting to omit.

Hog Island, made up of a couple hundred acres, is on the northeast side of Cedar Island. The island is bordered by Back Bay, Pamlico Sound and Cedar Island Bay. The name of this island probably came from the wild hogs that roamed its expanse. There was once a thriving little

town named Lupton here, and the island was inhabited until the mid-1900s, serving as a trading point for people from Cedar Island.

Phillips Island can be seen from the top of the Morehead City-Beaufort highrise bridge. Looking north, this two-acre island is in the Newport River and is easy to identify because of the brick chimney poking through the trees — a remnant of an old menhaden (fish) processing plant once operated on the island. The island is privately owned and in 1993 was leased to the National Audubon Society, making it part of the the society's North Carolina Coastal Sanctuary System. Considered one of eastern North Carolina's most important nesting sites for many species of wading birds including herons, egrets and ibises, Phillips Island has recently known less nesting activity. Birds are fickle that way.

Piver's Island is on the west side of the Beaufort drawbridge and is about 20 acres in size. The island is home to the Duke University Marine Laboratory and Biomedical Center and the National Oceanic and Atmospheric Administration/National Marine Fisheries Service Beaufort Laboratory. The majority of the island was bulkheaded for the construction of these facilities that dominate the island.

Radio Island is a 200-acre island on the south side of the Morehead City-Beaufort Causeway. For years the east side has been a favorite beach spot for locals. Beachgoers can park and walk a few steps to the beach. Small boats and sailboards can be launched from the beach, and divers converge on the south end and walk into the water next to the rock jetty for some interesting diving near the beach. The south end of the island is owned by the U.S. Government, and the broad cement ramp and pilings accommodate landing

craft that transport deployed troops from nearby military bases. The N.C. State Ports Authority (SPA) owns the rest. A daytime-only beach access area with parking and toilet facilities is managed by the Carteret County Parks and Recreation Department on the east side.

In Swansboro, there is another island of historical significance. **Russell's Island**, formerly known as Huggins Island, was the site of Huggins Island Fort. That Confederate earthworks fort was apparently built in the final months of 1861 to guard Bogue Inlet and West Channel, the principle access channel from the inlet into Swansboro. The fort consisted of earthworks, an underground bunker or magazine and barracks. It had six cannon and was garrisoned in January 1862 by a 200-man company commanded by Capt. Daniel Munn. Two months later, the troops were ordered to remove their guns and ammunition and go to New Bern to aid in the defense of that town. At New Bern, the guns and ammunition were captured. Huggins Island Fort was never regarrisoned. All that remains of the former fort are the brush-covered earthworks.

The Boardwalk By The Sea Arcade is the hub of meet-and-greet activity for the younger set in Emerald Isle.

Crystal Coast
Kidstuff

I went to find the pot of gold
That's waiting where the rainbow
ends.
I searched and searched and searched
and searched
And searched and searched and then—
There it was, deep in the grass,
Under an old and twisty bough.
It's mine, it's mine, it's mine at last . . .
. What do I search for now?

— Shel Silverstein

If the pleasure is in the search, not the treasure, there's a lot of kid in you. For that kid, and any other kids you have onboard, great explorations are ahead on the Crystal Coast. Of course the beaches at the ocean's edge are the main attraction, and the adventures and challenges they offer are as endless as imagination. But, when you reach the what-do-I-search-for-now point, the choices present you with another bountiful quest.

Set out for fun in the jungle, on a pirates' island or on a water-boggan slide. School up with other minnows at the North Carolina Aquarium, and explore things that live in the ocean. Make wonderful creations from stuff you find on the beach, go on a snorkeling adventure in the sound. Ride a Ferris wheel and see forever. Take the helm of a bumper boat, try your skills in a round of mini-golf or take a spin in a go-cart. We've got horseback rides on the beach and some of the best summer camps on earth. And, if you're interested in how the seashore environment works or want to learn how to sail a boat, the thing for you is North Carolina Maritime Museum's Summer Science School or Jr. Sailing Program. The courses are short, and the classes are out in the wild for only a few hours each day, so it won't take your whole vacation.

When you've exhausted the suggestions we've listed and you're told, "Go fly a kite!," you actually can! Flying anything is best on a North Carolina beach, you know. The Wright Brothers knew.

Many of the sites for adventures that follow are also described in other chapters and, for further details, we have referred you to them. We just thought you might appreciate having a concentration here in case you have the misfortune of finding a pot of gold.

SUMMER CAMPS

The Crystal Coast area is near some of the most prestigious summer camps in the eastern United States for campers 6 to 17 years old.

On the Neuse River in Arapahoe is **Camp Seafarer** for girls, 249-1212, and **Camp Sea Gull** for boys, 249-1111. Both are operated by the YMCA Association of Raleigh, 832-4744, and offer programs for varied interests but with a love for the water. Sailing and watersports, including ocean excursions from the Morehead City waterfront outpost, horsemanship, archery, golf, tennis and riflery are offered.

For more information about these and other camps in the Crystal Coast area, see the Sports, Fitness and Parks chapter.

THE CIRCLE
Atlantic Beach, MP 2¼   *no phone*

Depending on your age, you may well think of The Circle when you consider Atlantic Beach. This was the site of the beach's first arcade, the Idle Hour. The Pavilion always had the best bands and was the birthplace of all things that were cool. The younger kids were jostled all day and night on the rides in the center, and there was no place more fun than The Circle. It's still an active place for nightclubs that provide live music, dancing and entertainment far into the night, and it's the home of Fun 'n' Wheels amusements, 240-0050, that in the summer months features the largest Ferris wheel on the island and a go-cart track.

The Circle's continuing face-lift is still in progress to invite more family recreational use of the area. The boardwalk has been improved and beach volleyball courts added. This year The Circle will see the addition of parking areas, burying of utility wires, paving, guttering and landscaping.

JUNGLELAND
Salter Path Rd., N.C. Hwy. 58, MP 4½
Atlantic Beach   *247-2148*

This large amusement park has some-thing for the whole family. Here you will find bumper boats, miniature golf, an arcade, a snack bar and rides for the kids. Admission to the park grounds is free, and tickets (or day passes) are available for individual rides. The park opens daily at 11 AM from April through October. Jungleland is one of the best places to keep kids amused for hours.

PIRATE ISLAND PARK
Salter Path Rd., N.C. Hwy. 58, MP 10½
Salter Path   *247-3024*

The family will enjoy an active day at this Salter Path park with two giant twister waterslides, kiddie slides, a pool and bumper boats. A lounge area, showers and lockers are available for use before a round of miniature golf or a turn through the video arcade. Hot dogs and snacks are available. Group rates and a picnic area with volleyball are available for parties.

PLAYLAND
204 Islander Dr., MP 20½
Emerald Isle   *354-6616*

Playland in Emerald Isle has eight superfast waterslides and all sorts of rides for toddlers and youngsters, including bumper cars, bumper boats and slick and grand prix tracks. Home of "the original" Water Boggan, 354-2609, and Lighthouse Golf, 354-2811, an 18-hole miniature golf course, Playland also has a snack bar and a picnic area to keep the kids completely happy and give moms and dads a break. Playland is open daily during the summer months.

BOARDWALK BY THE SEA ARCADE
Islander Dr., Emerald Isle   354-4440

This is the hub of meet-and-greet activity for the younger set in Emerald Isle. Other than arcade games, the boardwalk features a beach volleyball court, a snack bar and a long boardwalk over the dunes to the beach. It's *the* place to see and be seen.

THE GOLFIN' DOLPHIN
Manatee St., Cape Carteret   393-8131

This expansive family entertainment complex, off N.C. Highway 24 in Cape Carteret behind Hardee's, is where athletes of all ages and stages can hone their competitive edges. The complex includes a 50-tee driving range, baseball and softball batting cages and an 18-hole miniature golf course. While the bigger kids are sharpening their skills, the little ones enjoy the arcade games, bumper boats and go-carts. The Golphin' Dolphin also has a snack bar and a pro shop that sells high-quality golf accessories. A party room is available for private birthday parties and celebrations. The complex is open daily, "9 AM until," from March through December.

WHITE SAND TRAIL RIDES
N.C. Hwy 12., Cedar Island   729-0911

Mount up, cowpokes. There are beach trails to explore on horseback about as far Down East as you can go before getting wet. Lots of packages are available, but Wayland Cato also offers a half-hour ride just for kids. The 45-minute drive from

Photo: Frances A. Eubanks

It's way cool down under.

Beaufort through Down East is a great exploration trip, too. Stop along the way at Harkers Island to visit the Core Sound Waterfowl Museum or at the Cedar Island Wildlife Refuge (see our Attractions chapter). In fact, this trip could pretty much devour a whole day.

KITE FLYING
Kites Unlimited, Atlantic Station
Atlantic Beach   247-7011

Kites Unlimited sponsors Sunday morning kite-flying exhibitions at Fort Macon State Park, and everyone is invited to join. Bring a kite because you'll want to try the things you see after the demonstrations. For the truly competitive kite fliers, the Carolina Kite Fest at Sands Villa Resorts in October (see our Annual Events chapter) is also sponsored by Kites Unlimited.

SPORTSWORLD
U.S. Hwy. 70 W., Morehead City   247-4444

The sport at Sportsworld is skating, and for the local crowd, it's the meet-and-compete spot for the younger-than-the-driving-age set. Sportsworld is well-maintained and supervised with all the right music and activity changes on the skating floor. A snack bar with arcade games is a comfortable vantage for viewing the skating without actually having to relearn the sport. Sportsworld is open year round. Call for hours and activities.

CARTERET LANES
U.S. Hwy. 70 W., Morehead City   247-4481

Everyone in the family can enjoy knocking down a few pins at Carteret Lanes. It's bowling in a family atmosphere with an arcade and snack bar available. Of course leagues and competitions bring out the matching shirts, but the unpolished amateurs also have lots of fun. Carteret Lanes is open year round.

SANDY'S KIDS CLUB
Sands Oceanfront Resort   247-2636
Atlantic Beach   (800) 334-2667

Kids ages 5 to 12 years old who vacation at A Place At The Beach, SeaSpray or Sands Villa Resort in Atlantic Beach and rent through Sands Rental Management register at a special kids' desk while their parents check in at the regular desk. Kids get an identification wristband so they won't get lost, a free gift and access to many fun activities of the kids' club. Daily, between mid-June and mid-August, club activities are scheduled at the resort pool and waterslide, on the beach or on field trips to exciting places like the North Carolina Aquarium, the North Carolina Maritime Museum, Jungleland or Fort Macon State Park. Everyday resort activities include fun stuff like pool games, T-shirt tie dyeing, kite flying, treasure hunts and lots of things parents don't want to do. Sandy, the kids' club mascot, sends each member a birthday and Christmas card each year to remember the summer fun.

SUMMER SCIENCE SCHOOL FOR CHILDREN
N.C. Maritime Museum
315 Front St., Beaufort   728-7317

This popular summer program of the North Carolina Maritime Museum (see our Attractions chapter) is for students entering 1st through 9th grades. The various hands-on study activities include explorations of delicate marine ecosystems with guidance of researchers and instructors at area marine laboratories. Maritime heritage projects are assisted by the museum staff. Most classes are offered in one-week sessions for about three hours a day. Five-day classes at Cape Lookout explore the wonders of the barrier island. Class sizes are small and activities are often wet. For schedules and applications, write or call the museum.

Insiders' Tips

That brilliantly colored purple balloon with pink tentacles washed up on the beach is a Portuguese Man-Of War. It can emit painful stings long after it's dead, so be sure to warn the kids before they find one.

It takes two to reel in the big ones.

PROGRAMS JUST FOR KIDS

N.C. Aquarium, N.C. Hwy. 58
Pine Knoll Shores 247-4004

Everything at the North Carolina Aquarium (see our Attractions chapter) will keep a kid fascinated, but each summer the aquarium plans programs and activities with a kid's point of view in focus. Activities are scheduled each week through the summer months for kids from 4 to 11 years old. The 1½-hour programs introduce preschoolers to marine life with live animals, craft projects, stories and films. The early grade students enjoy art projects, games and sea life videos; the older children learn about coastal environments and marine life via field trips as well as craft and live animal activities. Beginning snorkelers of any age are offered instruction on a regular basis at the aquarium during the summer months. Preregistration is required for all these activities, and we suggest making your reservations early.

JR. SAILING PROGRAM

N.C. Maritime Museum
315 Front St., Beaufort 728-7317

For kids ages 8 through 15, the Junior Sailing Program teaches basic through advanced sailing skills during the summer's eight two-week courses. Sailing courses also include seamanship, navigation skills and maritime traditions, but kids also learn safety, adapting to forces of nature, self-reliance, sportsmanship and respect for others, boats and the sea. Each student uses an Optimist Dinghy, and class size is limited to 14 students with two instructors per class. This is a first-class program and classes fill quickly. Call or write for a schedule and an application.

ARTS AND ENRICHMENT CAMPS

Morehead City Parks and Recreation
1600 Fisher St., Morehead City 726-5083

Art and Enrichment Camps are conducted at Morehead Elementary School at Camp Glenn throughout the summer for school-age children by the Morehead City Parks and Recreation Department. Week-long camps, full- or half-day, are designed for fun in art, dance, drama, computers and math. A small fee is charged.

CHARISMA KIDS

Glad Tidings Pentecostal Holiness Church
Morehead City 726-0160

The children's ministry at Glad Tid-

Photo: NC Aquarium

A field trip to the salt marsh makes learning fun.

ings on Country Club Road in Morehead City involves around 100 kids between the ages of 4 and 12 in a very active program that is met with a very positive response from kids. Charisma Kids meet for their own church on Sundays, 10:30 AM to noon in Glad Tiding's Family Life Center. For the kids, it's an exciting celebration that positively reinforces lifetime Christian habits. Their activities include music, mission trips, games, interesting community guests and involvement in the church through projects like their 1995 "Little Is Much" penny collection project that contributed $1000 to the Family Life Center church debt. This youth program is so highly motivating, we've heard of kids asking to be dropped off if their par-

ents aren't planning to attend Sunday services. Anyone is welcome, and parents are encouraged to participate.

SUMMER DAY CAMP
Morehead City Parks and Recreation
1600 Fisher St., Morehead City   726-5083

An eight-week summer day camp for preschool and school-age kids offers field trips, arts and crafts, swimming, skating, music, drama, sports, games and T-shirts. It's a lot of supervised entertainment for an incredibly reasonable price for both city residents and nonresidents.

N. C. KIDFEST
Morehead City Parks and Recreation Dept.
726-5058

Celebrated the first Saturday in June

at The Circle in Atlantic Beach, Kidfest is a full-day early summer festival staged for and by children. It involves entertainment on multiple stages, educational tents, puppet shows, storytelling, a petting zoo, a tractor-pulled train and other fun rides and booths where kids can sell products to benefit civic and charitable organizations focused on kids. It's a spectacular day that ends, spectacularly, with fireworks.

FISHING EVENTS FOR KIDS

Take-A-Kid Fishing is a project organized annually by the Carteret County Sportfishing Association, 726-5550, for underprivileged children from all over North Carolina. The August day of fishing involves every head boat on the Crystal Coast, at least 100 volunteers, loads of donated burgers and more than 300 young anglers. The event has grown geometrically since it began in 1989 and sponsorships are generous.

The **Triple S Marina Kids Tournament**, 247-4833, is held each summer in late July for kids ages 2 to 14. There is a 50¢ registration fee and awards are presented for the largest and smallest fish. A family cookout for residents and guests at Triple S Village follows the awards ceremony.

The **North Carolina Seafood Festival Kid's Fishing Tournament**, 726-NCSF, during the first weekend in October, brings close to 50 young anglers to Sportsman's Pier in Atlantic Beach. Prizes are awarded for the largest of any kind of fish caught, and each angler goes home with a tackle box.

For county residents age 65 and older there is no tuition charge, only the cost of materials, for courses in visual arts techniques at Carteret Community College.

Crystal Coast
Arts

The state of the arts on the Crystal Coast is active, visible and valued. Our most treasured annual events reflect the value of the arts to our communities. And as art often imitates life on the coast, the arts enjoy an important place in museums and public buildings and reflect the relationship of coastal people with the sea.

The active community of artists on the Crystal Coast is involved in an eclectic array of artistic production. Many artists find the pace of coastal living conducive to developing their talents and move here for that purpose. It's not unusual to meet professionals from other locations earning a living here painting, writing or making pottery. Arts organizations actively support artists' endeavors and welcome new members and volunteers.

Arts Organizations

CARTERET ARTS COUNCIL
704 Arendell St.
Morehead City 726-9156
This nonprofit organization, partially funded by the North Carolina Arts Council, is a distributing agent that funds arts events and education, promotes arts organizations, assists artists seeking grant support in their professional development and sponsors workshops and lectures. Every February it sponsors the *Art From The Heart* exhibition, which involves artists

from three surrounding counties. The council also sponsors the Carteret Arts Festival, a June weekend of music and exhibits by selected artists. Both events take place in Morehead City (see the Annual Events chapter).

CARTERET COUNTY
ARTS AND CRAFTS COALITION
Meg Forward 728-2633
What began in the late 1970s as a small group of professionally oriented artists seeking an outlet for their work has grown into a juried, professional art group of almost 75 members. The coalition conducts three major shows each year: one on Memorial Day weekend, another on Labor Day weekend and a two-week Christmas gallery show during the Thanksgiving holidays. New members are welcome, and jurying of new work takes place twice each year.

CORE SOUND DECOY CARVER'S GUILD
Wayne Davis 728-7316
Born from an idea of seven decoy carvers at a birthday party in 1987, the Decoy Carvers Guild now has a membership of more than 300 active decoy carvers, collectors, breeders, taxidermists and waterfowl artists in more than 25 states. The Core Sound Decoy Festival (see our Annual Events chapter) in December and Core Sound Waterfowl Museum (see our Attractions chapter) in Harkers Island are outgrowths of the efforts of the Decoy Carv-

ers Guild which always welcomes new members and meets each month at Harkers Island Elementary School.

Dance

The Crystal Coast has several dance studios, where everyone from toddlers to adults learn ballet and modern dance. Each performs recitals and often participates in area festivals, group functions and parades. Some of the studios also offer gymnastics, baton, tap and jazz. **Carolina Strut Performing Arts Centre**, Camp Glen Drive, Morehead City, 726-0431; **Dance Arts Studio**, 123 Bonner Avenue, Morehead City, 726-1720; and **Swansboro Dance Studio**, Cedar Point Village, Cedar Point, 393-6159, all offer dance lessons.

The **Gulls and Buoys Square Dance Club** of Carteret County stages an annual Square and Round Dance for adults. The event gathers dancers from nearby states and across North Carolina at the Crystal Coast Civic Center. The club meets weekly at the First Presbyterian Church in Morehead City, and new members are welcome. Call 223-4641 or 728-4219 for information. The **Hi-Tiders Square Dance Club** meets each week for dancing in Swansboro. For information about this active group, call 393-8242 or (910)326-5789. Line-dancing instruction is held regularly at the Carteret County Senior Citizens Center, 1600 Fisher Street in Morehead City. Call 247-2626 or 726-4648 for more information.

Music

The Crystal Coast is home to several choral groups that perform frequently and occasionally audition new prospects. We are fortunate to host some extraordinary concert series, a wonderful music festival weekend in the spring, and active jazz and folk arts music societies which promote, in concerts and education, America's most innovative music styles.

CARTERET CHORALE
Laurence Stith   *726-6193*

This group of more than 30 talented vocalists has worked together to create a chorale known widely for its topnotch performances. The chorale performs benefit concerts regularly in Carteret County and has taken its talent as far as Carnegie Hall, the National Cathedral and Russia. Annually, the group performs at Bruton Parish Church in Williamsburg, Virginia. Director Laurence Stith, retired professional pianist, vocalist and educator, is also a composer and the group often performs his original music.

CRYSTAL COAST CHORAL SOCIETY
Finley Woolston   *240-1173*

Originally formed in the mid-'80s in Swansboro to perform at the town's bicentennial celebration, the group has continued to appear in concert every year since and includes nearly 70 vocalists from Onslow and Carteret counties. Several members are retired professional musicians, and others are talented amateurs

Insiders' Tips

The Sunday Afternoon Concert Series at the First Presbyterian Church in Morehead City often features classical music on the church's remarkable pipe organ and by the Morehead Brass Consortium.

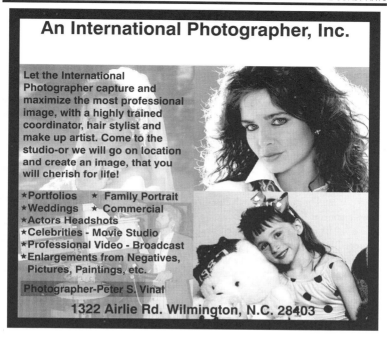
who rehearse each week at Swansboro United Methodist Church.

CARTERET COUNTY CHAPTER OF THE NORTH CAROLINA SYMPHONY

Philip Smith   726-6122

The Carteret County chapter of the North Carolina Symphony brings our superb state symphony to the area to perform three annual concerts. A well-supported annual fund drive, A Day for the Symphony in September, provides for an additional three free concerts for elementary and middle school students. Volunteers are always needed.

AMERICAN MUSIC FESTIVAL

Julie Naegelen   808-ARTS

An exquisite chamber music series, the American Music Festival is composed of five extraordinary concerts performed in the acoustically complementary North Carolina Maritime Museum auditorium in Beaufort. Now in it's sixth season, the concert series is supported by membership, sponsorship and a volunteer staff. From late fall 1995 through early spring 1996, the series brought Duke University's Ciompi Quartet, Beaufort native and Metropolitan Opera Audition winner Sandra McClain and East Carolina University's resident artist quintet, East Carolina Brass. Series memberships are $50 or, if you take chances, concert tickets may be available at the door.

COASTAL JAZZ SOCIETY

Marjorie Hoachlander   247-7778

The society's primary mission is jazz education for all ages. The organization also aims to increase awareness and enjoyment of jazz within coastal areas of the state. The Coastal Jazz Society presents well-known musical groups in concert at its annual Jazz Fest By The Sea in June and hosts other popular jazz-interest events including speakers on jazz history and development. The society welcomes the membership of anyone who enjoys listening to, learning about or playing jazz.

DOWN EAST FOLK ARTS SOCIETY

Judy Orbach   726-2399

If you think folk music sounds like the mountains, you need to hear more folk music by the sea. And, you can. Between September and May, each month brings a concert to the Crystal Coast for the Folk Music Series. Organized and sponsored by the Down East Folk Arts Society, concerts occur either at the Dock House on the Beaufort waterfront or in the Duke University Marine Lab auditorium on Pivers Island. Folk music, especially bluegrass, will not let an audience remain still, and occasionally someone instructs New England contra dancing which requires no partner and has no age requirements. Call for series membership information and concert schedules, or watch the newspaper for announcements.

CRYSTAL STRINGS DULCIMER CLUB

Donnell Meadows   726-7699

This group meets each month, except for the summer months, to make music with mountain and hammer dulcimers and other acoustic instruments. Interest is the only prerequisite; beginners and professionals are welcome.

LA MUSIQUE CLUB OF CARTERET COUNTY

Rachel Mundine   223-4538

This music fellowship is open to performers and music lovers. Members meet at 11 AM on the first Monday of each month at Webb Civic Center, 812 Evans Street, Morehead City. The group performs a number of concerts each year, including Civil War music at Fort Macon and benefit concerts.

BEAUFORT BY-THE-SEA MUSIC FESTIVAL

Beaufort Business and Professional Assoc.   728-6894

This beautifully organized annual spring weekend event is jam-packed with a complete range of music, performed in downtown Beaufort. The Beaufort Busi-

Art in nature takes many forms.

Photo: Scott Taylor

Simka Simkhovitch and the Post Office Murals

If you visit the Beaufort Post Office on a daily basis, they become easy to ignore. Most Beaufort residents barely give them a glance. But the three murals on the post office's upper walls are now treasures from the Great Depression's hungry years when the United States Government commissioned these now-famous murals for its newly built, small-town post office buildings under its Federal Arts Program.

The murals are signed "Simka Simkhovitch, 1940," hardly a local name, but it brings us to an interesting story that can be fully explored in files from the National Archives available at the  Carteret County Public Library on Turner Street in Beaufort.

Born in 1893 in Chernigov, Russia, near Kiev, Simka Simkhovitch attended the Art School of Odessa and the Royal Academy of Petrograd. In 1918, a year after the Russian Revolution, he was awarded first prize by the First Soviet Government, and his paintings were purchased for the Museum of the Winter Palace and the Museum of Art in Leningrad. The Cracow Museum in Poland also acquired his work. He taught art and flourished in Russia until 1924 when the government's attitude toward art changed. In an effort to solidify its position through traditional values, the Soviet government established that "radicalism" was out and "social realism" was in. Simka must have decided he was out, because he became a United States citizen in 1924.

At home in Greenwich, Connecticut, Simka was doing well. He had his first one-artist show in New York in 1927 followed by several years full of portrait commissions, critical praise and prizes. His paintings were collected by the Whitney Museum of American Art and the Chicago Art Institute as well as by many private collectors. His art, wrote one critic, shows "the rare merit of sound craftsmanship that so few of the moderns possess." Then came the Great Depression. In 1933, he was awarded recognition by the Worcester Art Museum, after which his files show no more achievements until his 1939 commission to paint the Beaufort Post Office murals.

During the decade between 1934 and 1944, the Treasury Department's Section of Fine Arts chose 600 artists through open competitions to create 1,000 post office murals, with the government's stylistic guidance aimed at reminding the people of small towns that hardships are made to be overcome.

Simka arrived in Beaufort in early March 1939 and must have gone straight to work, because by mid-April he submitted a portfolio to Washington that would bring a smile to any New Dealer's face.

The place of honor over the postmaster's door was given to the mural portraying the wreck of the *Crissie Wright* on January 11, 1886. This wreck is vivid in the local folklore because it happened within sight of town, and many locals tried valiantly to save the crew. All hands were lost, and some of the victims lie in the Old Burying Grounds on Ann Street. "A startling morning light illuminates the scene," Simka's file says of the mural, "reminiscent of the blazing bonfires which had been built on the shore the night before to buoy up the spirits of the shipwrecked men."

Things aren't stormy all the time, Simka and the Treasury Department remind us in the remaining two murals. Fair skies and "Sir Walter Raleigh sand ponies," as Simka called them, symbolize freedom, "a right of legend they have had since the day of Sir Walter Raleigh." And over the postal clerks' stations, the abundance mural showing Canada geese and fishing nets reminds us that, indeed, we are provided for on the Crystal Coast.

Washington was only a bit critical of the "emphasis on the telephone poles" in two of the murals. The Treasury Department was obviously unfamiliar with range markers used in the waterways.

The murals, as it turns out, were painted on canvas in Simka's Greenwich studio and are very well-hung on the post office walls to disguise that fact. Stop in to see them. They're quite a lift.

ness and Professional Association sponsors and schedules the festival.

SATURDAY IN THE
PARK CONCERT SERIES
Morehead City Parks and Recreation Dept.
726-5083

On Saturday evenings between Memorial Day and Labor Day, this popular concert series brings an interesting range of music to the Jaycee Park on the Morehead City waterfront. Gospel, flamenco guitar, acoustic rock, reggae — it's all there for the listening on those beautiful summer evenings. Just bring a chair or blanket. The rest is absolutely free.

Theater

CARTERET COMMUNITY THEATER
Richard Evans   *726-6340*

This group of amateur actors and actresses puts on a series of plays each year that are greatly appreciated by the community, including children's productions in summer and at Christmas, dinner theater and other staged performances. Always receptive to talented newcomers, the community theater welcomes everyone at widely advertised cast calls and meets monthly at Carteret Community College.

Writers' Organization

THE CARTERET WRITERS
Bob Van Wingerden   *354-3067*

This is an active group of professional writers and aspirants who gather on the second Thursday of each month for lunch and a scheduled speaker at Mrs. Willis' Restaurant in Morehead City. Carteret Writers sponsors workshops, seminars and competitions throughout the year as well as an ongoing outreach program in the public schools.

Regular Exhibits

The **N.C. Maritime Museum**, 315 Front Street, Beaufort, 728-7317, always exhibits the finest work by state and local artists complementing the museum's maritime focus. Monthly exhibits are sponsored by the **Arts for the Hospital** committee, and are shown at Carteret General Hospital, 3500 Arendell Street, Morehead City, 726-1616. The **Carteret County Museum of History and Art**, 100 Wallace Drive, Morehead City, 247-7533, features at least one local artist a month. The county's three public libraries sponsor artists in revolving displays that change monthly.

Carteret Community College, 3505 Arendell Street, Morehead City, 247-6000, displays work by students in the school's arts and crafts courses in the college library. The Upstairs Gallery at the college also features student work and work by other local and regional artists. And on Harkers Island, the **Core Sound Waterfowl Museum**, 728-1500, exhibits the best of hand-carved decoys and wildlife art.

Art Lessons

The Continuing Education Department of **Carteret Community College** offers courses in specific visual arts techniques each quarter. For county residents age 65 or older there is no tuition charge, only the cost of materials. Call 247-6000 for further information.

Commercial Galleries

To our great advantage, some coastal artists have also become involved in the business of art galleries that showcase and sell their works. Some galleries represent local and regional artists; others bring art works from much farther afield. Discover many of our treasured local artists at the following galleries.

Handscapes Gallery in Somerset Square, Front Street in Beaufort, 728-6805, represents local and regional artists in jewelry, pottery and varied media. **Down East Gallery**, 519 Front Street in Beaufort, 728-4410, represents the paintings of local artist Alan Cheek and publishes prints of his work. The **Mattie King Davis Gallery**, on the Beaufort Historic Site, 728-5225, exhibits and sells the varied works of more than 100 local and regional artists from Memorial Day through Labor Day.

In Morehead City, **Carteret Contemporary Art** exhibits an extraordinary selection of paintings and sculpture by regional, national and local artists at 1106 Arendell Street, 726-4071. **Windward Gallery**, 508 Evans Street on the Morehead waterfront, 726-6393, represents the paintings of local artist Alexander Kaszas. The **Painted Pelican Art Gallery**, 4645 Arendell Street, 247-5051, sells paintings of local artist/owner Beth Munden as well as prints and poster art.

In Atlantic Beach on Salter Path Road, the **Laughing Gull Gallery**, 726-2362, exhibits a nice collection of local and regional artists, as does Swansboro's **White Oak Gallery**, 137 Front Street, 326-3600.

The Havelock Chili Festival is a spicy competition that puts any lost heat back into late October.

Crystal Coast
Annual Festivals and Events

The full calendar of annually scheduled events on the Crystal Coast reflects the year-round nature of this once seasonal resort, and highly valued salty traditions spice the distinctive flavor of the area's festivals. While the simple pleasures of just being here provide a full plate, plans that include any of the following events will graciously enlarge the feast.

January

The **American Music Festival** chamber music series is a five-concert series with performances scheduled from late fall through spring in the auditorium of the North Carolina Maritime Museum in Beaufort (see our Arts chapter). Call 808-ARTS or the museum, 728-7317, for details. Tickets cost from $10 to $12 at the door if they are available; season tickets are $50.

February

Formerly Family Day at the North Carolina Maritime Museum, **Collector's Day** in early February invites family participation in a Saturday exhibit of personal collections. The focus is family participation, teaching and learning from each other.

Art From the Heart is an extraordinary two-week exhibition of original, innovative and traditional works created by selected area artists in mid-February. Proceeds benefit the local arts council and pro-

vide scholarships to Children's Art Camp. Carteret Arts Council in Morehead City, 726-9156, sponsors the exhibition, which is usually held at the Morehead Plaza in Morehead City.

March

The **Crystal Coast Home and Garden Show**, in early March assembles the services, wares and expertise of local businesses that focus on aspects of building, gardening and decorating. Gather ideas, good advice and the right products for do-it-yourself projects, or shop for professional services during the weekend show at the Crystal Coast Civic Center. For exact dates, call 247-3883.

The **St. Patrick's Day Festival** is a mid-March weekend of fun and games, corned beef and cabbage, music and wearing of the green in Emerald Isle. Most events take place at Emerald Plantation Shopping Center. Benefits from the festival help support local craftspeople and civic organizations. For more information call 354-3650.

In mid-March the **North Carolina Commercial Fishing Show** features boats and fishing equipment displays and offers information about the commercial fishing industry in North Carolina. For exact dates call the Crystal Coast Civic Center in Morehead City, 247-3883.

The **Swansboro Oyster Roast** offers all-you-can-eat oysters for one price at its annual scholarship benefit. The Swansboro Rotary Club, 354-6444, sponsors the mid-March event, which is held at the Cape Carteret Fire and Rescue Building. The meal — oysters, clams, and pig-pickin' with all the trimmings — costs $20 or $25, depending on your food selections.

April

The **Newport Pig Cooking Contest** is a huge barbecue competition that draws folks from all over eastern North Carolina for the best barbecue on earth, accompanied by homemade baked goods, live entertainment and children's activities. Delicious "Down East" barbecue goes on sale after the contest is judged. The event benefits numerous civic organizations and occurs in Newport Park on Howard Boulevard in early April. For more information call 223-7447.

Publick Days on Beaufort Historic Site in mid-April features the outdoor sale of flea-market merchandise and crafts, entertainment, mock trials and exhibits. Proceeds benefit preservation of historic structures through the Beaufort Historical Association, 728-5225.

On Easter weekend, the Beaufort Historic Site is the perfect setting for a traditional **Easter egg hunt** for kids. It's a bring-your-own-basket event heaped with small-town warmth and hosted by the Beaufort Historical Association, 728-5225. **Easter sunrise services** are celebrated at several locations across the county, many on the waterfront or beach. The *Carteret County News-Times* lists services the week before Easter.

Beaufort By-the-Sea Music Festival is a full weekend celebration offering fun for all ages and appealing to all musical tastes in late April. Free concerts, including classical, country, traditional, jazz, rock and reggae, are presented on various stages within a three-block area of downtown Beaufort. The Beaufort Business and Professional Association sponsors and schedules the weekend events. Bring a chair or blanket and a picnic to enjoy on the lawn or have lunch or dinner at any of the downtown restaurants. Parking is available at any of the downtown parking areas. Call 728-6894 for details.

The **Lookout Spring Road Race** in Morehead City adds 5K and 1-mile race competitions to the Beaufort Music Festival weekend. The event benefits local charities and civic organizations. For more information contact Lookout Rotary Club, 726-5831. There is an entry fee, call the Sports Center at 726-7070 for information.

May

In late April or early May, the **Spring Homes and Gardens Tour** of Morehead City is hosted by the Morehead City Woman's Club and Carteret County Historical Society. The tour includes at least 10 private homes, both new and historical, followed by tea at the Carteret County Museum of History and Art. Tickets are $10. For details and schedule call 247-7533.

Nelson Bay Challenge Sprint Triathlon in Sea Level includes a 750-meter swim, a 20K bike ride and a 5K run the first Saturday of May. Proceeds from the race, raised by entry fees, benefit the Sea Level Rescue Squad and various county youth programs. For more information call 247-6902.

The North Carolina Maritime Museum's **Traditional Wooden Boat Show** was the first and is the largest gathering of wooden watercraft in the Southeast. Not a commercial show, it's an early-May weekend of scheduled demonstrations, talks and races, assembling people

who share a well-honed interest in the art, craftsmanship and history particular to wooden boats. Call the Beaufort museum for details at 728-7317.

The **Salter Path Clam and Scallop Festival** is a lot of fun with good local seafood and music in the heart of Salter Path, which is a hard place to miss. Organized by and benefiting the Salter Path Fire and Rescue Department and the Crystal Coast Pentecostal Holiness Church, the festival is always held the first weekend in May. It begins with a clam chowder cookoff at the fire department on Friday night. Saturday's food and music, all local, is at the ballpark on the sound side. For details, call 247-7994.

Mile of Hope Weekend in early May is a beach getaway for pediatric cancer patients and their families. Local donors and sponsors provide lodging, food, entertainment and gifts to make it a very special weekend. The mile of beach between the Sheraton and Royal Pavilion Resorts is the site of a Saturday sandcastle building contest. Wonderfully imaginative structures evolve throughout the day. Music, food and entertainment add to the relaxed fun. Call for information 354-5400.

Emerald Isle Beach Music Festival features top beach music groups, a beauty pageant and other entertainment in mid-May at the Holiday Trav-L-Park in Emerald Isle. Benefits go to Children's Hospital of Eastern North Carolina and civic organizations. Tickets are $28 at the gate for a full day of music, sun, food and entertainment. For additional information contact Holiday Trav-L-Park in Emerald Isle at 354-2250.

The **Storytelling Festival** is a delightful, entertaining two-day event in mid-May. The Swansboro waterfront is the setting, stages and workshops are scheduled and organized by the Onslow Public Library, (910) 455-7354.

Annual Turtle Release returns rehabilitated sea turtles to their natural environment in late May. Loggerhead and other types of turtles are taken offshore and released into the sea by the N.C. Aquarium at Pine Knoll Shores. Anyone who has preregistered may go along, and a small fee is charged. Contact the aquarium, 247-4004, to register.

The **Memorial Day King Mackerel & Blue Water Tournament** is an annual holiday weekend fishing competition with a variety of categories. Hosted by Casper's Marina in Swansboro and sponsored by the Swansboro Rotary Club, proceeds from the tournament benefit local charities and civic organizations. Call 354-2787 for information.

Carteret County Arts and Crafts Coalition Spring Show is an outdoor exhibition and sale of arts and crafts by coalition members on Memorial Day weekend. Demonstrations, food and music enhance the festive atmosphere at the Beaufort Historic Site in the 100 block of Turner Street in Beaufort. For more information call 728-7297.

June

Kidfest occurs on the first Saturday of June, usually at the Morehead City waterfront, but the location is subject to change. With sponsorship from area businesses, the day is full of events "for kids, by kids" but is great fun for adults, too. See our Kidstuff chapter for details or call 726-5083.

Big Rock Blue Marlin Tournament, one of the oldest and largest sportfishing tournaments in the country, involves fish-fry festivities, parties and daily public weigh-ins on the Morehead City waterfront. The early-June event benefits charities and nonprofit organizations. For more information, call 247-3575.

Arts By the Sea, an arts and crafts festival, brings lots of music, food and people to the Swansboro waterfront in early June. Proceeds from the festival go to local civic organizations. Call (910) 326-7222 for specific information.

The **Carteret Arts Festival**, sponsored by Carteret Arts Council and the Downtown Morehead City Business Association in mid-June, brings artists and craftspeople and lots of art-related activities for youngsters to the city park in downtown Morehead City for a festive weekend. Mu-

sic, refreshments, dancers and art creation are part of the fun. Most activities are free. Funds raised support area art programs. For more information call 726-9156.

Worthy Is The Lamb, an outdoor passion play, begins its summer season in mid-June. Plays are presented each Thursday, Friday and Saturday through Labor Day, weekends through September, at Crystal Coast Amphitheater off Highway 58 in Peletier. Contact the theater, 393-8373 or (800) 662-5960. See our Attractions chapter for more information.

Beaufort Old Homes Tour, always the last weekend in June, opens some of this country's oldest private homes and buildings for narrated tours. New restorations and those in progress keep the tour fresh and interesting each year. Crafts, music, demonstrations and re-enactments occur throughout the weekend at the Beaufort Historic Site, where the tour begins. For information, call the Beaufort Historical Association, 728-5225.

An **Antiques Show and Sale** is held in conjunction with the Beaufort Old Homes Tour at the Crystal Coast Civic Center in Morehead City in late June. The large show features around 40 dealers and repair and restoration specialists. For more information call 728-5225.

July

Fourth of July Fireworks and festivities, including a street dance, are held on the Morehead City waterfront to celebrate Independence Day. For information, consult the *Carteret County News-Times* before the weekend or call the town office at 726-6848. Fireworks also light up the **Swansboro** waterfront every Fourth of July.

Down East Fish Fry features fish, shrimp and other seafood, plus live entertainment on the Fourth of July in Sea

Chrome Domes
Gather in Morehead

MOREhead, less hair — get it? Well, the Bald Headed Men of America got it and have been gathering for their annual September convention on the shores of the Crystal Coast for the last 21 years. This wacky, good-natured group of "chrome domes" has drawn national and international attention to the small coastal town of Morehead City.

Founder and local resident John Capps, whose head is as slick as a peeled onion, has more one-liners than you can shake a stick at: "If you haven't got it, flaunt it"; "No drugs, plugs or rugs"; "God gave some men hair and others brains"; or "The convention is a hair-raising experience." And that's just for starters.

John and his wife Jane own and operate Capps Printing, located — where else — on Bald Drive in Morehead City. John formed the Bald Headed Men of America organization more than 20 years ago after being rejected for a job. He was in his mid-20s, and the employer who turned him down told him his baldness made him look too old for the position and that he didn't project the image the company wanted. Since then, John has changed the minds of thousands of people and has led a campaign focusing on baldness as both a humorous and painful issue.

Since the formation of the group, which now has a membership of more than 20,000 around the globe, John and many of the members have appeared on virtually every entertainment news magazine show on TV. They have been featured in hundreds of magazines and newspapers, both in the United States and in foreign countries. In 1993, a segment on the news show "20/20"

Photo: Jimmy Sparkman

The second weekend in September brings bare heads from around the country and around the world to Morehead City for the Bald Headed Men of America's annual convention.

featured bald John and his Bald Headed Men of America, and the BBC came to Morehead City that year to film a re-created Bald Headed Men of America annual convention for a documentary.

Attendance at the group's annual September convention varies but is never less than several hundred. Polished pate pals travel across the country to join the fun, and members from such far-flung locations as Australia, London and Ireland often travel to the States to attend the convention. The annual gathering includes family members too, and many couples load up the kids and make the jaunt a fall vacation.

The three-day affair includes activities such as cookouts, golf, boat cruises, picnics, a social and the official bald banquet, where contest winners of such challenging competitions as "the sexiest bald head," "the smallest bald spot," "most kissable" and "smoothest" carry away prizes.

The annual get-together does have a serious side, though, and offers self-help sessions for wives of bald men, workshops for those having trouble coming to terms with their baldness and a variety of open forums. The organization contributes annually to the Aleopecia Areata Research Foundation, which conducts research in baldness, especially in children.

Collectively, the group is jovial about the bare facts of being bald. Their sense of humor is both infectious and inspirational. At the 1990 convention, Great Britain's Tim Hibbert showed up to write a feature story for the *Daily Mail*, a newspaper with a circulation of 4 million. Hibbert commented, "In England, people are too insular, too private, to ever get into a group like the Bald Headed Men of America. All these domes together, having a good time, would be unthinkable. At home, the thought of growing bald is traumatic, and the man suffers in private. But it's a silly thing to worry about. Here, believe it or not, they celebrate being bald. It's incredible. It would help if the English could be more like this."

Bald John eschews all the remedies on the market that are supposed to cure baldness. He labels them gimmicks and believes they instill false hopes among users and compound the stigma that bald is bad. Bald is just bald. Why is bald bad? Why isn't bald beautiful? To the Bald Headed Men of America, it is.

John's wife is as active in the group as her husband. In the office one day she fielded a call from an anxious and despondent Jim in Poughkeepsie, N.Y. After listening and chatting for a few minutes she said with a wide smile, "Jim darlin', you need some humor in your life. Come on down to the convention and you'll see a whole new side of things." Jim came . . . and he left smiling.

Level. Proceeds help to operate the Sea Level Rescue Squad, 225-7721.

The **Coastal Invitational Showcase** spotlights artists and craftspeople from all over the southeastern United States who demonstrate and sell work during the weekend show at the Crystal Coast Civic Center in Morehead City in mid-July.

The show is also conducted in December. Call 729-7001 for more information.

The annual **Historic Beaufort Road Race** includes a certified 10K, 5K and 1-mile walk and run starting in downtown Beaufort in mid-July. The popular race organized by Beaufort Old Towne Rotary and St. Egbert's Track Club brings out lots of participants. For information call 726-7070.

The **Bogue Sound Watermelon Festival** in late July celebrates one of our most valuable summer resources: watermelon. The festival, like Bogue Sound melons, is growing in Cedar Point. The day of fun and entertainment benefits the Carteret County Domestic Violence Program. Call 393-2281 for information.

The annual **Ladies King Mackerel Tournament** is a very popular event in Atlantic Beach in late July that involves only women anglers, although there are always lots of men involved in some capacity. The tournament is hosted by Crow's Nest Marina on the Atlantic Beach Causeway. Call 726-8452 for information.

August

North Carolina Ducks Unlimited's Band the Billfish Tournament tags and releases billfish. The early August tournament benefits state wetlands. For information call 247-2106.

Atlantic Coast Soccer-on-the-Sand Jam gathers statewide soccer and volleyball team competitors to Atlantic Beach for an early August weekend of sporting competition. The well-organized weekend is a great spectator sport too. Call 859-2997 or (800) 375-4625 for information.

Atlantis Lodge Sand Sculpture Contest began as one energetic family's pastime at a reunion and now draws some serious competition in early August for adults and children. Seeing is believing

every year, and it's well worth the trip. The competition entry fees benefit the Outer Banks Wildlife Shelter. Contact the Atlantis Lodge in Pine Knoll Shores, 726-5168.

September

Carteret County Arts and Crafts Coalition Fall Show is an outdoor show and sale of excellent quality and original arts and crafts on Labor Day weekend. Food and music add to the festive atmosphere at Beaufort Historic Site, 100 block of Turner Street, Beaufort. Call 729-7297 for information.

Hardee's Annual Atlantic Beach King Mackerel Tournament is the nation's largest all-cash king mackerel tournament. The mid-September tournament benefits local nonprofit organizations and includes a memorable fish fry. Contact the Sea Water Marina in Atlantic Beach, 247-2334 or (800) 545-3940, for more information.

Big Sweep is an annual statewide cleanup of waterways, beaches and roadsides by volunteers in mid-September. Locally, volunteers are organized by several interests including the Rachel Carson Reserve, 728-2170, and Carteret County's office of the North Carolina Cooperative Extension Service, 728-8421.

Bald Headed Men of America's Annual Convention includes self-help workshops, testimonials, golf games, picnics, contests for the most kissable head and other activities in mid-September. Proceeds benefit the Aleopecia Areata Research Foundation, which conducts re-

Santa arrives by sea to the towns of Beaufort and Swansboro during their annual Christmas boat flotillas.

Insiders' Tips

search in baldness, especially in children. The organization was founded by Morehead City's John Capps. Call 726-1004 for more information.

October

The **North Carolina Seafood Festival** brings close to 100,000 people to the Morehead City waterfront during the first weekend in October. The two-day outdoor festival highlights an endless variety of seafood prepared in a multitude of ways. Crafts, exhibits, music, street dances, educational exhibits and programs, games and contests are also part of the activities. For information call 726-6273.

Harvest Time at the Beaufort Historic Site in early October provides living history re-enactments of daily family life in a coastal village in the 1700s. School groups and visitors are treated to an interesting weekend of winter preparation activities and demonstrations. Call 728-5225 for additional information.

The **Mullet Festival** in Swansboro has been celebrated for more than 40 years with a parade, a street carnival of bountiful mullet and seafood, arts and crafts on the Swansboro waterfront. The festive early-October Saturday event benefits local civic organizations. For information call (910) 326-1174 or 326-4661.

The **Carolina Kite Fest** fills the skies in Atlantic Beach with kite demonstrations, competitions and night kite flying on the beach in late October. Kites Unlimited, 247-7011, in Atlantic Station sponsors the event.

The **Havelock Chili Festival** is a spicy competition that puts any lost heat back into late October. The sparks fly in Havelock City Park. Any smoldering issues concerning chili festival details can be resolved by calling 447-1101.

November

Mill Creek Oyster Festival is a family event in early November starring oysters, all you can eat for $12. The Saturday festival co-stars other seafoods for the less adventurous and also includes music and crafts. The event benefits and is held at the Mill Creek Volunteer Fire Department, 726-0542.

The **Saltwater Light Tackle Fishing Tournament** in early November offers anglers their choice of surf, pier or boat fishing for king mackerel, puppy drum or flounder. The largest fish takes the cash and the competition challenges more than 200 anglers each year hosted by Crow's Nest Marina, Atlantic Beach. Call 240-2744 for information.

The **Ducks Unlimited Banquet**, an annual fund-raising benefit for the preservation of waterfowl habitat, is an eagerly anticipated event on the first Thursday of November. Ticket price includes membership, a wonderful dinner and an evening at the Crystal Coast Civic Center with around 400 people committed to waterfowl habitat preservation. Call Mark Shouse, 240-1794, for information.

Swansboro By Candlelight is celebrated in mid-November. Downtown merchants host the evening event with open shops decorated for the Christmas season.

A **Community Thanksgiving Feast** is served on the Sunday before Thanksgiving at the Beaufort Historic Site. Beaufort restaurants contribute a traditional Thanksgiving feast. Proceeds from this ticketed event benefit preservation efforts of the Beaufort Historical Association, 728-5225.

Christmas Gallery Show is a two-week late-November show and sale of original juried artwork by members of the Carteret County Arts and Crafts Coalition. More than 40 local artists combine their work to create a gallery show that

Photo: Core Sound Decoy Festival

The Core Sound Decoy Festival, held each December at Harkers Island Elementary School, is fun for the whole family.

opens in the Morehead Plaza Shopping Center in Morehead City during the Thanksgiving holidays. Call 728-7297 for more information.

Coastal Invitational Showcase brings numerous crafters and their wares to the Crystal Coast Civic Center, Morehead City, 729-7001, in late November.

Christmas Flotilla is an evening parade of decorated and lighted boats bringing Santa to the Swansboro waterfront during the weekend after Thanksgiving. For more information call (910) 393-6997.

December

Core Sound Decoy Festival is held the first weekend in December at Harkers Island Elementary School on Harkers Island. The festival includes competitions in carving and painting decoys, exhibits and sales of old and new decoys, a loon-calling contest, special competitions and activities for children, educational exhibits and an auction. The event benefits the Core Sound Waterfowl Museum and is the area's larg-

est off-season event. Call 728-1500 for additional information.

Festival of Trees is sponsored in early December by Hospice of Carteret County and features more than 60 decorated trees displayed at the Crystal Coast Civic Center, a breakfast with Santa, a fashion show, a luncheon and a festive preview party. Call 247-2808 with questions.

Christmas Open House takes place at the North Carolina Aquarium of Pine Knoll Shores and at the North Carolina Maritime Museum in Beaufort in mid-December. It's a good time to meet those involved in activities and programs, to hear of forthcoming plans and to volunteer to help. Call the aquarium, 247-4004, or the museum, 728-7317.

Coastal Carolina Christmas Celebration opens historic homes and buildings decorated for Christmas in traditional styles in mid-December. The celebration at Beaufort Historic Site benefits preservation of historic structures through the Beaufort Historical Association. Call 728-5225 for information.

Carolina's Finest 30 MPH 100 Footer

CONTINENTAL SHELF

On the Waterfront in Morehead City
Year round Gulf Stream fishing

Deep Sea Fishing for
Snappers, grouper, bass & more

Departs Daily
at 6:00 a.m.
Half-day or Full-day
18 and 22 hour trips available

We also offer
moonlight cruises and charters.

800-775-7450
919-726-7454
P.O. Box 3397 Morehead City, N.C. 28557

Crystal Coast
Fishing, Watersports and Beach Access

The Crystal Coast is well-known as a perfect place for a variety of water-related activities. Surfers looking for ocean waves, windsurfers and water-skiers looking for calm sound waters and anglers looking for something in between will find what they want here, and the area's generally mild climate allows folks to participate in their favorite watersport year round.

In this chapter, we offer a look at the area piers, boat ramps, charter boats, fishing schools, marinas, boat and watersport equipment rentals and beach access areas. For businesses on Bogue Banks, we have given the milepost (MP) number to assist you in locating them.

Fishing

The Crystal Coast hosts numerous fishing tournaments, including one of the nation's largest king mackerel tournaments, the Hardee's Annual Atlantic Beach King Mackerel Tournament in September, and one of the largest and oldest blue marlin tournaments, the Big Rock Blue Marlin Tournament in June. Details and dates of the fishing tournaments are listed in the Crystal Coast Annual Events chapter.

Federal government studies have shown that a person's chances of catching fish in North Carolina waters are unsurpassed along the entire East Coast. Of the 21 recorded catches of Atlantic blue marlin

in excess of 1,000 pounds, five have been caught off the North Carolina coast. In fact, a 1,002-pounder is on display behind the Crystal Coast Visitors Center in Morehead City.

The Crystal Coast has many opportunities for anglers. Whether you fish from the beaches, piers, and barrier islands or aboard a private, charter or head boat, you're sure to catch your limit.

Fishing Reports

What's biting when and where is as important to some people as the world news is to others. Information about catches is available at most bait and tackle shops, marinas, piers or charter boat rental offices. Television station WCTI TV 12 offers a fish and game report during the sports segment of its news shows.

Tackle Shops

Tackle shops offer gear, supplies, bait and a bit of advice about what the fish are biting and where. We certainly can't list all the tackle shops in the area, but we will tell you about a few.

EJW Outdoors, 2204 Arendell Street, Morehead City, 247-4725, has been in business for more than 50 years and continues to offer gear for a variety of sports including hunting, biking and archery. But, the main focus is on fishing. EJW sells rods and reels and all kinds of bait and clothing, and also service rods and reels. The shop is owned by David Willis.

Freeman's Bait & Tackle, Atlantic Beach Causeway, 726-2607, is a complete saltwater tackle shop selling rods and reels, along with a repair and cleaning service. Freeman's also has bait, clothing and other supplies.

Pete's Tackle Shop, 1704 Arendell Street, Morehead City, 726-8644, is a N.C. Official Weigh Station for the citation program. Pete Allred sells rods and reels and is well-known for the repair and cleaning service his store provides. Pete offers everything an angler needs for offshore and inshore fishing, including specialized clothing and bait. He has been in business since 1977.

Photo: NC Travel & Tourism

A speckled trout is a fine catch from local piers.

Fishing Piers

Most of the fishing piers along the Crystal Coast are on Bogue Banks, offering access to the Atlantic Ocean. These piers are popular spots for fishing (or simply walking out to see others' catches) during the spring, summer and fall. Most piers close during the winter and those that don't only open during the day. The majority are privately owned and a fee, usually between $3 and $5, is charged for a day/night of fishing. We've listed the piers on Bogue Banks first.

Triple S Fishing Pier, MP½, 726-4170, is at the east end of Bogue Banks. Patrons are offered a lighted pier, tackle/snack shop and plenty of parking.

Sportsman's Pier, MP 1¼, 726-3176, carries the slogan, "You should have been here yesterday." The pier has a tackle shop and a cafe that serves sandwiches, seafood and steaks, and has all ABC permits.

Oceanana Fishing Pier, MP 1½, 726-0863, is beside the Oceanana Resort Motel. The pier is lighted, with a tackle/snack shop and plenty of parking.

Iron Steamer Resort and Pier, MP 7½, 247-4213, is beside the Iron Steamer Motor Inn. This 800-foot pier offers a tackle shop and fishing equipment rentals.

Indian Beach Fishing Pier, MP 12, 247-3411, is about 825 feet long and offers a grill and tackle shop, efficiency apartments, a camping area and plenty of parking.

Emerald Isle Fishing Pier, MP 15, 354-3274, has a snack/tackle shop. The pier extends 742 feet and is lighted.

Bogue Inlet Fishing Pier, MP 19½, 354-2919, is a lighted 950-foot pier that has a snack bar and tackle shop.

Causeway Pier, Morehead City-Beaufort Causeway, 726-7851, is at the east

foot of the high-rise bridge. This lighted pier offers a snack and tackle shop.

Straits Fishing Pier, no phone, is on Harkers Island Road and is maintained by the Carteret County Parks and Recreation Department, 728-8401. The pier extends over Back Sound, and there is no fee.

Boat Ramps

The Crystal Coast area has a great deal of boat ramps, large and small, public and private. Below is a short list of just a few of the state-maintained public ramps. Because most ramps don't have names, we've listed them alphabetically according to location. There are private ramps in every part of the Crystal Coast area, and most marinas and campgrounds have boat ramps. Remember, this is only a list of the free state-maintained ramps, so call the marina clos-

est to you and, chances are, you won't have to drive far to put your boat in the water.

BEAUFORT

Curtis A. Perry Park is a public ramp with four launching areas. The park is at the east end of Front Street near the tennis courts.

Two ramps and a dock are offered off **West Beaufort Road** beside Town Creek Marina. These are maintained by Carteret County Parks and Recreation Department.

CEDAR ISLAND

A ramp is beyond the Cedar Island National Wildlife Refuge office on **Lola Road** at the south end of the island.

The refuge also maintains a ramp on the west side of (and almost below) the new high-rise bridge, **N.C. Highway 12**, just west of the island.

CEDAR POINT

A ramp maintained by the N.C. Wildlife Commission is on the south side of **N.C. Highway 24** between Cape Carteret and Swansboro.

MOREHEAD CITY

Municipal Park behind the Crystal Coast Visitors Center on Arendell Street, U.S. Highway 70, has several launching areas and a large parking area. The park is just east of Carteret Community College.

SEA LEVEL

A ramp is maintained on the east side of the high-rise bridge on **Highway 70** just before you get to the Down East community of Sea Level.

Head Boats
and Charter Boats

The Crystal Coast offers many excellent opportunities to those interested in fishing. In addition to fishing from your own boat, there are several ways to get out on the big ones. Head boats are large vessels that take as many as 50 people out into the Gulf Stream for a day of fishing. The name came about because you pay by the head, or per person, for the trip. You don't hire the entire boat, just a spot on the deck. The crew provides the rods, reels and bait; you just take your personal belongings (maybe a cooler of drinks and snacks, some extra clothing, weather gear and sun protection).

Charter boats are smaller vessels that are generally hired by a private party of four to six individuals for a half day or a full day of fishing in the Gulf Stream. If you don't have a full party, a charter captain may be able to hook you up with another half-

party willing to share the expenses of chartering the boat.

Regardless of how you get there, once in the Gulf Stream, you will have a chance at red and silver snapper, king or Spanish mackerel, cobia, tuna, wahoo, blue fish, sailfish, dolphin, bass, grouper or other fish abundant in this area.

Space does not allow us to list all the fishing vessels available for hire, so we have tried to describe a few of the head boats — listing them in alphabetical order. We have also included a vessel that offers a chance to trawl for shrimp. The Crystal Coast is home to more than 50 charter boats with experienced captains ready to take you on a fishing adventure.

Most head and charter boats operate year round, with less frequent trips in the dead of winter. For more information about head and charter boats, we recommend you walk along the Morehead City waterfront and Atlantic Beach Causeway marinas, talk with other anglers and contact the Crystal Coast Charter Boat Association, Morehead City, 729-1661.

CAPT. STACY FISHING CENTER
Atlantic Beach Causeway   247-7501
Atlantic Beach   (800) 533-9417

There are more than 14 vessels in the Capt. Stacy fleet, including everything from sportfishing boats to an 83-foot head boat and a 65-foot head boat. The head boats offer half- ($30) and full-day ($40 to $50) trips along with a 22-hour trip ($100) and a 36-hour trip ($130, winter). The fleet's charter boats can be hired for half- and full-day trips, and prices vary. The Capt. Stacy Center also offers moonlight cruises and harbor tours and can handle private parties.

CAROLINA PRINCESS
Eight St., Morehead City   726-5479
Waterfront   (800) 682-3456

Owner Captain WooWoo Harker is

Keep Your Eyes on the Sea for Dolphins

If you're walking along the beach and see fins gliding in and out of the water just offshore, don't be alarmed. Chances are you're being treated to a passing display of bottle-nosed dolphins. If you're really lucky, you'll see one catapult itself from the watery depths to leap above the horizon simply for the sheer fun of it.

These friendly, sleek, streamlined marine mammals are permanent residents in waters along the Crystal Coast. People often call them porpoises, but on the Eastern Seaboard, porpoise range only as far as New Jersey. What we have here are bottle-nosed dolphins.

Worldwide, there are about 80 species of whales and dolphins. Several species live and pass through offshore waters along our coast, including spotted, striped and common dolphins. Technically, dolphins are small-toothed whales, and because they give live birth and nurse their young, they are marine mammals. During summer, when calves are born, dolphins tend to concentrate in tidal rivers and estuaries along our coast. These areas provide plenty of food and shelter from large sharks. Still, many dolphins swim in and out of the inlets and can be seen traveling in groups just beyond the breakers along shore.

Dolphins don't eat anything that can't be swallowed whole. In local waters, their main diet consists of crabs, mullet, menhaden, flounder and other small fish. Studies have shown that some dolphins are local residents, while others are seasonal, or migratory. Along the Crystal Coast, dolphins are commonly seen during the summer months in Back Sound, Core Sound, Bogue Sound, North River, Newport River, Nelson Bay, Straits and other estuary areas. Here they feed, mate and raise their young. Feeding activity can frequently be seen late on summer afternoons around the rock jetties off Radio Island and Fort Macon. In late fall, they leave the estuaries and head for open water, where they live and feed through April.

Dolphins are air breathers. They have lungs, not gills, and must come to the surface to breathe. Rather than breathing through a nose like humans, dolphins breathe through a blowhole in the top of their heads. Boaters anchored in creeks, coves and bays often hear dolphins blow nearby. Exhibiting an unusual friendliness and perpetual smile, dolphins often follow alongside boats, sometimes swimming ahead or body surfing on the boat's wake.

The intelligence of dolphins is hard to determine, although there seems little question that their brains are highly developed. Marine parks have trained them to perform amazing stunts, and the military has been able to teach them to carry out rather complicated maneuvers. In the wild, however, they don't always display dolphin-perfect judgment. They sometimes wind up in places they're not supposed to be — like stuck in water that's too shallow. Similar to a sailboat that's run aground, they have to wait until the tide rises before they can float to freedom. Such a predicament poses a threat to these animals because they can become overheated in the sun and die. If you see a stranded dolphin, call the local Marine Mammal Strandings Network at 728-8762.

Another perplexing behavior involves their eating habits. Stomach contents of dead dolphins have turned up cigarette lighters, fishing lures, rocks, camera lens caps and other foreign materials. Whether the dolphin ate them, or whether the dolphin ate a fish that ate them, is not known.

People often confuse the dolphin mammal with the dolphin fish. Believe us, when you see dolphin on a restaurant menu, you are not eating Flipper. The dolphin fish is now commonly listed on restaurant menus as mahi-mahi, dorado, or by other names to avoid confusion.

So, remember, when you are out on the beach, scan the area just past the breakers frequently and you might see these graceful marine mammals surfacing and descending in a smooth flowing line as they feed, play and enjoy their water world. Somehow just seeing them gives you the feeling that everything's OK.

Photo: Tabbie Nance

Dolphins are frequently seen in the waters along the Crystal Coast.

one of the area's best-known captains. The 95-foot *Carolina Princess* offers a variety of ways to enjoy the area and the Gulf Stream. Full-day ($50 to $55), 18-hour ($80) and 22-hour ($100) fishing trips are available year round, and half-day trips ($20 to $30) are offered each Wednesday. The *Carolina Princess* can accommodate 100 people. Group fishing trips, parties, receptions and weddings can also be arranged. The *Carolina Princess* also offers dinner cruises.

CONTINENTAL SHELF
400 Evans St.   726-7454
Morehead City   (800)775-7450

The *Continental Shelf* is a 100-foot head boat that goes out on full-day ($45 to $55), 18-hour ($80) and 22-hour ($100) trips. Half-day trips ($30 adult, $20 child) are offered on Tuesdays. The boat docks on the Morehead City waterfront beside the Charter Restaurant. Summer evening cruises aboard the boat offer guests a chance to see the surrounding area, islands and wildlife and enjoy a quiet, relaxing night. The *Continental Shelf* is available for private charter groups, fishing, evening cruising or daytime sightseeing.

MARY CATHERINE
Beaufort　　　　　726-8464, 726-6519

Here is a chance to have a new experience and fill your freezer with shrimp. The *Mary Catherine* is a 55-foot commercial trawler equipped with the latest fishing gear. Shrimp trawling charters are available from May through mid-October. After a trip, you take home the catch. The boat is licensed for up to six passengers and operates every day during the season.

Fishing Schools

Most anglers come to the Crystal Coast equipped with fishing skills and knowledge, but a growing number of people want to know more about fishing in area waters or want to improve their chances of hooking the big one. Lucky for them, there are a few fishing schools around and there is hope that the number of schools and workshops will grow in coming years.

Each fall the **N.C. Aquarium at Pine Knoll Shores**, 247-4004, presents a two-day program about surf fishing that usually includes a trip to Core Banks and Cape Lookout. The date and cost of the 1996 workshop had not been set at press time. Those interested should call the N.C. Aquarium and might also want to ask if other workshops have been scheduled.

Morehead Marine Inc., 4971 Arendell Street, 247-6667, offers a free one-day, lecture-type workshop each year, usually in

March. Speakers address a variety of subjects such as flounder and trout fishing, inshore bottom fishing, offshore trawling and live baiting. They also teach the all-important subject of how to throw a cast net.

Watersports And Rentals

Boating

The Sailing Place, Atlantic Beach Causeway, 726-5664, offers a variety of boats for rent and provides navigational information and charts with each boat. The Sailing Place also offers instruction for each type boat. Others places to rent boats include **Water Sports Rental**, MP 12, 247-7303, and **Causeway Marina**, Atlantic Beach, 726-6977.

Barrier Island Adventures, Beaufort, 728-4129, offers rental and charter boats for trips to Carrot Island, Shackleford Banks or Cape Lookout, and offers guided tours and fishing guide service. **Rose's Marina**, Harkers Island, 728-2868, rents motor boats from 16 to 30 feet in length.

Check the Ferries chapter of this book for information about local ferry services.

Jet Skis/Waverunners

AB Jet Ski Rentals, Atlantic Beach Causeway beside Marsh's Surfshop, 726-0047, rents Jet Skis and other personal watercraft. **Water Sports Rental**, MP 12 in Indian Beach, 247-7303, rents Jet Skis and other watersport equipment and offers lessons as well as half-day scenic guided Jet Ski tours. **Island Harbor Marina**, Old Ferry Road, in Emerald Isle, 354-3106, has Jet Skis and motor boats for rent.

If your Waverunner breaks down, **Morehead Marine Inc.**, 4971 Arendell

Street, 247-6667, will get you back into the waves. Morehead Marine sells and services Yamaha Waverunners.

Rowing

The **Beaufort Oars** is a rowing club headquartered at the N.C. Maritime Museum's Harvey Smith Watercraft Center on the Beaufort Waterfront. The group meets for fun and exercise, and new members are encouraged to join. For more information, call the museum, 728-7317.

Kayaking

As kayaking becomes more popular, the number of businesses offering rentals and tours is growing. **Island Rigs**, MP 12, 247-7787, rents and conducts tours and lessons. Kayaks, canoes and skiffs are available for rent at **Waterway Marina and Store**, 1023 Cedar Point Boulevard, Swansboro, (910) 393-8008.

Sailing

The **Sailing Place**, Atlantic Beach Causeway, 726-5664, rents sailboards,

Sunfish, daysailers, catamarans, power boats and canoes. The company also offers bareboat or captained charters of yachts from 19 to 45 feet, sailing lessons and sales of new and used sailboats. **Water Sports Rental**, MP 12, 247-7303, offers a variety of sailboats as well as sailing lessons. **Island Rigs**, MP 12, 247-7787, offers Sunfish rentals and lessons.

If you want to go sailing and get a lesson in coastal ecology, call Captain Ron White, 247-3860, owner of the 42-foot sailboat *Good Fortune*. This custom-built craft is available for half-day, full-day and 2-hour sojourns, educational trips, group and corporate charters and evening sails. Sunset excursions are completed with complimentary wine.

Scuba Diving and Snorkeling

The Crystal Coast is fast becoming a popular diving and snorkeling spot, and local businesses meet the demands of the sport. Diving in this area is a year-round activity thanks to the nearby warm waters of the Gulf Stream that lies about 35 miles off our shoreline. In summer, water temperatures range in the 80s, with visibility of 75 to as much as 150 feet. Ideally, the best dive months are June through September when most tropical fish are present.

A national scuba diving magazine recently selected a local site — that of a German submarine sunk off Cape Lookout in 1942 — as the fifth-favorite wreck dive. It was the only dive site on the list that is an actual wreck, not a man-made reef. Readers of *Rodale's Scuba Diving* magazine also voted **Olympus Dive Center**, 726-9432, of Morehead City third in the United States in both the "favorite resort/operator" and the "day boat operator" categories. Olympus Dive Center, operated by the Purifoy family, is on the Morehead City waterfront. With five custom diver boats, Olympus is a full-service shop offering full- and half-day dive charters, equipment rental and instruction. The shop is also a Nitrox facility.

Discovery Diving Company, Beaufort, 728-2265, can teach you to scuba dive or snorkel. On the water at 414 Orange Street, the company offers Professional Association of Diving Instructors (PADI) Open Water Diver training, rentals, repairs, service and dive trips.

Wreckreational Divers, Atlantic Beach, 240-2244, provides instruction (PADI approved), all types of training and rentals. These folks can also arrange for large or small group dive trips.

Skiing

We are talking water-skiing here! Is there any other kind? Most surf stores carry water skis and related information. Both **Water Sports Rental**, MP 12, 247-7303, and **The Sailing Place**, Atlantic Beach Causeway, 726-5664, can give you water-skiing lessons and then set you up in a boat for an hour or a day of practicing.

Favorite skiing spots include the Bogue Sound west of the Atlantic Beach high-rise bridge, the sound between Beaufort and Shackleford and Core Creek north of Beaufort. These all offer areas that are free from no-wake zones and are wide enough to allow for skier safety.

Surfing

Surfing is very popular along the North Carolina coast and always has been. There are plenty of places to catch the swell on the Crystal Coast. Any area surf shop can provide information about wave conditions and surf contests. Most local surf shops offer surfboard and boogie board rentals. Listed below are some of the area's surf shops.

Bert's Surf Shop, MP 2½, Atlantic Beach, 726-1730

Surf Zone Boards & Bikes, MP 4¾, Atlantic Beach, 247-1103

Marsh's Surf Shop, Atlantic Beach Causeway, 726-9046

Hot Wax Surf Shop, MP 20¼, Emerald Isle, 354-6466

Bert's Surf Shop, MP 19½, Emerald Isle, 354-2441

Sweet Willy's Surf Shop, MP 19½, Emerald Isle, 354-4611

77 Degree Surf Shop, Belk of Morehead City, 726-5121

Swimming

You can swim just about anywhere along the Crystal Coast, with the exception of a few posted areas. But even the most skilled pool swimmer may have difficulty dealing with ocean waves and undertows, so exercise caution and never swim alone. Riptides and undertows are very common along the North Carolina shoreline. If you find yourself being pulled

A sportfishing guide for North Carolina's Coast

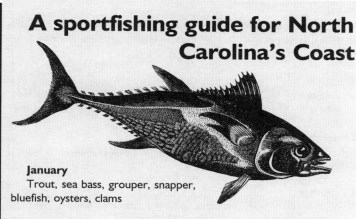

January
Trout, sea bass, grouper, snapper, bluefish, oysters, clams

February
same as January

March
Grouper, sea trout, sea bass, bluefish, croaker, snapper, oysters, clams, king mackerel, some yellowfin tuna

April
Bluefish, channel bass, grouper, snapper, croaker, sea trout, sea mullet, some king mackerel, some oysters, clams, tuna

May
King mackerel, bluefish, grouper, flounder, cobia, tuna, shark, sea mullet, crabs, soft crabs, blue marlin, sea bass, wahoo, dolphin, Spanish mackerel

June
Blue marlin, white marlin, sailfish, dolphin, wahoo, cobia, king mackerel, bluefish, tuna, summer flounder, snapper, grouper, Spanish mackerel, shark, crabs, soft crabs

July
Dolphin, wahoo, tuna, blue marlin, white marlin, sailfish, snapper, grouper, summer flounder, bluefish, Spanish mackerel, sea mullet, shark, crabs, soft crabs

August
Dolphin, wahoo, tuna, grouper, snapper, Spanish mackerel, bluefish, speckled trout, spot, sea mullet, shark, crabs, blue marlin, white marlin, sailfish, king mackerel

September

Grouper, snapper, Spanish mackerel, king mackerel, spot, shark, bluefish, speckled trout, sea mullet, channel bass, flounder, sea bass, dolphin, blue marlin, white marlin, tuna

October

King mackerel, bluefish, snapper, grouper, channel bass, spot, speckled trout, flounder, shark, oysters, sea bass, tuna

November

King mackerel, bluefish, speckled trout, flounder, snapper, grouper, shark, sea mullet, clams, sea bass, tuna

December

Bluefish, flounder, speckled trout, sea trout, snapper, sea bass, grouper, oysters, clams, some king mackerel

(Provided by NC Marine Fisheries)

by frightening currents, the most important thing to do is to stay calm. If you are caught in a riptide, relax and let it carry you toward the sea. Eventually it will dissipate. You should swim parallel to the shore to get out of the riptide, and then swim toward the shore. Some areas along Bogue Banks, such as the Atlantic Beach circle area and Fort Macon State Park, post lifeguards during the summer season. Swimming is not allowed around the park's rock jetties or on the inlet side. There are no public pools on the Crystal Coast, only those at hotels, condominiums, private communities and fitness centers.

Sailboarding

The popularity of this sport is growing quickly, and rental shops offering boards and lessons have come with that popularity.

The Sailing Place, Atlantic Beach Causeway, 726-5664, offers windsurfer rentals as well as individual or group lessons. **Island Rigs**, MP 12 in Indian Beach, 247-7787, offers sailboard rentals and lessons as well as rentals of kayaks, boogie boards, Sunfish and skim boards. The shop at Island Rigs carries a complete line of accessories, beachwear, sportswear, car and bike racks, footwear and sunglasses. The outside deck overlooking Bogue Sound is a good place to have a cold drink and watch the action.

Beach Access Areas

As is true in many coastal areas, getting onto the beach can be confusing. You aren't sure what is private property and what is public or where to park. The number of beach access areas is increasing, and that's a good sign. The areas listed here offer access to the water, and some offer parking and bathroom facilities and are handicapped accessible. Vehicle access is available for permitted vehicles at some access areas. Public Beach Access areas are usually marked with signs that feature blue letters and a sea gull flying in an orange circle. We have given the

milepost (MP) number for those on Bogue Banks. Some beach access areas have gates that open at first light and close at dusk.

Atlantic Beach

Atlantic Beach offers a pedestrian access area at the east end of the Sheraton Resort parking lot. A vehicular access area is provided at the south end of Raleigh Avenue.

SOUTH END OF ATLANTIC BEACH CAUSEWAY

The character of The Circle changes from day to night, and it might not be the place where Insiders would recommend you let your kids roam free at night. But, it is improving and provides good access to the beach. A go-cart track and Ferris wheel have recently been added in the center of The Circle, giving it more of a family atmosphere. The beach has been renourished after several storms that washed a lot of the sand away, so beachgoers will now find a larger stretch of beautiful beach, volleyball nets and plenty of parking.

WEST SIDE OF ATLANTIC BEACH CIRCLE

On the west side of The Circle, this facility offers limited paved parking, a bathhouse with outdoor showers, a ramp over the dunes and gazebo/picnic areas. It is equipped for handicapped beachgoers.

LES AND SALLY MOORE PUBLIC BEACH ACCESS
MP 1½, Atlantic Beach

This access area offers toilet facilities, outdoor showers, a covered gazebo and a boardwalk over the dunes to the beach. Parking meters are in operation during the summer. Once on the beach, the young and not so young will find swings, a climbing area and an old boat to hide in. This access is equipped for the handicapped.

FORT MACON STATE PARK
East End of Bogue Banks

Fort Macon State Park offers visitors miles and miles of sandy beaches on which to roam. The park has two popular access areas. The one at the west end of the park features a large bathhouse, outdoor showers, a seasonal refreshment stand, picnic shelters and outdoor grills. The other is near the fort and has a good deal of parking. The only amenity is the restroom facility at the entrance to the fort. For more information about Fort Macon State Park, see the Crystal Coast Attractions chapter.

Pine Knoll Shores

Town residents are provided access to the water at a few places, but there are no public access areas.

Indian Beach/Salter Path

SALTER PATH
REGIONAL PUBLIC BEACH ACCESS
MP 10¼, off Salter Path Rd.

This facility offers paved parking, a boardwalk over the dunes to the ocean, a picnic area and a comfort station with dressing area and outdoor showers. It is equipped for handicapped oceangoers as well.

PUBLIC BEACH ACCESS
MP 11, off Salter Path Rd.

This area, on the west side of Squatter's Restaurant, offers parking for cars and racks for bikes. The south end of the parking lot opens directly onto the beach to allow access to registered vehicles during the off-season.

Emerald Isle

THIRD STREET PARK
MP 12¼, at Second St.

Visitors to this park actually turn on Second Street just west of the Indian Beach town line. A small gravel lot offers parking for a few cars and a bike rack. A ramp over the dunes takes oceangoers to the beach.

BESIDE EMERALD ISLE PIER
MP 15, off Salter Path Rd.

This is a large access area that offers parking for more than 100 cars on a gravel lot. The area is beside the Emerald Isle Pier, and visitors will have a short walk to the ocean beach.

OCEAN DRIVE
MP 15¼, off Salter Path Rd.

This area offers no parking spaces, only access to the beach for walkers or cyclists and vehicles with permits.

WHITEWATER DRIVE
MP 17½, off Salter Path Rd.

Beachgoers will find a wooden walkway to the beach at this site and two vehicle parking places for handicapped visitors.

Photo: Scott Taylor

Beaufort Oars Rowing Club members scoot by a trawler in Taylor's Creek.

BLACK SKIMMER ROAD
MP 19, off Salter Path Rd.

This access offers visitors a place to walk to the beach and access for vehicles. No parking is offered.

CEDAR STREET
MP 19¼, off Salter Path Rd.

This sound access has a small gravel parking lot and a short pier over the water.

Beaufort

NEWPORT RIVER PARK
Causeway, U.S. Hwy. 70

On the east side of Beaufort-Morehead City high-rise bridge, this facility offers a pier, sandy beach, picnic area, bathhouse and a launching ramp sufficient for small sailboats. The entrance to this park is directly across from Radio Island.

RADIO ISLAND
Causeway, U.S. Hwy. 70

Radio Island is the largest island between the Beaufort-Morehead City high-rise bridge and the drawbridge into Beaufort. The island is home to a variety of businesses — marinas, boat builders and a fuel terminal complete with large tanks. The beach access area is a favorite spot for locals because it fronts Beaufort Channel, offers few to no waves and provides an impressive view of Beaufort and the surrounding islands. There's plenty of parking and portable toilets are provided.

CURTIS A. PERRY PARK
East end of Front St.

While this is not a swimming spot, the park does provide picnic tables, grills and a dock overlooking Taylor's Creek. Bathroom facilities and a boat ramp are also provided.

Crystal Coast
Marinas

North Carolina has the largest area of inland waters on the East Coast. The Outer Banks enclose several large inland sounds: Currituck, Albemarle, Pamlico, Core and Bogue, which are laced together north to south by 265 miles of the Intracoastal Waterway (ICW). This liquid highway of inland waters makes the numerous coastal resorts and historical points of interest easily accessible by boat.

Of Carteret County's total 1,063 square miles, 531 miles are water. The bountiful brine giving definition to the Crystal Coast challenges the greater portion of the populace and most annual visitors to see the area by water. The weather lures pleasure boaters and sailors almost year round. Even in the coldest months, you'll find a few days each week that are too pretty to stay ashore.

Because many boaters enjoy the shallow, protected waters along the Crystal Coast, numerous marinas are available to serve the fleet of water traffic. There are more than 35 marinas, most on or just off the ICW. And, via the ICW, boaters can sojourn to nearby Oriental and New Bern, where a number of marinas serve power and sailing vessels. See the New Bern Marinas chapter for listings.

Crystal Coast marinas have varying water depths, services, amenities, transient accommodations and proximity to sights and services. Many condominium developments provide owners the use of private docks. Here, we have provided a listing of Crystal Coast area marinas. Please call ahead or write to inquire whether a marina offers the specific services you'll need.

See our Fishing, Watersports and Beach Access chapter for locations of boat ramps.

Marinas

Atlantic Beach

Triple S Marina Village, E. Fort Macon Road, MP½, 247-4833

Anchorage Marina, 517 E. Fort Macon Road, MP 1½, 726-4423

Fort Macon Marina, E. Fort Macon Road, MP 1¾, 726-2055

Bailey's Marina, Atlantic Beach Causeway, 247-4148

For transient boaters weekending in the area, some marinas, especially those in Beaufort, offer courtesy vehicles for making necessary supply runs.

Angler Inn and Marina, Atlantic Beach Causeway, 726-0097

Captain Stacy Fishing Center, Atlantic Beach Causeway, 247-7501

Crow's Nest Marina, Atlantic Beach Causeway, 726-4048

Sea Water Marina, Atlantic Beach Causeway, 726-1637

Causeway Marina, Atlantic Beach Causeway, 726-6977

Emerald Isle

Island Harbor Marina, Old Ferry Road at the end of Mangrove Drive, 354-3106

Beaufort

Boaters who arrive in Beaufort via Taylor's Creek may drop anchor in the designated anchorage and out of the main channel. A number of moorings are privately owned, and boaters are asked to respect waterway courtesies of space and anchorage. There is no charge for anchoring and no limit for length of stay. A public dinghy dock and restrooms are available. The dock master at the Dock House is available to answer questions. Town Creek on the north side of Beaufort is also a designated anchorage with dinghy landing.

Beaufort Town Docks, Taylor's Creek, 728-2503

Beaufort Gulf Dock, Taylor's Creek (fuel only), 728-6000

Airport Marina, West Beaufort Road on South Creek, 728-2010

Sea Gate Association, N.C. Highway 101, 1 mile north of Core Creek Bridge on the ICW, 728-4126

Town Creek Marina, W. Beaufort Road, north of the Beaufort drawbridge, 728-6111

Radio Island Marina, Morehead City-Beaufort Causeway, 726-3773

Morehead City

Dockside Marina and Ship's Store, 301 Arendell Street, 247-4890

Portside Marina, 209 Arendell Street, 726-7678

Morehead City Yacht Basin, Calico Creek, north of the Morehead City high-rise bridge, 726-6862

Island Marina, Morehead City-Beaufort Causeway on Radio Island, 726-5706

Morehead Sports Marina, Morehead City-Beaufort Causeway, 202 Radio Island Road, 726-5676

Coral Bay Marina, Pelletier Creek, U.S. Highway 70 W., 247-4231

70 West Marina, Pelletier Creek, 4401 Arendell Street, 726-5171

Harbor Master, Pelletier Creek, 4408 Central Drive, 726-2541

Spooner's Creek Yacht Harbor, N.C. Highway 24, 726-2060

Western Carteret/Swansboro

Almost every home or business on the White Oak River or Bogue Sound has a

The fishing trawler, Anna Marie *slips into Beaufort followed by hungry pelicans.*

dock, boat ramp or both. But the commercial docks, particularly the ones big enough and with channels dredged deep enough to accommodate a very large motor or sailing yacht, are few.

Casper's Marine Service, on the ICW south of town at 102 Broad Street, Swansboro, 326-4462

The Flying Bridge, off the ICW north of town on N.C. Highway 24, Swansboro, 393-2416

Dudley's Marina, off the ICW north of town on N.C. Highway 24, Swansboro, 393-2204

Down East

Barbour's Harbor, Harkers Island, 728-6181

Calico Jack's Inn & Marina, Harkers Island, 728-3575

Fisherman's Inn, Harkers Island, 728-5780

Harkers Island Fishing Center, Harkers Island, 728-3907, (800) 423-8739

Morris Marina, 1000 Morris Marina Road, Atlantic, 225-4261

Authorized Sales and Service

We hope it doesn't happen to you, but unfortunately, boat motors have been known to fail. If you have a breakdown while boating along the Crystal Coast, one of these businesses should be able to help. For your convenience, we've organized the businesses according to the type of motor-repair services they specialize in. If you're in the market for a new boat

Strong sea breezes fill the sails for all sorts of wonderful craft.

or motor, call around or visit the businesses to find out who sells what.

Evinrude Outboards

Morehead Marine Inc., 4971 Arendell Street, Morehead City, 247-6667

Lane's Marina Inc., Morehead-Beaufort Causeway, 728-4473

Johnson Outboards

Boats Inc., 4838 Arendell Street, Morehead City, 726-2196

Crow's Nest Marina, Atlantic Beach Causeway, 726-6161

Fort Macon Marina, 417 E. Fort Macon Road, Atlantic Beach, 726-5676

Mercury Outboards

Morehead Sports Marina, Morehead-Beaufort Causeway, 726-5676

Precision Marine, 1058 N.C. Highway 24, Cedar Point, 393-3036

70 West Marina, U.S. Highway 70 W., Morehead City, 726-9993

Suzuki Outboards

Atlantic Beach Causeway Marina, Atlantic Beach Causeway, 726-6977
Walsh Marine, 213 U.S. Highway 70 W., Havelock, 447-BASS

Volvo Penta

Town Creek Marina, 232 W. Beaufort Road, Beaufort, 728-6111

Yamaha Outboards

Jones Brothers Marine, 5136 U.S. Highway 70 W., Morehead City, 726-8404

The Beaufort and Morehead City waterfronts and the beaches continue to be the most favored running and walking spots, and they are heavily traveled by exercisers in the early morning and evening.

Crystal Coast
Sports, Fitness and Parks

North Carolina's Crystal Coast has plenty to offer in the way of sports. Whether it be running, basketball, beach volleyball, bicycling or windsurfing, the year-round mild climate and wonderful coastal scenery make any activity easier to do. And, if the weather just won't cooperate or you need some equipment, there are also a few fitness centers in the area.

This section will introduce you to a few of the area's most popular sports and, in most cases, give you a contact. Watersports are described in a separate chapter appropriately titled Fishing, Watersports and Beach Access. At the end of this chapter, we have listed some of the county and city parks on the Crystal Coast. Information about state and national parks is given in the Attractions chapter.

Sports

Like most areas, the Crystal Coast has its share of sports enthusiasts who participate in their favorite events casually or as part of an organized team. Here we have listed popular sports and how to contact someone in the know.

Baseball and Little League

Teams for children and adults are sponsored by the Carteret County Parks and Recreation Department, 728-8401. The Kinston Indians, a minor league profes-

sional baseball team based in nearby Kinston, provide great family entertainment. Games are played on week nights and weekends during the season in a newly renovated park with all the extras. Kinston is a two-hour drive from Morehead City. For ticket information and a game schedule, call 527-9111 or (800) 334-5467.

Basketball

Most of the Crystal Coast parks have basketball courts, as do a few of the area fitness centers. The county Parks and Recreation Department, 728-8401, sponsors a basketball league.

Bicycling

Flat, coastal areas lend themselves to fun cycling. Regardless of the type of bike (road or fat tire) you have, Salter Path Road (N.C. Highway 58) on Bogue Banks is one of the area's best riding roads. No road in the area has enough shoulder for cycling, but this one comes close. Emerald Isle's Coast Guard Road now has a bike path. If you just want to cruise around, there is a posted route in and around Beaufort and maps are available at the Beaufort Historic Site on Turner Street. If you have an off-road bike, head for the beach on a low tide.

Fitness Centers

Emerald Isle Municipal Complex, Emerald Drive, MP 19 in Emerald Isle, 354-6350, is open to residents and nonresidents at a nominal fee. This facility offers a full-size gym for indoor tennis, basketball, volleyball, soccer and shuffleboard. Classes vary and often include aerobics, gymnastics and karate. There is also a weight room, a game room with pool and Ping-Pong tables, an exchange library and a fully equipped kitchen. Space for meetings and parties is also available. Outside you will find tennis courts, a basketball court and a children's play area.

The **Morehead City Recreation Department**, 1600 Fisher Street in Morehead City, 726-5083, is the area's most affordable fitness center with yearly rates of $30 for city residents and $40 for non-city residents. Members are offered use of a fully equipped weight room with free weights and equipment, a gym with a full-size basketball court and a game room with pool and Ping-Pong tables. The department offers aerobics, dance and karate classes, dog obedience classes and various youth sports programs such as basketball, T-ball and softball.

The **Sports Center**, 701 N. 35th Street in Morehead City, 726-7070, is the area's most complete fitness center, offering a fully equipped weight room, Nautilus equipment, fitness equipment, an indoor swimming pool, racquetball courts, an indoor walking/running track and classes of all kinds including karate, water and floor aerobics and swimming. Sports Center also has a basketball/volleyball court, tanning salon, stair climbers, treadmills and NordicTrack. A new Olympic-size outdoor pool with a waterslide and surrounding picnic tables has been added to the facility. For relaxing, you'll find saunas, a whirlpool and a steam room. The center has a vitamin and equipment store, a snack bar and child-care services.

Flying

The **Michael J. Smith Field** in Beaufort, 728-1777, offers services for private planes and private lessons. This airfield was named in memory of the pilot of space shuttle *Challenger*, which exploded January 28, 1986. A Beaufort native, Navy Capt. Michael Smith learned to fly at this airfield.

Horseback Riding

Acha's Stable, 223-4478, provides lessons and trail rides and offers boarding and stall rentals by the month for horse owners. The stable is just west of Morehead City.

Eterna Riverview Stables, 726-8313, offers trail rides, lessons and boarding. The stables are off Country Club Road in Morehead City.

WhiteSand Trail Rides, 729-0911, hosts rides along the beach during the day, at sunset and in the moonlight. With stables on Cedar Island, WhiteSand also offers camping trips. WhiteSand provides

the horses and you have the fun. Horse owners can bring their own horses to join the fun any time of the year.

Zeigler Stables, 223-5110, is off Howard Boulevard (across from the ballpark) in Newport. The stable offers riding lessons, boarding, summer riding camps and a tack shop.

Hunting

Guide services have long been a popular means for duck and goose hunters to experience a new area. Using a guide familiar with the area cuts down on the chances of spending time in the wrong spot.

The folks at the **Driftwood Motel and Restaurant** on Cedar Island, 225-4861, operate a guide service for hunting and fishing. Hunting dates depend on those set for the season but are usually mid-December through late January.

The Driftwood's hunting package includes guide service by a local and use of the boat, decoys and blinds, accommodations in the motel and hearty meals. Blinds are scattered along 1,100 acres of marsh from Cedar Island to Portsmouth, in Core Sound and on Core Banks. Hunters can rent waders, have their kill cleaned, buy hunting accessories or get a hunting license at the Driftwood. Folks come to the Driftwood from all parts of the country each year to have a crack at the abundant redheads, pintails and other ducks and geese.

Adams Creek GunSports, 447-7688

Photo: Wayland Cato

In Cedar Island, you can ride horses on the beach.

or 447-6808, provides guides for hunting quail, pheasant, duck, dove and deer. June and Rusty Bryan provide accommodations in an 1870 country farmhouse lodge overlooking Adams Creek, a part of the Intracoastal Waterway. Southern-style cooking, emphasizing seafood, beef and game, sends the hunters off in the morning and welcomes them on the return. Noon meals can be arranged.

Adams Creek GunSports maintains impoundments, natural woodland ponds, and marsh and floating blinds. They also have a regulation skeet field and a Sport-

ing Clays course consisting of targets in the woods and fields. An on-site pro shop and shooting instructors are also available. The Bryan's welcome hunting parties and the lodge is available for business meetings, parties and weddings.

Karate

Karate lessons are often offered by the Morehead Recreation Department, 726-5083, and several of the local fitness centers (see Fitness Centers entry in this chapter).

Beach volleyball is increasing in popularity and the Atlantic Beach waterfront is the place to watch, or take part in, the action.

Running/Walking

Running and walking are favorite forms of exercise along the Crystal Coast. This area's mild temperatures mean that one seldom has to miss a day of exercise and outdoor enjoyment. The Beaufort and Morehead City waterfronts and the beaches continue to be the most favored running and walking spots, and they are heavily traveled by early morning and evening exercisers.

For those runners who like to test their skills or just run with a group, there are a few races around. Most of the races also include walks.

Lookout Rotary Spring Road Race kicks off the local race season on the last weekend in April with a flat 5K and 1-mile run/walk beginning and ending at the Sports Center, N. 35th Street in Morehead City. The race is sponsored by the Lookout Rotary Club of Morehead City. For information call Sports Center, 726-7070.

The **Carteret County Parks and Recreation Department**, 728-8401, sponsors the Beach Run Series that usually begins in late May. This low-key weekday series attracts lots of local runners and walkers. The 1-mile run/walk, 5K and 10K are on the beach and begin and end at the beach access area at The Circle in Atlantic Beach. Dates vary depending on the tide.

The **Historic Beaufort Road Race** is the area's most popular race. Hundreds turn out in mid-July to tackle the 1-mile run/walk, 5K run/walk and 10K courses. The courses are flat and fast, and runners can be assured of plenty of heat and humidity. For information call Sports Center, 726-7070.

There aren't many choices with the **Twin Bridges Race**. You either run the 8K or stay on the porch. There aren't any hills at the coast, so race directors throw in two high-rise bridges. The race kicks off Saturday's events at the N.C. Seafood Festival, 726-6273, the first full weekend in October on the Morehead City waterfront. The race begins at the drawbridge in Beaufort and ends on the Atlantic Beach Causeway.

Soccer

There is a lot of action on the soccer fields across the area for children and adults. Carteret County Parks and Recreation Department, 728-8401, sponsors leagues for younger players and for women and men.

Softball

The county sponsors a men's and women's softball league each year. The teams are usually sponsored by local businesses and are very competitive. Call 728-8401 for information.

Summer Camps

The Crystal Coast is home to a number of camps that offer summer programs and are available for group use year round. A few of the largest camps are listed here.

Camp Albemarle, 1145 Hibbs Road, Newport, 726-4848, is a Presbyterian camp that operates year round and is open to the public. Summer camp sessions are divided into age groups, with weeks dedicated to campers from 3rd through 12th grades. Activities include swimming in the pool and sound, tennis, basketball, sailing and canoeing, along with other traditional camp activities. A sailing camp is also operated each summer. Overlooking Bogue Sound, the camp is on Highway 24 north of Morehead City.

Camp Sea Gull and **Camp Seafarer**,

Route 65 in Arapahoe, 249-1111 or 249-1212, are on the Neuse River in Arapahoe, which is about 27 miles north of Morehead City and 21 miles east of New Bern. The camps share an outpost and docks on the Morehead City waterfront. Camp Seafarer for girls opened in 1961, and Camp Sea Gull for boys has been in operation since 1948. Both are owned and operated by the capital area YMCA in Raleigh. Sea Gull and Seafarer feature a nationally recognized seamanship program including sailing and motorboating. The camps offer many camping acitivities such as archery, golf, tennis, soccer, riflery and group camping, and they offer environmental education programs serving schools throughout the state, corporate training and a conference center.

Tennis

The Crystal Coast is host to a number of tournaments each year. For more information, contact Spooner's Creek Racquet Club, 726-8560, or call Island Beach and Racquet Club, 726-2240. Public tennis courts are scattered throughout the area (see the Parks listing at the end of this chapter).

Triathlons

The **Nelson Bay Challenge** is a popular sprint triathlon that takes place in Sea Level in early May. The race includes a 750-meter swim in Nelson Bay, a 20K bike ride and a 5K run. For many, the race is a warm-up for the triathlon season ahead. It is a well-organized race that offers spectators easy viewing of the transition area and a great post-race clambake. The funding sponsor is J.M. Davis Industries of Morehead City, 247-6902. Money raised benefits local youth programs.

Volleyball

Beach volleyball is catching on. Tournament nets are on the main beach at The Circle in Atlantic Beach, and there is usually plenty of action there. For information about beach volleyball tournaments, call the Atlantic Beach Recreation Director, 726-2121. An indoor volleyball league is sponsored by the Carteret County Parks and Recreation Department, 728-8401.

Parks

County Parks

The first seven parks listed below are managed by the Carteret County Parks and Recreation Department, 728-8401, and all offer a picnic area and comfort station. Additional amenities are listed along with the location. Other area parks are included at the bottom of the list.

The **Salter Path Ball Field**, N.C. Highway 58 in Salter Path, is behind the community fire department and is used for sports as well as community events.

Freedom Park, off Lennoxville Road in Beaufort, is surrounded by woods and has lighted regulation and youth fields, basketball courts and a picnic and play area.

Newport River Park, on the east side of the high-rise bridge between Beaufort and Morehead, has a short fishing pier, a boat ramp sufficient for launching small sailboats, a picnic area and restroom facilities. The park entrance is directly across from the entrance to Radio Island.

Swinson Park, Country Club Road in Morehead City, is a popular spot for athletics. Beside the new Morehead City Primary School, Swinson Park offers lighted regulation and youth athletic fields, tennis and basketball courts and a picnic area.

Western Park, off Highway 58 in Cedar Point, offers a lighted youth softball/baseball field and a multipurpose field.

Eastern Park, U.S. Highway 70 in Smyrna, is a lighted park that features regulation and youth fields, basketball courts, tennis courts and a picnic area.

Mariner's Park, off Highway 70 in Sea Level, is across from the Sea Level Extended Care Facility and has lighted youth athletic fields and tennis courts.

Bogue Banks Parks

There are few parks on the island, so most residents and visitors use the beach access areas as picnic and play sites. For a listing of the access areas, see the Fishing, Watersports and Beach Access chapter.

Emerald Isle Parks and Recreation Department, 354-6350, maintains two small public parks. The park, behind the town hall on Emerald Drive at MP 19, has a children's play area and picnic tables. **Merchant's Park** is on the south side of Emerald Drive at MP 19½ and offers parking, picnic tables, shelter and restroom facilities.

Beaufort Parks

The town's most popular park, **Freedom Park**, is maintained by the county (see County Parks above). It is about three blocks from Front Street on Leonda Drive. The town does maintain two others, **Grayden Paul Jaycee Park** and **Curtis Perry Park**.

Grayden Paul Jaycee Park is on Front Street at the south end of Pollock Street. The small area offers a dock, a swimming

area, a gazebo and a grassed picnic spot, although there is no beach. The park was named for the late Beaufort raconteur Grayden Paul.

Curtis A. Perry Park is at the east end of Front Street across from the boat ramp. You'll find a basketball court, two lighted tennis courts, bathroom facilities, a dock and waterfront picnic areas complete with grills. The park was named in memory of the town's public works director.

Morehead City Parks

Morehead City Recreation Department, 726-5083, maintains several parks in town. Each offers different amenities. At 1600 Fisher Street, behind the recreation department, are two multipurpose fields used primarily for softball and baseball. Inside the facility, members are offered use of a weight room loaded with free weights and machines, a gym with a full-

Photo: NC Aquarium

"Bottom fishing" on the Crystal Coast is one way to catch the big ones, or at least see them swim by.

Photo: Burnie Batchelor

Campers from Camp Sea Gull explore the waters of the Neuse River.

size basketball court, and a game room with pool and Ping-Pong tables. Membership costs are very reasonable. The department also offers aerobics, dance and karate classes, dog obedience classes and youth sports programs (basketball, T-ball, softball, etc.) and more.

City Park, 1000 Block, Arendell Street, is a shady park that offers playground equipment and a few picnic tables.

Jaycee Park is on the water at the south end of 9th Street. This is a fairly new park that is the site of the city's Summer in the Park concert series hosted by the Parks and Recreation Department on Saturday evenings in summer. You'll find parking, picnic tables and a short pier at this park.

Municipal Park, behind the visitors center, Arendell Street, offers plenty of parking, picnic areas and a boat ramp. The park borders Bogue Sound, just west of the Atlantic Beach high-rise bridge.

Piney Park, 2900 Block, Bridges Street, just east of Morehead Plaza, is tucked away in some trees and offers a quiet picnic spot.

Shevans Park, 1600 Block, Evans Street, has four tennis courts (two are lit), four basketball goals, a practice field and a fence.

Swansboro Parks

Bicentennial Park is at the base of the bridge into Swansboro on N.C. Highway 24. The park was dedicated in 1985 and contains a life-size statue of Otway Burns, Swansboro's favorite privateer from the War of 1812, and a memorial to Theophilus Weeks, founder of the town. The park is the perfect place to fish from the sea wall, play or simply sit and enjoy the beauty of the White Oak River.

Crystal Coast
Golf

The Crystal Coast's championship courses await the golf enthusiast, and most of the area's exceptional club courses are open to the public. Courses are busy year round, and many Insiders consider fall the most favorable time to play. It is best to call ahead, especially on weekends, to reserve tee times. Several area hotels offer golf packages that include accommodations, meals, guaranteed starting times, greens fees and a few extras.

Below you will find the area courses that are open to the public. The slope ratings and course rating are given at the end of each course description. Two local driving ranges are listed at the end.

Courses

BRANDYWINE BAY
GOLF AND COUNTRY CLUB
N.C. Hwy. 24, Morehead City   247-2541

Located west of Morehead City, this 18-hole, par 71 championship course was recently ranked in *Golf Digest* as the best course in the area. A very popular course, it is set in dense woods and laced with streams and ponds. Originally designed by Bruce Devlin and redesigned by Ellis and Dan Maples, this coastal course plays 6611 yards from the championship tees, 6138 yards for regular men's and 5196 yards for women's. Golfers will find a pro shop, snack bar, lessons by appointment and putting greens.

Coy Brown is Brandywine's PGA professional and is well-known in the area. 119(72.7)

BOGUE BANKS
GOLF AND COUNTRY CLUB
N.C. Hwy. 58, MP 5, Pine Knoll Shores   726-1034

This par 72 course is 6100 yards with four holes overlooking Bogue Sound. Numerous lagoons and lakes meander throughout the narrow 419 bermudagrass fairways leading to lush 328 bermudagrass greens. Beautiful water oaks and lofty pine trees enhance the overall beauty of the course. From the blue tees it measures 6100 yards, from the white tees, 5757 yards and from the red, 5043 yards. A pro shop, snack area, tennis courts and daily and weekly rates are available. Golf and tennis lessons can be arranged. Jeff Austin is the course PGA professional. 116(68.8)

MOREHEAD CITY COUNTRY CLUB
Country Club Rd., Morehead City   726-4917

On the Newport River, this club offers a challenging 18-hole course and is Carteret County's oldest. The common bermudagrass fairways and greens are maintained beautifully year round by PGA professional Randy Fuquay and his staff. From the blue tees it measures 6383 yards, from the white, 6060 yards and from the ladies' tees, 4909 yards. 113(70.4)

SILVER CREEK GOLF CLUB

N.C. Hwy. 58, Cape Carteret   393-8058

On Highway 58 just north of Cape Carteret, this par 72 championship course, with bentgrass greens and beautiful bermudagrass fairways and tees, was designed by Gene Hamm. The course plays 7005 yards from silver tees, 6526 yards from blue tees, 6030 yards from white tees and 4962 yards from women's tees. A Southern-style clubhouse has a wide porch overlooking the course. Also on the grounds are a snack bar, locker rooms, a driving range, a putting green, a pro shop, tennis courts and a swimming pool. 122(73.3)

STAR HILL GOLF AND COUNTRY CLUB

Club House Dr., Cape Carteret   393-8111

This is one of the area's finest 27-hole championship courses, measuring more than 9000 yards. Comprised of the Sands, the Pines and the Lakes, Star Hill is at the junction of highways 24 and 58 and is nestled between the Intracoastal Waterway and Croatan National Forest. A 4,000-foot private airplane landing strip is nearby. Patrons will find a driving range, rental clubs, tennis courts, a swimming pool and a grill and snack area. You'll also find PGA Professional Instructors Phill Hunt and Phil Johnson on hand. Sands/Pines 115(70.4), Pines/Lakes 113(70.1), Lakes/Sands 118(70.8)

Driving Ranges

BOB'S GOLF DRIVING RANGE

N.C. Hwy. 24, Morehead City   240-4653

Just outside Morehead City on Highway 24, Bob's Golf Range offers a 250-yard

Photo: Scott Taylor

Thanks to increased environmental protection programs, pelicans are once again a delightful sight along the coast.

Brandywine Bay Championship Golf Course invites you to discover 18 holes of the finest golfing experience on the North Carolina Coast! This course, designed by Bruce Devlin, boasts over 6600 yards of rolling fairways and bentgrass greens, the challenge of 40 acres of water, fast putting greens and the well known 555 yard par 5 hole #10. This is truly a golfer's paradise for the novice or seasoned veteran,

-PUBLIC & GROUPS WELCOME-

LESSONS AVAILABLE
BENTGRASS GREENS
FULLY STOCKED PRO SHOP

Tee Time Reservations:
(919) 247-2541

Brandywine Bay Championship Golf Course
Hwy. 70 West
Morehead City, NC 28557

Photo: NC Travel and Tourism

For some golf is a way of life, and the Crystal Coast offers some of the area's best courses.

driving range. Patrons can hit from T-mats or grass areas. The range is open throughout the year, although the winter hours vary.

GOLPHIN' DOLPHIN
N.C. Hwy. 58, Cape Carteret   393-8131

This business offers a 300-yard driving range, an 18-hole miniature golf course with elevations up to 22 feet, a batting cage, a pro shop, a go-cart track, bumper boats and more. The batting cage is for softball and baseball and golf equipment is offered in the pro shop. The go-cart track is new and is loads of fun. A separate room is available for parties or meetings. Golphin' Dolphin is behind Hardee's in Cape Carteret and is open every day during the summer. Winter hours vary.

Silver Creek Golf Club

18 Championship Holes
Greens Fees Available
Electric Carts
Tennis Courts
Swimming Pool
Grill Serving Lunch

Hwy 58 Swansboro, NC
(919) 393-8058
Call for Tee Times

Crystal Coast
Ferries

A number of state-owned and private ferries serve the Crystal Coast, offering visitors and residents a timesaving and enjoyable transportation alternative via the Intracoastal Waterway. The state's ferries operate under the administration of the North Carolina Department of Transportation (DOT) and are large, seaworthy vessels.

State Ferries

The **Cedar Island-Ocracoke Ferry Service** is the most popular state-operated ferry, carrying passengers and their vehicles between the Crystal Coast and Ocracoke Island. The Cedar Island terminal is a little more than 30 miles east of Beaufort, but allow at least an hour and a half for the trip. Reservations must be claimed 30 minutes before departure time, or they will be cancelled.

The **Cherry Branch-Minnesott Ferry** is essential for commuters from Oriental who must travel with their cars across the Neuse River to work in Havelock and surrounding areas. On the Crystal Coast side, the Cherry Branch terminal is off N.C.

Highway 101, about 5 miles south of Havelock. Signs along the highway give directions to the terminal. This ferry takes you on an interesting exploration north to Oriental and is an especially nice route to Belhaven.

The small, "people only — no cars" ferry at **Hammocks Beach State Park** provides transportation from the park headquarters terminal to Bear Island. The ferry terminal is off N.C. Highway 24 about 2 miles west of Swansboro at the end of State Road 1511. The ferry operates daily from Memorial Day weekend through Labor Day; in May and September it runs Wednesday through Sunday; in April and October it runs Friday through Sunday. If you are visiting Bear Island in season, get to the ferry landing early to avoid long waiting lines. Pets are not allowed on the ferry, and alcoholic beverages are prohibited in the park (see our Attractions chapter).

Regardless of the ferry you choose, you can almost always be assured of a calm crossing with plenty of time to look around. All ferry schedules and tolls are subject to change without notice, and ferries do not operate in rough weather. For more information about state-owned ferry crossings, contact the N.C. Department of Transportation Ferry Division, Maritime Building, Morehead City 28557, 726-6446 or 726-6413. Information about state ferries can also be obtained by tuning to New Bern's radio station 1610 AM. No reservations are required if you are traveling as a pedestrian or with a bicycle. Following is a list of state-operated ferry schedules and fares.

Cedar Island - Ocracoke Toll Ferry

2¼ HOURS CROSSING - 50 CAR LIMIT
RESERVATIONS RECOMMENDED
Summer Schedule, May 22 - Oct. 1

Depart Cedar Island	Depart Ocracoke
7 AM	7 AM
8:15 AM	9:30 AM
9:30 AM	10 AM*
Noon	10:45 AM
1:00 PM*	Noon
1:15 PM	3 PM
3 PM	4:15 PM*
6 PM	6 PM
8:30 PM	8:30 PM

*Additional departures Memorial Day through Labor Day

Nov.1 - April 2
April 17 - May 7

7 AM	7 AM
10 AM	10 AM
1 PM	1 PM
4 PM	4 PM

April 3 - April 16
May 8 - May 21
Oct. 2 - Oct. 31

7 AM	7 AM
9:30 AM	9:30 AM
Noon	Noon
3 PM	3 PM
6 PM	6 PM
8:30 PM	8:30 PM

Fares (One Way)

Pedestrian	$1
Bicycle Rider	$2
Motorcycles	$10
Vehicle and/or combination less than 20 feet	$10
Vehicle and/or combination 20 feet to 40 feet	$20
Vehicle and/or combination up to 55 feet	$30

Call the ferry terminals at Cedar Island, 225-3551, or Ocracoke, 928-3841, for reservations and to verify times.

Ocracoke - Swan Quarter Toll Ferry

2½ HOURS CROSSING - 28 CAR LIMIT
RESERVATIONS RECOMMENDED
Year-round Schedule

Depart Ocracoke	Depart Swan Quarter
6:30 AM	7 AM*
12:30 PM	9:30 AM
4 PM*	4 PM

*Additional departures Memorial Day through Labor Day.

Fares are the same as those for the Cedar Island - Ocracoke Toll Ferry. For departures from Ocracoke, call 928-3841; from Swan Quarter, call 926-1111.

Ocracoke - Hatteras Inlet Free Ferry

40 MINUTE CROSSING - 30 CAR LIMIT
NO RESERVATIONS ACCEPTED

Depart Ocracoke	Depart Hatteras
Summer Schedule, May 1 - Oct. 31	
5 AM	5 AM
6 AM	6 AM
7 AM	7 AM
Every 30 minutes:	Every 30 minutes:
7:30 AM-6:30 PM	8:30 AM-6:30 PM
7 PM	7 PM
8 PM	8 PM
9 PM	9 PM
10 PM	10 PM
Midnight	11 PM

Winter Schedule, Nov. 1 - April 30
Leaves Ocracoke every hour from 5 AM through
11 PM.
Leaves Hatteras every hour from 5 AM through
10 PM and at midnight.

Cherry Branch - Minnesott Beach Free Ferry

20 MINUTE CROSSING - 30 CAR LIMIT
NO RESERVATIONS ACCEPTED
Year-round Schedule

Dep. Cherry Branch	Dep. Minnesott Beach
Every 20 minutes:	Every 20 minutes:
5:45 AM-7:45 AM	5:45 AM -7:45 AM
Every 30 minutes:	Every 30 minutes:
7:45 AM-12:15 PM	7:45 AM-12:15 PM
Every 30 minutes:	Every 30 minutes:
1:15 PM-3:45 PM	1:15 PM-3:45 PM
Every 20 minutes:	Every 20 minutes:
4:15 PM-6:15 PM	4:15 PM-6:15 PM
Every hour:	Every hour:
6:45 PM-12:45 AM	6:15 PM-1:15 AM

Hammocks Beach State Park Ferry

25-MINUTE CROSSING - NO VEHICLES
NO RESERVATIONS ACCEPTED
Operates seasonally
Memorial Day - Labor Day
Monday - Tuesday
Every hour on the half-hour from 9:30 AM -
5:30 PM
Wednesday - Sunday
Every half-hour from 9:30 AM - 5:30 PM
May and September
Wednesday - Sunday
Every hour on the half-hour from 9:30 AM -
4:30 PM
April and October
Friday - Sunday
Every hour on the half-hour from 9:30 AM -
4:30 PM

Fares (Round trip)
Adult	$2
Children ages 4-12	$1
Younger than 4	Free

Call Hammocks Beach, 326-4881, to
verify times.

Private Ferries

A number of privately owned vessels
also stand ready to carry passengers to just
about any destination along the Crystal
Coast. Of course, you always have the options of hiring a luxurious sailboat complete with crew and catered meals or renting a small motorboat to do your own navigating. Whatever your choice, there is a lot
to explore.

Along with state-owned ferries and privately owned vessels, the National Park
Service (NPS) authorizes specified concessionaires to operate under NPS guidelines and take passengers and/or vehicles
to the uninhabited Cape Lookout National Seashore (see our Attractions chapter). The seashore is a 56-mile stretch of
barrier islands made up of North Core
Banks, home of Portsmouth Village;
South Core Banks, home of Cape Lookout Lighthouse; and Shackleford Banks,
home to wild ponies.

The NPS allows two privately owned
ferries to carry passengers and vehicles to
North and South Core Banks and Portsmouth Village. These small ferries operate
out of Down East communities and don't
have all the extras you will find on the
state ferries. They do have medium-size,
seaworthy vessels that are equipped to

Photo: NC Travel & Tourism

Even commuting to work is a great escape on a ferry.

carry one or two vehicles, a few passengers and some equipment. They normally operate between April and November, although schedules and fees vary. Most concessionaires require reservations, so it is best to call ahead to see what schedule the ferry is operating on, to check current fares and to see if there is room aboard for you. Each concessionaire can provide information on cabins and camping (see the Camping chapter). Federal regulations prohibit pets on any of these ferries.

Alger Willis Fishing Camps Inc., operating out of the Down East community of Davis on U.S. Highway 70, 729-2791, carries passengers, vehicles and all-terrain vehicles (ATVs) to the northern end of South Core Banks. Fares are $13 round trip per adult and about $65 round trip for a standard-size vehicle. Cabins, delivered

supplies (ice, groceries, bait, etc.) and island transportation can be arranged at the office. For more information about the fishing camps, see our Accommodations Chapter.

Morris Marina, Kabin Kamps and Ferry Service Inc., operating out of the Down East community of Atlantic on Highway 70, 225-4261, transports passengers, vehicles and ATVs from the community of Atlantic to Portsmouth or to the south end of North Core Banks at Drum Inlet. Transportation costs vary according to the season but usually are $13 round trip per person and around $65 round trip for a vehicle. Owners Katie and Don Morris can also arrange island transportation as well as cabins and supplies (ice, groceries, etc.).

A few other passenger ferries are permitted by the NPS to transport island hoppers to Core Banks, Portsmouth Village and Shackleford Banks. Most of these can also be hired for service to other areas or just for a cruise around the harbor. Charter and rental boats are available for getting around the area's waterways (see the Fishing, Watersports and Beach Access chapter). The concessionaires with the NPS are listed below in alphabetical order. Keep in mind, however, that there are other privately run services.

per person, $6 for passengers younger than age 6 and $15 for overnight campers. Group rates are offered. Once at the lighthouse, visitors can take the quarter-mile boardwalk to the ocean or hitch a ride on the jitney at a cost of $3 to the beach, $8 to Cape Point. On a hot July day, the jitney is definitely worth the money. The ferry leaves from the Harkers Island Fishing Center on Harkers Island. Call for departure times and to make reservations.

BARRIER ISLAND TRANSPORTATION CO. INC.

P.O. Box 400   728-3908
Harkers Island   (800)423-8739

Barrier Island provides passenger ferry service to Shackleford Banks and the Cape Lookout Lighthouse area. No vehicles are accommodated. Fares are $12 round trip

OUTER BANKS FERRY SERVICE

328 Front St.
Beaufort   728-4129

The Outer Banks Ferry Service, owned and operated by Perry Barrow, offers transportation to Carrot Island, Shackleford Banks and Cape Lookout. The service runs on schedule and by res-

Photo: Scott Taylor

Bottlenose dolphins are frequently seen playing offshore beyond the breakers.

ervation year round. The ferry office, open from 9 AM to 5 PM, is in the Atlantic Coast Realty office on Front Street. Group rates are available.

SANDDOLLAR TRANSPORTATION

Harkers Island   *728-3533*

This ferry service provides transportation to Shackleford Banks and the Cape Lookout Lighthouse area by reservation. It departs from Barbour's Harbor Marina on Harkers Island. Round-trip fare per adult is $12; for children younger than 6, it's $6. Call reservations and departure times.

ISLAND FERRY SERVICE

300 Front St.
Beaufort   *728-6888*

In spring and summer, Capt. Ronnie Lewis leaves every 30 minutes between 9 AM and 5 PM for Shackleford Banks and Carrot Island. Island Ferry Service is at the end of Orange Street behind Harpoon Willie's Restaurant. During late fall and the winter months, service is on demand. Guided tours of Shackleford Banks are offered by reservation.

In Atlantic Beach, Indian Beach and Salter Path, there are a number of older homes that sometimes sell for less than what could be considered market value because of the age of the house or its lack of modern amenities.

Crystal Coast
Real Estate and Neighborhoods

If you are seriously considering purchasing property or relocating to North Carolina's Crystal Coast, this is the section for you. We, as Insiders, think you are making a wonderful decision. Welcome!

This chapter is designed to introduce you, first, to the neighborhoods that make up the expansive Crystal Coast and then to acquaint you with some of the area's real estate companies and builders. The lists are by no means complete but will familiarize you with the area and help you locate neighborhoods, businesses and services.

We begin this chapter looking at neighborhoods at the beach, which is actually the island of Bogue Banks including the townships of Atlantic Beach, Pine Knoll Shores, Indian Beach, Salter Path and Emerald Isle. From there we move to delightfully different historic Beaufort, then to the central town of Morehead City, westward to Swansboro and finally to the Down East reaches of the county.

Like everywhere else, homes on the Crystal Coast vary tremendously in price, and location is everything. Here, good locations are determined by proximity to water, historic districts or golf courses and upscale subdivisions. While you may find very comfortable living quarters in the $60,000 to $70,000 range, you can also spend hundreds of thousands for a large, plush home in an exclusive waterfront neighborhood with a slip for your boat. A great deal of

recent development has taken place away from the water, and a wide range of housing is available.

A note on zoning: If the property you are considering is not in an incorporated city or subdivision, ask your real estate agent or the county planning office what uses are permitted in that area. Large portions of Carteret County are unzoned and may permit certain uses you have not bargained for. Then again, some folks are looking for that kind of freedom. Ask questions so you'll know before you commit.

The agencies and businesses suggested throughout this section are listed alphabetically. These are not the only companies of their type; there are many other fine and reputable firms, but we simply couldn't list them all. This book is revised annually, and we welcome your input concerning additions or omissions in the next edition.

Like most beach resorts, the Crystal Coast has a large number of condominium developments. We've mentioned a few here; however, for a more complete list of what is available, check with a real estate agent. Also, for information on time-share and fractional ownership possibilities, check our Crystal Coast Vacation Rentals chapter.

There is no specific relocation service on the Crystal Coast; however, rest assured that most agents will move heaven and earth to ensure that your move is smooth.

After all, they are in the business of sharing with newcomers what we Insiders have already learned — this is a great place to be!

Neighborhoods

Bogue Banks — The Beaches

Many newcomers move to the Crystal Coast for one reason: to live at the beach. In Atlantic Beach, Indian Beach and Salter Path, there are a number of older homes, sometimes selling for less than what could be considered market value because of the age of the house or its lack of modern amenities. Newer homes, condominiums and townhouses have been built in recent years.

Emerald Isle and Pine Knoll Shores are the more recently established towns. Both have many new structures and home sites in a variety of price ranges; so, whatever you want, you can probably find it on the beach.

ATLANTIC BEACH

Atlantic Beach has a nostalgic air about it — a throwback to the 1950s when beach houses were built to be functional and rambling, when small cottages nudged right up next to ponderous two-story clapboards on narrow streets running parallel to the ocean. Today, some see Atlantic Beach as a bit ramshackle and hodgepodge while others are inspired to reminisce about red convertibles, Sandra Dee and beach blankets. But changes are afoot. The Circle, where most beach entertainment businesses used to centered, is being renovated and new businesses are moving in.

Today, private homes and vacation rentals are mixed throughout the small oceanfront town and, over the years, building has extended several blocks back from

the water to N.C. Highway 58, or Salter Path Road. Most all dwellings in Atlantic Beach are within walking distance of the ocean, and the majority of new homes are concentrated on the eastern end of the island, along Fort Macon Road. Here, too, are a number of condominium and townhouse developments, such as **Seaspray**, **A Place At the Beach**, **Southwinds**, **Sands Villa Resort**, **Island Quay** and others. **Angler's Cover** is one of Atlantic Beach's newest waterfront condo developments. On the causeway, this development offers five three-story buildings with 18 units starting at $164,000.

The residential area known as **Hoop Hole Creek** on Bogue Sound, a few miles from the downtown center, is a beautifully forested area with a few remaining lots. Condos and townhouses such as **Dunescape Villas**, **Island Beach and Racquet Club**, **Coral Bay East and West** and others are also in this section. **Ocean Ridge II** is a new small oceanfront community with 18 lots. The lots offer great views of the ocean and Bogue Sound, are covered by restrictive covenants and begin at $39,000.

PINE KNOLL SHORES

The developers of Pine Knoll Shores deserve credit for their farsightedness. Built in a maritime forest, the development has done an admirable job of minimally impacting the environment. Drive through and you will see what we mean — there are trees everywhere. Restrictive covenants require a complete survey of all trees larger than 3 inches on each lot. Before you can get a permit to build, you have to prove you will save as many trees as possible and disturb the land as little as possible. The process can be tedious, but the result is worth it, as most all residents will agree.

The area is nearly 75 percent developed,

and both large and small homes come on the market fairly regularly. Lot prices start at $35,000, and homes range from the low $100,000s to the mid $200,000s, depending on the proximity to canals, open water or the area's 18-hole golf course. Within the central portion of the town, a good many homes are built on canals, with the option of private docks.

Pine Knoll Townes, **Bogue Shores Club** and **Beachwalk at Pine Knoll Shores** are townhouse and condominium developments between MP 6 and 7 on Highway 58. All are on the ocean and in a lovely maritime forest setting. Design features include courtyards, sun porches, gourmet kitchens, private balconies and other upscale luxuries. Prices range from $80,000 to as much as $300,000 for plush living accommodations.

Beacon's Reach, MP 8½ through 9¼, is a large development in a maritime forest on land once owned by the Roosevelt family. It includes both multifamily and single-family dwellings. Each village is carefully planned, and residents have access to lighted tennis courts, swimming pools, parks on the ocean and the sound, as well as a marina. Villages include **Ocean Grove**, with three- and four-bedroom units; **Westport**, with one- two- and three-bedroom units and both soundfront and freshwater lagoon-front units; the **Breakers**, with oceanfront condominiums; **Fiddlers' Walk** with soundside condominium units; and **Maritime West**, with oceanfront units.

Condominiums and single-family homes range from $99,000 to $600,000 or more on the ocean. Soundside and oceanside lots range from $35,000 to just more than $200,000.

SALTER PATH/INDIAN BEACH

Many of the longtime residents in these two small communities are descended from fishermen, and many still make their living from the sea. Some homes are low, rambling structures on the soundside, nestled under windswept live oaks bent from prevailing winds. If you are lucky enough to find one of these cottages on the market, you will have a piece of paradise.

The **Summerwinds** condominium complex is a large, oceanfront development offering spacious living quarters with prices starting at just more than $100,000. Recreational facilities include an indoor, heated swimming pool, a whirlpool, saunas, exercise rooms, a spa and racquetball courts. Outside are three oceanfront pools with sundecks and a boardwalk. Units at the oceanfront **Windward Dunes** in Indian Beach range between $90,000 and $149,500 with pools, saunas and tennis courts.

EMERALD ISLE

The western end of the Emerald Isle is family-oriented, and not until a few years ago did a substantial number of residents become "year rounders." Originally, the only access to the island was by boat and, later, ferry. It wasn't until the 1970s that the B. Cameron Langston high-rise bridge opened the area to tourists and newcomers. Emerald Isle is the fastest growing area of the county. Areas along Coast Guard Road, off N.C. Highway 58, have seen an astounding amount of development in recent years. Some of the nicer subdivisions are here.

You'll find many of the town's recently built residences quite impressive. Homes and cottages come in all styles, but most are multi-storied, with wide porches and decks, so residents can take advantage of the beach view and sea breezes. Although some developers have bulldozed dunes and cleared much of the natural vegetation, others have left stands of maritime forest. There are a number of condominium and townhouse developments as well, such as **Pebble Beach**, **Queens Court**, **Sound of the Sea** and others in the price range between $59,900 and $139,000.

Lands End is an exclusive planned residential community on Coast Guard Road off Highway 58 near the Point in Emerald Isle. Ownership includes use of a spacious clubhouse, a pool, four lighted tennis courts, stocked freshwater lakes and a lighted boardwalk to the beach. All roads are private, and utilities are underground. Homes range from $149,000 to $2.1 million. Lots start around $45,000.

Emerald Plantation is a relatively new soundside subdivision that extends from Highway 58 to Bogue Sound. A mixed-use development with single-family homes, townhouses and patio homes, amenities include a clubhouse, a pool, a boat ramp, tennis courts and a security gate. Lot prices range from $18,000 to $135,000, and homes range from $110,000 to $300,000. The **Wyndtree** subdivision is a large tract near **Emerald Isle Point** that has restrictive covenants as to sizes of houses but offers a wide diversity of sites from oceanfront to ocean view. Lot prices range from $35,000 to about $49,000, and single-family homes from $110,000 to $400,000.

The Point on Coast Guard Road off Highway 58 at the westward tip of the island is one of the most established areas and has a wonderfully wide beach. Homes range from $162,500 for new constructions to $400,000.

Deerhorn Dunes, **Sea Dunes** and **Ocean Oaks** are three well-planned subdivisions that are almost indistinguishable from one another. On Coast Guard

We Represent Buyers and Sellers

Buyer's Agency

Buyer's Agent vs. Sales Agent

Traditionally, all agents involved in a real estate transaction legally represent the Seller (both the "Listing Agent" and the "Selling Agent.") When a Buyer's Agent is involved, the person buying the property is represented by the "Selling Agent," who is now known as the "Buyer's Agent."

What is a Buyer's Agent?

A Buyer's Agent is a Real Estate Agent who legally represents a Buyer in a real estate transaction and acts solely on belhalf of the Buyer.

Benefits of Buyer's Agency

A Buyer's Agent can legally:
- Advise and counsel a Buyer with unrestricted assistance,
- Prepare an estimate of value and future salability to insure the true value of the property.
- Investigate any situation that might jeopardize the best interests of the Buyer.
- Negotiate with the Selling Agent and Seller to obtain the lowest price.
- Show all properties on the market - regardless of whether they are listed with Multiple Listing Service.

Sun-Surf Realty
7701 Emerald Drive
Emerald Isle, NC 28594
800-849-2958   919-354-2958

Photo: Francis A Eubanks

There are lots of housing possibilities on the Crystal Coast.

Road off Highway 58, all are relatively new and were built around the same time. They are made up primarily of single-family homes, nicely landscaped on spacious lots. Lot prices begin at $35,000, with ocean view lots less than $70,000. Single-family homes range between $110,000 and $200,000, with oceanfront homes climbing to as much as $400,000.

Windfall is one of the newer subdivisions in Emerald Isle off Highway 58. It is a small development made up of about 24 lots that offer second, third and fourth row locations away from the ocean. Lot prices range from $70,000 to $96,000, with homes from $175,000 to $250,000.

Cape Emerald off Highway 58 on the soundside of Coast Guard Road is a subdivision of primarily permanent residents.

Amenities include a clubhouse, a heated pool and a spa and two tennis courts. It also has a security entrance and a community sewage system. Lots range from $20,000 to $95,000, and homes from $100,000 to $350,000. **Emerald Landing, Royall Oaks, Dolphin Ridge** and **Pointe Bogue** are four new, beautifully landscaped developments that offer peace and privacy in a verdant, spacious wooded setting. Off Coast Guard Road, lots vary from 75-feet wide to 30-feet wide on ocean- and road-fronts. Interior lots also vary in size due to efforts to preserve the area's wetlands. Lot prices begin at $50,000. Emerald Landing, Pointe Bogue and Royall Oaks have soundfront sites, and Dolphin Ridge has oceanfront building sites.

Beaufort

Beaufort's geographic design lends itself to small residential areas built around roads and water. Most new development is east of Beaufort along U.S. Highway 70 or north along N.C. Highway 101. This small port town is a haven for boaters and is a hub of activity during the summer months. Many of its historic homes have been restored as residences or bed and breakfast inns. Its lovely waterfront is a natural setting for music and socializing at outdoor cafes. The town's many shops, restaurants and tourist attractions give Front Street a festive air. Runners, strollers, exercise walkers and bike riders flow constantly along the main Front Street thoroughfare, and the Historic District can easily be covered on foot.

Beaufort's Historic District is the oldest residential area in town, covering about 15 square blocks. Homes here date back to the 1700s, and exterior characteristics are governed by guidelines of the Beaufort Historic Preservation Commission. Charged with assuring the integrity of the area, the commission reviews all proposals for exterior changes such as paint color, siding, window treatments, redesign and other building changes.

Businesses and signage in the historic district are also regulated. The historic commission was not formed until the 1980s, so you will see a few things that do not meet their standards. Property prices vary greatly in the historic district, depending on distance from the water, size and age of the house or building and its condition. You could be looking at a $425,000 waterfront home, a $90,000 residence a couple of blocks away from the water or a home at the far end of Ann Street for somewhere in the $70,000s.

Beaufort homes outside the historic district also carry a variety of price tags, again depending on the distance from the water as well as size, age and condition. Deerfield Shores, Gibb's Landing, Howland Rock, Jones Village, Tiffany Woods and Sea Gate are examples of subdivisions north of the downtown area. **Taylor's Creek** is the newest development on the east end of Taylor's Creek on the Beaufort waterfront, and Graystone Landing is the newest development along Highway 101.

Deerfield Shores, off Highway101, is in an attractive area on the Newport River and Intracoastal Waterway. Central to the development is the Carolina Marlin Club, a private boating (sail and motor) club complete with a 73-slip marina, a clubhouse and a swimming pool. Slip owners own the marina and clubhouse, which is also used by the Morehead-Beaufort Yacht Club. Interior lots in Deerfield range from $12,000 to $35,000; marina-front lots begin at about $40,000 and riverfront lots sell for about $75,000 to $100,000.

Gibb's Landing is a small subdivision on North River, reached by following Highway 70 east and turning right on Steep Point Road. Subdivision amenities include a community dock, pool and gazebo. Large lots range from $70,000 on the waterfront to $25,000 for lots across the street from the waterfront.

Howland Rock might be considered one of Beaufort's most prestigious neighborhoods. The entrance road is on Highway 70, just across from the Food Lion grocery store. This older subdivision offers residents such amenities as a boat ramp, a recreational area and a homeowners association. Most of the homes were custom built with attention to detail. Price tags start at about $135,000

and go up to $350,000. Some lots are still available, including a few on the waterfront that can go for as much as $175,000.

Jones Village is in the Beaufort town limits and is one of the area's oldest subdivisions. There are several entrances from Live Oak Street (Highway 70) to the subdivision, which wraps around behind Jones Village Shopping Center. The development is a quiet, well-settled area that seems to attract a pleasant mix of people. You'll find retirees living alongside young couples. Homes sell for $70,000 to $125,000.

Tiffany Woods is a new development about 4 miles east of Beaufort on Highway 70. Developers are offering large wooded lots for about $16,000 and up. Several cul-de-sacs extend from the lighted main road, giving the neighborhood a feeling of privacy. This is one of the nicer new neighborhoods in the area. **Sea Gate** is a waterside resort community 7 miles from Beaufort on Highway 101 at Core Creek. The development is on the Intracoastal Waterway with a deep-water marina, a ships' store, gas and diesel fuel, a clubhouse, a playground, a swimming pool, tennis courts, a boat ramp and a security entrance. Homes range from $60,000 to $250,000. Waterfront lots range from $27,000 to $45,000.

The **Taylor's Creek** development at the east end of Lennoxville Road is a pricey new development of only 10 gorgeous building sites at the east end of Taylor's Creek. Lots are offered from near $70,000 to $200,000 and include pool and dock use.

Graystone Landing is about 3 miles up Highway 101 from Beaufort. This new neighborhood offers about 60 building lots. A few waterfront lots are offered, although the majority are wooded interior lots in quiet surroundings. Lots range from about $20,000 to $120,000.

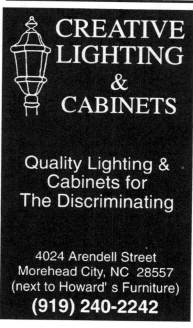

Morehead City

Morehead City is the area's largest city, so you'd expect it to have the most neighborhoods, and you're right. Most early communities began at the water's edge because that's where the work was. Today, people continue to live by the water, but not so much for the work as for the beauty of the views and the breeze.

The city's earliest inhabitants lived near what is now the N.C. State Port, bounded by Bogue Sound, the Newport River and Calico Creek. As the area filled up, homes were built farther west.

Although Morehead City's downtown has not seen as much restoration activity as Beaufort's, it is happening. Between Arendell Street and Bogue Sound, from about Ninth to 14th streets, is a neighborhood of small, wood-sided homes of ac-

tive fishermen known as the **Promise Land**. Some of these houses were moved to the mainland by sailing skiffs at the turn of the century when severe storms almost destroyed the once-flourishing fishing village of Diamond City on Shackleford Banks. Homes were dragged out of the water and rolled on logs to their new foundation. It is said that one spectator commented on the sight, "It looks like the Children of Israel coming to the Promise Land." The name stuck.

The town has expanded as its population has grown. Now, with improved access and all-weather bridges, more and more developments are popping up along the outskirts of town, many in the direction of **Crab Point** via N. 20th Street, Country Club Road and Barbour Road. Once an isolated farm community, Crab Point is one of Morehead City's oldest subdivisions and also the site of some of the newest developments, so prices vary greatly. Clustered within each development are houses of a broad range of prices, mainly because of the high prices demanded by houses on the water.

Joslyn Trace is a relatively new subdivision on N. 20th Street at the junction of Country Club Road. Homes here are both one and two story, and lots range from $14,500 to $16,500. Creek Pointe and Mandy Farms are two neighborhoods just off Country Club Road, with homes ranging from $75,500 to $115,000.

South Shores is a new, private waterfront community on the Newport River. It offers members of its homeowners association lighted streets, curbs and gutters, a swimming pool and tennis courts. Lots begin at about $20,000 and go up to $45,000.

Country Club Road is a main thoroughfare along the backside of Morehead City. West Carteret High School is at the western end, and the Morehead City Country Club is toward the eastern end. In between lies mostly long-settled neighborhoods, although a few new developments have gone up in recent years. In most areas the lovely old trees have been left in place, and some homes are suitable for retirees or as first homes. An equal number are huge and obviously expensive. Generally speaking, the closer you get to the Morehead City Country Club, the more expensive the real estate becomes. In the more exclusive areas, there are very few lots left, but homes are being resold here as in all areas of the Crystal Coast.

Country Club East is a newer development across from and fronting the golf course. Here, two- and three-storied homes are the norm. Prices vary, depending on the size and features. Established homes with amenities such as a fireplace and two-

car garage can sell for $134,500. A four-bedroom, two-story home with a partially finished attic can sell for up to $250,000.

River Heights lies to the east of the country club and is one of the older suburbs. Homes here are rarely on the market, and when they are, they are sold at premium prices.

Hedrick Estates on the west side of Country Club Road features nice one-and two-story homes, with well-landscaped yards. Lots are available, and established homes range from about $73,000 to $100,000. Adjacent to Hedrick Estates is **Westhaven Village**, made up of one- and two-story homes on large wooded lots. Homes here range from around $90,000 to $130,000.

West-Car Meadows off Country Club Boulevard is a well-established development, backed by Swinson Park and close to the new primary school, the high school and shopping areas. This is a good location for young families with children. **Northwoods** is a fairly new development off Country Club Road, with single-family dwellings on large tree-covered lots. A three-bedroom, two-bath home with a formal dining room and living room, screened-in porch, deck and garage can sell for between $100,000 and $160,000.

Bonham Heights, **Mansfield Park** and **Mitchell Village** are older, spacious and well-established neighborhoods along the sound off Highway 70. Homes vary from modest bungalows to two- and three-story residences. Most residents have lived in these areas for a number of years; however, homes do occasionally go on the market. Prices can vary from $85,000 several blocks away from the water to $350,000 for soundfront. Many waterfront homes have deep-water access at their back doors. It's worth a drive through these areas to see what is available.

IMAGINE . . .
LAND THAT FULFILLS
YOUR DREAMS.

Solitude was once the home to dreams, the place where spirits were

renewed and senses restored by bountiful Southern waters and clean,

gentle breezes. Today, rustic visionaries can find this same quiet beauty

on the shores of eastern North Carolina, just 45 minutes from the historic

towns of New Bern & Bath, with homesites beginning at $29,900.

Imagine . . . a new home, a new life.

Weyerhaeuser Real Estate Company, New Bern, NC
800-622-6297

The Bluffs is a condominium development at the end of Mansfield Parkway, overlooking Bogue Sound. Units are individually owned townhouses or condominiums, with a sound view from most units. A three-bedroom, two-bath condominium can sell for around $110,000; a four-bedroom, four-bath unit will sell for around $189,000.

Western Carteret County

As the county's population increases and annexation takes place, development in the western part of Carteret County continues, especially in response to the incoming personnel needs at Cherry Point. This area has some long-established neighborhoods, but many new ones are springing up along Highway 24 between Morehead City and Cape Carteret and along Highway 70 between Morehead City and Havelock.

Spooner's Creek and **Spooner's Creek East** are long-standing neighborhoods, built around the marina at the mouth of Spooner's Creek and along Bogue Sound. The area features large homes, many with their own private docks. Homes are within walking distance of Spooner's Creek Marina, which has rental dockage and enough deep water for large yachts. **Spooner's Creek Racquet Club** has lighted tennis courts. Homes here are affordable to those in the upper income brackets. **Spooner's Creek North** is a new development in the area and offers many lots with boat slips. Building lot prices range from $44,000 to $200,000, depending on water access.

Brandywine Bay is an exclusive planned subdivision, stretching from Bogue Sound to Highway 70. Begun in 1972, the project was built around the Earle Webb estate. The Webb Mansion, an impressive brick structure surrounded by lumbering live oaks high on a bluff overlooking Bogue Sound, is now a private home. The waterfront portion of Brandywine Bay consists of a noncommercial marina with a community boat launch ramp surrounded by residential building lots. Marina slips are individually owned. Three separate townhouse projects surround the harbor with space available for future construction. There are single-family residences and lots available on either side of the townhouses and harbor. Across Highway 24 is the main residential section of **Brandywine**, which surrounds a beautiful 18-hole championship golf course. While some homes here were built in the 1970s, there is usually a nice selection of resales of both houses and lots. A new section, **The Honors**, recently opened.

Gull Harbor, Soundview, Ho-Ho Village and **Barnesfield** are all established developments along Bogue Sound on Highway 24. While some homes are quite large and elaborate, others are moderate in size and style. Many have deep-water docks, and a few lots may still be available. Homes range from around $150,000 and up.

Somerset Plantation is one of the newest developments off N.C. 24 and features a swimming pool, tennis courts, a boat ramp, a residential day dock, boat slips and a secured entrance. Lot prices range from $33,000 to $145,900, depending on proximity to the water. Houses can range from $100,000 to $229,000, depending on size and water proximity.

In the Broad and Gales Creek areas are **Bluewater Banks, Fox Lair** and **Rollingwood Acres**. These are new subdivisions close to Broad Creek Middle School. Bluewater Banks is a soundfront development, and Rollingwood Acres is on Broad Creek. Home prices vary greatly, depending on location and water access. In Fox Lair, a nonwaterfront development, homes range from $90,000 to $140,000, whereas in Bluewater Banks prices range from $124,000 up.

Farther up Highway 24 are **Pearson Subdivision**, **Bogue Sound Yacht Club**, **Blue Heron Bay** and **Hickory Shores**. Again, some of these developments are longer settled than others. Homes vary from spacious and elaborate to small and practical. A few select lots remain for sale at Bogue Sound Yacht Club, beginning at about $40,000 and going up to $150,000. Blue Heron Bay is one of the newest developments, with lots ranging from $21,000 to $115,000 and homes from $100,000 to $350,000. Hickory Shores has interior lots, beginning at $17,500, and going up to $75,000 for waterfront.

Swansboro

Swansboro offers a variety of housing opportunities, including historic houses near the business district, mobile homes on the outskirts of town and charming new homes on unbelievably beautiful lots overlooking the water.

The **Swansboro Heights Extension** area is a 34-lot, fully built development with homes reselling in the $70,000 range. In the town itself, there are basically three types of homes. In the oldest part of town are the historic homes, some rehabilitated and restored and others in need of attention. Around the fringes of the business

district and extending several blocks in all directions are houses that were built about 50 years ago. They, like the older homes, are a mix of beautifully restored and maintained residences, with some that would be on the market as fixer-uppers. Closer to the city limits are homes built within the past 25 or 30 years. Most are still in good condition but not terribly distinctive in design.

In recent years, new developments have been opening, bringing a totally new look to Swansboro's housing picture. The **River Reach** development is perhaps the most dramatic change in Swansboro's real estate market and is almost fully settled. However, a few lots remain on the White Oak River and Stevens Creek, selling for around $60,000. Homes sell in the $150,000 to $200,000 range.

Plantation Estates is another waterfront subdivision on the White Oak River, with homes ranging from $125,000 to $150,000. **Hurst Harbour** is an exclusive new subdivision near the ferry landing at Hammocks Beach State Park. Prices begin in the $135,000 range, with interior lots starting around $55,000. **Oyster Bay** offers moderately priced homes and lots and is being settled by the area's young professionals. Prices average from $100,000 up to $150,000. **Walnut Landing** was designed for more economical residences, with costs averaging between $70,000 and $80,000.

Port West Townhouses are beside Swansboro Primary School and are made up of 13 buildings with four units each.

Most units are rentals; however, some are owner occupied. The townhouses feature one, two or three bedrooms and range from the mid $40,000s to mid $50,000s.

Down East

Traditionally, the Down East communities themselves have made up the majority of neighborhoods. They string along the highway and the waterfronts and revolve around the church, or the volunteer fire/rescue department. You should keep in mind that living Down East isn't for everyone. Newcomers must be ready to forfeit the conveniences of town living and be able to entertain themselves with the simple pleasures of day-to-day life. If you are ready to make those trade-offs, then you may have found your little piece of paradise.

Many of the county's traditional fishermen and boatbuilders live Down East, an area along Highway 70 that merges into Highway 12 and extends from Bettie to Cedar Island. As you cross the area's many bridges, it is not unusual to see clammers hip-deep in water with an inner tube in tow, harvesting the salty-tasting mollusks from the sound bottom. Boat sheds are more common than garages, and the whir of saws and smell of wood chips are sure signs of happy boatbuilders. Fishing and shrimp boats ply the waters year round, and egrets, herons, ospreys and other shorebirds live in the marshes and wetlands along the highway.

Like many people who hold on to land settled by their ancestors and look to Mother Nature for their livelihoods, the indigenous people who make up these communities are reserved and self-sufficient. They are fiercely independent and expect others to be the same. But in times of trouble or crisis, you will find none more kind or gracious than those living in the little fishing villages that make up the area known as Down East.

As more people move to Carteret County, its eastern sector has seen the development of a few subdivisions outside the fishing communities. Homes and acreage are also available from time to time. If you want to get away from it all, this is the place to do it.

None of the Down East area is zoned and therefore falls under county jurisdiction.

Harbor Point in Straits has two sections and was established several years ago. Home sites are on a secluded peninsula, and the development offers a park area and boat ramp. Interior lots sell for around $20,000, with waterfront lots at about $46,000. **Osprey Isle** in Smyrna has homes and lots on the water and paved streets. **Nassau Heights** is a new development in Williston, with lots ranging from $18,900 to $24,900. **Ward's Creek Plantation** and **Tranquility Estates** in Otway are both new developments. Ward's Creek offers waterfront, water view and water access lots, with prices starting at $12,500. Tranquility Estates is a waterfront and interior lot subdivision on Ward's Creek, with lots ranging from $13,500 to $62,000. Owner financing is available. **Whitehurst Landing** offers residential creekfront homesites in the Down East community of Straits. These large wooded lots are in peaceful surroundings and begin at $44,000.

Real Estate Companies

Like most coastal areas, the Crystal Coast has plenty of real estate companies and agents to serve you. There are many good real estate firms in the area, and here we have listed, in geographical and alphabetical order, some of those that are most active. Most all of those listed are members of the Multiple Listing Service (MLS) and can show you any listing in the area; however, many companies and agents specialize in a certain geographic area — usually the town or community where their office is located and the adjacent communities. It's always a good idea to ask agents what areas they specialize in and whether they will show you property that other companies have listed.

In the past, North Carolina law authorized real estate companies to work for sellers because agents are paid by the sellers. Today, a new procedure also allows companies to operate as a buyer's agency, meaning they can negotiate price and terms in the best interest of the buyer. This procedure can be advantageous to those interested in purchasing a home or property. Ask if your agent offers this service.

The Morehead City-Carteret County Board of Realtors, 247-2323, can answer questions you have about companies that operate in the area. Again, here is a list of a few of the area's companies. Check with the Board of Realtors or other Insiders for additional recommendations.

Atlantic Beach

AL WILLIAMS PROPERTIES

407 Morehead Ave.	726-8800
Atlantic Beach Causeway	(800) 849-1888

Offices for this real estate sales and development business are in the Causeway Shopping Center. Listings often include exclusive condominium properties and waterfront homes on the beach and in Morehead City as well as building lots and acreage. Al Williams' Realtors are available to show you any of them.

ALAN SHELOR REALTY

Crow's Nest Shopping Center	247-7700
Atlantic Beach Causeway	(800) 849-2767

This company offers listings in every area of the Crystal Coast. Six Realtors are on staff to assist clients in sales of residential, resort and commercial properties, acreage and building lots. The company also offers a selection of resort rentals (call 240-7368 or (800) 786-7368). Alan Shelor Realty has been in business for more than 20 years.

CANNON & GRUBER, REALTORS

509 Morehead Ave.	726-6600
Atlantic Beach Causeway	(800) 317-2866

Formed in 1995 and combining more than 20 years of experience in local real estate, Cannon & Gruber offers many enviable listings not often on the market as well as beach and soundfront condominiums. Contact them for a listing of currently listed properties.

CENTURY 21 COASTAL PROPERTIES

Atlantic Beach Causeway   726-4700
                                  (800) 637-1162

This full-service agency handles both sales and rentals with 20 agents on staff. It deals in properties throughout the county, including the western sector and Down East. Properties include condominiums, single-family homes, acreage, exclusive building lots and commercial sites. Other services include a building department that offers home design and construction services, and Auction Marketing Inc., which handles property auctions.

COLDWELL BANKER
SPECTRUM PROPERTIES

515 Morehead Avenue   247-5848
                                  (800) 334-6390

The Coldwell Banker firm is a full-service agency in Atlantic Beach with offices in Emerald Isle, 354-3070, (see Emerald Isle section) and Greenville, 756-3000. The two offices each offer about 24 agents who specialize in properties throughout the county. It handles condominiums, homes, home sites and commercial property as well as long-term and seasonal rentals, 247-1100, and professional property management services.

GULL ISLE REALTY

611 Morehead Ave.,   726-0427
Atlantic Beach Cswy.   (800) 682-6863

In business for more than 20 years, Gull Isle Realty has earned a reputation of providing professional and individual attention to each client. This agency handles the sales of condominiums, homes, building lots and investment properties on Bogue Banks and the mainland. Gull Isle Realty also offers a number of resort rentals, 726-7679. The firm has a state-licensed appraiser. Call owner-broker David Waller for any real estate need.

OMNI REAL ESTATE

513 Morehead Ave.   247-3101
Atlantic Beach Causeway   (800) 334-2727

Omni, a Tetterton Management Group Company, specializes in condominiums and homes for sale on the beach and in Morehead City including the new nine-unit condominium development on the Atlantic Beach Causeway, Marlin Harbor. The full-service company also offers property listings county-wide and manages rentals for investment buyers. A vacation guide is published by Omni each year showing vacation rental properties. Its onsite rental office can lead you to the vacation location that fits your needs.

NATIONAL
SOUND N' SEA REAL ESTATE

205 Morehead Ave.   247-7355
Atlantic Beach Causeway   (800) 682-7368

Owned and managed by Demus and Ellen Thompson, Sound N' Sea is a full-service company, specializing in the sale

Insiders' Tips

Those enormous brown piles at the N.C. State Port at the base of the Morehead City-Beaufort high-rise bridge are wood chips ready to be exported to Japan to be used in the production of fine quality paper.

of homes, condos and commercial properties both on the island and mainland as well as vacation rentals, 247-RENT. The company is the oldest continuously owned and operated full-service real estate firm in the Atlantic Beach-Pine Knoll Shores area.

REALTY WORLD - JOHNSON REALTY

407 Morehead Ave.   247-0077
Atlantic Beach Cswy.   (800) 849-4801

Realty World - Johnson Realty's team concept combines years of real estate experience in Carteret and surrounding counties. The group focuses on selling and marketing existing homes — those on the oceanfront or on the mainland. Realty World is noted for its professional property management group, which provides service-oriented care for properties. For information about seasonal rentals offered by Realty World - Johnson Realty, see the Vacation Rentals chapter of this book.

Pine Knoll Shores

SUNNY SHORES

N.C. Hwy. 58 (Salter Path Rd.)   247-7347
Pine Knoll Shores   (800) 624-8978

Sunny Shores is a full-service company operated by a couple of veteran Pine Knoll Shores Realtors. The company offers sales, vacation rentals, property management and maintenance. Robert Lewis handles sales and partner Carol Piner handles rentals and property management. Sunny Shores' specialty is meeting unique rental requirements. For rental information, call 247-2665 or (800) 626-3113.

Emerald Isle

BLUEWATER ASSOCIATES
BETTER HOMES AND GARDENS

200 Mangrove Dr.   354-2128
                                      (800) 326-3826

Across from the K&V Plaza, this full-service firm offers condominium and home sales on the beach and mainland with emphasis on sales of new constructions, building lots and resales in Emerald Isle and Cape Carteret. The company has its own construction arm that builds or finishes to client specifications. Its rental department, 354-2525, handles vacation and long-term rentals. Agents and other staff serve clients in Emerald Isle.

CENTURY 21
COASTLAND REALTY INC.

7603 Emerald Dr.   354-2131
                                      (800) 822-2121

The first realty franchise on the beach, this full-service company has been in business since 1980. It offers many completed homes, both new and previously owned, in some of Emerald Isle's most exclusive locations. It also sells building lots, constructions in progress and acreage on Bogue Banks and the mainland. Condominium resales and pre-construction sales are also their specialty. The staff includes 10 sales agents and a rental department handling vacation and long-term rentals.

The shingle-covered dome on the north side of the Morehead City-Beaufort high-rise bridge keeps phosphates from the Texasgulf mining industry in Aurora out of the air as the chemical is processed for export from the N.C. State Port.

Insiders' Tips

COLDWELL BANKER
SPECTRUM PROPERTIES
7413 Emerald Dr.   354-3070
(800)682-3423

The Coldwell Banker firm is a full-service agency in Emerald Isle with offices in Atlantic Beach, 247-5845, and Greenville, 756-3000. The Emerald Isle office provides an extensive inventory of homes, condominiums and building lots in Emerald Isle and Cape Carteret with knowledgeable agents to match new homeowners with affordable property in the right locations. The Emerald Isle office also has a good reputation for its vacation and annual rental department, 354-3040, (800) 367-3381, and property management details.

EMERALD ISLE REALTY
7501 Emerald Dr.   354-4060
(800) 849-3315

This agency has been a tradition on the coast for 31 years and hosts thousands of vacationing families each year. This family-owned property management, rental and sales firm is now in its new headquarters offering nearly 600 vacation rental properties, an online rental reservations system and in-house maintenance and housekeeping departments. Rentals can be arranged by calling 354-3315. The company's sales team is equally strong, handling resales of homes and condominiums, commercial properties and building sites.

EMERALD PROPERTIES
9100 Emerald Dr.   354-4488
(800) 398-8612

This agency is a small real estate firm that specializes in property sales in Cape Carteret and Emerald Isle. It offers residential and commercial properties, building lots and condominium resales. It also coordinates sales of remaining building lots in the Windfall and Wyndtree developments and the spectacular Tanglewood Ridge 1-acre oceanfront lots.

ERA CARTERET PROPERTIES
7801 Emerald Dr.   354-3289
(800) 448-2951

This full-service agency handles all types of properties both on the island and the mainland and has been in business since 1969. It is also very prominent in the property management field, with some 100 available rentals, 354-3005. Five agents conduct commercial and residential sales of new and established homes and offer business opportunities as well as lots and acreage. In addition, the firm offers other services that can be advantageous to clients, and it can help with custom construction and design.

KETTERER REALTY
N.C. Hwy. 58 at Mangrove Dr.   354-2704
(800) 849-2704

This agency has a solid reputation earned through 22 years of service to home buyers on the Crystal Coast. Company agents offer both new and resale homes in Emerald Isle and the western sector of the county as well as commercial sites, building lots and acreage. As exclusive agents for Dolphin Ridge, Royall Oaks, Emerald Landing and Pointe Bogue developments, Ketterer Realty's services extend to guidance in developing house plans and construction details.

LOOK REALTY
9101 Coast Guard Rd.   354-4444
(800) 849-0055

A full-service real estate operation with sales agents and a rental and property management staff, LOOK Realty offers a variety of properties in the Emerald Isle/Cape Carteret area including resales, building lots, waterfront acreage and com-

mercial properties. It handles sales for Crystal Shores in Cedar Point and, if you are in the market for new construction, the company offers on-site contractors and home design services.

PRUDENTIAL SUN-SURF REALTY

7701 Emerald Dr.   *354-2958*
                                    (800) 849-2958

This company is a full-service agency that receives very high marks from other Realtors in the area. It has its own construction firm, Staebler Homes Inc., for custom-built homes and offers a variety of homes, vacation homes, building lots and condominiums on the island. It also has a very successful, professionally operated vacation rental program, 354-2658, (800) 553-7873. Like other real estate firms, it represents sellers. Unlike other firms, it is also a buyer's agency, meaning it negotiates price and terms in the best interest of the buyer. A free brochure explaining the firm's buyer's agency policy is available.

WATSON-MATTHEWS REAL ESTATE

9102 Coast Guard Rd.   *354-2872*
                                    (800) 654-6112

Originally Rouse-Watson Realty, this business has been active since 1979 with sales of condominiums, single-family dwellings and duplexes as well as investment and commercial property. Watson-Matthews offers building sites in Lands End and other developments and pre-construction packages. The firm's agents will work with you in finding the perfect buy, whether it is a second home or a primary residence.

Beaufort

ATLANTIC COAST
REAL ESTATE SERVICES

328 Front St.   *728-6793*
                                    (800) 645-9379

On the Beaufort waterfront across the street from the N.C. Maritime Museum, this full-service company offers commercial and residential properties, rentals, investments and property management.

BEAUFORT REALTY COMPANY

325 Front St.   *728-5462*
                                    (800) 548-2961

This company specializes in residential and commercial property in the Beaufort historic district and handles some of the most handsome historic properties offered for sale. The company also offers sales of properties in Beaufort subdivisions, Down East, in Morehead City and on the beach. The company does appraisals and also offers annual and vacation rentals.

CENTURY 21 DOWN EAST REALTY

415 Front St.   *728-5274*
                                    (800) 849-5795

As the name implies, Century 21 Down East Realty specializes in property in Beaufort and Down East. It also handles property in Morehead City and is affiliated with the Morehead City Century 21 office. The firm handles residential and commercial sales, as well as appraisals. It is Beaufort's oldest full-service real estate company, and its agents are knowledgeable and helpful.

HOMEPORT REAL ESTATE

400 Front St.   *728-7900*
                                    (800) 948-5859

Realtors and brokers Pat Kindell and Candy Rogers have lived in the area and operated businesses for more than 21 years. Upstairs in the Somerset Square building just off the Beaufort boardwalk, the company specializes in historic and resort properties as well as retirements and relocations along the Crystal Coast. Agents also work as buyers' brokers for clients. The company handles commercial and residential properties on the beach, mainland and Down

East and also offers short- and long-term rental services.

Morehead City

BROWN AND SWAIN REAL ESTATE
4659 Arendell St.   247-0055

From Beaufort to Brandywine Bay, from points Down East to Cherry Point, owner-broker Betty Brown Swain always has interesting listings. She offers a range to interest any client from mobile home lots to Beaufort waterfront homes and always has a good buy in a fixer-upper. She handles sales of building lots in many area subdivisions as well as commercial property and acreage.

CENTURY 21 NEWSOM-BALL REALTY
4644 Arendell St.   240-2100
                                (800) 849-5794

Ben Ball and Alan Leary own both the Morehead City business and the Century 21 office in Beaufort. Both Realtor/brokers and the 14 sales associates working with them in the Morehead City office have well-rounded knowledge of the area. The company offers complete services, emphasizing the sale of homes, businesses and acreage. Century 21 also provides appraisals, property management services and rentals.

CHALK & GIBBS REALTY
1006 Arendell St.   726-3167

This Better Homes and Gardens agency has been in operation since 1925. It handles sales of single-family dwellings, townhouses and condos as well as building lots and acreage. The company also offers property management and annual rental services for Morehead City and Beaufort as well as certified appraisals. In addition to real estate, Chalk & Gibbs has a complete insurance branch.

CHOICE SEACOAST PROPERTIES
1512 Arendell St.   247-6683
                                  (800) 444-6454

This real estate firm is owned and operated by Trish and Tom Dale who, along with four other agents working with them, represent a variety of properties and innovative services. "Mailmost" increases exposure of homes listed through weekly mailings to qualified buyers, and "Netmost" enables buyers and sellers to save money through lower commissions. Choice lists residential and commercial properties, lots, acreage, condos and townhouses and offers property management services. For long-term rental information, call 808-2114.

GOLF & SHORE PROPERTIES
Brandywine Bay, U.S. Hwy. 70   240-5000
                                  (800) 523-4612

Golf & Shore Properties specializes in properties in Brandywine Bay, which is on Highway 70 in Morehead City. The company also represents properties throughout the county, and its experienced agents can help you select lots, single-family homes and townhomes.

HOME FINDERS
ROBINSON AND ASSOCIATES
304 N. 35th St.   240-7653

Alan and Sharon Robinson own and operate this family business, with the assistance of an additional agent. Alan Robinson has been in the real estate business since 1979, and his wife joined him in 1988. The company handles single-family homes from Morehead City to Newport plus lots and acreage. It also offers property management services and works with several builders in the area to offer building plans and construction.

PUTNAM REAL ESTATE COMPANY
3800 Arendell St.   726-2826

Putnam Realty is one of those companies that other real estate agencies recommend. It is a full-service agency that specializes in the sale of new and established homes and commercial properties throughout the county as well as building lots and constructions in progress in fast-growing Newport developments. Its agents also handle townhouses and mobile homes. The company offers full appraisal services, property management and long-term rentals.

RE/MAX MASTERS REALTY
4459 Arendell St.   247-3629
                                  (800) 849-1144

In Colony Square on Highway 70, this agency offers new homes and resales as well as townhouses, lots, acreage, condos and commercial property throughout the county. In addition, the firm assists clients in selecting and modifying house plans to meet their needs in Newport's recently developed Deer Park. The agency also offers commercial buildings and business opportunities as well as buyer's agent services.

SAUNDERS REAL ESTATE COMPANY
28th and Arendell sts.   247-7444

In the center of Morehead City, this company offers a great variety of properties from homes in some of the area's most exclusive residential districts to fixer-uppers with investment potential. The company offers lots and acreage and specializes in commercial business opportunities. The firm employs five agents and can provide appraisals and property management services.

Photo: Scott Taylor

Castles in the sand are easy to find — and build — on the Crystal Coast.

Western Carteret and Swansboro

BALLARD REALTY

N.C. Hwy. 24 at Nine Foot Rd.   240-2121
Broad Creek   (800) COAST-NC

Broker/owner Brenda Ballard specializes in the western section of the county and especially in the subdivisions off N.C. 24 such as Fox Lair, Bluewater Banks, Soundview Park, Rollingwood Acres, Silver Creek and others. Ballard Realty also markets properties in Newport and Swansboro and manages long-term rental properties.

SHACKLEFORD REALTY

415 W.B. McLean Dr.   393-2111
  Cape Carteret   (800) 752-3543

With more than 20 years of experience, Shackleford Realty is well-known in the county for its market expertise in and around Cape Carteret, Swansboro, Cedar Point and Emerald Isle, as well as in subdivisions along Highway 24. The agency handles many of the sales in the Star Hill and Hunting Bay housing divisions and also offers town houses, lots and acreage. Ethel Shackleford operates the business, and the agency is recommended by other Realtors around the county.

CENTURY 21 WATERWAY REALTY

N.C. Hwy. 24, Swansboro   (910) 326-4152

This agency, one of the oldest in Swansboro, sells building lots, new homes and resales in the Swansboro/Cape Carteret/Emerald Isle area. Most of the company's agents are longtime residents of the area and can give you the real scoop about where the best buys are and about the best financing. The company also handles commercial properties, lots and acreage along the White Oak River and the Intracoastal Waterway and long-term rentals.

Down East

Most real estate agencies in Beaufort and Morehead City handle property east of Beaufort, and there are only a few real estate companies with offices actually in the Down East area. We suggest you contact your favorite Realtor if you are interested in property in the eastern sector of the county. Chances are he or she will be able to help you.

CORE SOUND REALTY

2622 U.S. Hwy. 70 E.   728-1602
                   (800) 211-8202

Core Sound Realty handles all types of real estate — residential, commercial, acreage and lots — all over the county. They specialize in waterfront properties and act as a buyer's broker. With an office just outside Beaufort, Barbara Berrini can be reached by phone, through the Internet at http://www.jtr.com/CSR/, or by e-mail at bberrini@coastalnet.com.

EASTERN GATEWAY REALTY

U.S. Hwy. 70, Bettie   728-7790
                   (800) 205-5765

Eastern Gateway office in Bettie

handles properties all over the county and specializes in properties Down East. The company offers an enviable number of waterfront listings, lots and acreage. The firm's agents are all experienced and knowledgeable in Down East property, and best of all, they're right there.

Builders

To find a builder in the Crystal Coast area, contact the **Carteret County Home Builders Association**, 223-5527. This organization is a membership group of builders that includes real estate companies, contractors and banks as associate members.

Building Supplies

There are a number of area businesses that provide building supplies. Here is a very brief list of those carrying the most complete lines of materials.

Community Lumber and Supply, Highway 24 W., Swansboro, (910) 326-5051

Guy C. Lee Building Materials, Highway 70 W., Morehead City, 726-0114

Huntley's Building Supply, Junction of Highway 70 E. and Highway 101, Beaufort, 728-3111

Lowe's, Highway 70 W. at Highway 24, Morehead City, 247-2223

Morehead Builders Supply, 2514 Bridges Street, Morehead City, 726-6877

Safrit's Building Supply, 1308 Mulberry Street, Beaufort, 728-3843

Wickes Lumber, Highway 70 W., Morehead City, 726-6801

East and West Carteret High Schools put on wonderful theater productions throughout the year. Don't miss them.

Crystal Coast
Schools and Child Care

Educational opportunities in Carteret County include public and private schools. This section is designed to give you information about schools and child-care facilities on the Crystal Coast. The Higher Education and Research chapter in this book contains information about the local community colleges and area research facilities.

About 8,200 students attend prekindergarten through 12th grade in the county's 14 public schools. Each school is accredited by both the N.C. Department of Public Instruction and the Southern Association of Colleges and Schools. The local school system employs about 920 people. Carteret County public schools are governed by an elected five-member board of education. Members serve four-year terms and are chosen in county-wide, nonpartisan elections. School board members meet in open session each month.

Elementary school students follow a basic state curriculum that features reading/language arts, math, science, social studies, health, physical education, music and art. The middle school concept is used in the three public middle schools and to varying degrees in grades 6 through 8 at other schools. This approach groups teams of students and educators to work together to create consistency for each group.

Technology is vital to instruction and the amount of computer equipment each school has for its students to use continues to increase. A $29 million school bond referendum passed by voters in November 1994 provided more than $6.2 million for technology in the schools, allowing for an increase in computer equipment and software for student use and the networking of all county schools. The remaining bond funds were for construction and renovation projects.

The county's two high schools and three middle schools offer a comprehensive management program. This program emphasizes high expectations in the areas of discipline and class attendance. Extended-day classes are part of this program. Students who need remediation are required to attend the after-school classes, and other students voluntarily attend for enrichment opportunities.

Each high school offers a handbook listing specific course offerings. Vocational education is offered in several areas: agriculture, home economics, distributive education, health occupations, business, occupational exploration and introduction to trade and industry.

Carteret County offers a voluntary year-round school for those living in the Newport district who choose to attend. The county's alternative high school, grades 8 through 12, offers innovative teaching methods for students having difficulty with traditional methods.

Student services include guidance counselors, psychologists, social workers and nurses. Bus transportation is provided to and from school for students who live at least 1.5 miles from the school. Lunch is served at each school, and breakfast is served at several schools. Free or reduced-rate meals are available to those who qualify.

New students should register at the appropriate school prior to the fall school opening, if possible. Students entering kindergarten and 1st grade must have immunization and physical examination records.

Each school has an advisory council that meets monthly to discuss issues. The councils report to the Board of Education. Most schools have a Parent-Teacher Organization (PTO) as well as booster organizations.

If you have questions about the school system, contact the Carteret County Schools Central Office (Board of Education), P.O. Box 600, Beaufort 28516, 728-4583. Information booklets are available.

Schools

Public Schools

BEAUFORT

Two schools are within the Town of Beaufort, and one school is on the outskirts. **Beaufort Elementary School**, 801 Mulberry Street, 728-3316, serves about 560 students in prekindergarten through the 5th grade. Once students have completed 5th grade, they attend **Beaufort Middle School**, 100 Carraway Street, 728-4520. The middle school has an enrollment of about 370 students in the 6th, 7th and 8th grades. Once students have completed 8th grade, they attend **East Carteret High School**, on Highway 70 E. just outside of town, 728-3514. About 800 students in

grades 9 through 12 attend East Carteret. The school offers students 20 clubs/organizations and 16 areas of athletic competition, and the band is well-known for outstanding performances. Students who complete 8th grade at Atlantic, Smyrna, Beaufort Middle or Harkers Island schools attend East Carteret High School.

MOREHEAD CITY

In the Morehead City area, children in the public school system follow a path from primary to elementary to middle to high school. Which school children attend depends on these basic rules: Children living in the town limits of Morehead City or down Bogue Banks as far as Indian Beach attend a Morehead City school; children living at the west end of the county or Bogue Banks start school at **White Oak Elementary School**, Cape Carteret, 393-8354, then advance to **Broad Creek Middle School**, Highway 24, 247-3135. From there students from the western end of the county go to West Carteret High School, along with students from Morehead City. Call the county School Board office, 728-4583, to find out which school district your home is in.

Several attendance zones in the western part of the county will change in 1998 and in 1999, when a new elementary school and a new high school are completed. Both will be off Highway 24, just west of the existing Broad Creek Middle School. The construction of both new schools was part of a $29 million school bond referendum county voters passed in November 1994.

Morehead City Primary School, 4409 Country Club Road, 247-2448, opened in 1994 and serves more than 800 students in prekindergarten through 3rd grade. **Morehead City Elementary School** at Camp Glenn, 3312 Arendell Street, 726-1131, serves about 460 students in 4th and 5th grade in a newly renovated building.

Morehead City Middle School, 400 Barbour Road, 726-1126, is the third school in the progression for students in the Morehead City area. It serves almost 700 students in 6th, 7th and 8th grades. Upon completion of 8th grade, students advance to **West Carteret High School**, 4700 Country Club Road, 726-1176. With an enrollment of about 1,600 students, West Carteret is the largest of the county's two high schools. A new addition houses 17 classrooms and four labs. Work ended in January on an expanded media center, four new computer labs, and new guidance and administrative offices. The school offers about 25 clubs/organizations and 20 areas of athletic competition, and the band and choral departments are award winners.

Cape Lookout High School, 1108 Bridges Street, 726-1601, is the county's new alternative school, serving students in grades 8 through 12. Class sizes are limited to ensure a lower student-teacher ratio.

SWANSBORO

The four schools in Swansboro fall under the jurisdiction of the Onslow County Board of Education, Jacksonville, 455-2211. **Swansboro Primary School**, 126 School Road, 326-4574, offers curriculum for students in prekindergarten through 2nd grade. The school is one block off Highway 24. **Swansboro Elementary School**, 119 Norris Road, 326-5350, includes 3rd, 4th and 5th grades and is just off Highway 24. **Swansboro Middle School**, 240 W. Corbett Avenue, 326-3601, is attended by students in grades 6, 7 and 8.

Swansboro High School, 201 Queen's Creek Road, 326-4300, serves about 640 students in grades 9 through 12. The school is just off Highway 24.

Voters in Onslow County approved a $40 million school bond in November 1994. This provides for new construction and major renovations throughout the county, and the Swansboro area is included on the list. A new elementary dining hall has been built at Swansboro Elementary and a new elementary school will be constructed just outside Swansboro.

DOWN EAST

There are three schools in the Down East area of Carteret County. Each of these schools is named for its community, and each serves students through the 8th grade. Upon completion of 8th grade, students from these three schools attend East Carteret High School.

Atlantic Elementary School, 550 School Drive, 225-3961, has an enrollment of about 180 students in grades prekindergarten through 8th. **Harkers Island Elementary School**, Island Road, 728-3755, serves about 185 students from kindergarten through 8th grade, and it is the smallest school in the county system. **Smyrna Elementary School**, Marshallberg Road, 729-2301, has an estimated 380 students attending prekindergarten through 8th grade.

WESTERN CARTERET COUNTY

Three schools are in the western part

Environmental educational programs for children are offered by the Core Sound Waterfowl Museum year round. Call 728-1500 to find out more about the programs offered.

Insiders' Tips

of the county. **White Oak Elementary School** on Highway 24 in Cape Carteret, 393-8354, offers curriculum to about 580 students in kindergarten through 5th grade. **Newport Elementary School**, 34 Chatham Street, 223-4201, has about 950 prekindergarten through 5th grade students. After completion of the 5th grade, students from White Oak and Newport attend **Broad Creek Middle School**, Highway 24, 247-3135. The middle school provides instruction to about 780 students in 6th, 7th and 8th grades. After completing 8th grade, students attend West Carteret High School.

Private Schools

Several private schools serve county students seeking an alternative to public education. Most offer instruction in four or five grade levels, with only two serving students from kindergarten through 12th grade. There is also a small group of home-school participants. For information about home schools, contact the Carteret County Schools Central Office, 728-4583.

Beaufort Christian Academy, Highway 70 E., Beaufort, 728-3165, is a ministry of Beaufort Free Will Baptist Church and enrolls students from kindergarten through 12th grade. This academy also offers before- and after-school care for public school students. **Grace Christian School**, 4723 Country Club Road, Morehead City, 726-1044, shares a facility with Grace Fundamental Baptist Church and serves 5 year

olds through 12th graders. Grace School and Church plan to move to Newport within the next year. **Gramercy Christian School**, Highway 70, Newport, 223-4384, provides instruction for students in kindergarten through 12th grade.

Carteret Academy, 1600 Fisher Street, Morehead City, 808-2398, is the county's newest private school. This private Christian school opened last August and serves students in grades 6 through 9. The **Tiller School**, 1950 Highway 70, Beaufort, 728-1995, is in its third year and serves students in kindergarten through 6th grade. The Tiller School is not church affiliated.

St. Egbert's Catholic School, 1705 Evans Street, Morehead City, 726-3418, is affiliated with St. Egbert's Roman Catholic Church and provides instruction to students in kindergarten through 5th grade. **White Oak Christian Academy**, Highway 24, near Cape Carteret, 393-6165, is affiliated with the White Oak Church of God and serves students from 3 years old through 12th grade.

Newport Development Center, Church Street, Newport, 223-4574, specializes in training for handicapped children and adults who need more specialized attention than regular classrooms can offer.

Child Care

Reliable sitters for children are available on the Crystal Coast. **Nancy's Nannies**, P.O. Box 3375, Morehead City, 726-6575, is used widely and offers responsible adult sitters for children, as well as

Insiders' Tips

The Beaufort Historical Association presents Harvest Days each fall, offering students from across the state a chance to step back in time. Demonstrations include cooking, spinning, bullet making and hunting.

the elderly, for a day, night, weekend or longer. A few day-care centers offer extended hours on weekends.

Fees for day-care services vary and are often based on the age of the child, the number of hours the child spends at the facility and the number of siblings attending the facility. Many facilities provide transportation to and from school if needed, and most offer summer programs. There are also a number of qualified, caring nannies who will provide care for your child in your home or theirs.

BEAUFORT

Beaufort has several child-care facilities. **Ann Street United Methodist Church**, 500 Ann Street, 728-5411, provides preschool care for three, four and five year olds. Day care and an after-school care program are also offered. **Beaufort Christian Academy**, Highway 70 E., 728-3165, offers day-care services during the week for children ages 2 through 5 and after-school care for older students. **Colony Day Care Center**, 103 Fairview Drive, 728-2223, offers care for children from 6 weeks to 12 years of age. Colony offers day care, preschool and before- and after-school care.

MOREHEAD CITY

Morehead City has several child-care facilities. **My School**, 105 Eaton Drive, 247-2276, serves youngsters from 6 weeks of age through elementary-school age with preschool and before- and after-school programs. **Colony Day Care Center**, 700 N. 35th Street, 247-4831, recently expanded and offers child care for kids from 1 to 5 years of age.

ABC Day Care, Mandy Plaza N. 35th Street, 240-2222, serves children from 6 weeks to 12 years old and offers before-and after-school care. **Miss Nancy's Early Learning Center**, 204 N. 18th Street, 247-

2006, serves children from 6 weeks to 12 years of age with preschool, day care and after-school care. **Kids Kampus**, 600 N. 35th Street, 247-1866, is designed for children from 5 to 12 years old in need of before- and after-school care.

SWANSBORO

Swansboro area residents can find services at several centers. These are all in the 910 area code. **Coastal Kiddie College**, 783 Corbett Avenue, 326-3386, serves children from 6 weeks to 12 years of age with day care and before- and after-school care. **Hug A Bear Day Care**, Mount Pleasant Road, 326-7002, cares for children from infancy to age 12. **Swansboro United Methodist Child Care and Preschool**, Highway 24, 326-3711, accepts children from 6 weeks to 12 years of age and offers preschool and after-school programs.

WESTERN CARTERET COUNTY

Western Carteret County residents will find the larger child-care facilities in the community of Newport. **Miss Pat's Learning Center and Child Care**, 100 Fort Benjamin Road, 223-3432, serves children from ages 3 to 12 with preschool and before-and-after-school programs. **Newport Child Care Center**, 51 Chatham Street, 223-3500, serves children from 6 weeks to school age with a preschool program, and offers before-and after-school programs. **Newport Kids Inc.**, 30 E. Chatham Street, 223-4303, offers before- and after-school care for school-age children as well as a summer program. **St. James Day Care and Preschool Center**, 1011 Orange Street, 223-3191, offers day care for children from 6 weeks through 2nd grade. Before- and after-school programs for older children are provided.

CARTERET COMMUNITY COLLEGE

3505 Arendell Street, Morehead City, NC 28557-2989
(919) 247-6000

"You supply the dream, we'll supply the education!"

We offer the following programs of study:

Administrative Office Technology
Basic Law Enforcement Training
Business Administration
College Transfer
Cosmetology
Criminal Justice
Electrical Installation & Maintenance
Interior Design
Marine Propulsion Systems
Medical Assisting
Medical Transcription
Microcomputer Systems Technology
Nursing Assistant
Paralegal Technology
Phlebotomy
Photography Technology
Practical Nursing
Radiologic Technology
Respiratory Care Technology
Teacher Associate
Therapeutic Recreation
Welding

"When the week ends, let education begin! "

We offer Saturday Classes and
Telecourses!

For more information call (919) 247-6000

An Equal Employment Opportunity Educational Institution Serving the Community Without Regard to Race,
Creed, Sex, National Origin, or Disability

Crystal Coast
Higher Education and Research

Two higher educational institutions are accessible to Crystal Coast students interested in pursuing additional education or residents seeking enrichment. The area is also home to many well-known and respected research laboratories.

Higher Education

Carteret Community College (CCC), 3505 Arendell Street, Morehead City, 247-6000, is part of North Carolina's 58-campus community college system. The college has programs for traditional college students and for trade students seeking to upgrade their skills. The college offers associate degrees in a number of programs as well as courses in adult basic education and high school completion. Through East Carolina University in nearby Greenville, the college has transferable general education courses. CCC offers vocational courses, such as heating and cooling systems, auto mechanics, welding, computers, boat building and photography. CCC provides educational support and customized skills training to area businesses and industries. Day and evening classes are available, and there are several off-campus class sites throughout the county.

Coastal Carolina Community College, (910) 455-1221, is also part of the state's community college system. Based in Jacksonville, it provides many of the same programs as Carteret Community College.

Research Facilities

The Crystal Coast is home to numerous research facilities and will soon have one of the largest concentrations of marine scientists on the East Coast. That will come with the completion of the **Center of Marine Sciences and Technology**. In 1995 North Carolina State University received appropriations for this center from the General Assembly, and the center will be built on the west side of the Carteret Community College campus in Morehead City. The appropriation also provided for renovations to the existing **Institute of Marine Sciences**.

Most of the existing research facilities have something to do with the surrounding water and resources. These facilities offer research, product development and personnel training for corporations around the world.

Area laboratories have been involved in developing many exciting products. Contract research has included work with companies such as Strohs Brewery, W. R. Grace, Hercules Chemical, Biosponge Aquaculture Products, International Paint, Allied Chemical, Sunshine Makers, Aquanautics, Mann Bait Company, 3M Corporation and General Dynamics.

Duke University Marine Laboratory was established by Duke University on Piver's Island near Beaufort in 1938. This interdepartmental facility has two objectives — research and teaching. The laboratory's large resident academic staff and innumerable visiting professors and researchers from throughout the United States and abroad have contributed to its worldwide reputation. The laboratory maintains a campus and two research vessels. The largest is the *R/V Cape Hatteras*, a 131-foot ship owned by the National Science Foundation. The ship is designed to carry out basic and applied research and education as required to meet national, state and private needs.

Also on Piver's Island is **Duke University Marine Biomedical Center**, supported by the National Institute of Health. The center focuses research on marine organisms and their relationship to humans and environmental health. This is one of four such centers in the nation.

The University of North Carolina Institute of Marine Sciences has a facility in Morehead City with activities directed toward understanding basic aspects of the marine sciences. Established in 1947, this is the oldest state-supported marine research laboratory in North Carolina.

The **National Oceanic and Atmospheric Administration** (NOAA) operates the Southeast Fisheries Center on Piver's Island near Beaufort. Here, research focuses on fish that are important to recreational and commercial fishing groups. This Beaufort laboratory is one of six labs operated as part of the Southeast Fisheries Center.

NOAA also operates a weather forecast center near Newport. The **NOAA National Weather Service Center** provides state-of-the-art weather tracking and forecasting and includes a Doppler weather radar system with advanced weather capabilities.

The **North Carolina Division of Marine Fisheries** has a large facility in Morehead City. Charged with stewardship of marine and estuarine resources in coastal creeks, bays, rivers, sounds and the ocean within 3 miles of land, this state agency is often in the midst of conflict between lawmakers, environmentalists and fishermen.

The Rachel Carson component of the **North Carolina National Estuarine Research Reserve** is just across Taylor's Creek from Beaufort. It may look like just a bunch of islands, but this system is an active research and classroom area. Public educational trips to the island are frequently offered. Congress created the reserve system in order to maintain undisturbed estuaries for research and education on the natural and human processes that affect the coast. The other three components that make up the state Research Reserve are Masonboro Island, Zeke's Island and Currituck Banks. For more information about the Rachel Carson component, call 728-2170 and see our Attractions chapter.

Crystal Coast
Commerce and Industry

Tourism and commercial fishing play the lead roles in the area's economic picture, but there are a number of domestic and international companies that call Carteret County home. The Carteret County Economic Development Council Inc., 726-7822 or (800)462-4252, and the Carteret County Chamber Of Commerce, 726-6350, can provide detailed information about area businesses and industries. Below is a brief look at a few of the area's major businesses.

The **North Carolina Port** at Morehead City is the most visible industry in the county. Situated on the east end of Morehead City, the 116-acre main facility offers a foreign trade zone and one of the deepest channels and turning basins of any East Coast port. This is one of two state-owned ports; the other is in Wilmington.

The large piles of wood chips seen along the highway at the port are brought to Morehead City on trucks and train cars by **Weyerhaeuser** and **Canal Wood Corporation**. The chips, which are used for the production of fine quality paper, are exported via ships to Japan.

PCS Phosphate (formerly Texasgulf) exports phosphate-based materials throughout the world and utilizes the Intracoastal Waterway to barge these materials from the company's Aurora mine to the port.

A new customer at the port is **Waterman Steamship Co.**, a barge line running to and from the Far East. Although this company handles a number of products, it is best known for importing rubber for Goodyear. Locally, much of the rubber is taken to the two North Carolina plants — one in Fayetteville and one in Reidsville.

The Port at Morehead City facility is the port of embarkation and debarkation for the Second Division of the **U.S. Marine Corps** at Camp Lejeune, North Carolina. The port includes much of the land on Radio Island, which is the body of land on the southeast side of the Morehead City-Beaufort high-rise bridge.

Atlantic Veneer Corporation in Beaufort is the largest manufacturer of hardwood veneers in North America. With manufacturing facilities on three

Photo: Scott Taylor

Commercial fishermen work hard to bring fresh seafood to your plate.

continents, the company also produces lumber, plywood and edgebanding. It exports about half of its products. With about 550 employees, this corporation is the county's largest manufacturing employer.

Veneer Technologies in Newport employs about 100 people and manufactures a variety of products, including flexible veneer and endbands.

Bally Refrigerated Boxes Inc., is the Crystal Coast's newest manufacturing firm. Located off U.S. Highway 70 in Morehead City, Bally makes walk-in re-

frigerated units, coolers and freezers. The company anticipates employing 200 people by mid-1996.

Several apparel companies have their headquarters on the Crystal Coast, including **Cross Creek Apparel**, makers of Cross Creek Apparel and Russell Athletic Wear, and **Creative Outlet Inc.**, producers of healthcare apparel.

Of Carteret County's 90,000 acres of farmland, 44,000 acres make up **Open Grounds Farm**. It is the largest farm east of the Mississippi River and produces corn, soybeans, beef cattle, wheat and cot-

Insiders' Tips

Contact the Economic Development Council, 726-7822 or (800) 462-4252, for county business and economic information.

P.O. BOX 825 • MOREHEAD CITY, NC 28557 • 919.726.7822 • 800.462.4252 • 919.726.4215 fax

Dear Carteret County Visitor,

       Thank you for your interest in Carteret County. I hope you have an opportunity to visit the county and enjoy our unspoiled beaches, our great sportfishing and our historic sites. In addition to its wonderful quality of life, Carteret County offers many business advantages for companies considering an expansion or relocation to this area.

       The state-owned and operated port in Morehead City is one of the deepest and most accessible ports on the east coast. PCS Phosphate and Weyerhaeuser are examples of companies which ship substantial cargoes through the Morehead City Port. Carteret County is also the only North Carolina county offering a direct port/rail/four-lane highway connection to the Global TransPark.

       Carteret County excels in education at the primary, secondary, community college and post-graduate levels. Carteret Community College offers prospective employers free customized training programs. The marine science laboratories of Duke University, the University of North Carolina-Chapel Hill, N.C. State University, and the National Marine Fisheries Service have established Carteret County as a world-renowned research center, with excellent opportunities for business research and development.

       Carteret County offers an abundant and proud labor force, supplemented with skilled labor from nearby military facilities at Cherry Point and Camp Lejeune. Developed acreage tracts are available for industrial, commercial and resort development opportunities. Carteret County Economic Development Council is available to provide you with confidential site assistance, local permit assistance, and labor needs. I hope that you will consider the business opportunities available in Carteret County... "where business is a pleasure."

                    Sincerely,

                    Donald A. Kirkman

                    Donald A. Kirkman
                    Executive Director

Aquaculture Down East

A Down East agricultural tour would take you through fields of cabbage, collards, sweet potatoes, turnips and corn. But, in Harkers Island there's a native crop grown on an unlikely farm you'd never notice. The routines on this farm are the same as those on other farms: germinating, planting seedlings, harvesting, grading and shipping to market. However, it's different from the usual farm in that the farmers are scientists and inventors working in the water to merge the 20th and the 21st centuries in seafood production and meeting market demands. This farm's crop is clams and its field, Core Sound.

Carolina Cultured Shellfish is only six years old. Among the first of North Carolina's commercial shellfish aquaculture ventures, its history from first planting in February 1990 to first harvest in 1993 is a story of approximation, experimentation, invention, trial and error. "All the research for this was done out of state," said assistant manager Ken Brennan, "and successful conditions in Virginia or South Carolina don't necessarily apply in Core Sound." In fact, conditions that result in significant differences in harvesting time vary within stone's throw distances in Core Sound or any tidal water. As Brennan summarized the trial-and-error nature of the shellfish aquaculture business: "If you haven't lost 900,000 (clams), you're just not doing it."

The order requisite to shellfish aquaculture has a lot of appeal. Beginning in the nursery, rows of cylinders contain the seed clams that grow from barely visible spats to around 4 millimeters. Nurtured by constantly circulating water from the sound, their growth is noted in byssal threads. At a size slightly larger than the holes in window-screen mesh they become recognizable as clams. Because the breeding stock is chosen for growth performance that shape characteristic growth patterns, about 75 percent of Carolina Cultured Shellfish clams are recognizable by their specific growth patterns. "It's a tattoo, a brand of sorts," says Brennan. "Keeps the poachers away."

From the cylinders the thousands of growing mollusks, now the size of nail heads, go on to the raceways. Raceways are a resting place for the seedling clams to grow strong before bedding down in the Core Sound mud. They appear as happy as clams in the raceway's fuzz of filters, which are extended to grab invisible nutrients from the still circulating Core Sound water.

Next stop, Core Sound. Uniform north-south rows in beds measuring 10-by 25-feet are densely planted. It is here that a strong competitive streak is valued in a clam. There's food to compete for and predators to avoid in the real world of Core Sound mud.

Density, another trial-and-error factor, involves a balance between production necessities and survival factors. "You plant as many clams as you can at a safe size and hope for the greatest survival rate," explained Brennan. "The more room you give them, the less competition they have for food and the greater the survival rate." But that way fewer clams are produced. That is why the best competitors, the fittest survivors, the fastest growers are selected for breeding.

Ken Brennan reveals a whole world of clams.

It requires an average of three years for a clam to grow from spat to harvest-size, which is one reason why everyone Down East isn't interested in shellfish aquaculture. Other retarding factors are the ever-tightening regulations governing commercial fishing and leases of bottom or water columns (surface to bottom) in public waters. But other factors that evade the traditional Down East farmer smile on the shellfish aquaculturist.

"Harvest responds to the market," explained Brennan. "As it is for other livestock, it's not like you can't leave the crop in the field. The money-size clam is about the size of a quarter. Harvested smaller, clams can be tossed back into the appropriate bed to finish growing or, at market size, to wait until the market calls. There is little waste in the efficiency of growth and harvest once the correct bed density/survival balance in the Core Sound lease is known."

The continuous efficiency refinements of Down East shellfish aquaculture has made the traditional commercial clammer a rare sight in 1995. Although the number of commercial aquaculture operations can be counted on one hand, they are meeting broad market demands. One reason aquaculture is becoming so popular is that the crop of clams is available year-round instead of seasonally.

"Our clams go to New Jersey, New York — the North and Midwest — Cleveland, Philadelphia. . .," Brennan said from the barge-like harvester custom-fashioned to this Core Sound farm's production requirements. From Atlantic City Clams Casino to the Cleveland Fire Department's annual clambake, the trained eye can recognize a Carolina Cultured Shellfish clam.

The untrained eye will definitely miss the farm. Haphazard stakes are the only evidence of a potentially large, unobtrusive industry and clams, by nature, always leave the water cleaner.

Photo: Scott Taylor

Fishing plays a major role in the area's economic picture.

ton. Owned by the Ferruzzi Group, one of Italy's largest companies, the farm stretches from Merrimon Road outside Beaufort east to Highway 70 near Sea Level. Individuals can get a look at the farm by checking in at the main gate. Permission to enter is most often granted, although visits are not recommended on Sundays or during busy planting or harvesting times.

Beaufort Fisheries at the east end of Front Street opened in 1934 and is called the oldest existing industry in the area. Where there were once many, this is the only menhaden plant now operating in the state. Menhaden, an oily, high-protein fish, are caught by company vessels and brought to the docks along Taylor's Creek to be processed into fish meal, oil and solubles. Fish meal is used as a protein component in many animal feeds. Fish oil is used primarily in margarine, cosmetics and paints. Fish solubles are high protein liquid by-products also used

in the feed market. During processing, a unique smell can travel through the seaside town. Locals, particularly the older folks who remember when fish plants were the biggest businesses in town, call it "the smell of money." Annual production at Beaufort Fisheries is estimated at 10,000 tons of meal and 300,000 to 450,000 gallons of oil.

Parker Marine Enterprises specializes in the construction of fiberglass fishing and pleasure boats. The company plant is on Highway 101 outside Beaufort. Boats are sold through authorized dealers.

Aquaculture and mariculture are exciting new forms of agriculture being promoted by the state. This production provides a dependable, year-round supply of seafood for wholesale and retail markets. **Carolina Cultured Shellfish** is one of the region's largest aquaculture operations and has facilities on Harkers Island.

There are also a number of large seafood dealers in the area. Two of the largest are **Luther Smith & Son Seafood** and **Clayton Fulcher Seafood**. These two family-owned and operated businesses work from fish houses in the Down East community of Atlantic. Smith operates several steel-hulled trawlers in waters up and down the East Coast and has a second fish house in Beaufort. Fulcher buys seafood directly from independent commercial fishermen and has a second fish house on Harkers Island.

The American Association of Retired Persons (AARP) has two active chapters on the Crystal Coast.

Crystal Coast
Retirement and Senior Services

The mild year-round climate and relatively low property taxes attract great numbers of retirees to North Carolina each year. The Crystal Coast is one of the areas frequently chosen for retirement life because there is much more bang for the retirement buck here. Property values on or near the water are, relative to other coastal communities, low. The Crystal Coast enjoys a fast-growing population of highly educated, well-traveled and active retired senior citizens.

As our number of older residents increases, the county and its various towns are developing more activities directed toward suiting the needs and interests of the senior set. With the variety of sports, hobbies, volunteer opportunities and entertainment available, most retirees stay as busy as they like.

Housing requirements can change quickly during the retirement years. Many townhouse and condominium developments are perfect for retirees who also decide to retire from house and lawn maintenance. All real estate companies can guide you toward more simplified living arrangements in beautiful locations.

Housing exclusively for older citizens on the Crystal Coast is available in a variety of settings, from federally subsidized accommodations for the elderly and handicapped to exclusive retirement complexes where you buy the unit and pay a monthly maintenance fee, which includes taxes, meals, laundry and around-the-clock security service. In addition, there are several nursing homes, rest homes and family care centers for those who need extra attention.

If you are shopping for one of these alternatives, it is very important to make several visits to the places you are considering. Information about all nearby facilities is available at the Department of Social Services, 2822 Neuse Boulevard in New Bern, 637-1703 or, of course, at the facilities.

Housing Options and Facilities

HARBORVIEW TOWERS
812 Shepard St., Morehead City   726-0453

Harborview Towers is in a downtown residential neighborhood on the Morehead City waterfront overlooking Bogue Sound. The modern 10-story, 50-apartment complex is adjacent to Harborview Health Care Center, a skilled and intermediate care facility for 125 patients and two family care facilities. Apartments are sold to residents, and a monthly fee includes maintenance, housekeeping, laundry, emergency and scheduled transportation, one meal a day in the dining room, all property expenses except telephone, property taxes and homeowner's policy on apartment contents. There are efficiency apartments and one- and two-bedroom units. All but the smallest units have balconies providing views of either Newport River or Bogue Sound. There is outdoor parking, with some covered parking on the building's ground floor. The newly renovated facility has an activities director, full-time security, and a live-in administrator, owner Doris Jernigan.

EKKLESIA APARTMENTS

Ekklesia Dr., Morehead City   726-0076

Ekklesia Apartments is a HUD-subsidized retirement complex in a quiet part of town on Barbour Road. The complex was built by four area churches, who retain much of the management authority. About two blocks from Morehead Plaza Shopping Center, Ekklesia includes 74 one-bedroom units and six two-bedroom units, all arranged in one-story clusters around the community center, which houses laundry facilities, a mail room and a large meeting room complete with a kitchen. The site manager and activities director offices are also in the community center. Regular activities include monthly birthday parties, special holiday parties, bingo, club meetings, a support group for the visually handicapped and such special events as the annual Watermelon Festival.

AMERICARE OF EASTERN CAROLINA

3020 Market St.   223-2600
Newport   (800) 948-4333

Recently opened in November 1994, Americare offers 16 beautifully furnished two-bedroom apartments, each accommodating four residents who are able to live independently with some assistance. Assistance includes three nutritious meals a day (with special diet considerations) served in the dining room, laundry, housekeeping services, medication monitoring and administering, scheduled transportation and a variety of social, recreational and educational opportunities. The community-within-a-community complex is designed around an exterior courtyard with a gazebo-style bandstand for special performances and events or a village green for community gatherings. Each apartment has a courtyard patio. Monthly rental includes all services and an enthusiastic staff that is available at all times.

SAILORS' SNUG HARBOR

U.S. Hwy. 70 E., Sea Level   225-4411

Sailors' Snug Harbor is a retirement facility built specifically for retired Merchant Marines and operated by one of the oldest charitable trusts in this country. The facility is more than 160 years old although the building and location in Sea Level is less than 20 years old. The trust was penned by Alexander Hamilton in the late 1700s for his friend Capt. Robert Richard Randall who wanted to build a "marine hospital for aged, decrepit, and worn out seamen" to be called "The Sailor's Snug Harbor." Properties of the trust included a small tract of land on Manhattan Island, now called Greenwich Village. The mariners, as Capt. Randall specified the resident retired Merchant Marines should be called, enjoy a lovely facility in a beautiful setting.

Nursing Homes

Nursing homes, by law, must provide

registered nurses on duty at least 8 hours a day, seven days a week, with licensed nurses on duty around the clock under the supervision of the director of nursing. The following facilities provide both short- and long-term care. Generally, physical therapy and speech therapy are provided, according to doctors' orders. The homes provide planned activities, meals, regular classes and worship programs for the ambulatory.

CRYSTAL COAST REHABILITATION CENTER
Penny Ln., Morehead City   726-0031
Crystal Coast Rehabilitation Center is a facility that provides skilled nursing care for 92 patients who require intermediate or acute care. On-site staff members provide speech, physical and occupational therapy, and a full-time activities director keeps ambulatory patients active and alert. Center activities include current events, ceramics, painting, church activities, parties and other social functions. The center accepts Hospice patients, and 11 Medicare beds are available.

HARBORVIEW HEALTH CARE CENTER
812 Shepard St., Morehead City   726-6855
Harborview Health Care Center has an in-house therapy department and in-

cludes a nursing home for 125 patients who require skilled and intermediate nursing care. The center provides three nutritional meals daily, and both the second and third floors have two large glassed-in solariums that overlook Bogue Sound and Morehead City. It is certified for Medicare and Medicaid and is a member of the N.C. Health Care Facilities Association and the American Health Care Association. A staff activity director plans programs, and volunteers also conduct a variety of events for residents. Church services, Bible study, communion services, music therapy and other interactive functions are offered.

Rest Homes

Rest homes provide custodial care, not nursing care, and have a doctor on call but only registered nurses on staff. There are trained nurses' aides on duty at all times under the direction of trained supervisors. While some residents use the facility for short-term care, most residents make use of the home on a long-term basis.

CARTERET CARE REST HOME

Professional Park, Morehead City   726-0401
Carteret Care Rest Home is three blocks from Carteret General Hospital in Professional Park. The care facility is licensed for 60 patients, and residents are involved in programs aimed at keeping them active and interested. Twenty-four hour care is provided, and an in-house, facility-maintained physician's office is available to an assigned physician who visits once a month. Nurse's assistants and medication assistants are on staff, as is an activities director. The facility provides transportation for residents, and volunteers conduct church-related programs and activities. Local garden club members maintain gardens and bird feeders.

SEA LEVEL EXTENDED CARE FACILITY

U.S. Hwy. 70 E., Sea Level   225-4611
This extended care facility is housed in the former Sea Level Hospital building and provides acute and intermediate nursing home care, plus a home for the aged. It also offers a unique guest care service for those whose caregivers need a respite (see our Accommodations chapter).

Family Care Centers

Family care centers provide a home-like atmosphere for those who need some care but can basically live independently. Residents must be ambulatory and perform some light housekeeping duties. They usually have kitchen privileges. They generally live in semiprivate bedrooms with a shared bath, have meals together and use the living room or other facilities jointly with other residents. There is a resident supervisor who does the heavy housework and cooking and, in general, looks after the residents. Transportation for medical attention, worship and shopping is provided. Medicine is under lock and key and is dispensed by the supervisor according to the doctors' directions.

CRYSTAL COAST FAMILY CARE CENTER

238 Copeland Rd., Beaufort   728-6065
In a quiet rural setting off N.C. Highway 101, Crystal Coast Family Care Center offers private rooms with shared baths and common-use living areas for 12 residents. Each of the two homes comprising the facility has a live-in supervisor to prepare meals, dispense medicines or any needed attention 24 hours a day. Meals are served family-style. Planned activities are scheduled including cookouts, transportation, church and shopping. Owned and administered by Dean and Carolyn Graham, the Crystal Coast Family Care Cen-

The Crystal Coast has a world of opportunities for retirees.

Photo: NC Travel & Tourism

ter for ambulatory and semi-ambulatory residents has been operating since 1991.

HARRIS FAMILY CARE CENTER AND WADIN' CREEK FAMILY CARE CENTER
N.C. Hwy. 101, Beaufort   **728-7490**

These are two separate care facilities in a country setting north of Beaufort. They are owned and operated by George and Millie Harris. Each house is licensed for six residents. The Harris house has only women residents, and the Wadin' Creek house can accommodate men or women. Each has three double bedrooms and two large bathrooms. Some outings and activities are planned. The live-in manager cooks, dispenses medicine and does heavy cleaning.

Organizations

The **American Association of Retired Persons** (AARP) has two active chapters on the Crystal Coast. The Morehead City chapter meets on the third Monday of each month for lunch at 11:30 AM at the Ramada Inn, MP 8¾, in Pine Knoll Shores. A speaker is scheduled for each meeting, and a newsletter is published to keep members apprised of goings-on of interest. To join the membership for lunch, reservations are taken in advance at either 726-4596 or 726-8405. Lunch is $6 per person. The White Oak Chapter of the AARP meets at the Western Carteret Community Center in Cape Carteret on the second Monday of each month. Lunch reservations for this chapter meeting are taken at 354-2336 or 354-3413.

Agencies and Services

CARTERET COUNTY SENIOR CITIZEN CENTER
1610 Fisher Street, Morehead City **247-2626**

The Senior Citizens Center provides a variety of programs for those older than 60. Classes, exciting trips, workshops and entertainment events are planned for senior citizens, and facilities are also used for a variety of community activities, including lively lessons in line dancing, exercise, billiards, table tennis, club meetings and the like. A hot lunch is available but arrangements need to be made at the center. The center also serves as headquarters for the SHARE food co-op. Each fall the center holds a Volunteer Opportunity Fair with representatives present from dozens of county institutions to share information on volunteer opportunities in the area. The center is open weekdays from 8 AM until 5 PM.

In 1995, property was secured by Carteret County on which to build the Leon Mann Jr. Enrichment Center for Senior Services on Galantis Drive in Morehead City. When built, this center will replace the current center that is on Fisher Street. Goals for the new center include improved accessibility, modernization, expanded facilities including space to expand for future tennis courts and swimming pool. Current plans include space for large meeting rooms, classrooms, a library, a game room and a health center.

THE SENIOR HEALTH INSURANCE INFORMATION PROGRAM
1610 Fisher St., Morehead City   247-4366

The Senior Health Insurance Information Program (SHIIP) is a service of the Retired Seniors Volunteer Program (RSVP) that refers senior citizens' health insurance questions to trained volunteers. The volunteers help compare the benefits and disadvantages of various policies so seniors can make an educated buying decision. They also help file insurance and Medicare claims and find solutions to insurance problems.

LIFELINE PROGRAM
Carteret General Hospital   247-1616

The Lifeline Program operates out of the emergency room at Carteret General Hospital and was set up to help older or chronically ill persons live independently. The subscriber has a special machine attached to his or her home telephone and wears a small device at all times. In case of sudden illness, a fall or other emergency, the subscriber simply depresses the button on the portable unit, which activates an alarm in the hospital emergency room where a staff member will respond. Newer devices include the capability of transmitting voice messages to and from the subscriber. If there is no answer or if the answer indicates an emergency, help is sent right away.

MEALS-ON-WHEELS
Mary O'Connell, coordinator   354-3130

Area Meals-On-Wheels programs

Photo: Scott Taylor

Breezy summer days are just great for snoozing in the sunshine.

provide home delivery of hot meals, usually one a day, five to seven days a week. The program is designed to help the elderly, shut-ins, those recuperating from surgery and handicapped persons. Some systems require full payment for meals, some seek contributions and others operate entirely on donations. Volunteers deliver the meals. Meals-on-Wheels operates out of Beaufort, 728-3356; Morehead City, 354-3130; Newport and Broad Creek, 223-4534; and the White Oak River area, 326-5333.

SENIOR GAMES
1610 Fisher St., Morehead City   247-2626

Carteret County has its own Senior Games program for residents 55 and older. Local games are held each May, and a year-round program leads up to the annual games in July. Competitions include tennis, golf, swimming, biking, table tennis, horseshoes, croquet, walks, runs, jumps and shot-put. Get the picture? It's active. Games also include Silver Arts competition in painting, sculpture, writing, heritage crafts, instrumental and vocal music. Local winners compete in the state Senior Games during the summer and advance from there to the nationals. The Senior Games committee sponsors workshops to prepare the prospective athlete or artist to participate.

WEEK AT CAMP
Carteret County Parks and Recreation Dept.
728-8401

Another special senior activity is Week At Camp, a week-long camping experience in August at a 4-H camp in the foothills outside Reidsville, North Carolina. Participants come from all over North Carolina and other states through both managing agencies, the Carteret County Parks and Recreation Department and the Dare County Cooperative Extension Service, 473-1101. For a fee of about $200 per person, campers get transportation, insurance, room and board, nonstop entertainment, workshops and other extras. In addition, for those seeking a little more challenge, the High Adventure option takes participants white-water rafting and outdoor camping for two days out of the week. The camp has a swimming pool for exercise and a freshwater lake for paddleboating and canoeing and fishing. Classes and workshops are scheduled daily, and there's entertainment each evening. Meals are served family-style.

Veterans' Groups

Because of the proximity of several military bases and military hospitals, many people retiring to Carteret County are veterans. There are numerous veterans' organizations in the area, and all welcome new members. And, for the veteran with a problem, there's the **Veterans' Service Office** in Beaufort, 728-8440.

American Legion, Post 99, Jimmy Range, Beaufort, 728-3675

Disabled American Veterans Chapter 41, Wesley Jones, Newport, 223-5468

Veterans of Foreign Wars Post 2401, Marvin Knox, Beaufort, 728-3362

Veterans of Foreign Wars Post 9960, Jim Broadus, Swansboro, 393-6278

Veterans of Foreign Wars Post 8986, Gary N. Bills, Newport, 247-2619

Vietnam Veterans of America, Jerry Birch, 728-5652; Charles Odell, 808-3766

Since the nearest emergency room and hospital facilities are in Morehead City or New Bern, Newport Family Practice Center offers needed medical services in the Newport community.

Crystal Coast
Hospitals and Medical Care

Routine and specialized medical care, diagnostic procedures, treatment and surgery are available and practiced routinely on the Crystal Coast. In cases requiring equipment or specializations not presently available here, referrals are usually to New Bern or Greenville, which are no more than 2 hours away. In cases of emergency, residents and visitors receive medical attention on a walk-in basis at several locations around the county during weekday business hours. At other times, Carteret General Hospital's emergency room is the best bet.

In almost every town or community throughout the county, there are clinics or specialized practices with one to a half-dozen doctors. It is not unusual, however, for routine appointments to be scheduled months in advance, although sickness and emergency cases are generally worked in. When moving to the Crystal Coast, it's best to arrive with a referral from your most recent doctor. Otherwise, as there is no medical referral service in Carteret County, ask a few Insiders for their recommendations and take the consensus.

Hospitals

CARTERET GENERAL HOSPITAL
3500 Arendell St.
Morehead City   247-1616
Emergency room   247-1540

Carteret County's sole community hospital is Carteret General Hospital. The hospital's expanding medical staff includes 48 full-time physicians representing most medical specialties. The 117-bed facility offers 24-hour emergency services plus top-quality patient services including lithotripsy for kidney stone treatment, vascular surgery, cancer treatments and cardiac care which includes a newly implemented outpatient rehabilitation program. The hospital's full service laboratory, imaging services and CT scanner provide state-of-the-art diagnostic services. The Raab Clinic provides outpatient chemotherapy and neurology services and other outpatient procedures. Construction of a new birthing environment and a new radiation therapy center for cancer patients should be completed in 1997. The renovation of all patient care rooms should be completed in 1996. The hospital recently took over the county's home health services, providing a continuum of care. Continual additions of facilities, services and equipment keep Carteret General Hospital abreast of the latest developments in medical diagnosis and treatment.

If other facilities are needed, the hospital makes arrangements to air-evacuate patients by helicopter to Pitt County Memorial Hospital in Greenville or to other larger city hospitals. This is sometimes necessary in the event of an extremely premature birth, severe burn or major head injury.

CRAVEN REGIONAL MEDICAL CENTER
2300 Neuse Blvd., New Bern   633-8111

This major medical facility includes 24-hour emergency room service, outpatient surgery, diagnostic services, critical care units, cardiac care services offering diagnostic catheterization and open-heart surgery and radiation oncology. Magnetic resonance imaging (MRI), CT scanning, home care, long-term care for older adults, speech and language therapy, rehabilitation, adult psychiatric services and women's health services are also offered. For more information, see the New Bern Medical Care chapter.

BRYNN MARR
BEHAVIORAL HEALTHCARE SYSTEM
192 Village Dr., Jacksonville (910) 577-1400
Helpline counselor   (800) 822-9507

Brynn Marr Hospital extends comprehensive services throughout eastern North Carolina in treatment of emotional and behavioral problems, mental illness, substance abuse and chemical dependencies for individuals of all ages. Designed to offer the least restrictive level of care needed by clients, Brynn Marr's Behavioral Healthcare System offers outpatient care, day treatment programs or full hospitalization for critical care needs. Brynn Marr's Helpline is a free crisis and referral service that offers round-the-clock telephone assistance with confidentiality in identifying needs and recommending an appropriate next step toward problem solution. One may see a counselor at Helpline offices in the Crystal Coast area, in Jacksonville or in Hampstead for a no-cost evaluation. For senior citizens, the hospital's New Beginnings day treatment programs address the specific mental health issues of elderly adults. Brynn Marr also offers numerous support services and outreach programs to the community, including no-cost professional workshops on mental health topics and free community education programs.

ONSLOW MEMORIAL HOSPITAL
317 Western Blvd., Jacksonville   577-2345

This hospital is used by some residents of western Carteret County because Jacksonville is only about 20 miles from Swansboro. The facility offers 24-hour emergency service and admissions, ambulatory surgery, an oncology clinic, private birthing suites and in-and-out treatment for minor illnesses, injuries or emergencies. Considerable remodelling has improved the hospital's efficiency by relocating outpatient and administrative services. A new urgent care clinic, opened in 1996, provides nonemergency care services on an appointment or walk-in basis. The hospital houses its own poison control unit and has physicians on staff with a wide variety of specialties.

PITT COUNTY MEMORIAL HOSPITAL
Stantonsburg Rd., Greenville   551-4100

This large facility is affiliated with the East Carolina University School of Medicine and East Carolina Children's Hospital. It offers a wide spectrum of treatment, specialized staff and facilities that range from its well-known emergency room to a neonatal nursery used by smaller hospitals

Insiders' Tips

A mixture of Avon's Skin So Soft and water is a soothing, good-smelling insect repellent for people and dogs.

across the region. The hospital also has an orthoscopic surgery clinic, and the new Leo W. Jenkins Comprehensive Cancer Center provides radiation therapy, chemotherapy and oncologic surgery.

NAVAL HOSPITALS

Camp Lejeune	451-1113
Cherry Point	466-5751

For active duty and retired military and their families, there is the Naval Regional Medical Center at Camp Lejeune, the U.S. Marine Corps Base at Jacksonville and the completely new Cherry Point Naval Hospital at the U.S. Marine Corps Air Station at Cherry Point, Havelock.

Urgent Care

WESTERN CARTERET MEDICAL CENTER
N.C. Hwy. 24E., Cape Carteret   393-6543

The Western Carteret Medical Center, a subsidiary of Carteret General Hospital, is in the Cape Carteret shopping center. The clinic provides services by appointment with primary-care physicians as well as walk-in care for minor emergencies. Open weekdays from 8:30 AM until 5 PM, the clinic also offers blood pressure clinics and diabetic counseling.

EASTERN CARTERET MEDICAL CENTER
U.S. Hwy. 70, Sea Level   225-1134

Eastern Carteret Medical Center, also a subsidiary of Carteret General Hospital, offers the same services as the Western Carteret Medical Center. It was established to serve the eastern part of the county and is open from 8:30 AM until 5 PM weekdays.

EMERALD ISLE PRIMARY CARE
7901 Emerald Dr.   354-6500
Emerald Isle

Three medical doctors and a physicians assistant are available in Emerald Isle seven days a week for complete outpatient medical services. Offices are in Suite #7, Veranda Square. Services by appointment or on an emergency walk-in basis include internal medicine, pediatrics, gynecology, minor surgery and sports medicine.

MED CENTER ONE
Atlantic Beach Causeway   247-2464
Atlantic Beach

Med Center One is on the Atlantic Beach Causeway, not far from the base of the high-rise bridge between Morehead City and Atlantic Beach. This privately owned facility has in-house X-ray services and a pharmacy. Med Center One provides emergency and other services on a walk-in basis. Hours are from 8 AM until 6 PM Monday through Friday, 9 AM to 6 PM Saturday and noon to 5 PM on Sunday. In addition to minor emergencies, the clinic schedules appointments and sees walk-in patients for general medical care.

NEWPORT FAMILY PRACTICE CENTER
Howard Blvd., Newport   223-5054

Since the nearest emergency room and hospital facilities are in Morehead City or New Bern, Newport Family Practice Center offers a needed service in the Newport community. This privately owned

The touch tank at the NC Aquarium at Pine Knoll Shores is always popular with kids.

clinic is open from 8 AM to 5 PM weekdays and from 9 AM to noon on Saturday. The center prefers seeing patients who have made appointments in advance, but in an emergency, they accept walk-ins.

Private Medical Practices

FAMILY MEDICINE

Carteret Family Practice Clinic, 2 Medical Park Court, Morehead City, 247-5177

Cas Cader, M.D., 5 Medical Park, Morehead City, 726-8414

James Crosswell, M.D., 97 Campen Road, Beaufort 728-3875

Morehead General Medicine, 500 N. 35th Street, Morehead City, 726-2282

Seaside Family Practice, U.S. Highway 70 E., Bettie, 728-7176

INTERNAL MEDICINE

Carteret Internal Medicine and Cardiology Center, 212 Penny Lane, Morehead City, 247-5426

Downeast Medical Associates, 3610 Medical Park Court, Morehead City, 247-2013

Eastern Carolina Internal Medicine, 532 Webb Boulevard, Havelock, 447-7088

NEUROLOGY

Coastal Neurological Associates, 3110 Arendell Street, Morehead City, 240-1574

OBSTETRICS AND GYNECOLOGY

Carteret OB-GYN Associates, 302 Medical Park, Morehead City, 247-4297

Carteret Women's Health Center, 302 Penny Lane, Morehead City, 726-8016

OPHTHALMOLOGY

Coastal Eye Clinic, 3110-6 Arendell Street, Morehead City, 726-1064; and 802 McCarthy Boulevard, New Bern, 633-4183

EAR, NOSE AND THROAT

Coastal Ear, Nose and Throat and Facial Plastic Surgery, 3601 Bridges Street, Morehead City, 247-3257

J.M. Esposito, M.D., 208 Professional Circle, Morehead City, 247-3016

PEDIATRICS

Carteret Clinic for Adolescents and Children, 221 Professional Circle,

Sketch: Tim Ruane

The 1859 Apothecary Shop and doctor's office is at the Beaufort Historic Site.

Morehead City, 726-0511; Cape Carteret, 393-2134

Coastal Children's Clinic, 315 E. Main Street, Havelock, 447-8100

Coastal Pediatric Care, 212 N. 35th Street, Morehead City, 247-5212

SURGERY

Carteret Surgical Associates, 306 Medical Park Court, Morehead City, 247-2101

Way Surgical Associates, 3 Medical Park, Morehead City, 247-4769

Support Groups and Services

In Carteret County there are a number of active support groups with concerns related to children and family difficulties, mental and physical health, lifestyle changes, challenges and substance abuse. Most support groups meet at the Neuse Center, Carteret General Hospital or at area churches, but that certainly doesn't cover all of them. Following are some of the many groups who meet regularly in the area. For information, call the contact numbers listed. If the list doesn't include a group related to your concern, contact the **Neuse Center for Mental Health**, 726-0515, or **Helpline**, 247-3023.

AIDS and HIV-positive support group for individuals and families, 240-2675

Alzheimer's Group, 726-0031

Autism Society, 223-4108

Battered Women Support Group, 726-3362

Bereavement/Grief Support Groups, 726-5580, 726-3151

Better Breathers Support Group, 247-6000

Breast Cancer Support Group, 393-7293

Cancer Support Group, 247-4338

Children of Divorced/Divorcing Parents, 247-2202

Codependents Anonymous, 726-1757, 728-1730

Diabetes Support Group for Patients and Families, 726-7990

Growing Through Divorce, 726-4840

Hospice of Carteret County, 247-2808

Lesbian Support Group, 726-6202

Lifeline, 247-1530, provides a direct, electronic link between Carteret General Hospital and people needing emergency care

Multiple Sclerosis Support Group, 726-0515

Nervous Disorders Support Group, 728-5460

Neuse Center for Mental Health, Morehead City, 726-0515; New Bern, 633-4171

Overeaters Anonymous, no contact number. Meets at 8 PM Wednesdays at the Webb Center, Evans Street, Morehead City.

PAC: Positive Alternatives and Choices Tutoring for dropout prevention, 728-4096

Post-traumatic Stress Disorder Support Group, 728-4930

Stop Smoking Support Group, 247-1616

Toughlove Parent Support Group, 726-3556

Unpaid Family Caregivers Support Group, 728-8430

Victims of Sexual Assault and Abuse, 728-4460

Widows' and Widowers' Support Group, 247-6664

Crystal Coast
Volunteer Opportunities

Countless organizations on the Crystal Coast rely on volunteers of all ages to render their time, talents and services. Through varied volunteer opportunities, residents are involved directly in nurturing herbs, narrating historical tours, directing tourists, caretaking the lighthouse keepers quarters and greeting visitors at Cape Lookout, building houses, assisting hospital patients and delivering food and presents to families who need help at Christmas. Volunteering adds a heightened level of interest to many people's lives — while sharing their time and skills with their fellow citizens, they are given the chance to meet other people with common interests.

People who like history, meeting the public or showing tourists around interesting historical restorations will enjoy channelling some spare time in the direction of the aquarium, museums and historic sites. If you'd enjoy lending a hand and hammer, you will be welcomed into the fold at Habitat For Humanity, and Hammocks Beach State Park will be equally glad to see you help with inevitable repairs. All the public libraries employ volunteer help in children's programs, one-on-one assistance for patrons and outreach programs. To make a lasting contribution to the community, volunteer to help with reading or other programs in one of the schools.

Volunteers preferring the company of animals will be delighted with the opportunities at the Outer Banks Wildlife Shelter or at the Humane Society's animal shelter. The Hospital Auxiliary places volunteers in every area at Carteret General Hospital. Meals-on-Wheels and Hospice both depend on volunteered kindness to deliver meals or offer relief to caregivers. The Domestic Violence and Rape Crisis programs train volunteers who are interested in offering specific care in crisis situations. Helpline, the 24-hour crisis telephone line, is fully staffed by trained volunteers who are available to lend an ear and offer referral information. The Retired Senior Volunteer Program (RSVP) is very active and recognized for its matchmaking of retired volunteer expertise with appropriate recipients.

Whether or not you are new to the area, if you have some time to share, the range of interesting possibilities through volunteer efforts will open new doors. Consider the following list of organizations that are always welcoming and training new volunteers. You can learn something new or teach others something you do well. Your call will be welcomed and your experience broadened.

Public Sites and Parks

Core Sound Waterfowl Museum, Harkers Island, 728-1500

Beaufort Historical Association, 138 Turner Street, Beaufort, 728-5225

Cape Lookout National Seashore, 131 Charles Street, Harkers Island, 728-2250

Carteret County Historical Society, 100 Wallace Drive, Morehead City, 247-7533

N.C. Maritime Museum, 315 Front Street, Beaufort, 728-7317

N.C. Aquarium at Pine Knoll Shores, Salter Path Road, Highway 58, 247-4004

Fort Macon State Park, E. Fort Macon Road, Highway 58, Atlantic Beach, 726-3775

Hammocks Beach State Park, 1572 Hammocks Beach Road, Swansboro, (910) 326-4881

Carteret County Public Library, 210 Turner Street, Beaufort, 728-2050

Bogue Banks Public Library, Pine Knoll Village, Pine Knoll Shores, 247-4660

Newport Public Library, Howard Boulevard, Newport, 223-5180

Animal Care Services

Outer Banks Wildlife Shelter, 5810 Arendell Street, Morehead City, 240-1200

Humane Society of Carteret County, Hibbs Road, Morehead City, 247-7744

Human Care Services

Big Brothers/Big Sisters, 727 Arendell Street, Morehead City, 240-1024

Big Brothers/Big Sisters of the Lower Neuse, Country Aire Suites, 240-2165

Carteret County Habitat For Humanity, 312 Live Oak Street, Beaufort, 728-5216

Carteret County Domestic Violence Program, 402 Turner Street, Beaufort, 728-3788

Guardian Ad Litem, 402 Cedar Street, Beaufort, 728-8574

Hope Mission, 1412 Bridges Street, Morehead City, 240-2359

Newport Developmental Center For Handicapped Children, 903 Church Street, Newport, 223-4574

Retired Senior Volunteer Program (RSVP), 17th and Fisher streets, Morehead City, 247-4366

Foster Grandparent Program, 17th and Fisher streets, Morehead City, 726-5219

Senior Games, 17th and Fisher streets, Morehead City, 247-2626, 728-8401

Hospice of Carteret County, Webb Memorial Library and Civic Center, Ninth and Evans streets, Morehead City, 247-2808

Martha's Mission Cupboard, 901 Bay Street, Morehead City, 726-1717

Meals-on-Wheels, Mary O'Connell, Coordinator, 354-3130

Carteret Literacy Council, Carteret County Public Library, 210 Turner Street, Beaufort, 728-2050

Project Christmas Cheer, Daisy Hilbert, 726-5970

Carteret County Hospital Auxiliary, Carteret General Hospital, Morehead City, 247-1532

Carteret County Public Schools, Beaufort, 728-4583

Helpline, Morehead City, 247-3023; Beaufort, 728-1554

Environmental Services

Big Sweep, N.C. Cooperative Extension Service, Carteret County, 728-8421

Rachael Carson Reserve, 430-B West Beaufort Road, 728-2170

N.C. Coastal Federation, 3609 Highway 24, Ocean, 393-8185

Several churches host Easter sunrise services on the beach, with the most popular taking place at Fort Macon State Park.

Crystal Coast
Places of Worship

Residents, visitors and newcomers can choose from hundreds of worship centers on the Crystal Coast. Whether you're interested in attending a service, admiring architecture or learning about history, each Crystal Coast church has something to offer.

There seems to be a church around every corner, but that's not unusual for an area many refer to as the "Southern Bible Belt." Even the smallest of communities may have two or three churches.

Many of the area's oldest churches are in Beaufort. For the most part, these are wooden structures preserved to look just as they did years ago. Each church in the area is distinct; some are modern structures, some are classic brick designs, others are weathered and vine-covered. Each has its own legends and stories held dear to members of its congregation.

It would be impractical to list the hundreds of worship centers scattered around the Crystal Coast. We have described a few of the area's most noted churches, whether that be because of the building's age, size of the congregation or convenient location.

For more information about other churches in the area, check the Yellow Pages.

EMERALD ISLE CHAPEL BY THE SEA
6712 Emerald Dr. 354-3210
Emerald Isle

This interdenominational church sprung out of the Bogue Banks Resort Min-

isterial Association, which was formed in 1968. The association was asked to assign a minister to Emerald Isle for the summer months, and services began in the town hall beginning in May 1969. In 1971 plans were made for the church to become independent of the association and to have services during the winter. Ground was broken for the chapel in 1972, and the first meeting was held on Easter Sunday 1973. Today the church is attended by locals along with visitors from across the state and country.

ANN STREET UNITED METHODIST CHURCH
Ann and Craven sts. 728-4279
Beaufort

Built c. 1854, the church features curved wooden pews and beautiful stained-glass windows. An unusual feature of the church is the handcarved rosettes in the ceiling. The steeple of the church, stretching high above the houses on the low coastal land, was shown on old mariners' charts as a point of reference, a beacon to aid those at sea. It is one of three churches surrounding the Old Burying Ground. The church's modern educational building stands across the street and is used for community events.

PURVIS CHAPEL AME ZION CHURCH
217 Craven St. 504-2605
Beaufort

Purvis Chapel was built in 1820 and is Beaufort's oldest continuous-use church. It stands on the same block as Ann Street United Methodist Church. Originally built by the Methodist Episcopal Church, it was later deeded to the AME Zion congregation and is still owned by that group. The bell in the church was cast in Glasgow, Scotland, in 1797. The building is listed on the National Register of Historic Places.

St. Paul's Episcopal Church

209 Ann St.   728-3324
Beaufort

St. Paul's Episcopal Church, c. 1857, is the area's oldest Episcopal church. The church building was built in two years by local shipbuilders. Visitors will notice that the interior of the sanctuary bears a striking resemblance to an upside-down ark. It is reported to be one of the 10 most acoustically perfect buildings in North Carolina. Holy Eucharist is on Sunday and a midweek Eucharist is conducted each Wednesday.

Purvis Chapel is one of Beaufort's oldest churches and is beside the Old Burying Ground.

St. Stephen's Congregational Church

Craven and Cedar sts.   No phone
Beaufort

St. Stephen's Congregational Church was built in 1867 along with the neighboring two-story school building that housed the Washburn Seminary. Records show the lot was purchased for $100 in 1867, and the seminary served as a school for many years.

First Baptist Church

Ninth and Bridges sts.   726-4142
Morehead City

Morehead City's First Baptist Church is one of the town's oldest churches. The congregation originally shared a small building near the waterfront with the town's Methodists. After the War Between the States, the congregation built the current new structure.

The new 18,000-square-foot family life center at First Baptist Church is available for community activities such as meetings and weddings. The center can handle such activities as basketball games, parties and dinners for up to 800 people. A fancy light and sound system allows for excellent quality concerts.

First United Methodist Church

Ninth and Arendell sts.   726-7102
Morehead City

Standing on the corner of Ninth and Arendell streets, this church is home to one of the oldest Methodist congregations in eastern North Carolina. The church congregation's roots go back to Shepard's Point in 1797. The original chapel was built in 1879 and later was converted to a bakery by the Union Army in 1862. Today's sanctuary was dedicated in 1952.

St. Egbert's Catholic Church

1612 Evans St.   726-3559
Morehead City

St. Egbert's parish had its start in

Photo: Scott Taylor

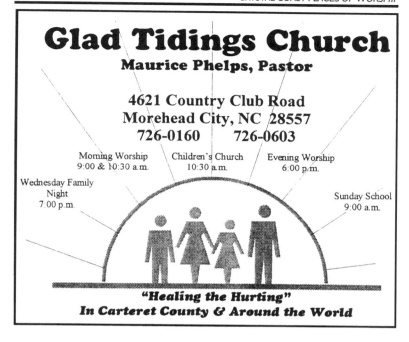

Glad Tidings Church
Maurice Phelps, Pastor

4621 Country Club Road
Morehead City, NC 28557
726-0160   726-0603

Morning Worship
9:00 & 10:30 a.m.

Children's Church
10:30 a.m.

Evening Worship
6:00 p.m.

Wednesday Family
Night
7:00 p.m.

Sunday School
9:00 a.m.

"Healing the Hurting"
In Carteret County & Around the World

Morehead City in the early 1920s. The church now has its own school for students from kindergarten through 6th grade. In late 1991 it completed extensive renovations and additions to the church and parish house. Community service is emphasized, with support groups regularly meeting in church facilities. Parish services are offered Saturday and Sunday, and Mass is held on various weekdays.

ST. ANDREW'S EPISCOPAL CHURCH
2005 Arendell St.   247-6909
Morehead City

St. Andrew's, constructed in 1957, is a beautiful church wonderfully designed with many unusual wooden features. Park in the lot behind the church on Evans Street. The church has a large active congregation and offers three Sunday services and one Wednesday morning service.

UNITARIAN COASTAL FELLOWSHIP
1300 Evans St.   240-2283
Morehead City

The Unitarian Universalist congregation was organized in Carteret County in 1980 and has grown to a church with about 90 members. Services are conducted at 10:30 AM each Sunday in a renovated building that features a fellowship hall, kitchen and religious education rooms.

GLAD TIDINGS CHURCH
4729 Country Club Rd.   726-0160
Morehead City

The new family life center at Glad Tidings provides 10,400 square feet of space for activities. There is a large open area, 11 classrooms, a kitchen, storage areas and offices. This center is often available for weddings, conferences and meetings.

Cherry Point
is the leading
military employer of
Carteret County
residents with about
2,000 civilian
employees and 700
military employees
residing in the
county.

Crystal Coast
Military

Military bases and training facilities dot North Carolina's Central Coast, but they haven't spoiled its beauty. They have just added a few more people, a little noise, extra traffic every now and then and a lot of patriotism.

Occasionally residents express concern about low flying aircraft, the noise a night training flight might cause or the increased traffic on two-lane roads, but overall the military bases are excellent neighbors. They provide employment and income and contribute to the commu-

Military Base Tours

Cherry Point Marine Corps Air Station conducts base tours throughout the month. From September to May, tours are scheduled on the first and third Thursday morning. During June, July and August, there is a tour every Thursday morning. Call 466-4906 for more information.

New River Air Station in Jacksonville arranges tours by appointment. Write H&HS, MCAS New River, PSC Box 21002, Jacksonville, NC 28545.

Tours of Camp Lejeune in Jacksonville may be scheduled by writing Commanding General, Attn. Public Affairs Office, MCB PSC 20004, Camp Lejeune, NC 28542.

nity through many, many volunteer projects. Military crews often volunteer to tutor students, clear and construct school athletic fields, help nonprofit groups with projects and raise funds for holiday programs.

Of the surrounding bases, Marine Corps Air Station Cherry Point has the greatest impact on the Crystal Coast. Cherry Point, with its Naval Aviation Depot and the Marine Corps Air Station, is the leading military employer of Carteret County residents with about 2,000 civilian employees and 700 military employees residing in the county. In 1994, those 2,700 workers earned approximately $107,000,000 out of a total Cherry Point payroll of $469,467,000. About 9,280 of Carteret County's 57,000 year-round residents are impacted by Cherry Point. That figure includes the employees, retired miliary, and military and civilian dependents.

The Port of Morehead City is the port of embarkation and debarkation for the Second Division of the U.S. Marine Corps at Camp Lejeune. This base is near Jacksonville and military troops often travel Highway 24 from Swansboro to Morehead City. Another area establishment is Seymour Johnson Air Force Base in Goldsboro, which is about a three-hour drive from the Crystal Coast.

What follows is a detailed description of a few of the closest military establish-

Photo: Bill Russ

The 150-year-old restored fort at Fort Macon State Park near Atlantic Beach was originally used to protect colonists from hostile seafarers. The fort stood guard over Beaufort Inlet during the Civil War and World War II.

ments. For information about Marine Corps Air Station Cherry Point, see our Havelock chapter.

MARINE CORPS
AUXILIARY LANDING FIELD
Bogue Field, off N.C. Hwy. 24   *393-2027*
This 875-acre landing field fronts Bogue Sound. The field primarily is used for field carrier landing practice, and pilots perform many of these landings at night to simulate landing on an aircraft carrier.

ATLANTIC OUTLYING FIELD
AND PINEY ISLAND (MARINES)
These two facilities are in the Down East area. Atlantic Outlying Field is a 1,514-

acre facility in the community of Atlantic. Piney Island, or BT-11 as the military refers to it, is a 10,000-or-so-acre electronic practice range at the eastern tip of Carteret County. As part of the Mid-Atlantic Electronic Warfare Range (MAEWR), Piney Island is used by various military groups, including active duty personnel and reservists. While planes actually do fly over the area, bombing simulations are recorded and scored electronically via computers to lessen the environmental impact.

COAST GUARD BASE FORT MACON
Fort Macon Rd.
Atlantic Beach   *247-4598*
Coast Guard Base Fort Macon is at

the east end of Bogue Banks and is the home port of several large cutters and smaller vessels. The base is charged with patrolling the area from Drum Inlet on Core Banks south to the North Carolina-South Carolina border. Coast Guard missions include search and rescue, and law enforcement.

Coast Guard
Station Swansboro

Station St.
Emerald Isle 354-2462

This station is at the west end of Bogue Banks in Emerald Isle. When the station was first established, Emerald Isle was not a town, so it was named after Swansboro, the town to the north. The name never changed. This station's vessels patrol an area from Marker 21 in Bogue Sound, which is in the area of Gales Creek community, south to the Surf City swing bridge in Pender County.

The *Carteret County News-Times* is published on Wednesday and Friday afternoons and Sunday mornings.

Crystal Coast
Service Directory

This directory offers an abbreviated listing of some useful information about services on the Crystal Coast. Most of the businesses we recommend are tried-and-true establishments. This list is only a sampling, so we suggest you check the local phone directory for additional service providers.

Emergency Phone Numbers

COAST GUARD

Information	247-4598
Search and Rescue Emergencies	247-4545
Swansboro Lifeboat Station in Emerald Isle	
	354-2719

CARTERET OR
ONSLOW COUNTY SHERIFF

Emergency	911
Carteret business number	728-3772
Craven business number	636-6620

FIRE , POLICE OR RESCUE SQUAD

For any emergency, regardless of your location, dial 911.

POLICE DEPARTMENTS

For business calls, dial the appropriate number below. If a number isn't listed in your community, use the sheriff's office business number.

Atlantic Beach	726-4040
Beaufort	728-4561
Cape Carteret	393-2183

Emerald Isle	354-2021
Indian Beach	247-6700
Newport	223-5111
Morehead City	726-5361
Pine Knoll Shores	247-4353
Swansboro	(910) 326-5151

OTHER IMPORTANT NUMBERS

Crime Stoppers	726-INFO
Crisis Helpline	247-3023
Magistrates	728-8516
State Highway Patrol	726-5766
Carteret General Hospital	247-1616
Neuse Center for Mental Health	726-0515
Alcoholics Anonymous	726-8540
American Red Cross	240-1002
Carteret County Health Department	728-8550
Carteret County Department of Social Services	728-3181
Poison Control Center	(800) 672-1697

Animal Services

Most incorporated towns have leash laws for dogs and most of the towns require that dogs and cats have registration tags. Many require owners to pick up the waste their dogs leave on town property or on the property of others. Pine Knoll Shores also requires owners to pick up waste left on the beach. For detailed information about requirements in the area you live in or are visiting, contact the town hall. Stray or lost pets can be reported to the **Humane Society of Carteret County Animal Shelter**, 247-7744, or the **Crystal Coast Animal Protection League**, 247-3341.

Veterinarians

Guy Jaconis, 814 W. Beaufort Road, Beaufort, 728-7600

David Bird, 176 N.C. Highway 24, Morehead City, 393-6581

David Hall or **Roxanne Taylor**, 5015 Executive Plaza, Morehead City, 726-4033

John Puette, 1074 Cedar Point Lane, Cedar Point, 393-6581

Walter Westbrook, P.O. Box 1090, Newport, 223-5115

Kennels

Nelson's Kennels, 4115 Arendell Street, Morehead City, 247-2026

Hadnot Creek Kennels, N.C. Highway 58, Cape Carteret, 393-2855

Crystal Coast Kennels Inc., Sam Garner Road, Newport, 223-3007

Lake Road Boarding Kennel, Lake Road, Newport, 223-4183

Wildlife

If you see or find an injured, sick or orphaned wild animal, call **Outer Banks Wildlife Shelter** (OWLS), 240-1200. You can either take the creature to the facility on U.S. Highway 70 at the junction of N.C. Highway 24 beside Lowe's, or you can have a trained volunteer pick up the animal. This local organization was established to counteract the adverse pressure of development on the wildlife of the Crystal Coast. OWLS works to rehabilitate and release wildlife. It relies on donations and volunteers.

Area Codes

The Crystal Coast, New Bern and Havelock are within the 919 telephone area code. Swansboro and Wilmington are in the 910 area code. The dividing line between the codes is at the Carteret County-Onslow County line, which is marked by the White Oak River. All telephone numbers in this book are in the 919 area code unless otherwise noted.

Bus and Taxi Service

Bus Station of Morehead City, 105 N. 13th Street, 726-3029

A-1 Yellow Cab Co. (Service to Atlantic Beach, Beaufort and Morehead City), 728-3483

Crystal Coast Cab (Service to Atlantic Beach, Beaufort, Down East, Morehead City, Newport), 728-5365

Yellow Cab Co. (Service to Atlantic Beach, Beaufort and Morehead City), 726-3125

Emerald Isle Taxi (Service to Swansboro, Emerald Isle and Cape Carteret), 393-8866

Presidential Limousine (Service anywhere in the tri-county area), 726-8109

Car Rentals

Arrangements for rental cars should probably be made in New Bern or a nearby larger area. In Carteret County,

Insiders' Tips

Recycling is easy and popular along the Crystal Coast. Most towns offer curb-side pick up of recyclable items. Residents outside town limits can call the county office, 728-8450, for directions to the closest drop-off point.

Carteret-Craven Electric Cooperative

Locally owned and locally controlled by 27,000 member-owners

◆

Serving Morehead City Havelock Salter Path

A vital part of growth in Carteret and Craven Counties since 1940

---

try the **Michael J. Smith Airfield**, Beaufort Airport, 728-1777; **Merritt-Williams Ford**, Highway 70 W. in Morehead, 247-2131; or **Enterprise Rent-A-Car**, Highway 70 W. in Morehead, 240-0218.

Government Offices

Town Halls

Atlantic Beach, MP 2½, W. Fort Macon Road, 726-2121

Beaufort, 217 Pollock Street, 728-2141

Cape Carteret, 204 W.B. McLean Drive, 393-8483

Cedar Point, Lois Lane, 393-7898

Emerald Isle, 7500 Emerald Drive, MP 19, 354-3424

Indian Beach, Salter Path Road, MP 11, 247-3344

Morehead City, 706 Arendell Street, 726-6848

Newport, 402 Howard Boulevard, 223-4749

Pine Knoll Shores, 100 Municipal Circle, MP 7, 247-4353

Swansboro, corner of Church and Webb streets, (910) 326-4428

Libraries

The three public libraries on the Crystal Coast are part of a multi-county system. Therefore, if a book is not on the shelf at one library, ask and it might be in another and available for a loan to your library. Most libraries offer special programs for children and adults. A traveling bookmobile service is offered throughout the county.

Bogue Banks Library, 320 Salter Path Road, MP 7, Pine Knoll Shores, 247-4660

Carteret County Public Library, 210 Turner Street, Beaufort, 728-2050

Newport Public Library, 431 Howard Boulevard, Newport, 223-5108

Onslow County Public Library Branch, N.C. Highway 24, Swansboro, (910) 326-4888

Webb Memorial Library, 812 Evans Street, Morehead City, 726-3012

Media Information

Newspapers

CARTERET COUNTY NEWS-TIMES
4034 Arendell St.
Morehead City   726-7081
Carteret County has no daily news-

paper, but is well-covered with the *Carteret County News-Times*, published Wednesday and Friday afternoons and Sunday mornings. A comprehensive county publication, the paper covers all area activities. The paper includes news and features on the Crystal Coast and surrounding areas. State and national sports are included. *Carteret County News-Times* is published by Carteret Publishing Company, Morehead City.

NewsTalk 24 is a computerized phone service provided by the *News-Times*. Residents and visitors to the area can dial 247-NEWS and then access a number of information files. These files are advertised regularly in the newspaper and include information about area activities, schools, NASCAR, area businesses, and more. For more information or a listing, call the NewsTalk 24 office, 726-7081.

TIDELAND NEWS
101-2 Church St.
Swansboro   *(910) 326-5066*

Tideland News is published each Wednesday from its office in Swansboro. Owned by Carteret Publishing Company of Morehead City, the paper covers news and activities in the western part of the county — Swansboro, Cape Carteret, Cedar Point and Emerald Isle.

HAVELOCK TIMES
13 Park Ln.
Havelock   *444-8210*

Published each Wednesday, the *Havelock Times* covers news and features happening in the Havelock and Newport areas. The paper is owned by Carteret Publishing Company of Morehead City, and it is based in Havelock.

JACKSONVILLE DAILY NEWS
Bell Fork Rd.
Jacksonville   *(910)353-1171*

The *Jacksonville Daily News*, a daily morning paper, includes state and national coverage and primarily covers Onslow County and the U.S. Marine Base at Camp Lejeune. The paper also covers Carteret County activities and county-wide issues.

THE MAILBOAT
P.O. Box 3
Harkers Island   *728-4644*

The Mailboat, published on Harkers Island, is a quarterly publication that includes anecdotes, recollections and stories about life as it used to be in Carteret County's Down East communities. Each publication is a treasured addition to local libraries. *The Mailboat* also puts out an annual booklet of Christmas recollections, which is included in the subscription price or may be purchased from area book stores.

COASTER MAGAZINE
201 N. 17th St.
Morehead City   *240-1811*

Coaster is published seven times year with the majority of issues in the summer. About 210,000 magazines are printed at each publication and distributed at no charge to the public through 150 visitor locations on the Crystal Coast and out of

Insiders' Tips

The Crystal Coast has just about the same services that you would find in any big city. You might have to look a little harder to find them, but the casual lifestyle here makes it well worth it.

the area. Now in its 14th year, *Coaster* provides details on local events and attractions, traditional culture and legends.

CRYSTAL COAST VISITOR'S GUIDE
1724 Virginia Beach Blvd., Ste.108
Virginia Beach   (800) 422-0742
Crystal Coast Visitor's Guide provides a variety of information for both the visitor and the resident. The magazine focuses on Crystal Coast entertainment and attractions, shopping, restaurants, real estate and more.

Television Stations

TIME WARNER CABLE CHANNEL 10
U.S. Hwy. 70, Newport   223-5011
Time Warner Cable Channel 10 supplies cable television to most areas of Carteret County. The station airs a variety of programming varying from school and health issues to sports and talk shows. Studio manager Marty Feurer focuses on community events and works hard to disseminate information about community projects and community-service activities. "Coastal Headline News" is shown twice an hour and "Do What?," a guide of local events for visitors and residents, is scheduled at various times.

WFXI-FOX
U.S. Hwy. 70, Morehead City   240-0888
Television Channel 8 shows the regular Fox programming and offers a local news show at 10 PM.

WCTI
225 Glenburnie Dr., New Bern   638-1212
Television Channel 12, the local ABC affiliate, provides comprehensive local coverage as well as ABC programming. The station offers local news coverage, sports and weather each weekday at 6 AM, noon, 5, 6 and 11 PM. A fish and game forecast is given during the news sports segment.

WITN
Hwy. 17, Chocowinity   946-3131
Television Channel 7, the local NBC affiliate, has its studios in Chocowinity. Along with NBC programming, the station has area news coverage, including high school and college sportscasts.

WNCT
3221 S. Evans St., Greenville   355-8500
Television Channel 9, the local CBS affiliate, includes a morning local talk show and local news and sports shows along with its network programming.

Radio Stations

WTKF 107.3 FM
U.S. Hwy. 70, Newport   247-6343
North Carolina's first talk FM, WTKF carries news, talk, sports and NASCAR. "Wake Up Carolina", a local talk show, is featured each weekday from 8 to 9 AM. Listen to the nation's hottest talk hosts with the nation's hottest talk topics. Rush Limbaugh, Alan Colmes and Bruce Williams entertain and inform

Many Insiders keep a stash of "hurricane food" in their kitchen cabinets. That might include unopened jars of peanut butter, canned meats and fruits, crackers, jellies and instant breakfast mixes. It's also a good idea to have plenty of matches, candles and batteries on hand during hurricane season.

Insiders' Tips

while area hosts feature local news and newsmakers. The station also features a dozen local daily newscasts plus TV-12 weather twice an hour.

WBTB 1400 AM

209 Ocean St.
Beaufort 728-1635

WBTB features Christian talk from the Moody Bible Network. It has nondenominational programming with a Christian perspective on issues of the day. Call-in shows, news programs and children's programming make WBTB a well-rounded source for news and family entertainment.

WMGV 103.3 FM

207 Glenburnie Dr., New Bern 247-1033

V 103.3 offers a variety of adult contemporary music that appeals to all ages. The station offers news in the morning and weather at 10 minutes past the hour all day long.

WMBL 740 AM

5058 U.S. Hwy. 70 W.
Morehead City 240-0740

WMBL provides the best of 1940s, '50s and '60s. This easy listening station is very popular on the Crystal Coast. Morning host Jay Cobb often talks with community members from 7 to 9 AM and the show provides information about community projects and programs. Big Band music is featured each Sunday morning and Mary Alford's show titled "Reminisce" can be heard at 9:50 AM Monday through Friday. CNN news is featured at the top of the hour.

WRHT 96.3 FM

Little Nine Rd.
Morehead City 247-2002

WRHT, Sunny 96.3 FM, offers listeners top 40 and contemporary hits. It features "Charlie Byrd's Beach Music Show" each Sunday from 7 to 11 PM. The station's request line is 726-9600.

WTEB 89.3 FM

800 College Court, New Bern 638-3434

This National Public Radio station offers "Morning Edition" weekdays from 6 to 9 AM and "Weekend Edition" from 8 to 10 AM Saturday and Sunday. The popular "All Things Considered" is aired weekdays from 5 to 7 PM. Saturday evening features ballroom music and Sunday evening features jazz.

WRNS 95.1 FM / 960 AM

Rt. 2 Box 182, Kinston 522-4141

Based in Kinston, this station plays the latest and hottest country music. The station always has a contest going and offers all kinds of prizes including concert tickets and trips. The station also features Paul Harvey. The request line number is (800) 682-WRNS.

Rental Services

If you couldn't bring it with you or just plain forgot it, there are places ready to rent it to you whether you're a visitor or resident in need of a few extra things. If you are looking for vacation-type rentals (linens, cribs, high chairs), check the Vacation Rental chapter of this book. The Watersports chapter has information about watersports equipment rentals.

COUNTRY AIRE RENTAL

Hwy. 70, Morehead City 247-4938
Hwy. 70, Beaufort 728-2955

This company rents a little bit of everything — beds, baby furniture, tools, equipment (tillers, mowers, trailers, sanders, tractors, paint sprayers, etc.) tents of all sizes and wedding and catering supplies.

Photo: Clay Nolan

Boat builders on Harkers Island use plans that have been refined and handed down from father to son for many years to build boats in their backyards.

GENERAL RENTAL

Hwy. 24 east of Cape Carteret   393-2220

General Rental rents beds, baby furniture, car seats, all kinds of home repair tools (saws, drills, sanders), carpet cleaners, party tents, mowers, tillers and midsize construction equipment.

PR RENTALS AND SALES

4803 Arendell St.   247-9411

PR offers furniture, appliances, vacuums and electronics rentals.

WALSTON'S TRUE VALUE HARDWARE

Cedar Point   393-6111

Walston's rents carpet cleaners and all types of tools from a half-inch drill to a ditchwitch. They also have ladders, tillers and mowers.

Storm and Hurricane Information

Carteret County Emergency Management Office can be reached by calling 728-8470.

Hurricane season lasts from June 1 through November 30. Each time a storm threatens, residents and visitors are urged to heed warnings and take precautions. Evacuation routes are marked on the area's main roads to guide people away from the dangerous coastline in case of a storm. While some people may find a storm exhilarating, the damage of prior storms has let those of us on the coast know that it is prudent to be informed and take precautions.

Residents of Bogue Banks, the barrier

island strip from Atlantic Beach to Emerald Isle, are required to obtain re-entry passes from their respective town halls before a hurricane hits. While nonresidents are prohibited from entering a damaged storm area, residents can use the pass to return to the island after an evacuation.

Improved communications greatly increase the chance for escape before a storm hits. But, in order for the warnings to be effective, they must be heeded. The following definitions are used in announcing the condition of an approaching hurricane:

A hurricane WATCH means it is possible that, within 36 hours, hurricane conditions may exist in a specific area.

A hurricane WARNING is announced when it is possible that hurricane conditions may be 24 hours or less away from a particular location.

In low-lying areas or places such as Carteret County's barrier islands and parts of the Down East area, emergency management officials may decide to evacuate an area in preparation for what appears to be a rapidly approaching storm. In these cases, shelters open at announced sites, usually schools, to provide a place for residents to wait. If you go to a shel-

ter, it is recommended that you take important personal papers, food, water, clothing, medicines, blankets, baby foods, diapers, formula and other specialized items required for a wait of hours or days. Battery-powered radios and flashlights are useful also. Pets are not allowed in the shelters.

When a hurricane makes landfall, both wind and water are sure to create mayhem with property and will likely take human lives, if the people have not taken cover when advised to do so. In the center of the high winds is the eye of the hurricane. Should the eye pass over, it will allow a temporary calm, but this is not a signal that the storm has ended. After a brief respite when the eye is overhead, the winds and rains will resume with at least as much force and violence as before.

Strong winds pounding waves onto the shore, heavy rains and abnormally low pressure within the hurricane produce what is called a storm surge. In addition to being extremely forceful, a surge may raise water levels as much as 20 feet above normal. The storm surge of Hurricane Hugo was measured at 17 feet. It is essential that you avoid being trapped in

Photo: Scott Taylor

A pelican prepares for a safe landing.

your car, mobile home or other structure in a low area. Leave in time if an evacuation is ordered.

Tax Rates

The Carteret County 1995-96 tax rate and municipal rates are based on a $100 valuation.

Carteret County	50.5¢
Atlantic Beach	45¢
Beaufort	40.5¢
Cape Carteret	35¢
Cedar Point	5¢
Emerald Isle	20¢
Indian Beach	19¢
Morehead City	45¢
Newport	46¢
Pine Knoll Shores	21¢

The 1995-96 Onslow County tax rate and Swansboro rate are also based on a $100 valuation.

Onslow County	61.5¢
Swansboro	50¢

In addition to property taxes, North Carolina residents pay a 7 percent state income tax and a 6 percent sales tax. Call the N.C. Department of Revenue at 726-7910 for more specifics. The office is only open on Mondays.

Utility Services

Utility services on the Crystal Coast vary from area to area. Regardless of whether you are buying or renting, you can usually expect to have the gas, electricity, water and sewer services turned on within 24 hours. Telephone service could take three to four days to be connected, and cable TV service could take a week.

Deposits or connection fees vary among service providers; some depend on whether you have had service with that company before, some are refunded if you are in good standing with that company after a year.

Utility service for each area is listed separately below. If you have questions about the service provider you need to contact, ask a real estate agent, the town hall, county office staff or the previous resident.

Electricity

CAROLINA POWER & LIGHT
3504 Bridges St.
Morehead City   726-7031

CP&L offers electricity to the majority of residents and businesses. The amount of the deposit required depends on the size of your house or apartment, the service area and your credit. This deposit is refundable after one year if good credit is established. CP&L provides electricity to about 22,000 customers in Carteret County and in the Havelock area of Craven County.

CARTERET-CRAVEN ELECTRIC MEMBERSHIP COOPERATIVE
1300 Hwy. 24
west of Morehead City   247-3107

Providing electrical service to much of western Carteret County, this member-owned corporation has about 28,000 members. It services all residents of Bogue Banks except those living in Atlantic Beach; all residents in Cape Carteret, Cedar Point and along Highway 58 to Maysville; residents along Highway 24 toward Morehead City and down Nine Foot Road and Lake Road to Havelock; residents along Highway 70 from Morehead City to the old residential district in Newport; and all Morehead City residents in the Country Club and Crab Point areas. A deposit is required when making an application.

HARKERS ISLAND ELECTRIC MEMBERSHIP
849 Island Rd.
728-3769

Providing electricity to residents of Harkers Island, this is an electric distribution cooperative owned by the people it serves. The co-op was formed in 1939 and continues to provide electric utility service to residential property owners and commercial businesses on the island.

CAROLINA POWER & LIGHT
1099 Gum Branch Rd.
Jacksonville   455-1375

Call this CP&L office to arrange for electrical service in Swansboro.

Gas

Propane gas is provided through any number of private area businesses. Check the Yellow Pages for a list of bottled gas providers.

Telephone

Apply for service by calling **Carolina Telephone**, 903 Arendell Street, Morehead City, 633-9011 (toll-free). Depending on your previous record, you may be asked to pay a deposit. That deposit usually is refunded after a year. Connection could take three or four working days, longer if there has not been telephone connection at that address before.

360° Communications (formerly Sprint Carolina Telephone) in Jacksonville, 300 New Bridge Street, 633-9011 (toll free), can arrange for service in Swansboro.

Water and Sewer

The number you call to get water and sewer connection depends on where you live. If you live in a town, apply to the water and sewer department at the town hall. If you live outside town limits, chances are you will rely on a well and septic tank.

Check with the county office; some rural areas are served by a water supplier. If you get service from your town or a provider, you will be required to pay a hookup fee, which varies from system to system.

West Carteret Water Corporation, 247-5561, is a member-owned cooperative with offices at Pender Park in Broad Creek on Highway 24. The company provides water to areas in the western part of the county, not including Bogue Banks. The service area mainly focuses on Highway 24 from Gull Harbor to Cedar Point and the many sideroads along that stretch north along Highway 58 for several miles. The company expects to continue expanding across the western portion of the county. They deal with water only; there is no sewer system serving the western part of the county. Instead, people have septic tanks.

Carolina Water Service, 247-4216, provides water to residents of Pine Knoll Shores and Brandywine Bay. Brandywine Bay has sewage service.

Bogue Banks Water Company, 7412 Emerald Drive, 354-3307, provides water to residents of Bogue Banks from Salter Path to Emerald Isle. They offer no septic tank service.

Trash/Recycling

Trash is picked up within town limits on varying days. Special arrangements can be made for picking up large trash items, lawn trimmings and limbs. Curb-side recycling programs have been started in most towns, but not in rural areas of the county. For information, contact your town hall (see listings in this section), or call the county office at 728-8450. Green box sites (dumps) are located throughout the county.

Photo: Evan Roderick/North Carolina Aquarium

Rescued baby loggerhead turtles can be seen at the North Carolina Aquarium before they are released into the sea.

Zip Codes

Atlantic	28511	Marshallberg	28553
Atlantic Beach	28512	Morehead City	28557
Beaufort	28516	Newport	28570
Cape Carteret	28584	Oriental	28571
Cedar Island	28520	Salter Path	28575
Cedar Point	28584	Sea Level	28577
Davis	28524	Smyrna	28579
Emerald Isle	28594	Stacy	28581
Gloucester	28528	Stella	28582
Harkers Island	28531	Swansboro	28584
		Williston	28589

We average a home bought or sold by our customers every minute. Think what we could do for you in a day.

With $1 trillion in real estate transactions over the past 25 years, you can count on the CENTURY 21® system to help you find the right home fast. In fact, the CENTURY 21 system averages a home bought or sold by its customers every minute, every day. Let us get started this minute, showing you that when you're #1, you can do things others can't. **Call #1.**

ZAYTOUN RAINES
REAL ESTATE
1-800-548-3122
(919) 633-3069

Inside
New Bern

To really understand the New Bern of today, it's important to know its past. This river town maintains its heritage by standing guard over its Colonial, Georgian, Federal, Greek Revival and Victorian architectural styles. And, its citizens still maintain an attitude of friendliness and Southern gentility.

The town's Swiss look comes honestly. It was settled in 1710 by Swiss and German immigrants who named it after the Swiss capital of Bern. Officially founded by Swiss Baron Christoph deGraffenried, New Bern is distinguished by its red-brick clock tower above city hall just like any Swiss city. The town emblem, as in old Bern, is a black bear and that symbol appears frequently throughout the city.

New Bern has been fought over by Native Americans, Swiss, British, Colonials, Yankees and Rebels. After each skirmish, it pulled itself up by its boot straps and plodded onward. The result is a panoply of American history along tree-lined streets that have just the slightest look of old Switzerland. It's an odd mix that makes the town quite picturesque.

Historic markers point out the houses where the first elected assembly in the Colonies met in defiance of the crown in 1774, where a signer of the U.S. Constitution lived and where George Washington slept — twice. Markers also show you where noted jurist William Gaston, the first chief justice of the state Supreme Court and composer of the state song, had his office.

The second-oldest city in North Carolina, New Bern is the site of many firsts. It was in New Bern that the first state printing press was set up and the first book and newspaper were published. The state's first public school opened here. The first official celebration of George Washington's birthday was held in New Bern, and it was here that the world's first practical torpedo was assembled and detonated. In the 1890s C. D. Bradham, a local pharmacist, invented Brad's Drink in New Bern. The drink later became known as Pepsi-Cola.

Without question, New Bern's centerpiece is Tryon Palace, the lavish Georgian brick mansion named after William Tryon, the British Colonial governor who

"General George" is a longleaf pine in the Croatan that was a sapling in the Revolutionary War.

Insiders' Tips

New Bern

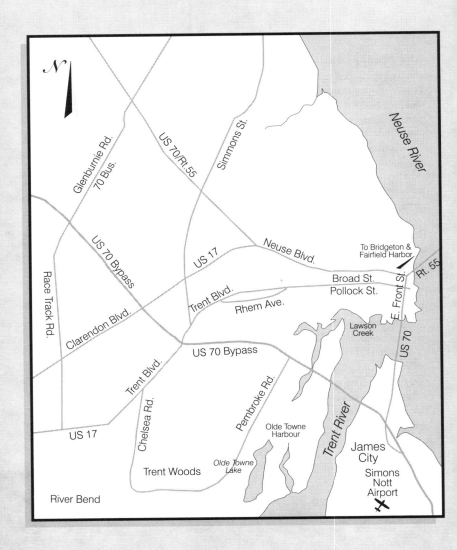

New Bern
HISTORICAL DISTRICT

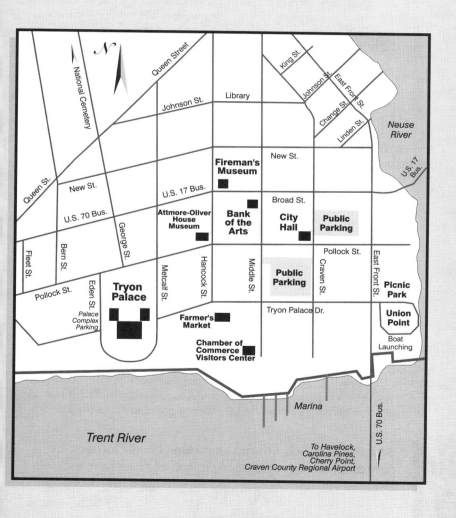

had it built in 1770. It is a sumptuous showplace inside and out. Twin rows of oaks leading up to the entrance provide a stately introduction, and the scenic backdrop is the wide and lovely Trent River. The palace is where delegates gathered for the first State Legislature meeting in 1777.

But even before all that, before the palace, the school and the white man's voice, the site captured the interest of the Tuscarora Indians. It is believed the Indians may have had hunting camps and villages here for thousands of years. Who could blame them?

Downtown New Bern sits on a point of land at the confluence of the Neuse and Trent rivers. Once the main hub, its downtown fell into great disrepair in the early 1970s due to the development of shopping malls and suburban housing outside the business district.

That all changed, however, in 1979 when local government gave Swiss Bear Inc., a nonprofit corporation composed of civic leaders, the authority and responsibility to revitalize the downtown area. Today, art galleries, specialty shops, antiques stores, restaurants and other businesses have resurrected downtown, turning it into a bustling hub of activity.

Progressive and exciting improvements are continuously underway. Built and dedicated in 1995, James Reed Lane is a lovely downtown mini-park and pedestrian walkthrough on Pollock Street across from Christ Church. The pleasant respite amid downtown activity was planned and funded through efforts of Swiss Bear Inc., in honor of the first rector of Christ Church. In October 1996 a downtown Welcome Center housing the Craven Convention and Visitors Bureau and the Greater New Bern Chamber of Commerce will open to visitors at the corner of Middle Street and Tryon Palace Drive. Swiss Bear Inc. and the City of New Bern are renovating the park at Union Point in several phases beginning in 1996 with new bulkheading, railings and a riverside promenade. The entire 300 block of Middle Street is undergoing a facelift, inspired by the restored Kress Building at Middle and Pollock streets, restoring all the building facades to their turn-of-the-century elegance. The Swiss Bear downtown revitalization initiative has been very visibly successful.

Just a few miles upstream from downtown, the Neuse River slows and quickly broadens into a mile-wide concourse. Joined by the Trent River, the Neuse takes a lumbering left turn and widens to 4 miles across, making it the widest river in the United States. The two rivers converge at downtown's Union Point Park. Sitting on a park bench by the docks, you can look downriver for what seems like forever.

This inviting link to the broad, shallow Pamlico Sound and the Atlantic Ocean helped shape New Bern's destiny. The town long thrived on the richness of its rivers and the fertile soil surrounding them. In Colonial times, West Indian and European vessels would dock here to trade cargos of merchandise. The river

Photo: Kenny Barrow

The clock tower above City Hall is the focal point of the downtown historic area.

led inland to pitch, tar and tobacco and, of course, to local hospitality. Now the rivers serve as the focus of the area's recreational activities: water-skiing, sailing and fishing. Hotel-based marinas for modern-day skippers edge toward the Trent River channel from both banks between Union Point Park and the railroad trestle and also front the Neuse. New Bern's rivers are a tremendous source of area pride, and recent pollution symptoms in the Neuse have stirred tremendous state and local efforts in restoring its health.

New Bern's southeastern boundary is only a few miles from the Croatan National Forest, a 157,000-acre preserve that shelters deer, bears, alligators and the rare Venus' flytraps. Canada geese and osprey are common sights along the rivers, as are the resident great blue herons. Given the right weather conditions and saltwa-

ter intrusion, the Neuse River has been known to hide 8- and 10-foot sharks.

New Bern has three historic districts with homes, stores and churches dating back to the early 18th century. Within easy walking distance of the waterfront are more than 200 homes and buildings listed on the National Register of Historic Places. Several bed and breakfast inns, most of the area's best restaurants, banks, antiques and specialty shops, Tryon Palace, city and county government complexes and many of the town's 2,000 crape myrtles are also nearby.

The crape myrtle is New Bern's official flower, and it's no wonder. On those hot summer days when you feel like drooping, the crape myrtle seems to laugh with energy as it bursts forth in a profusion of blossoms. New Bern does its gardening quietly. Led by the example of the professionally pampered Tryon Pal-

The Great Fire of 1922

Friday, December 1, 1922. It was the most tragic day in New Bern's modern history. The day after Thanksgiving. The morning was gray and overcast with a gale blowing out of the south. At 8 AM, the fire department was called just outside of town to the Rowland Lumber Company, the largest sawmill in North Carolina and the largest employer in town. Every piece of firefighting equipment and all personnel were required to fight the huge blaze that engulfed the mill.

Meanwhile in town, at the home of Henry and Hester Bryan on Kilmarnock Street, family members were gathered at the table for breakfast when someone called from the street that the chimney was on fire. Dr. Samuel Bryan was the youngest of the Bryan family at the table. He remembers, "Family members began immediately removing the furniture from the house. In the excitement of moving the furniture, it was discovered that I was still inside the house eating. A Mr. Chapman came in and took me from the table. Flame caught in the gable of our house, but men saved the house by beating out the flames. While houses burned all around, our house remained standing and served as a haven to several families . . ."

The December 2, 1922 issue of *The New Bernian* reported the sequence of events as follows:

"By an irony of fate it is very likely that had it not been for the fire at Rowland Mill an hour or so earlier the devastation of a portion of New Bern would not have occurred. But such was the fate and when, in answer to the alarm calling firemen to the new scene of the conflagration, the driver of the hose wagon found that there was no nozzle to be attached to the hose and it was necessary to rush back to headquarters after this. In the meantime the fire gained headway, burst beyond all bounds and the devastation of the city was consummated."

Fire was carried by the wind from house to house, easily igniting the wooden shingles that were typical in the area of town which is now Craven Terrace. Before the day ended, 3,200 people were homeless, nearly 1,000 buildings were destroyed, hundreds of jobs were lost and an area of forty blocks was destroyed in New Bern. That night, families were taken in all over town, but many slept with their salvaged belongings on open train cars and in Cedar Grove Cemetery.

Photo: George Multon in Memories of New Bern by Emily Herring Wilson

A tent city was erected in New Bern to house the victims of the devastating fire of 1922.

In the days and months that followed, the town fed thousands of displaced fire victims at West Street School, and in the James City area of town a tent city was constructed as temporary housing. Because of the loss of jobs, many victims were forced to move away.

The fire changed the lives of all residents of New Bern in some way. As New Bern resident Dorcas Carter remembers it, "The big fire of December 1, 1922, caused me and my family to become scattered from our homes and my birthplace, church site and make new adjustments for another mode of life . . . To me, it seems as if I have been scattered from everyone ever since."

Personal recollections are based on interviews from the oral history *Memories of New Bern* by Emily Herring Wilson, published in 1995 by the New Bern Historical Society Foundation.

ace gardens, the town's residents have a yen to make things grow. During the spring explosion of dogwoods and azaleas, a ride through the DeGraffenried neighborhood, about a mile from downtown, is breathtaking.

Gardens, both public and private, extend throughout the city and its suburbs. Summertime brings day lilies, dahlias, zinnias, black-eyed Susans and petunias. Home gardens produce tomatoes, chives, squash, corn and other favorites. In fall, it seems everyone goes ga-ga for chrysanthemums. Flowering cabbage and pansies brighten the winter.

Besides the downtown historic district, New Bern also has the Ghent and Riverside neighborhoods, both of which carry official historic neighborhood designations. Ghent, across Trent Road from the DeGraffenried neighborhood, was the town's first suburb, and the dogwood-planted median on Spencer Avenue was once the bed of a trolley. The neighborhood displays an eclectic collection of architectural styles.

Riverside, developed at the turn of this century and across town from Ghent, runs between the Norfolk Southern railroad tracks and the Neuse River to Jack Smith Creek. It has a sort of baron-and-worker feel to it, with imposing mansions along National Avenue, giving way to the less sumptuous residences on neighboring streets.

Tucked between New Bern and the Trent River is Trent Woods, one of the wealthiest of North Carolina's incorporated towns. Here is the New Bern Golf and Country Club, the Eastern Carolina Yacht Club and some of the priciest real estate around. And Trent Woods' costly, pine-shaded real estate is more and more in similar company within New Bern's housing market. About 5 miles south of town off Highway 17 is River Bend which began as a planned development but later incorporated. Like Trent Woods, it has

Insiders' Tips

Stands of tall old pines in the Croatan National Forest serve as habitat for endangered red-cockaded woodpeckers that nest in the heart wood.

its own country club, golf course, tennis club, marina and waterfront acreage along the Trent River and canals that lead to it.

Both River Bend and Fairfield Harbour, another planned community about 8 miles east of New Bern on the Neuse River, have attracted retirees primarily from the Northeast. Fairfield Harbour's amenities include a couple of golf courses, two swimming pools, tennis courts, a marina, a restaurant and lounge, miniature golf, horseshoes and walking and riding paths.

If all this sounds boringly nice, take heart. There are a few trouble spots. Insiders' brows furrow when they talk about the town's traffic lights and its lack of nightlife.

First, the traffic lights. Those approaching New Bern on the two-laned Highway 17 north of town, will find that New Bern's drawbridge and traffic lights offer a major hitch in the flow of your trip. As you follow signs through the downtown area, the small Colonial-sized city blocks, widely varying levels of traffic and ill-timed traffic lights give you a chance to pause and read the historic markers, whether you want to or not. If you're headed south, you can expect another bottleneck around the road's intersection with Highway 70. These traffic problems won't be the case much longer, however, because changes are looming over the Neuse.

Construction of a four-lane high-rise bridge began in October 1995. The bridge will span the Neuse River and go from Bridgeton on Highway 17 to James City on Highway 70. The new bridge will replace the John Lawson drawbridge now approaching New Bern from the north. Construction is expected to be complete in 1999.

That brings us to New Bern's nightlife. There are a few lounges, some live music, a few movie theaters and a bowling alley, but those with a hankering for more may not hit town at the right time. There are good professional and amateur acting groups in town, a profes-

Middle Street at the turn of this century was part of New Bern's bustling commercial waterfront.

sional dance company, a subscription performance season and an annual jazz concert worth the wait.

The town also has wonderful festivals, shows and fun-for-all conventions — the Chrysanthemum Festival, the New Bern Preservation Foundation's Antique Show and the Clown Convention are among the favorites. Residents gather for special occasions on the Trent River waterfront — on July 4 for the fireworks and in early December for the Christmas flotilla. But, otherwise, the town's social life takes place in private homes and social clubs and at various civic and charity functions that are staged on an annual basis.

To really get to know New Bern, you have to take it as it is. Think of the river city as a slow treasure hunt where gems are revealed as you walk its streets. It's

there that you will discover the real New Bern. Visit its museums — the Bank of the Arts, Tryon Palace Historic Sites and Gardens, the New Bern Academy Museum, the Fireman's Museum and the Civil War Museum. Take time to read the historic markers and talk to the people in their gardens and on their porches.

You're likely to find a sailor from California, a cyclist from New Zealand, a city refugee from New York or a retired shop owner from Honolulu sharing your park bench. Ask them why they chose to live here. New Bernians like to talk about their town.

New Bern is a gentle place, a place where one can still enjoy the passing scene, where people know how to appreciate a pretty day. It's just that kind of town.

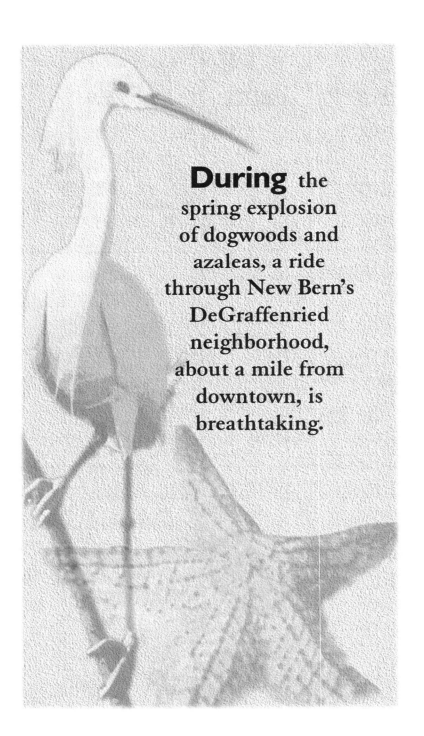

During the spring explosion of dogwoods and azaleas, a ride through New Bern's DeGraffenried neighborhood, about a mile from downtown, is breathtaking.

New Bern
Getting Around

New Bern is growing in many ways — the number of retirees and new residents moving to the area is on the up and up, and the number of tourists coming here to explore the area's many treasures increases every year. No matter how they arrive — by land, by air or by sea — all routes lead to attractions that everyone will enjoy.

By Land

From the north by land, U.S. Highway 17 leads directly into the heart of New Bern. From the west, Interstate 95 leads to U.S. Highway 70, which continues straight into New Bern. From the north or south, Highway 17 is the most direct route to the area. From the east, the drive here is along Highway 70 from the Morehead City area.

Construction of a new bridge from the north side of New Bern to James City on the southeast side is underway and should be completed by 1999. This will allow travelers coming from the south or the north headed directly to the beaches to by-pass the heart of New Bern. However, if you bypass New Bern on the way to the beach, make sure you include it in your return plans. There is much to see and do in this city, and your visit to the area will not be complete without a stop here.

Carolina Trailways, 504 Guion Street, 633-3100, offers bus transportation in and out of town.

By Air

Arriving by plane is as easy as flying into the **Craven County Regional Airport**, 638-8591. Situated about 2 miles southeast of downtown New Bern, the airport offers daily flights on USAir Express for passengers coming or going to the large hub airport in Charlotte. Charter services are available with Carolina Air, 633-1400.

Michael J. Smith Field, 728-1777, is in nearby Beaufort and offers charter air service. Beaufort Aviation is the fixed-base operator and handles all fueling, rental, flight instruction and charters. The other closest airport is **Albert Ellis Airport**, (910) 324-1100, in Jacksonville, about 30 miles west of New Bern. This airport offers commuter service to larger airports.

As you travel Highway 17 through New Bern, keep your eyes open for the interesting historic markers along the highway.

Photo: William Russ

Tryon Palace is a restoration of an elegant Georgian building used in the 18th century in 1770 as the residence of the Colonial governor and meeting place of the Colonial assembly. Later it was the first State Capitol.

Raleigh-Durham International Airport, 840-2123, is a major international airport that is about a 2½-hour drive from New Bern. This airport is a major hub for domestic and international travelers and is served by all major and several feeder carriers.

By Sea

Boaters arriving on the water come up the Intracoastal Waterway and then travel the Neuse River to New Bern. The Neuse River flows into the Pamlico Sound and has well-marked channels.

New Bern also fronts the Trent River, which flows into the Neuse. A complete description of the rivers, bridge schedules and channel markers is offered in the chapter titled New Bern Fishing, Watersports and Boating.

Once You're Here

If you arrive by air or water, a rental car would be a good investment if you are interested in truly exploring all New Bern has to offer. Rental car agencies are based at the airport and are detailed in the New Bern Service Directory Chapter of this book. There is no public transportation in New Bern.

Bikes are another wonderful way to get around the downtown and waterfront areas of New Bern. However, because of the narrow shoulders and the increasingly heavy traffic, we wouldn't recommend biking along the highways that immediately lead to and from New Bern.

Walking still remains the most popular way to travel in the downtown area.

Regardless of how you arrive in New Bern, if you are a visitor contact the Craven County Convention and Visitors Bureau, 219 Pollock Street, 637-9400. (The bureau will move in October 1996 to Middle Street and Tryon Palace Drive.) Maps, brochures and friendly staff make this a good place to get started. Ask about the narrated trolley trips.

If you are exploring the possibility of relocating to New Bern or the surrounding area, contact the New Bern Chamber of Commerce, 637-3111, for lots of information. There you will find maps and brochures to help out.

Getting around New Bern is easy, so relax and enjoy your stay.

If you're looking for good seafood, you'll love dining out in New Bern. In fact, you would be hard-pressed to find a restaurant that does not offer some type of shellfish or other seafood.

New Bern
Restaurants

An exciting variety of dining options is available to New Bern residents and visitors. Restaurants feature culinary fare from around the world; you'll find everything from traditional Southern home cooking to fine European cuisine.

If you're looking for good seafood, you'll love dining out in New Bern. In fact, you would be hard-pressed to find a restaurant that does not offer some type of shellfish or other seafood.

The following guide alphabetically highlights some of the better-known restaurants and those we've found particularly tempting for reasons we've explained. We did not list the chain and fast food restaurants with which you are probably familiar. We encourage you also to ask locals for recommendations and to call ahead for hours of operation.

The price codes we use in our discussions reflect the average price of a dinner for two which includes appetizers, entrees, desserts and coffee. The code is explained below. Prices are also subject to change. The majority of these establishments accept most major credit cards.

Less than $20	$
$21 to $35	$$
$36 to $50	$$$
$51 and more	$$$$

ANNABELLE'S RESTAURANT & PUB
Twin Rivers Mall   633-6401
$-$$

Annabelle's offers a variety of foods in a relaxed atmosphere. The same menu is presented for lunch and dinner, and it includes something for everyone. Choose from a variety of beef, ribs, chicken and seafood entrees. The restaurant also has international selections, including Mexican fare. Annabelle's has a children's menu and early-bird specials Monday through Thursday. The hot-fudge cake is a favorite dessert. The bar serves beer and wine and has all ABC permits.

THE BAGEL COTTAGE
712 Pollock St.   636-1775
$

Originally a take-out bagel shop, this is now a good stop for breakfast, lunch or daytime snacks. Behind an old home across from Tryon Palace, the shop offers a dozen varieties of fresh-baked bagels and almost as many homemade spreads, chicken salad, shrimp salad and homemade soups. There are special salads, quiches and muffins each day, along with tempting desserts and bagel chips for snacking. You can eat inside the small shop or take advantage of the outside tables overlooking the Tryon Palace Cutting Gardens. There are also a few rocking chairs on the porch where you can make yourself comfortable.

THE BERNE RESTAURANT
2900 Neuse Blvd.   638-5296
$

For hearty country-style cooking and

seafood, the Berne Restaurant is the place to go. On the corner of one of New Bern's busiest intersections, this large establishment bears the telltale sign of good food to be found within: The parking lot is always full at meal times. A traditional country breakfast is featured everyday, and a breakfast buffet is offered Saturday and Sunday. Home-style dinners are featured, from the regional specialty of pork barbecue to a rib-eye steak dinner. The Berne also has a large selection of seafood and shellfish including trout, flounder, oysters (in season) and shrimp served fried or broiled. There is a children's menu and banquet facilities that can accommodate more than 200 people.

BILLY'S HAM AND EGGS

1300 S. Glenburnie Rd.   633-5498
$

Open 24 hours a day, Billy's Ham and Eggs serves more than just that. Everything on the menu is home cookin' just like grandma used to make. Try ham and eggs, country-style fried potatoes, a Belgian waffle or a pork chop along with grits, pancakes or homemade biscuits. For hamburgers the way you remember them — before fast-food days — try Billy's Big Beef Burger, a hefty helping of ground beef cooked to order and served on a sesame-seed bun with all the fixin's. There are lots of home-style veggies on the menu. Seafood specialties include trout, shrimp, oysters, clam strips and crab cakes. Other selections include ham, chicken, meat loaf, hamburger steak, roast beef, spaghetti and pork chops. There is also a children's menu and, of course, there are plenty of homemade cakes and pies.

CAPTAIN BORDEAUX'S BAR AND GRILL

104 Marina Dr.
Fairfield Harbour   637-2244
$$

This is a great place to end a day. Overlooking the Northwest Creek Marina at Fairfield Harbour, this hospitable establishment offers sunsets, refreshing beverages and casual dining on deck or inside. The menu offers a nice range of fare from light supper options such as burgers, salads, soups or a terrific Reuben to Cajun-style shrimp Creole, New York strip steak or Texas ribs. Board specials are announced nightly. A variety of sandwiches, soups and salads is also available for lunch. Reservations are not accepted.

CHARBURGER

1906 Clarendon Blvd.   633-4067
$

The Charburger is a good place to find a real hamburger served with hot — not greasy — fries, in a no-nonsense setting. Before you place your order at the counter, check out the daily specials. Then take a seat in a booth and enjoy. Fried chicken, hot dogs, hamburgers, shrimp, trout and steak sandwiches are among the specialties. For dessert, try the apple turnover or an ice cream sundae. Charburger serves lunch and dinner.

THE CHELSEA — A
RESTAURANT AND PUBLICK HOUSE

325 Middle St.   637-5469
$-$$$

You'll want to see the newly restored details of this 1912 building which was a drugstore of pharmacist Caleb Bradham, the inventor of Pepsi-Cola. But come to The Chelsea for the delight of good food. The value of fine detail is apparent in every preparation from Chef Karl's kitchen. His training is traditional French, but in practice, the chef offers a fusion cuisine. Among the varied selection of appetizers try the Arroyo Rolls, a Southwestern egg roll stuffed with a blend of cheeses, roasted chicken, pico de gallo and black-bean salsa. For an exciting blend of tastes try the lunch sandwich combining smoked turkey, bacon, Monterey Jack cheese, lettuce and tomato in herbed pita bread and served with raspberry mayonnaise. Taste surprises are mixed with taste traditions on the menus that are nicely varied so anyone can be pleased. The Chelsea serves a Sunday brunch which includes the 325 Middle Benedict — a poached egg with a crab cake served on a potato pancake and topped with Hollandaise sauce. After this, you'll never forget the restaurant's address. The Chelsea offers a wide selection of domestic or imported beers and wine and mixed drinks. This is a popular nightly gathering place (see the New Bern Nightlife chapter), and there is often live entertainment.

The Flame

2303 Neuse Blvd.   633-0262
$$-$$$

The unique Victorian decor, elegant meals and irreproachable service make dinner at The Flame a memorable event. For a special occasion, try The Flame's steak and lobster. You'll want to add one of the specialties of the house: the stuffed baked potato. Other specialties include grilled shrimp and teriyaki chicken. And don't pass up a trip to the gourmet salad and soup bar. Evening specials are offered on some weekdays and could include steak-and-lobster-for-two combos or a second steak at a fraction of the cost of the first. The restaurant has all ABC permits and specializes in fine wines.

Fred and Claire's

247 Craven St.   638-5426
$

This cozy little establishment in the downtown historic district offers a variety of intriguing and delicious dishes, all prepared fresh daily. Dishes include cheese

and broccoli casserole, shepherd's pie or crab quiche served with fresh fruit, a muffin and sherbet. Lasagna, salads, soups, breads and desserts are all featured. Specialty sandwiches include spicy sausage subs, fillet of flounder on a French roll and homemade pimento cheese. You'll also find burgers and hot dogs. For dinner, Fred and Claire's offers wonderful omelettes, seafood, and chicken livers and onions. Your favorite domestic or imported beer and wine are available to complement your meal.

FRIDAY'S 1890 SEAFOOD

2307 Neuse Blvd.   637-2276
$-$$

The decor of Friday's gives you the feeling of being below the deck of one of the many pirate and merchant ships that frequented the North Carolina coast in the 1800s. It's rustic, and the tables are tucked away for privacy. Friday's offers a varied menu that includes the all-time seafood favorites of shrimp, flounder, trout, lobster and crab legs served with all the traditional fixings. Landlubbers' favorites include pork barbecue, rib eyes, hamburger steaks and chicken. Entrees come with a potato, hush puppies, coleslaw and a cup of clam chowder or a trip to the salad bar.

THE HARVEY MANSION

221 Tryon Palace Dr.   638-3205
$-$$$

This restaurant and lounge are in a restored building constructed by John Harvey in the 1790s. Through the years, the building served as a home, mercan-

tile establishment, boarding house, military academy and even the early home of Craven Community College. The restaurant opened in 1979, and its award-winning Swiss chef, Beat Zuttel, has a devoted following. Diners at the Harvey Mansion are treated to seasonally inspired menu selections for lunch, dinner and Sunday brunch and luncheon. Dinner might start with an appetizer of duck with pear and ginger compote or sauteed escargot. For your entree, consider one of the chef's Swiss specials such as veal morsels with mushroom sauce and Swiss potato. A choice of fresh seafood is featured each night — grilled, poached or sauteed. Homemade desserts include Key lime and berry tartlettes, banana-nut-chocolate torte and yogurt moussecake. Downstairs Harvey's Cellar Lounge offers an intimate atmosphere and a unique copper bar (see our New Bern Nightlife chapter). The Cellar offers private dining areas and a pasta, seafood and prime-rib menu. Guests can enjoy an extensive selection of wines, champagne by the bottle or glass, mixed drinks and domestic and imported beers.

HENDERSON HOUSE RESTAURANT

216 Pollock St.   637-4784
$$$

This award-winning restaurant in a restored, historic New Bern home, features a collection of original art work and offers service in private party rooms. Henderson House offers an elegant candlelit atmosphere for dinner and requires appropriate dress. The menu in-

Photo: Benners Studio

Nightlife and entertainment continuously change New Bern and might even offer a night on a hot-air balloon.

cludes dishes created with veal, duck, lamb and pheasant. Entrees offered might include tornadoes of beef with Béarnaise sauce, veal chop with chanterelles, pheasant in port wine, shrimp almondine or a delicious seafood casserole. There is an extensive wine list that favors French vintages but also includes wines from the world over. Mixed drinks are available. Dinner at the Henderson House is highly recommended and will certainly be a time to remember.

HOUSTON'S STEAK HOUSE AND SALOON

2000 S. Glenburnie Rd.   *637-2206*
$$

Formerly Clancy O'Hara's Restaurant and Lounge, Houston's continues the tradition of being the locals' favorite for steak and ribs. The interior has rough-hewn timbers salvaged from old homes and Victorian furnishings, creating a civilized cowpokes atmosphere. Lunch sandwiches, salads and burgers include Philly-style subs with steak, chicken or shrimp. Dinner selections are largely steak and ribs but there are also chargrilled chicken and shrimp entrees. Live entertainment is scheduled on weekends and may be Texas-style or local, such as the Crisis Band. Houston's has full ABC privileges and banquet facilities with a private bar to accommodate as many as 80 guests. Afternoon senior discounts are extended, and a kid's menu is available.

KRESS CAFE

309 Middle St.   *633-9300*
$

Opened in early 1996, the Kress Cafe is an authentic diner. Beautifully designed

Little Did Caleb Bradham Know...

Could a would-be pharmacist ever have believed that a drink concocted in the back room of a drugstore in the 1890s would, more than 100 years later, be advertised by legendary crooner Ray Charles, singing, "You got the right one, baby, uh-huh"?

Probably not.

Today, Caleb Bradham's syrupy concoction is known around the world as Pepsi-Cola. The location of his first drugstore, where the original mix was first brewed, is marked by a historical marker at the corner of Middle and Pollock streets in downtown New Bern.

Caleb Bradham had aspirations to be a pharmacist, but was forced to leave school and return home when his father's business failed. In his drugstore, sometime during the 1890s, he concocted a new soda fountain drink he called Brad's Drink. He advertised it as "exhilarating, invigorating and aids digestion." By 1898, young Bradham had given the new carbonate the name Pepsi-Cola.

Bradham began his cola operation on an organized basis in 1903. The company, headquartered in the back room of the drugstore, packaged the syrup for sale to other soda fountains. The bottling process was on the rise but still in second place to over-the-counter sales at soda fountains.

Business boomed until right after the war years, 1917-18, when sugar jumped from 5.5¢ a pound to 22.5¢ a pound. For Pepsi-Cola, which was retailing at a nickel per bottle, it spelled disaster.

After collapsing into bankruptcy, the company changed hands four times before winding up in 1931 as a subsidiary of Loft, the parent of the internationally known Pepsi of today.

Today, the only extant buildings with a direct link to Caleb Bradham are his home on the corner of Johnson and E. Front streets and a building on the corner of Broad and Middle streets that was leased by the Bradham Drug Company. It was known as the Broad Street Store. Mr. Bradham's attorneys had their offices upstairs and Bradham's state-of-the-art pharmacy was on the street level. The building is now the Chelsea Restaurant which houses a wall mural depicting the Pepsi Cola story.

Photo: Swiss Bear

Pepsi was served at Bradhm's state-of-the-art Broad Street drugstore.

as the centerpiece of the newly renovated downtown mall known as the Kress Building, the cafe is all 1950s chrome, neon and rock 'n' roll. You'll wish you had worn your poodle skirt. Jump in a booth for breakfast, lunch or dinner. Eggs any style, pancakes and omelettes are served in the morning. Lunch salads, sandwiches, burgers and dinner blue plate specials adhere to the theme throughout the day — it's all American. So order that milk shake and get two straws.

LATITUDE 35

I Bicentennial Park
Sheraton Hotel and Marina   638-3585
$$

Although the elegant decor and menu at this hotel restaurant suggest strictly fine dining, don't be put off if you've just jumped off your boat. You can come as you are and enjoy the cuisine and the panoramic view of the Neuse River and hotel marina. Latitude 35's breakfast buffet, with its selection of egg dishes, grits, breakfast meats, French toast, waffles, muffins, wonderful biscuits, fresh fruit and cereals, is a favorite of locals and visitors. Weekday lunches offer sandwiches, soups and creative salads along with light plates featuring pasta, salad, seafood or meat. Attention turns to seafood in the evening. You'll find all types of fish and shellfish that can be broiled, baked, fried, grilled, peppered or blackened. The salad bar is included with each entree. For landlubbers, Latitude 35 offers pasta, chicken and beef, and there is an extensive children's menu.

MOORE'S BARBECUE

U.S. Hwy. I7 S.   638-3937
$

Moore's specializes in eastern North Carolina chopped barbecued pork, but offers more. Whether you eat in or take out,

Fine dining has been a tradition in New Bern for over 200 years.

the food at Moore's is good, home-style cooking. A meal of pork or chicken barbecue is served with coleslaw, french fries and hush puppies. There's also a seafood plate — shrimp, flounder and trout — and an honest shrimp burger. Moore's features both meals and bulk orders as take outs. But before you decide what you want, check the specials. Moore's can cater small, large or huge events or put on a North Carolina-style pig pickin'.

MUSTARD'S LAST STAND

Tryon Palace Dr. and U.S. Hwy. 70 638-1937
$

Mustard's Last Stand is a movable concession stand that offers the very best in hot dogs and Polish sausages on freshbaked rolls. The hot dogs are better than those at the ballpark, and you don't have to fight for a parking space. The stand is next to the Exxon station at the corner of Tryon Palace Drive and Highway 70 and is the perfect place to stop while on a walking tour of New Bern. Mustard's also offers drinks, chips and more.

POLLOCK STREET
DELICATESSEN AND RESTAURANT
208 Pollock St.   *637-2480*
$-$$

In an old house in New Bern's downtown historic district, this restaurant serves wonderful New York-style cuisine for breakfast, lunch and dinner. Whether you eat downstairs, upstairs or on the patio, you can choose something as simple as a bagel with cream cheese or a homemade salad, or have a full meal with cheese-stuffed pasta shells, veal, chicken or sea scallops with pasta. The delicatessen offers an assortment of hot or cold sandwiches and sandwich platters. Daily specials are usually offered for lunch and dinner. Try the quiche or soup of the day served with fruit, a sub or a Reuben. Beer and wine are available. Homemade desserts include Key lime pie, cheesecake and chocolate mousse. Salads, deli-sliced meats and sandwiches can be ordered to go. Live music is often played, and the restaurant can accommodate special events. The Deli offers full-service catering.

RAGAZZI'S ITALIAN RESTAURANT
425 Hotel Dr.   *637-5090*
$-$$

At the Highway 70 overpass at Clarendon Boulevard, Ragazzi's was welcomed to New Bern in 1996. A small chain of thematic restaurants in eastern North Carolina, Ragazzi's features creative pasta combinations with a choice of pastas, toppings and sauces. Chicken, veal, seafood, steak and stuffed-pasta entrees are available in addition to the invincible pizzas and calzones. Light selections are available for those counting fat grams and calories, and all entrees are presented with fresh-baked bread and soup or salad. Special prices on selected menu items are offered during lunch hours, and everything is available for take out. Working locals often call ahead and pick up dinner at Ragazzi's.

RAMADA INN'S ANGUS STEAK HOUSE
101 Howell Rd.   *636-3637*
$-$$$

If you're looking for a good steak, try the certified Angus beef served at the Ramada. Each cut of meat is aged for tenderness and prepared with care by either slow roasting or cooking on a real hickory wood grill. You can order rib eyes, New York strips, tenderloin or prime rib. The Ramada offers steak Oscar and beef tips. Although the specialty is Angus beef, the Ramada also serves a variety of poultry and seafood selections. You'll find crab cakes prepared with jumbo lump crabmeat, shrimp, live Maine lobster and grilled catch of the day. The Ramada overlooks the Neuse River and Ramada Inn marina, and you can eat indoors or out on the deck. They are open for breakfast and dinner. The Sunday brunch buffet offers a wonderful selection of breakfast items, plus made-to-order omelettes. The Ramada Lounge also offers seafood and a light dinner menu.

Insiders' Tips

Extended local telephone service, new in spring 1996, means that calls between New Bern and Morehead City are now local calls. So pick up the phone and make reservations for dinner. It's a small world after all.

SANDPIPER RESTAURANT

2403 Neuse Blvd.   633-0888
$

If you are looking for seafood at a reasonable price, consider the Sandpiper. The restaurant offers lunch and dinner from one menu and specializes in oyster stew and clam chowder, shrimp and oyster cocktails and steaks. Full meals include fried seafood platters with fish, shrimp, oysters, deviled crab and scallops. A typical house special might include fried trout fillets, fried shrimp, French fries and a hearty serving of coleslaw. One of the nice things about the Sandpiper is that each meal is preceded with hot hush puppies and butter.

SARAH POCKET TEA ROOM

303 Metcalf St.   636-3055
$

Specializing in "doing lunch," this is a lovely stop for soup, salads, sandwiches or quiche in either the tea room or the adjacent sandwich shop. Civilized English teas and lace table linens encourage lingering for gingerbread or fruit pie desserts before continuing a tour of colonial restorations or racing back to work.

SCALZO'S

415 Broad St.   633-9898
$$

For outstanding authentic Southern Italian creations, dine at Scalzo's. Founded by Chef Mario Scalzo, the restaurant's word in food and ingredients is fresh. For starters, try the sauteed shrimp or calamari, lamb meatballs, antipasto, roasted peppers or Italian bean salad. The variety of different pasta dishes is enormous, with 18-plus sauces that can be matched with one of eight homemade pastas. The pasta selection includes meat or cheese ravioli, gnocchi and capellini. The sauces range from the familiar marinara to an unusual black olive and capers creation. There is a mixed seafood sauce, red or white clam sauce and several vegetable or meat sauces. Create your own meal with pasta, sauce and veal, eggplant, beef or chicken. Veal Gorgonzola, a house specialty prepared with cheese, white wine and fresh tomatoes, is a favorite with Scalzo's loyal patrons. For dessert, choose from among several delicious Italian confections. Scalzo's has an extensive international wine list.

SONNY'S RAW BAR & GRILL

235 Craven St.   637-9000
$$

A favorite downtown spot for lunch and dinner, Sonny's focuses on seafood but still serves a muy bueno enchilada, taco and burrito. Our lunch favorite is sauteed shrimp or scallops served with pasta and a vegetable of the day. The dinner menu shows seafood specialties such as stuffed fluke flounder served with vegetable, hush puppies and choice of potato, slaw or wild rice. Sauteed soft-shell crabs are offered with pasta. Sonny's raw bar steams shellfish from September through spring. The bar serves mixed drinks, wines and beers including a nice selection of Mexican beers.

SWEET BEARS PASTRY

Pollock & Middle sts.   635-5325
$

Freshly baked breads and pastries tempt even the most disciplined dieters from this corner bake shop, formerly Dixon's Soda Shop. Just-baked breads range from yeasty traditionals to herby and adventurous varieties such as sun-dried tomato bread. The inventory of pastries, cookies and muffins is extensive, so be forewarned. Coffee choices are perfectly matched to any selection from the baked sweets, and the seating provides a comfortable vantage for watching New Bern's activity.

TRENT RIVER COFFEE COMPANY

208 Craven St.   514-2030
$

This complete coffee bar and retail coffee shop is the social gathering place for downtown retailers on most weekday mornings for endless coffee and a nice selection of breakfast breads and pastries. This continues throughout the day, and on announced evenings this is the staging place for the Down East Folk Arts Society live performances and George's Dinner Club, intimate alternative classic theater performances. Coffee is always brewing.

YANA'S RESTAURANT

242 Middle St.   636-5440
$

In late 1995, Yana's brought to downtown New Bern the same food and atmosphere that has long kept the population of Swansboro happy. Yana's serves breakfast and lunch faithfully every day, and real ice cream milk shakes, sundaes, splits and malts into the afternoon. Yana's opens with delicious fruit pancakes, omelette specialties and even low-fat breakfasts. Breakfast fades to lunch when burgers roll out among the 1950s Chevys that adorn the booth-and-lunch-counter setting. Yana's has brought a shrimp burger to downtown New Bern as well as a chicken-salad sandwich that continues to form lines for lunch in Swansboro. Don't forget that shake.

New Bern
Nightlife

New Bern offers a nice variety of nightlife, although it isn't overrun with entertainment spots — a refreshing factor for a riverfront city. Nightlife here revolves around smaller gathering places where friends meet to mix and mingle. Several lounges are on the waterfront so guests can relax inside or outside and watch the sunset over the river.

Information about laws regulating liquor sales is included at the end of this chapter.

New Bern is home to a professional acting group, a professional dance troupe and a community theater organization. These groups stage a number of performances throughout the year, and there are several performances for children. The **Craven Arts Council**, 638-ARTS, has information about these groups. See our New Bern Arts chapter for more information.

Nightlife takes various forms here in New Bern. There's a six-screen movie theater at **Southgate Cinema 6** on Trent Road, 638-1820. You'll find three screens at **Cinema Triple** on Neuse Boulevard,

633-4620. **B&R Lanes** at 1309 Tatum Drive, 633-3424, is a local bowling alley.

As for the wander-in, sit-down-and-enjoy-yourself type of nightlife, New Bern has that to offer too. Although there are others, the nightspots that follow are among the more popular.

CITY SIDE CAFE
Sheraton Hotel and Marina   638-3585

City Side is one of New Bern's most exciting gathering places. The atmosphere is lively and upbeat for those nights when you might want to stay up late. Entertainment varies and includes comedians, dance contests, pool tournaments and live bands playing beach, classic rock and top-40 music. The City Side Cafe serves international food and imported beers and coffees and has all ABC permits. Favorite menu items include the top-your-own pizzas and burgers.

OAR HOUSE LOUNGE
I Marina Rd., River Bend   633-2006

If you're looking to party and have lots of fun, head to the Oar House. On

According to North Carolina law, a person is legally impaired when his or her blood-alcohol level is .08 or higher.

Insiders' Tips

the Trent River in River Bend, the Oar House can be reached by car or boat — just dock at a slip beside the lounge. Inside you'll find a large dance floor, a bar serving mixed drinks, bar snacks and plenty of fun. Sunday afternoons are for beach music and the T-Bird Shag Party. (The shag is the indigenous dance of the coastal Carolinas and is danced to a type of music called beach music.) Other nights you'll find a jukebox or a DJ.

RAMADA LOUNGE
101 Howell Rd.   *636-3637*

This is a spot that might be comfortably peaceful one night and buzzing with activity the next. Attracting a mixture of locals and visitors, the lounge offers guests lots of windows from which to view the river and downtown New Bern. Live entertainment is offered some weekends; a DJ spins tunes on weeknights; karaoke is featured on Wednesday and Saturday; and there is a jukebox on other nights.

PRO SAIL CLUB
1 Bicentennial Park
Sheraton Hotel and Marina   *638-3585*

Named after a professional sailing competition series, the Pro Sail is the place to enjoy casual relaxation in a sailor's haven. The club features a long, irregular-shaped bar, comfortable seating and lots of windows overlooking the harbor. There is also an outside deck. Live entertainment is offered on most weekends, and there is a large-screen television.

THE CHELSEA
335 Middle St.   *637-5469*

The Chelsea is a popular downtown gathering place for those interested in mingling with friends or soon-to-be friends. The bar is in the restaurant area (see the New Bern Restaurants chapter) and serves mixed drinks, beers and wine. The building and the decor are interesting in themselves, with lots of Pepsi memorabilia.

HARVEY'S CELLAR LOUNGE
221 Tryon Palace Dr.   *638-3205*

As the name implies, this lounge is in the cellar of the Harvey Mansion, which offers patrons an upstairs restaurant serving lunch and dinner (see the New Bern Restaurants chapter). This intimate lounge features a small, unique copper bar and offers a bar menu and mixed drinks. Call ahead; there is often live entertainment that might include music or scenes from a play.

ANNABELLE'S PUB
U.S. Hwy. 17
Twin Rivers Mall   *633-6401*

The Pub is part of Annabelle's restaurant and offers a casual, relaxed atmosphere. The bar serves beer, wine and mixed drinks and features at least one drink special each day. For information about the restaurant, see the New Bern Restaurants chapter.

HOUSTON'S STEAK HOUSE AND SALOON
2000 S. Glenburnie Rd.   *637-2206*

This popular lounge and restaurant

is a good place to wind down. The lounge has full ABC privileges and also serves wine and beer. More information about Houston's is in our New Bern Restaurants chapter.

Liquor Laws And ABC Stores

Craven County voters were among the first in North Carolina to take advantage of local-option mixed-drink sales. A 1980 referendum to settle the issue passed by a slim 50 votes.

ABC stores are the only establishments in the state allowed to sell liquor by the bottle. Beer and wine are sold in grocery and convenience stores and in specialty food shops throughout the area. All ABC stores are open Monday through Saturday, but the hours vary. Purchases must be made with cash, MasterCard or VISA. No personal checks are taken, and only those 21 years old or older are allowed in the stores.

ABC Store No. 1, 318 Tryon Palace Drive, 637-3623

ABC Store No. 4, 1407 Neuse Boulevard, 637-9744

ABC Store No. 5, 2005 Glenburnie Road, 638-4847

For guests of the New Berne House Inn, a tandem bicycle is available for those who enjoy leisurely cycling around town.

New Bern
Accommodations

Overnight lodgings are increasing in New Bern, and the river city now has several major hotels silhouetting its skyline. There are also a number of excellent bed and breakfast inns, at least one of which is said to be inhabited by a friendly spirit. However, those seeking less spiritual digs have a number of other options to choose from.

Hotels positioned along the city's picturesque waterfront offer lovely views of the Trent and Neuse rivers, and a number of economy and budget motels are near the downtown area. Cozy and architecturally interesting bed and breakfast inns are sprinkled throughout the historic district.

The listing here is alphabetical and not intended to recommend one place over another. Room prices fluctuate with the seasons, but for the purpose of reflecting rate information, we have shown high-season rates for double occupancy. Winter rates may be substantially lower. Rates are subject to change, therefore we urge you to verify rate information when making your reservations. All hotels and bed and breakfasts accept most major credit cards. The following scale is used to represent rate ranges.

$25 to $52	*$*
$53 to $75	*$$*
$76 to $99	*$$$*
More than $100	*$$$$*

THE AERIE
509 Pollock St.   *636-5553*
$$$ *(800) 849-5553*

Just one block from Tryon Palace, this bed and breakfast inn is in a Victorian-style home that was built in the 1880s. It is furnished with fine antiques and reproductions, and a player piano graces a downstairs sitting room. Each of the seven guest rooms comes with either twin, queen or king beds, a private bath and cable television. The inn provides complimentary wine, beer, soft drinks, light refreshments, a wealth of games, reading materials and books of local lore. A full gourmet breakfast is served each morning in the dining room.

The Tea Room at The Aerie is open Wednesday through Saturday serving teas, coffees, cocoa, scones with cream and jam, tarts and an assortment of tea cakes. Even if you're not staying the night, you're invited to enjoy afternoon tea at The Aerie.

COMFORT SUITES AND MARINA

218 E. Front St.   636-0022
$$-$$$ (800) 228-5150

This new hotel has a Colonial look and a warm, friendly atmosphere. It features 100 suites, many with waterfront balconies that offer beautiful views of the mile-wide Neuse River. All suites have refrigerators, microwaves and coffee makers; whirlpool suites are also available. Other amenities include free local calls, complimentary continental breakfasts, an outdoor pool with a waterfront courtyard, an outdoor heated whirlpool, a fitness center, a guest laundry room, a board room and meeting facilities. Room service is available with dinners prepared by the kitchen of the Harvey Mansion. Vouchers for golf privileges are available, and special golf packages can be arranged. The hotel's new 24-slip marina accommodates boats up to 120 feet. Slips can be rented by the day, week, month or long-term. Boat and Jet Ski rentals by Shorebird are available right at the marina. The hotel is within walking distance of New Bern's downtown area and historic sites.

DAYS INN

925 Broad St.   636-0150
$ (800) 329-7466

Recently refurbished, New Bern's 110-room Days Inn offers guests tastefully appointed units, an outside pool and a deluxe continental breakfast. Conveniently

onsite is the delightful restaurant and lounge, the Broad Street Bar & Grille. The inn is only two blocks from Tryon Palace and New Bern's historic downtown district. A large banquet room can accommodate 300 guests, and smaller conference facilities are available to accommodate conventions, workshops or family functions. Laundry service and free local calls are offered to guests, and historic walking tours can be arranged.

FAIRFIELD HARBOUR

750 Broad Creek Rd.   638-8011
Variable rates

Any of Fairfield Harbour's 237 time-share units is available for rent. Units range in size from a small condominium for two to a two- or three-story house that can accommodate eight guests. Units can be reserved on a weekly basis through area real estate offices or on a monthly basis at the onsite Fairfield Realty office. Renting guests are offered a full range of recreational amenities. Fairfield Harbour features two golf courses, a country club with an outdoor pool, nine tennis courts, a recreation center with indoor and outdoor pools, an exercise room, a game room, video rental and a miniature golf course. For those activities requiring a fee, Fairfield guests receive a reduced rate.

HAMPTON INN

200 Hotel Dr.   637-2111
$-$$ (800) 448-8288

Off U.S. Highway 17 at the U.S. Highway 70 bypass, this modern 101-room hotel opened in May 1993. Taste-

Insiders' Tips

Don't feel embarrassed to wander residential streets or stop and gaze at any of the houses in the historic district. Everyone appreciates your admiration.

fully furnished like other hotels in its chain, it is equipped with a pool, a Jacuzzi, an exercise room and meeting facilities. It also offers free local calls and free in-room movies; 75 percent of its rooms are designated for nonsmoking guests. A free continental breakfast is offered, or guests may dine at one of many nearby restaurants. Twin Rivers Shopping Mall is just across the highway. Golf packages can be arranged, and tour packages of New Bern's historic district, which is about 3 miles from the hotel, can be arranged by the hotel staff. Government discount rates are offered, and the hotel has a special third-and-fourth-adults-stay-free plan. Children stay free with their parents.

HARMONY HOUSE INN

215 Pollock St.   636-3810
$$$-$$$$ (800) 636-3113

The rocking chairs and swing on the long front porch and the two front doors (you'll see what we mean) distinguish this Greek Revival-style bed and breakfast in the downtown historic district from all others. The original part of the house was built sometime before 1809. Additions and porches were added and, around the turn of this century, the house was sawed in half and the west side was moved nine feet to accommodate a new hallway and staircase. The inn now has nine guest rooms and one romantic suite, all furnished with antiques and reproductions. All rooms have private baths and decorative fireplaces. A full breakfast, which may include house specialties such as orange French toast, stuffed pancakes, egg and bacon casserole and fresh-baked coffeecake, is served each morning in the dining room. A social hour is hosted each evening offering guests a selection of beverages, and before bed a glass of sherry or port is available.

KING'S ARMS INN

212 Pollock St.   638-4409
$$$ *(800) 872-9306*

Built in 1847, the King's Arms Inn was a private residence until 1980 when it was established as an inn, New Bern's first bed and breakfast. Named for a New Bern tavern said to have hosted members of the First Continental Congress, King's Arms has eight guest rooms, each with television, telephone, private bath and furnished with antiques and reproductions. A housetop suite offers a beautiful river view. Breakfast is served in-room and includes cinnamon coffee, specialty teas or juice and home-baked breads, muffins and fresh fruit. Complimentary soft drinks and home-baked treats are always on hand, and the hosts happily make arrangements and reservations for their guests to enjoy the best of New Bern.

THE MAGNOLIA HOUSE

315 George St.   633-9488
$$$ *(800) 601-9488*

Formerly the Margaret M. Hanff House, c. 1870-80, this Charleston-pink bed and breakfast inn is just a stone's throw from Tryon Palace and within walking distance of the town's center and waterfront. Hosts John and Kim Trudo offer three cozy guest rooms, each with its own decor including one room decorated with pieces from the East Lake period when the house was built. Rooms are fully heated and cooled and have private baths. House furnishings include family treasures, locally gathered antiques, estate pieces and local art. An onsite gift shop makes antique finds available to guests or anyone who catches the antiques bug while in New Bern. Guests are welcomed each morning with fresh-baked breads and muffins, seasonal fruits and fresh-ground coffees. A full breakfast is also offered. Afternoon tea with scones, tarts and finger sandwiches is served at 4 PM.

NEW BERNE HOUSE INN

709 Broad St.   636-2250
$$$ *(800) 842-7688*

This Colonial Revival-style bed and breakfast is about a block from the Tryon Palace Complex. Among the furnishings in the seven guest rooms is a notorious brass bed said to have been rescued from a burning brothel in 1897. All rooms are air-conditioned and have private baths and telephones. Rooms accommodate two people and are furnished with either twin, queen or king beds. Lounging in the front porch swing is encouraged. Refreshments and beverages are served, and guests are treated to a full, home-cooked breakfast. The house library is always open, and a tandem bicycle is available for those who enjoy leisurely cycling around town. The inn also conducts monthly mystery weekends, which have proven to be great fun for the innkeepers and their guests.

PALACE MOTEL

Hwy. 17 S.   638-1151
$

Long a mainstay for New Bern travelers, the 66-room economy Palace Motel has a pool and a full-service restau-

Insiders' Tips

Avoid Neuse Boulevard during commuter hours. Take Glenburnie Road or Simmons Street to reach either end of town.

rant that features homestyle Southern cooking and banquet facilities. All rooms have telephones and cable television. Guests will need transportation to see area attractions.

RAMADA INN
WATERFRONT AND MARINA

101 Howell Rd.	636-3637
$$$-$$$$	(800) 228-2828

One of the newer hotels in New Bern, the 112-room Ramada is across the Trent River from the city's downtown area. All rooms, offered with numerous discounts, have water views, in-room coffee makers and complimentary fruit baskets. The Ramada also offers four suites with Jacuzzis. The hotel's Angus Steakhouse specializes in certified Angus beef. For a more casual atmosphere, the Ramada Lounge offers light dinners and appetiz-

ers overlooking the marina or service on the expansive, covered outdoor deck. Both eateries provide lovely waterfront views. Guests may also enjoy the hotel's swimming pool. For boaters, a 144-slip floating dock marina comes complete with showers, phone hookups, electricity, lock boxes, cable and HBO hookups. Dockage is offered for transients and for longer stays of a week, a month or even a year.

THE SHERATON GRAND
NEW BERN HOTEL AND MARINA

1 Bicentennial Park	638-3585
$$$-$$$$	(800) 326-3745

One of the attractions of this downtown hotel is that all 100 guest rooms overlook the Trent River and the hotel's marina. A new addition recently added 72 guest rooms, suites and mini-suites in the style of grand Southern inns. The inn is attached to the hotel via a covered walkway and offers guests both waterfront and city-side views. The inn addition has an executive level made up entirely of suites. To serve the hotel and inn, two restaurants and two lounges offer dining and relaxing. Latitude 35 overlooks the marina and features full breakfast, lunch and dinner menus spotlighting the chef's signature entrees. The City Side Cafe offers casual dining and a lighter menu and features live entertainment. The Pro Sail Lounge is a great place for a relaxed day's end, and the Quarterdeck Gazebo & Bar extends the night under the stars with outdoor entertainment. The Sheraton has ample meeting facilities, a swimming pool, an exercise room and boat and bike

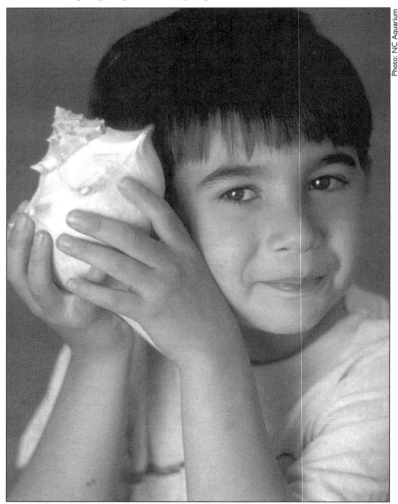

Photo: NC Aquarium

There are times when the ocean calls and even young ones get a far away look in their eyes.

The Harbour
A UNIQUE WATERFRONT RESORT
NEW BERN, NC

*Three pools, six lakes, eleven tennis courts,
weight room, whirlpool spa, miniature golf,
two 18-hole golf courses, golf lessons,
driving range, bicycle rentals, marina,
boat rentals, fishing, water sports,
one and two bedroom accommodations,
full kitchens, jacuzzis, sundecks,
waterviews, fireplaces...*

Vacation Resorts International
"perfecting the art of hospitality"
For more information **800-625-4874** *Reservations*

rentals. Golf and tennis privileges at area clubs can be included in your stay. Group rates are available.

VACATION RESORTS INTERNATIONAL
Broad Creek Rd.   *633-1151*
Variable rates

A professional management company since 1964, Vacation Resorts International manages properties in the Fairfield Harbour community offering fully furnished one- to three-bedroom condominiums on a daily, weekly or monthly basis. All units at Fairfield Harbour will accommodate six to eight people and are on one of the two 18-hole golf courses in the development. Guests are extended all development amenities including the

300-slip marina, rental boats, country club with restaurant, three swimming pools and two golf courses. For rentals on a daily basis, a minimum of three days is required.

ZIEGLER MOTEL
1914 Trent Blvd.   *637-4498*
$

Set amid a virtual forest of dogwoods and azaleas one block off Highway 17 S., this neat, clean, 11-room, family-run motel offers modest accommodations. Two cottages are also available. It is in a primarily residential section of town, and transportation will be necessary to visit area attractions.

New Bern
Camping

If you enjoy communing with nature by camping, you have the option to either rough it or do it with some flair in the New Bern area. You'll find commercial campgrounds ready to provide a number of services and you will also find primitive camping areas well off the beaten path. The Croatan National Forest has several camping areas and an additional campground farther down the highway close to Cape Carteret off N.C. Highway 58. The forest rangers allow primitive camping anywhere in the national forest except in picnic areas and parking lots.

The forest service camping facilities have been recently upgraded, and most can now accommodate any size recreational vehicle. For a more complete discussion of the Croatan National Forest, see our Crystal Coast Attractions chapter. For camping information, call forest headquarters, 638-5628, or stop in and pick up a map of the camping areas at the ranger station on Fisher Avenue, 9 miles south of New Bern off Highway 70 E.

NEUSE RIVER CAMPGROUND
U.S. Hwy. 17 N., Bridgeton   *638-2556*
This campground, about 3 miles north of New Bern, is the kind of place you can't miss. The back side of the park, which has 83 spaces for visitors, is on the Neuse River. Some camp sites are specially designed for tents, while others have full RV hookups. The campground provides a comfort station, a laundry room, a dump station, an outdoor theater, a pizza and sub shop, an indoor arcade, a dance floor and jukebox, a boat ramp and a swimming pool. A man-made swimming lake, surrounded by a white sandy beach and filled with treated water, awaits your leisure. It is open year round with nightly fees ranging from $12 for tent sites to $17.50 for full hookups.

FISHERS LANDING
Croatan National Forest
U.S. Hwy. 70 E., Riverdale   *638-5628*
Perched on a bluff above the Neuse River about 8 miles south of New Bern, Fishers Landing can be reached by turning left across Highway 70 E. at the Riverdale Mini-Mart. This recreation area offers only the barest of man-made amenities, but what it lacks in creature comforts is more than compensated for by the chance to be among some unusual

---

Insiders' Tips

Camping in boat ramp areas is discouraged by the park service in an effort to keep these areas easily accessible to launch for fishing and boating. Please camp outside the parking areas.

creatures. Take an early morning walk along the crescent-shaped sandy beach, accessible by wooden stairs set into the cliff, and you'll see ospreys, egrets, sea gulls and herons. Between the small parking lot and the bluff is a wide, grassy area, backed by a row of trees. The river is swimmable, but shoes are suggested for protection against rocks and tree stumps on the bottom. The site offers unimproved walk-in camping and picnicking, non-flush toilets, grills, drinking water and picnic tables. It is open year round, and nondeveloped trails for exploring wind through the thick surrounding forest.

NEUSE RIVER
CROATAN NATIONAL FOREST
U.S. Hwy. 70 E.   638-5628

Locally known as Flanner's Beach, this area is 10 miles south of New Bern on secondary N.C. Highway 1107, Flanner's Beach Road. Twenty-four camp sites are available plus picnicking facilities, a bathhouse, swimming, hiking, fishing, flush toilets and a dump station. Fees are $8 per site per night. The area is normally open April through October or November; however, that is subject to change at the beginning and end of each specified season. This recreation area is a favorite of locals.

CEDAR POINT
Croatan National Forest
Cape Carteret   638-5628

On the White Oak River a mile north of Cape Carteret (follow signs from Highway 58), this area is a bit of a drive from New Bern. But, it is a good stopover if you want to experience a coastal marsh and maritime forest in their truest forms. The site offers 41 camp units, picnicking,

drinking water, toilets, electric hookups, a shower building and an unimproved boat ramp. It is well-suited for group camping and has an interpretive nature trail nearby that winds through hardwood and pine forests. Boardwalks cross marshes and open water, and viewing blinds are set up for bird-watching. Camp fees are $15 per night. Formerly open year round, this camping area now closes for the winter and is open April through October.

NEUSIOK TRAIL
Croatan National Forest   638-5628

This area is strictly for those who enjoy roughing it. There are no camping facilities along the trail, but you may primitive camp if you pack out your garbage. You will need to bring along drinking water and wear boots to cross wet areas. The trail begins on the Newport River and ends on the Neuse River at Pinecliff Recreation Area. It passes through pine and hardwood forests and interesting areas of pocosin and dense titi brush. The total length of the trail is approximately 21 miles, and it crosses several paved and non-paved roads. Because of biting, stinging and zinging insects, fall, winter and early spring are best for camping and hiking.

Catfish Lake and **Great Lake** allow additional primitive camping. Boat ramps are available at Brice's Creek, Cahooque Creek and Haywood Landing. Locals favor these areas for their natural beauty and handy access to water; however, insects can be prolific in the summer months. For directions to these areas, call forest headquarters or stop in and pick up a map at the ranger station on Fisher Avenue.

New Bern
Shopping

New Bern offers a variety of shopping opportunities from large department stores to specialty shops and boutiques.

Twin Rivers Mall, 633-2800, has about 50 stores, making it New Bern's largest collection of stores under one roof. At the junction of U.S. Highway 17 and U.S. Highway 70, the mall is anchored by Belk, JCPenney and Kmart. Nearby is **Rivertowne Square** with Wal-Mart and Brendles as anchors, and **Berne Square** with Roses and Kerr Drug as anchors.

As downtown New Bern continues to develop and grow, so do the shopping opportunities. Looking at the downtown shops today, it is hard to imagine that in the mid-1970s stores were vacant.

Scattered along Pollock Street near Tryon Palace and through downtown, a selection of shops exists that should make anyone's must-shop list. The experience is known as **The Governor's Walk**. We've highlighted just a few of the shops on the walk and a few others in the area. These shops are certainly not the totality of the New Bern shopping experience. But they'll whet your shopping appetite. Antiques shops are featured at the end of this section.

Elusive Treasures, 301 Pollock Street, is the place for custom-crafted gemstone jewelry. Patrons will find an intriguing collection of jewelry as well as home and office decorations created from earth's natural treasures: minerals, fossils, geodes and collector gemstones. The shop's craftspeople can create custom jewelry in sterling silver, gold (10-24 karat) and platinum and can wire-wrap jewelry, crystal or glass jewelry. Stop by to have that special piece designed and crafted. The shop also has a Jewelry Hospital with on-premises services such as ring sizing, polishing and cleaning, prong repair, remounts, chain repairs, stone replacement, and bead or pearl restringing.

Carolina Creations, 226 Middle Street, is a combination of many things and is the favorite store of many Insiders. It is a weaving studio, knit shop, art studio and gallery. Weavers, spinners and knitters will find looms, spinning wheels and a wonderful selection of fibers, including silk, cotton, linen, rayon and wool. There is also plenty of spun yarn ready for use and cross-stitch supplies and patterns. North Carolina pottery is featured along with beautiful stained-glass creations. Ink drawings and watercolor pieces depicting New Bern and other areas are for sale. The shop offers some classes.

Crafter's Emporium, 210 Craven Street, housed in an old foundry, offers a wonderful collection of work by area artists and craftsmen. The shop appears small from the outside, however, one step inside reveals otherwise. Shoppers will find nautical and wood crafts, ceramics, needlework, paintings, American Indian art, photographs, carvings, notecards, baskets, clothing items, jewelry and many supplies. The Emporium also offers bird houses, garden items, flags and craft supplies.

Saints' Creations, 809 Pollock Street is in the beautiful old All Saints Chapel and is run and staffed by volunteers from the New Bern Historical Society. The shop features original hand-crafted gifts by area artisans. There are paintings, prints, notecards, gifts and sometimes a decoy or two.

Tryon Palace Gift and Garden Shops, 600 Pollock Street, has two separate stores, one featuring New Bern and Colonial memorabilia and gift items, and the other devoted totally to garden things. The gift shop faces Pollock Street, and the garden shop is on the palace grounds. Insider gardeners visit the Garden Shop every spring to get old-time plants and herbs that are hard to find elsewhere.

Hill's, 219 Middle Street, was established in 1910 and is a quality men's haberdashery and ladies' specialty shop. Hill's offers the finest in men's and ladies' styling from the traditional to the fashionable.

The Four C's, 252 Middle Street, is a trail and nature shop offering gifts and active outdoor wear for women and men. They carry Atlantis clothing and Teva sandals. You'll find New Bern T-shirts, books, cards, kites, jewelry and a nice selection of duffle bags and totes.

Stop at **Captain Ratty's Gear & Gifts**, 202 Middle Street, if you're looking for a particularly memorable gift for someone who is into sailing. They have marvelous seagoing gifts, unusual souvenirs from New Bern, marine clocks, lanterns and instruments, antique charts and prints. Captain Ratty's also carries foul-weather gear, embroidered clothing and nautical and local books. This is also the place to shop for the Sunday editions of out-of-town newspapers.

Long a fixture of downtown New Bern, **Bryant-McLeod Ltd.**, 321 Pollock Street, features haberdashery for gentlemen. Monogramming, tailoring and free gift wrapping are offered to customers.

Branch's of New Bern, 309 Pollock Street is really much more than the office supply store it appears to be. Among the fine gift items on display are David Winter cottages, Baldwin brass and Tom Clark figurines. There is also a wonderful selection of bird feeders and lawn and garden ornaments. Branch's has a sister store in Morehead City.

New Bern is the only officially-designated daughter city of Bern, Switzerland. **Bern Bear Gifts**, 303 Pollock Street, reflects that relationship. The store carries Swiss, German, Austrian, North Carolina and New Bern gifts and novelties. There are also flags from New Bern and the state, Swiss music boxes, German clocks and steins, Swiss Army knives and Swiss chocolates.

In the old City Hall building, **Favorite Gifts & Things**, 220 Craven Street, features unusual gifts and decorative ac-

Photo: Scott Taylor

Even in the peak summer months, you can find a quiet niche on the beach.

cessories. Patrons will discover lovely lawn and garden accessories, bird feeders and supplies, children's items, educational books, gourmet food items and tasteful seasonal decorations.

Mitchell Hardware -Since 1898, 215 Craven Street is a place you have to experience. The window display is like a historic showing of farm and garden equipment. Step inside to find an eclectic offering of traditional hardware items in a turn-of-the-century setting. Mitchell's carries a com-

plete line of hardware, garden and yard equipment, practical gifts, cast-iron and enamel ware, garden seeds and bulbs. There is also a large country store section with everything from country hams to crockery and pottery.

Backyard Bears, 718 Pollock Street, is the perfect shop for a teddy bear lover. Inside you will find teddy bears for all ages along with limited editions, collectibles and gifts. Plus, the gourmet country fudge is sure to please everyone.

The shop also features 3-D windsocks, greeting cards and more.

The **Farmer's Market**, 421 Tryon Palace Drive, 633-0043, housed in a new building, is the place to go for fresh vegetables and fruits, seafood, flowers and crafts. The market is between Middle Street and Tryon Palace. Hours vary depending on the season; call ahead.

Cooks & Connoisseurs, 3310 Trent Road, is a wonderful specialty food store that offers gourmet and international foods from around the world. A variety of coffees and cheeses, necessary cooking tools and gadgets, and an extensive selection of wines and beers are for sale. Gift baskets can be prepared for that special friend, and fresh bread, croissants, muffins and cookies are prepared daily. A cooking school is also offered.

Hearne's Jewelers, Rivertowne Square, offers quality men's and women's jewelry and is a trusted, well-established company. Founded in 1972 by Mickey Hearne, the business combines courtesy with integrity. Hearne's offers exquisite rings, earrings, necklaces and bracelets, as well as a fine line of watches including those made by Seiko and Citizen. This is also the place to go for jewelry repairs, remounts and watch repairs.

Antiques

New Bern offers plenty of antiques shops to nose around in and discover lost treasures. We've included just a few to get you started. The New Bern Preservation Foundation hosts an antiques show in February that features invited dealers. For more information, contact the New Bern Preservation Foundation, P.O. Box 207, New Bern 28563, 633-6448.

Seaport Antique Market of New Bern, 504 Tryon Palace Drive, is a multi-dealer shop specializing in quality antiques and collectibles. The antique market is a great place to browse and look at all the treasures.

Will Gorges Antiques and Civil War Items, 308 Simmons Street, has just about everything in the way of memorabilia and collectibles from the Civil War. The shop is run by Will Gorges, a Civil War buff himself. There are all kinds of authentic Civil War memorabilia, including muskets, pistols, uniforms, books and other items. Will Gorges also operates the Civil War Museum on Metcalf Street.

Visit **Middle Street Flea Market**, 329 Middle Street, and you'll find dealers that offer a lot of good stuff. The market features antiques, collectibles, furniture, silver, china, some jewelry and lots more. The market also buys items.

Poor Charlie's Flea Market and Antiques, 206 Hancock Street, features 15 dealers with booths offering just about everything a shopper could imagine. An old warehouse houses the booths and gives the feeling of an old-style market. Patrons will find reproduction furniture, household accessories and lots of nostalgic items.

As the name implies, **Tom's Coins and Antiques**, 244 Middle Street, offers coins and antiques of all types and much

For just plain fun nothing beats a bumper boat.

more. The shop has beautiful antique and reproduction furniture, estate jewelry, stamps and sports cards. There are lots of nostalgic items and collectibles.

The **Antique Depot**, 626 Hancock Street, offers household items, antique and reproduction furniture, old jewelry, china and glassware on consignment.

Jane Sugg Antiques, 228 Middle Street, offers period and reproduction furniture, lamps, silver, crystal and an assortment of boxes.

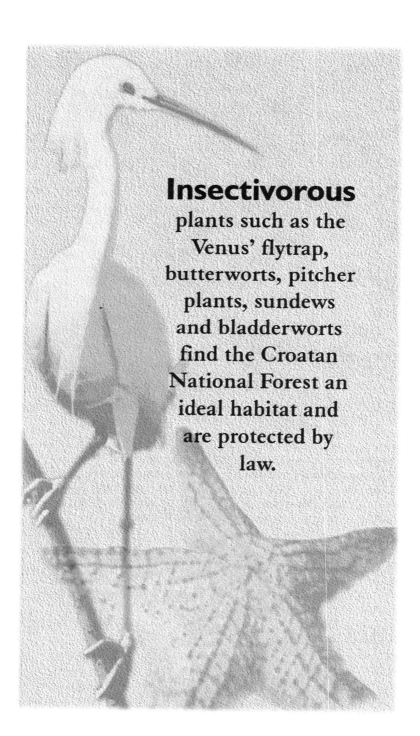

Insectivorous plants such as the Venus' flytrap, butterworts, pitcher plants, sundews and bladderworts find the Croatan National Forest an ideal habitat and are protected by law.

New Bern
Attractions

The importance of New Bern's history cannot be overemphasized. What exists today is attributable to a history that predates the founding of America by Europeans.

Shortly after its settlement in 1710, New Bern was nearly wiped out by Tuscarora Indians. Gradually the Indians were forced to move inland, and New Bern, with its ideal location at the confluence of the Neuse and Trent rivers, began to flourish as a farming and shipping community.

The city soon became an important port, exporting naval stores and later, tobacco and cotton. The captains of the ships that hauled these high-demand products used the spires of New Bern's churches to guide them up the Neuse River that at the time had few navigational aids or other landmarks. Several of the older homes have widows' walks projecting above the roofs, where wives would watch for their husbands' ships returning from long sea voyages.

Pirates also found the dark coves and creeks along the rivers ideal for subversive activities and, of course, for hiding treasures. Blackbeard is supposed to have stayed in a huge house by the Neuse, where he planned his raids on oceangoing ships carrying rich cargo between the American colonies, England and the West Indies.

New Bern can credit its gentility to the once-thriving area plantations that produced exportable products to be shipped around the world. The plantations themselves often became small cities, but today little remains of the beautiful estates that depended on the dark waters of the Neuse and Trent rivers for livelihoods. What does remain are the moss-hung oak and cypress trees guarding the many creeks and sloughs along the winding Trent and broad Neuse. Like other cities, New Bern endured the pangs of growth and change, eventually developing a character all its own. It did not, however, forget its past.

History taught New Bern many hard lessons, one of which was to value its heritage. To that end, a great number of old homes and churches have been restored, and, in cases of potential loss, relocated, thanks to groups such as the New Bern Preservation Foundation. Salvaged structures now number more than 150, and restoration efforts are ongoing.

While the historical museums, homes and buildings are the focal point of New Bern, there are additional attractions in the river city and surrounding area. A growing community of reputable artists grace New Bern with their work, which is often exhibited at the Bank of the Arts, the public library, ART Gallery Ltd., Carolina Creations, City Art Works and in the town's public buildings.

Because of its cultural activities, New Bern was known as "the Athens of North

Carolina" in the first quarter of this century, a title it is regaining today. Fine antique and art shops have opened in recent years and browsers are always welcome. Not listed in any guidebooks (except this one) but known to New Bernians are its churches, each distinctive and worthy of a sightseeing visit. For a listing of historic churches and other houses of worship, see our New Bern Places of Worship chapter.

Of the area's seven historic houses of worship, it is perhaps Christ Episcopal Church on Pollock Street that has the most interesting lore. Included in the church's regalia is a silver communion service donated by King George II. The service survived two fires and reconstruction but, according to local history, was stolen in the 1960s or '70s. The thief, so goes the tale, fenced it with a man who recognized it for what it was and returned it to the church.

In addition to the official sights of New Bern, walking tours of the historic district are very popular. Attractions open to the public primarily center on the town's history; however, many of the historic homes are private residences and are closed to the public. Nonetheless, walking the streets and viewing the architecture and landscapes of these grand old homes will truly give you the feel of the city's Colonial heritage.

Most of the attractions are within walking distance of each other, and we have listed a number of the sites here. For a detailed walking map and description of the more than 100 historic locations, let your first stop be the **Craven County Convention and Visitors Bureau**, 219 Pollock Street, 637-9400 or (800) 437-5767. Everyone there is very helpful with orienting you to their town. Hours are 8 AM to 5 PM Monday through Friday; 10 AM to 5 PM, Saturday; and 1 to 4 PM, Sunday. The new location of the Visitors Bureau at the cor-

ner of Tryon Palace Drive and Middle Street is expected to open in October 1996.

For those who enjoy the woodlands as well as the city, nearby Croatan National Forest provides a close-up look at coastal marshes, estuaries and maritime forests. The 157,000-acre preserve is home to insectivorous plants, uncommon wildflowers, marsh and shorebirds and a variety of forest animals such as black bears, alligators, deer and wild turkeys. Forest hiking trails and overnight campsites are popular with nature lovers. For a detailed discussion, see our Crystal Coast Attractions chapter.

TRYON PALACE
HISTORIC SITES AND GARDENS

Pollock and George sts.   514-4900
(800) 767-1560

Tryon Palace, built in 1770 by Colonial Gov. William Tryon, was known at the time as one of the most beautiful buildings in America. The elegant, Georgian-style mansion is mostly a reconstruction of the original building that stood at the same site. After its use both as a colonial and state capitol, the palace fell into grave disrepair. At the time the reconstruction was undertaken in the 1950s, only one wing — the stables — remained standing. The palace now houses an outstanding collection of antiques and art, and the grounds are devoted to extensive landscaping, ranging from English formal gardens and a kitchen garden to wilderness garden areas.

Included as part of the main palace complex are the John Wright Stanly House (1783) on George Street and the Dixon-Stevenson House (1828) on Pollock Street. The Stanly home, which was originally on New Street and moved to its present location in the early 1960s, was built by a Revolutionary War patriot who entertained George Washington on two occasions. The Dixon-Stevenson House is a prominent Federal-style home noted for its rare neoclassical antiques. The 1810 Robert Hay House on Eden Street across from the palace is a new addition to the historical complex. Its restoration, which should be complete in late 1996, will accurately reflect the lifestyle technology of its time. The palace also has dominion of the New Bern Academy Museum at New and Hancock streets.

Historical re-enactments supplement the daily palace and garden tours during special times in the summer months. Annual events include the colorful Christmas Celebration tours in December, Decorative Arts Symposium in March, Gardener's Weekend during New Bern's Historic Homes and Gardens Tour in April, King George III's Birthday and Festival of Colonial Life in June, the July Independence Day Celebration and the Chrysanthemum Festival in October. Monthly Garden Workshops and bimonthly Saturday Sampler Series lectures concerning research and findings at the historic site are offered year round. Cooking, blacksmithing and weaving are among regular craft demonstrations. The palace gift shop in the Daves House and the crafts and garden shop behind the palace east wing are open daily. An audiovisual orientation program is shown at the visitors center for all guests.

The palace is open year round from 9:30 AM to 4 PM Monday through Saturday and from 1:30 to 4 PM on Sunday. The last tour begins at 4 PM. The palace is closed on Thanksgiving Day, December 24-26 and New Year's Day. A number of tour options are available including two-day and annual passes, and group discounts are extended to pre-arranged groups of 20 or more. For current price information or group reservations, call 514-4900 or (800) 767-1560. The historic sites and gardens are partially equipped for handicapped visitors.

JOHN WRIGHT STANLY HOUSE
307 George St.   514-4900, (800)767-1560

On his Southern tour in 1791, President George Washington dined and danced at Tryon Palace, but his two nights in New Bern were spent at the nearby home of John Wright Stanly. Washington described his overnight accommodation as "exceeding good lodgings."

During the Revolutionary War, Stanly's merchant ships plied the waters as privateers, capturing British ships to aid the American cause. The elegance of Stanly's house, built in the early 1780s, reflects the wealth of its owner. Distinctive American furniture of the period complements the elegant interior woodwork, and Stanly family history provides a fascinating chronicle of father and son, epidemic and duel, war and wealth. Admission is charged as part of the Tryon Palace Complex admission.

DIXON-STEVENSON HOUSE
609 Pollock St.   514-4900, (800) 767-1560

Erected in 1828 on a lot that was originally a part of Tryon Palace's garden, the Dixon-Stevenson House epito-

You haven't seen New Bern until you've meandered the residential streets in the historic district and along the waterfront.

Insiders' Tips

mizes New Bern's lifestyle in the first half of the 19th century when the town was a prosperous port and one of the state's largest cities.

The house, built for a New Bern mayor, is a fine example of neoclassical architecture. Its furnishings, reflecting the Federal period, reveal the changing tastes of early America. At the rear of the house is a garden with seasonal flowers, all in white. When Union troops occupied New Bern during the Civil War, the house was converted to a regimental hospital. Admission is charged as part of the Tryon Palace Complex admission.

ATTMORE-OLIVER HOUSE

511 Broad St.   *638-8558*
Parking entrance on Pollock St.

Built in 1790 by prominent New Bernian Samuel Chapman, the Attmore-Oliver House today is the home of the New Bern Historical Society. It was enlarged to its present size in 1834 and houses 18th- and 19th-century antiques, a doll collection and Civil War memorabilia. Of particular interest is the fine Greek Revival portico and two-story porches at the rear of the house. It is open seasonally Tuesday through Saturday from 1 to 4:30 PM and closes from mid-December until the Spring Homes and Gardens Tour weekend. (In 1996 this will be the second weekend of April.) Otherwise, it is shown by appointment. The house may be reserved for private functions and is not handicapped accessible.

WALKING TOUR ATTRACTIONS

As mentioned earlier, a number of New Bern's historic homes are private residences; however, a leisurely stroll along river walks through the historic district will allow you to observe the landscapes, architecture and gardens of these vintage homes. Walking will give you a real sense of the many Old World customs that characterize this Colonial town. Self-guiding brochures are available at the Visitors Bureau at 219 Pollock Street and after July in its new location at the corner of Middle Street and Tryon Palace Drive. Guided walking tours, organized by **New Bern Tours**, 637-7316, for six or more people, depart from the Commission House across from the Tryon Palace gate. A few of the more noted residences and buildings are listed here.

The **John Horner Hill House**, 713 Pollock Street, is a Georgian period dwelling built between 1770 and 1780. It is noted for its rare nine-over-nine sash at the first-floor windows.

The **Henry H. Harris House**, 718 Pollock Street, was built in 1800 and is a well-preserved example of vernacular Federal period architecture.

The **Anne Green Lane House**, 804 Pollock Street, is a transitional late Georgian-early Federal house built between 1790 and 1800. It was remodeled during the Victorian period.

The **All Saints Chapel**, 809 Pollock Street, is a good example of Gothic-style architecture. It was built c. 1895 as a mission chapel by Christ Episcopal Church.

Photo: NC Travel & Tourism

The Tryon Palace gardens in the spring are simply magnificent.

The **John H. Jones House**, 819 Pollock Street, is a small Federal house with an unusual central chimney. Its original separate kitchen remains at the rear.

The **White House** at 422 Johnson Street is a simple sidehall Federal house built c.1820-30. It is noted for its two end chimneys with a small closet in between.

The **Cutting-Allen House**, 518 New Street, is a transitional late Georgian-early Federal sidehall house built in 1793. It is considered unusual because of its flanking wings and large rear ballroom. It was saved from demolition in 1980 and moved to its present location.

The **Hawks House** at New and Metcalf streets offers a side-by-side comparison of styles. Dating from the 1760s, the western part of the house is Georgian, and the eastern section is Federal, added by Francis Hawks, son of John Hawks, architect of Tryon Palace.

The **Clark-Taylor House**, 419 Metcalf Street, was built between 1795 and 1804. It is one of several gambrel-roofed houses in the historic district.

The **Attmore-Wadsworth House**, 515 Broad Street, is an unusual one-story Italianate-style house built c. 1855. Several Italianate-style homes are part of the city's historic architecture.

The **McLin-Hancock House**, 507 Middle Street, is unique for its strict symmetry and diminutive scale.

The **W.B. Blades House**, 602 Middle Street, was built in 1903 and is noted for its elaborate Queen Anne design.

The **Jerkins-Duffy House**, 301 Johnson Street, was built c. 1830 and is unusual because of its exterior Federal design and interior Greek Revival elements. It is also noted for its captain's walk and exposed-face chimneys.

The **George Slover House**, 209 Johnson Street, was built c. 1890 and is an eclectic combination of Queen Anne and shingle-style architectures.

The **Charles Slover House**, 201 Johnson Street, is a stately brick townhouse built in 1847 that was selected as headquarters by Gen. Ambrose Burnside during the Civil War. C. D. Bradham, inventor of Brad's Drink (now known as Pepsi-Cola) purchased the house in 1908.

The **Eli Smallwood House**, 524 E. Front Street, is one of the finest of New

Bern's Federal brick sidehall houses, built c. 1810. It is noted for its handsome portico and elegant interior woodwork.

The **Dawson-Clarke House**, 519 E. Front Street, was built c. 1808 and is one of several historic homes exhibiting the use of double porches, a popular style in the coastal region.

The **Coor-Gaston House**, 421 Craven Street, is a Georgian home (c. 1770) built by architect, builder and patriot-statesman James Coor. It was purchased in 1818 by Judge William Gaston and was the scene of the founding of St. Paul's Roman Catholic Church. Gaston was a brilliant orator, lawyer, member of Congress, State Justice and author of the state song.

The **David F. Jarvis House**, 220 Pollock Street, is good example of neoclassical Revival architecture.

The **Edward R. Stanly House and Dependency**, 502 Pollock Street, was built c. 1849 in Renaissance Revival style. The cast-iron grills over its windows are unique in New Bern.

The **Wade House**, 214 Tryon Palace Drive, was built in 1843 and remodeled before 1885 in the Second Empire style. The cast-iron crest on the mansard roof and the iron fence are notable surviving features.

THE NEW BERN ACADEMY MUSEUM
New and Hancock sts.   *514-4900*
(800) 767-1560

Founded in 1764 and built in 1809, New Bern Academy is the oldest public school in North Carolina and one of the oldest in America. It was used as a school recently enough to still be remembered by a number of New Bern's residents. After it closed, it sat vacant for several decades. In the 1980s, it was purchased and renovated by Tryon Palace and today houses exhibits illustrating the 300-year history of New Bern and eastern North Carolina.

The Academy Museum is open daily for self-guided touring. Admission is charged as part of the Tryon Palace Complex admission.

BELLAIR PLANTATION AND RESTORATION
1100 Washington Post Rd.   *637-3913*

The last and largest brick plantation country house of the 18th century in North Carolina, the Bellair Plantation (c. 1734) is a majestic three-story brick building approached from Highway 43 N. by two long driveways, one lined by lavish old cedars. Georgian handcrafted woodwork greets visitors at the imposing eight-panelled door and continues through the main rooms. Original family furnishings are still in the house, probably because Bellair was specifically guarded from harm during the occupation of Federal Forces during the Civil War by order of Gen. Ambrose Burnside. The written order, dated March 20, 1862, still hangs on the wall at Bellair. The basement holds the cooking fireplaces with crane, tools and ironworks of the period. One-hour tours of the historic site are offered hourly from 1 to 5 PM Saturdays and Sundays. The last tour each day begins at 5 PM.

THE CIVIL WAR MUSEUM
301 Metcalf St.   *633-2818*

Opened in 1990, the New Bern Civil War Museum houses one of the finest in-depth private collections of Civil War memorabilia and weapons in the United States. Included are rare uniforms, battlefield artifacts and other items. Articles from the museum have been featured in Time-Life Books, *Mid-Atlantic* magazine and numerous other periodicals. In 1992, a display from the museum won Best in Show at the Old North State Civil War Exhibition. History buffs and Civil War scholars say it is a site not to be missed.

Less than a block from Tryon Palace, the museum is open from April 1 to September 30 from 10 AM to 4 PM Tuesday through Saturday. From October 1 to March 31, it is open weekends only from 11 AM to 4 PM and by appointment. Admission is $2.50 for adults and $1.50 for students. The museum has a gift shop and access for people with handicaps.

BANK OF THE ARTS
317 Middle St.   *638-2787*

A former bank built in 1912, the interesting granite structure now serves as headquarters for the Craven Arts Council and Gallery. The classical facade of the building features Ionic columns leading into the open, two-story gallery. Detailed pilasters and Corinthian columns have been highlighted by colors in the Beaux-Arts motif. Changing exhibits of various media — painting, sculpture, photography, pottery, fiber art and other art forms — showcase the work of local and Southeastern artists. Many special events, such as concerts, lectures and receptions, are offered here throughout the year.

The Bank of the Arts does not charge an admission fee and visitors are welcome to browse at the Bank of the Arts, open Monday through Saturday from 10 AM to 5 PM. The arts building is handicapped accessible.

FARMER'S MARKET
421 Tryon Palace Dr.   *633-0043*

Bringing fresh local produce to downtown New Bern throughout the year, the Farmer's Market is a town treasure operated by the Cooperative Extension Service. From fruits to flowers and through the range of baked, canned and prepared goods, the Farmer's Market is a favorite stop, but you have to keep the days and hours in mind. From June 15 through September 15, days of operation are Tuesday, Thursday and Saturday from 6 AM to 1 PM. After September 15 and before June 15, the Farmer's Market is open Saturdays only, 6 AM to 1 PM.

Photo: Kenny Barrow

Fire Wagon Number One is displayed at New Bern's Fireman's Museum.

FIREMAN'S MUSEUM

410 Hancock St.   636-4087

The New Bern fire company is one of the oldest in the country operating under its original charter. The restored museum is just behind the fire department's Broad Street headquarters and houses steam pumpers and an extensive collection of other early fire-fighting equipment. Also on exhibit are rare photos, Civil War relics and even the mounted head of the faithful old fire horse, Fred, who, according to stories told by fire fighters, died in his tracks while answering an alarm.

Museum hours are Tuesday through Saturday from 9:30 AM to noon and 1 to 5 PM, and on Sunday from 1 to 5 PM. The museum is open year round, except for a week around the Fourth of July and a week around Christmas. Admission is $2 for adults and $1 for children. The museum is handicapped accessible.

CEDAR GROVE CEMETERY

Queen and George sts.

If you're one of those people who loves wandering through old graveyards, this is one you'll not want to miss. Statuary and monuments beneath Spanish moss-draped trees mark burial traditions from the earliest days of our nation. One smallish obelisk lists the names of nine children in one family who all died within a two-year time span. Although the causes of their deaths are not known, a disease of some sort is most probable. The city's monument to its Confederate dead and the graves of 70 soldiers are also here. The cemetery's main gate features a shell motif, with an accompanying legend that says if water drips on you as you enter, you will be the next to die.

REBECCA LEE RIVER BOAT

I Bicentennial Park   638-8800

Docked behind the Sheraton Grand Hotel at Bicentennial Park, this 150-passenger, 80-foot paddlewheel river boat is enjoying her first season in New Bern in 1996. *Rebecca Lee* cruises the Trent River on scheduled 90-minute cruises at 1 PM, at sunset and at other times for private events. She requires a minimum of 10 passengers.

Built in 1993 by her captain, Dan Hallock, the sternwheeler operated in Long Island, New York before her arrival in New Bern. Captain Hallock keeps it simple aboard and offers a sightseeing tour only. No meals are served, a cash bar is available and you may certainly bring your own picnic.

Sternwheeler cruises are somewhat traditional in New Bern. According to Capt. Hallock, cargo and passengers were regularly transported by such a river boat in the mid-1800s. Passages were made from New Bern to Washington and Elizabeth City. River cruises aboard *Rebecca Lee* are $10 for adults, $5 for children. Children younger than 5 ride free.

NEW BERN TROLLEY TOURS

Tryon Palace, Pollock St.   637-7316
                       (800) 849-7316

Touring the town by trolley is a comfortable and interesting alternative to a walking tour if you've arrived without your sneakers. Narrated 1½-hour tours depart Tryon Palace between April 1 and December 31 at 11 AM and 2 PM on most weekdays and at 2 PM on Sundays. Tours or charters for special groups or occasions may also be arranged. Professional guides narrate the tours with attention to historical and architectural interests and spice the narrative with folk-lore and local knowledge. Trolley tours are $10 for adults and $5 for children 12 and younger. A 30-minute "Get Acquainted Tour" of the Historic District departs Comfort Suites twice a day. Fares are $5 for adults, $2 for children. For reservations and further information, call 637-7316 or (800) 849-7316. Tickets are also available at Cherishables Gift Shop at 712 Pollock Street near Tryon Palace.

UNION POINT PARK

Tryon and E. Front sts.   *636-4660*

This lovely waterfront park is often the site of outdoor activities and offers a welcome respite for weary visitors who want to take a load off their feet. Music is sometimes featured here. It is an excellent place to simply sit and watch the world float by. There are lovely river views, and the site is particularly pleasant for evening sunset viewing. On-site facilities accommodate picnicking, boat launching and creature comforts.

Extensive renovations of Union Point Park have been planned to take place in phases. Phase one involves new bulkheading and the construction of a waterfront promenade with railings, which should be completed in 1996.

CROATAN NATIONAL FOREST

141 E. Fisher Ave.   *638-5628*

Croatan National Forest is an expansive nature preserve bordered by New Bern, Morehead City and Cape Carteret. It is headquartered on Fisher Avenue, which is approximately 9 miles south of New Bern just off Highway 70 E. Well-placed road signs make the office easy to find.

Within the forest's boundaries are en-dangered animals and rare plants. Black bears, otters, deer, raptors and other forest creatures live in this coastal woodland. Insectivorous plants such as the Venus's-flytrap, butterworts, pitcher plants, sundews and bladderworts find the forest an ideal habitat and are protected by law. The forest is also well-known for its beautiful wildflowers. Pamphlets on the wildflowers and insectivorous plants are available at the Fisher Avenue headquarters. Because of the forest's coastal location, many unique features can be found here. Some of the ecosystems present include pocosins, longleaf and loblolly pine and bottomland and upland hardwoods. Sprinkled throughout the Croatan are 40 miles of streams and 4,300 acres of wild lakes.

The forest areas are excellent for hiking, swimming, boating, hunting, fishing and picnicking. Miles and miles of unpaved roads lace through the woodland, providing easy if sometimes roundabout access to its wilderness. Recreation areas are available for a day's outing or for longer visits. Camp fees vary, so call headquarters, 638-5628, for season rates.

Because the Croatan is so expansive and undeveloped, it is best to stop in at headquarters on Fisher Avenue and pick up a forest map before heading out. The best times for venturing into coastal woodlands are fall, winter or early spring. Summer can be very hot and buggy, so prepare yourself with insect repellent. Some forest areas are closed November through March. For more information on the Croatan National Forest, see the Crystal Coast Attractions chapter.

For kids 10 and older, the Storytelling Club meets at New Bern-Craven County Public Library on the second and fourth Wednesdays of the month after school.

New Bern
Kidstuff

Once upon a time, there was a beautiful place at a point where two rivers met. It was such a beautiful place that even the first person who ever saw it, a Tuscarora Indian, wanted to live there. In fact, the entire tribe decided it was the best place to live. And, it was. There were lots of fish in the two rivers, and there was a big forest with many trees that the Indians could use to build all the things they needed, such as boats.

One day, some other people arrived in the beautiful place. Their leader was from a faraway place called Bern, Switzerland. The people saw that the two rivers came together here and saw the big forest with wood they needed to build things, and they also decided that this was the best place in the new world to live. They called the place New Bern to remind them of their old city. Except for once or twice, the people of New Bern got along pretty well with the Tuscarora Indians, but that's another story.

The people of New Bern built quite a fine town with pretty houses and their town became a capital where the king sent a governor to rule the whole land. The people built a palace in New Bern for the governor. Everyone loved the palace, and people came from all over the land to enjoy it. Even pirates came up the river from the sea to enjoy the town with the palace. And because it was always a beautiful place to live, people kept coming to New Bern.

Over the years, the people of New Bern got together to build a fort for their children to play in, and a Cow Cafe where their children have parties and eat ice cream. Today, they help their children put on plays that everyone enjoys and they bring wonderful performers from far away to teach and entertain the kids. They even have an arts camp in the summer and craft classes before Christmas and a fishing contest in the rivers for the kids in the summer.

And while the people of New Bern continue to live happily ever after, people still come from near and far to New Bern to enjoy the town with their kids. And this is hardly The End. Read on for the details.

A favorite summer destination for a day with the kids is Flanners Beach, a Croatan National Forest recreation area on the Neuse River. It's 10 miles south of New Bern off Highway 70 E. on Flanner's Beach Road.

Insiders' Tips

CHILDREN'S PERFORMING ARTS SERIES
Craven Arts Council
317 Middle St. 638-2577

This delightful performing arts series, held each spring for preschool and school-aged children, is sponsored by the Craven Arts Council (see our New Bern Arts chapter). The series offers three programs from February through April, each staged at Orringer Auditorium on the Craven Community College campus. The cost for the entire series is $10.50. Individual performances are $4 at the door and group rates are offered.

THE COW CAFE
301 Ave. C 638-1131

Treat yourself and take a kid to the Cow Cafe at the Maola Milk and Ice Cream Company's processing plant. Inside is a window on the world of milk processing. Everything looks like a cow, from the cafe seats to the toilets to the unimaginable range of gifts. Snacks and lunches — no burgers! — include hot dogs, milk shakes and malts. If you're limited to only one selection, take the Death By Chocolate. It's our choice of execution.

THE FIREMAN'S MUSEUM
410 Hancock St. 636-4087

The Fireman's Museum houses steam pumpers and other early fire-fighting equipment that was used by the New Bern Fire Department, one of the country's oldest fire departments. Rare photos, Civil War relics and the mounted head of Fred, the faithful fire horse who died while answering an alarm, are part of the collection. The museum is open Tuesday through Saturday from 9:30 AM to 5 PM and Sunday from 1 to 5 PM. See our New Bern Attractions chapter for further information.

KIDSVILLE PLAYGROUND
1225 Pine Tree Dr. 636-4061

Kidsville is a beautifully planned and constructed, active and interactive fort-like play environment that captivates both children and adults. Next to the West New Bern Recreation Center on Pine Tree Drive near the intersection of U.S. Highway 70 and N.C. Highway 17, Kidsville is the product of the fund-raising efforts of two mothers and a town with enough heart to contribute all that was needed to make it real. Efforts in 1994 raised $100,000 for the necessary materials, and all the labor and the location were donated. With or without a kid, Kidsville merits a visit. Whether you choose to slide, climb or clamber through its interesting maze or you spend your time taking note of the plaques naming the many contributors, Kidsville will wow you. You may arrange for large group visits by contacting the New Bern Parks and Recreation Department.

SUMMER ARTS CAMP
Craven Arts Council and Gallery 638-2577

Sponsored by the Craven Arts Council and Gallery, the Summer Arts Camp for children ages 4 to 13 is a one-week arts program designed to be fun and educational. Students strengthen their creativity by working in a variety of arts disciplines such as creative drama, music, creative movement and visual arts. Classes for particular age groups are limited in size, so early registration is a good idea. Transportation is provided from central pick-up locations and fees are $42 for arts council members, $47 for nonmembers.

KIDS' FISHING DAY
Croatan National Forest Service 638-5628

Kids' Fishing Day in June is organized by the Croatan National Forest Service for

When there's water close by, it's not hard to keep kids happy.

kids of all ages. Participants in 1995 ranged from ages 1½ to 15. Local businesses and organizations sponsor prizes for the largest, smallest and most fish caught.

NEW BERN-CRAVEN COUNTY PUBLIC LIBRARY CHILDREN'S PROGRAMMING
400 Johnson St.
Pam Machle, Children's Librarian   638-7815
The children's library at the New Bern-Craven County Public Library is well-organized for pre-schoolers to teens to enjoy selecting from the collection of books, video and audio tapes and compact discs. Help is plentiful. Weekday programs for children are planned each week. Time Out For Toddlers on Friday mornings is a program of stories, songs and finger plays for children younger than 3. Preschool Storysteps for ages 3 to 5 occurs twice on Tuesday mornings, offering stories, puppet plays, music and other fun. For kids between the ages of 5 and 9, the Children's Story Hour is held on Thursday afternoons. It involves storytelling, movies and age-specific activities. For kids 10 and older, the Storytelling Club meets on the second and fourth Wednesdays of the month after school. The club is a membership activity with goal-oriented projects that involve learning techniques of storytelling, puppetry and drama. Call the Children's Librarian for further information.

PUTT-PUTT GOLF COURSE
4172 Hwy. 17 S.   635-1570
When you have a day to spend with the kids, invite a few more and take a carload to the new 18-hole miniature Putt-Putt Golf Course on Highway 17. There are some interesting holes to play, even for the seasoned golfer, and facilities are available for 19th-hole relaxation, picnics or birthday parties.

If you're on a tour of the visual arts in New Bern, don't miss the wall mural at Kafer Park on George Street.

New Bern
Arts

For the first three decades of the 20th century, New Bern was known as the "Athens of North Carolina" because of its many artistic and educational endeavors. While the Great Depression put a halt to much of the activity, a rebirth occurred in the 1970s, and today locals enjoy performances and exhibits from an ever-increasing number of area and touring artists.

The **Craven Arts Council and Gallery** on Middle Street supports and features all art disciplines and is a ticket outlet and information center for almost any art event taking place in Craven County. The council sponsors the popular New Bern Sunday Jazz Showcase, the Children's Performing Arts and Craven Concerts series and many other visual and performing arts events throughout the year.

The **New Bern-Craven County Public Library** at the corner of Johnson and Middle streets, 638-7800, selects an artist of the month and displays his or her work in its recently expanded buildings. Photographers and other visual artists have been the most popular.

The evidence that activity in the arts is treasured in New Bern is most visual on a walk through downtown. Galleries are proliferating in renovated buildings, and teaching studios are active in and above shops and galleries. Local artist Doug Alvord will install a mural this year on the exterior of the First Citizens Bank on Broad Street depicting the working waterfront of New Bern in the 1800s. "I don't know why so many artists are in New Bern," says Alvord. "But there is a lot of activity. Most professional artists continue to work at other things still, but in 10 years, that will probably change." Art activity attracts artists, and the activity in New Bern is, simply, visible.

Among those artists to whom New Bern "just feels right" is stained-glass artist Michaele Rose. She and her husband relocated to New Bern from Florida, bought a Middle Street building, renovated the downstairs as a retail gallery and studio. New Bern had the right composite of ingredients: proximity to water, an active arts community, affordable real estate. She is active in instruction, with commissions for renovations and in the retail aspect of her business. She says her story of relocation is one she hears others repeat frequently.

New Bern is also home to an active community theater group, the New Bern Civic Theater, which has its own performing hall, the Saax Bradbury Playhouse, a former movie theater on Pollock Street. The group stages a number of productions annually. Alternative and repertory theater groups are also active in town as are numerous musical groups and dancers including historical dancers. Atlantic Dance Theater, professional touring dancers, gives a number of performances throughout each year in the public schools and also gives a public performance.

Here, we've described our arts organizations. If a group doesn't have a street address or regular office, we have given the contact person's name and phone number.

CRAVEN ARTS COUNCIL AND GALLERY
317 Middle St.   *638-2577*

Besides nurturing local artists, this organization provides exhibition space for local, regional and national artists in the Bank of the Arts, a reclaimed 1912 bank building that also houses the arts council's administrative offices. The large, open main gallery is the staging area for nine exhibits each year. Popular traveling exhibits are often featured, and overall works include a variety of media, ranging from traditional to contemporary. At Christmas, the gallery becomes a huge gift shop for the sale of art works, cards, fine crafts and other original creations. As part of its continuous support of the arts, the council organizes and runs Arts in Education, an outreach program of performances and artists' presentations designed to enrich and integrate the arts throughout educational curriculum. The program includes the acclaimed Day at the Improv workshop designed for fourth and fifth grade students. The workshop uses creative drama to strengthen communication and cooperative skills. Evening workshops are also free and open to the public. The energetic support of the Craven Arts Council and Gallery in integrating arts activity throughout the county and region

is recognizably effective in its explosive growth. The council publishes a monthly newsletter, *Luminary*, that informs of upcoming arts events. Classes in oil, watercolors and other art forms are often taught and conducted at the Bank of the Arts.

NEW BERN CIVIC THEATER
414 Pollock St.   *633-0567*

A community group, the civic theater relies on a bevy of part-time performers and behind-the-scenes technicians and assistants to produce a variety of performances at the Saax Bradbury Playhouse. The group's theatrical productions range from serious drama to lively musicals, including original works. Plans for 1996 include productions of *Noah*, *Paint Your Wagon* and *The Cemetery Club*. Their children's performing group, StageHands, stages entirely unique performances simultaneously in sign and spoken language.

ATLANTIC DANCE THEATER
Elizabeth Pope   *636-1760*

A professional touring dance troupe, the company's dancers come from across the United States to put together dance programs for students in public schools. For school performances, the company performs traditional ballet as well as other dance styles to give young audiences a broad view of dance as an art form. One concert performance each year is given to the general public.

CRAVEN HISTORICAL DANCERS
Paige Whitley-Bauguess   *633-9622*

Now totaling about 15 members of

all ages, this unique dance troupe performs 18th-century social dances in costume. Their dances include reels, country dances, minuets, cotillions and jigs. They entertain at holiday and fund-raising madrigal dinners, where they perform 16th-century dances. Craven Historical Dancers are often included in Tryon Palace's holiday festivities. They have danced at the Hope Plantation in Edenton and traveled as far as New York to dance at a Baroque music festival. The group meets weekly, and new members do not need previous dance experience to join.

DOWN EAST DANCE

2500 Trent Rd. 633-9622

This dance studio involves students of all ages in an impressive range of dance variety. Under the direction of Paige Whitley-Bauguess, the faculty and students performed *The Nutcracker* in 1995 with guest artist Thomas Baird and participating members of the Craven Historical Dancers.

FAIRFIELD HARBOUR CHORUS

Pat Rivett 638-8470

This chorus began with 24 enthusiastic members in 1984. Today, membership totals approximately 60 vocalists. The group performs about 15 concerts each year, featuring all types of music, including show tunes, gospel, Broadway hits, holiday arrangements, pop and contemporary. It has given numerous performances in area churches, rest homes and retirement homes and has combined its talents to perform with other choruses at Cherry Point and Craven Community College. Members must be residents of Fairfield Harbour. Rehearsals are conducted on Monday evenings at 7 PM at the Fairfield Community Center. Rehearsals begin the first Monday after Labor Day and continue until mid-May. The group is subsidized by a grassroots grant from the Craven Arts Council.

CRAVEN CONCERTS

Gene Fegley 636-5935

This organization schedules five musical concerts each year, staged at Grover C. Fields Middle School auditorium on Clarendon Boulevard. Attendance is by subscription membership only, with membership fees of $35 for adults and $5 for students. Productions include a wide variety of performances and always include one concert by the North Carolina Symphony. The 1995-96 calendar includes performances by classical guitarist Terrence Farrell and mezzo soprano Brenda Boozer. A membership campaign is conducted each spring, and membership forms and information are available at the Craven Arts Council and Gallery on Middle Street.

CRAVEN COMMUNITY CHORUS

Ruth Bumbera 636-2864

This large choral group has 70 members and performs locally, as well as in surrounding counties and out of state. There are no auditions, and membership

Insiders' Tips

In the early months of the year, Craven Arts Council's annual Children's Performing Arts Series brings professional touring performers to the Craven Community College's Orringer Auditorium for delightful events for preschool and school-age children.

is open to anyone who can carry a tune and enjoys singing. The group likes to include musicians whenever possible and usually plans its shows around a theme. Performances have featured Dixieland standards, Old West favorites, Big Band hits and classic '50s rock 'n' roll. The singers also perform folk songs, patriotic compositions, spirituals, swing, pop, some classical works and holiday favorites.

PRO MUSICA OF NEW BERN

Pat Rowett   *638-5144*

This a cappella singing group, formed in the late 1970s, is a local favorite which performs a variety of music from opera to pop, but its specialty is madrigals. Composed of about 12 members, Pro Musica is most frequently heard at occasional madrigal dinners, which occur in New Bern churches. Semiannually, the group performs a progressive Christmas concert.

STARDUST

Frank Swanson   *808-2204*

This newly formed musical group consists of 15 local musicians whose specialty is Big Band sounds as well as boogie

and blues with original musical arrangements. The group performs in concert and for dances.

TWIN RIVERS ART ASSOCIATION

Kathy Pickett   *636-3422*

The Twin Rivers Art Association sponsors two shows each year. Work is limited to two-dimensional paintings in any medium, including multimedia. Group shows are staged in the spring and late fall; however, members exhibit paintings throughout the year at various locations in New Bern and surrounding counties. Membership is $15 per year; show fees are $15 per show. Meetings are held at 7:30 PM on the first Wednesday of each month, except in July and August, at PJR Studio on Shoreline Drive in River Bend. The group exhibits its work at River Bend Town Hall, Bank of the Arts and Twin Rivers Mall.

VOCI ALLEGRI VOCAL ENSEMBLE

Lorraine Hale   *638-5295*

These four or five women form a very flexible and professional a cappella vocalist group that has performed together

Photo: Benners Studio Collection

New Bern's early 1900's working waterfront will be remembered on a downtown mural to be painted in 1996 by artist Doug Alvord.

Photo: Clay Nolan/NC Travel & Tourism

A re-enactor gives a weaving demonstration at Tryon Palace.

for around five years. Voci Allegri schedules a Friday Refresher Concert Series between the fall and spring months of the year featuring four late afternoon concerts at the Bank of the Arts. The ensemble performs a variety of music: Gilbert and Sullivan, folk songs, Broadway tunes, madrigals, opera, music of the Italian Renaissance. Undaunted by any musical challenge, they obviously enjoy themselves.

Commercial Galleries

ART AND ACCESSORIES
230 Middle St.   633-2209
Offering original paintings by local artists, this is an interesting stop for decorative arts for the home.

ART GALLERY LTD.
502 Pollock St.   636-2120
On the second floor of the Edward Stanly house, this gallery offers fine works in contemporary North Carolina arts including paintings, limited-edition prints, glass, sculpture, jewelry, stoneware, porcelain and tapestry.

ART MATERIALS
220 Middle St.   514-2787
An exhibiting artist is frequently at work in this downtown hub of arts activities. Active artists find all necessary supplies here and studio classes are on going.

BENNERS STUDIO
206 Middle St.   636-2373
A portrait photography studio, Benners also does copy and restoration

work with photographs and has a processing lab for black-and-white and color photography.

CAROLINA CREATIONS
226 Middle St.   *633-4369*

An art studio and gallery, Carolina Creations offers exclusively North Carolina arts including pottery, stained glass and jewelry. This is also an active studio for fabric arts where knitting supplies and weaving classes are offered.

CITY ART WORKS GALLERY
225 Middle St.   *636-3434*

Representing works of fine contemporary artists of the southeastern United States, this gallery reliably shows an interesting variety of original paintings in watercolors, oils and pastels as well as jewelry, pottery and sculpture.

CRYSTAL LADY
217 Middle St.   *637-9880*

This is an interesting, active spot for custom stained-glass and gemstone designs. An active studio offering a variety of classes, Crystal Lady also offers all supplies for artists in beads, stones and stained glass.

TOKELA INSTITUTE
515 Broad St.   *636-1111*

An exhibiting gallery housed in the Attmore-Wadsworth house, Tokela is home of artists who produce Native American masks and bookplate master print photography. It is also, philosophically, an enlightening sociological teaching center.

A living nativity, community caroling along the waterfront and lighting of the community Christmas tree in the yard of Christ Episcopal Church at Pollock and Middle streets each December will soften any Scrooge.

New Bern
Annual Festivals and Events

"The Athens of North Carolina" has been New Bern's fond and familiar epithet since Colonial times, and living up to it, the town does an Olympian job of entertaining and educating throughout the year. Tryon Palace hosts a variety of special events, and the Craven Arts Council and Gallery sponsors art exhibitions, music and dance performances year round. Sailing regattas take place all year, and the city has been known to throw itself a party at the drop of a hat.

Each year, New Bern hosts the Craven Concerts Series including an annual concert by the North Carolina Symphony, solo artists and dancers. Performance dates change with each year's calendar. The New Bern Civic Theater schedules a variety of dramatic presentations year round, as do neighborhood dramatic groups. Numerous musical and art organizations annually schedule shows and perform at city functions and festivities. The New Bern Farmer's Market hosts dance bands for the public at various times during the year, the Downtown Business & Professional Association offers an entertaining day's end function that invites folks to enjoy downtown at special times, and interesting things are always brewing at Tryon Palace. Current calendar information may be obtained through the Craven Arts Council, 638-2577.

January

Because of the area's mild climate, Tryon Palace tries to accommodate local green thumbs with monthly **garden workshops** beginning in mid-January. The workshops combine a historical perspective on the art of gardening with practical advice on timely topics throughout the year. In 1996 garden workshops occur on the second Tuesday of each month. Gardening experts offer expertise on winter gardening, water gardening, wild flowers and carnivorous plants, antique roses, color design, holiday greenery and Victorian gardens. Garden workshops are conducted in the Tryon Palace Visitor Center. Admission is by purchase of a $4 garden ticket or annual pass. No advance reservations are necessary. For informa-

On the corner of Pollock and Middle streets is a cannon buried muzzle down. The cannon was taken from the Revolutionary British ship-of-war *Lady Blessington* following an engagement with a privateer owned by New Bern patriot, John Wright Stanley.

Insiders' Tips

tion about any of these popular workshops, phone 514-4900 or (800) 767-1560.

The **Shrine Winter Ceremonial** occurs annually during the third week of January, bringing Shriners to New Bern from all over North Carolina. Numerous nobles put on the most colorful parade possible on Saturday of convention week in downtown New Bern.

February

The town goes cosmopolitan in early February for two performances of some of the finest jazz you'll hear anywhere. The **New Bern Sunday Jazz Showcase**, sponsored by the Craven Arts Council and Gallery, takes place at the Sheraton Grand Hotel. The annual jazz showcase assembles some of the most recognized names in modern jazz. Both afternoon and evening performances are always a sellout so reservations are a must. Performances are at 1:30 and 7:30 PM. For information, call 638-2577.

Antiques also take the stage in mid-February when the New Bern Preservation Foundation sponsors its annual two-day **Antique Show and Sale** at the Sudan Temple on E. Front Street. The show hosts as many as 30 dealers who sell and exhibit 18th- and 19th-century American antiques. Proceeds benefit the Preservation Foundation's restoration projects, particularly the city's historic Union Station which is now underway. Tickets are $3.50 in advance and $4 at the door. For information, call 633-6448.

March

In addition to their gardens, New Bernians also proud of the authenticity of their vintage belongings. Here again, Tryon Palace fills the bill with its annual **Decorative Arts Symposium** in mid-March, illustrating regional styles in decorations. Co-sponsored by the East Carolina University Division of Continuing Education, the event includes nationally recognized speakers as well as meals, social events and special tours. A registration fee is required, and a brochure is printed each year outlining the events. For information, call 514-4900 or (800) 767-1560.

The **Coors Light-Ramada Regatta** opens the area's spring sailing season each year. Hosted by the Ramada Inn since 1991, the regatta is open to several classes of sailboats. For information, call 636-3637.

April

Many people enjoy visiting New Bern in mid-April for the **New Bern Spring Homes and Gardens Tour**. The event is now co-sponsored by the Historical Society and the New Bern Preservation Foundation, and the town puts on its prettiest face to welcome visitors. The tour includes private homes, gardens and churches in the historic district, with guides and location maps provided. The tour can best be enjoyed on foot and is an ideal opportunity to explore selected homes and landmarks in the river city. During the two-day event, Tryon Palace opens its gardens for free and offers palace tour tickets at a discount to tour ticket holders. Homes and Gardens Tour tickets may be purchased on tour days at the headquarters for both sponsoring organizations and the Attmore-Oliver House at 510 Pollock Street, 638-8558. Tickets can also be ordered by mail in advance.

The weekend of the New Bern Historic Homes and Gardens Tour is the same as **Gardeners' Weekend** at Tryon Palace. Palace gardens are open free throughout the weekend, and walking tours of the gardens are guided by horticultural staff members on Sunday. Thousands of gloriously colored tulips are in bloom, along with expansive plantings of blazing daffodils and pansies. For specific information, call 514-4900 or (800) 767-1560.

If golf is your game, sign on for the annual **Two-Man Classic Invitational Tournament** in mid-April. Sponsored by the New Bern Area Chamber of Commerce and the Greater Havelock Chamber of Commerce, tournament play is held simultaneously at The Emerald Golf Club and at Carolina Pines. For information, call the New Bern Chamber of Commerce at 637-3111.

Photo: Swiss Bear

Wander the streets of New Bern during most any festival and you'll see remarkable sights.

May

In early May, the Craven Arts Council stages a two-day **Cinco de Mayo Fiesta** in the parking lot of the El Cerro Grande Restaurant in Havelock. The free festival is in celebration of the Mexican holiday and features arts of the Hispanic culture including music, food, crafts, pinatas, dancing and other entertainment. School children are bused in to enjoy the traditional celebration, and the public is welcome both Friday and Saturday. For information call 638-2787.

In late May, the Neuse River Foundation sponsors **Neuse River Day**, a Saturday festival to celebrate and save a valu-

able natural resource. The day's activities take place at Union Point on the Trent and Neuse rivers and include boat rides, a ski show, a yacht parade, a fish fry, food booths, sailboat races, amusement rides and informational exhibits, speakers and demonstrations that increase awareness of the impact we have on the delicate balance of river ecology. Proceeds from the event help to fund the River Keeper program that employs a full-time professional and provides numerous volunteers to monitor the health of the Neuse River and its tributaries. For further information, contact the Neuse River Foundation, 637-7972.

Mid-May in New Bern brings in the clowns for the annual **Colonial Clown Convention**. That's right. It's a three-day weekend with more than 200 clowns about town. Clowns in training are taught by the pros how to walk the walk. Wannabes can develop an entire personality through costuming, makeup, walking, talking and acting. Slapstick, juggling, puppetry, magic, gospel routines, the difference between circus and town clowning, it's all there, so take it away! Performances are frequent and audiences are vital to training clowns. For registration information, call 638-8697. Whether as clown or audience, it's a good time to be in New Bern.

Beginning the last weekend in May are Tryon Palace's **Drama Tours**, daily living history presentations by characters who enact a typical day in the palace in the year 1771. The tours continue through mid-August. During Memorial Day Weekend, the gardens of Tryon Palace are open free of charge and a regimental encampment occurs on the palace grounds. For information, call the palace at 514-4900 or (800) 767-1560.

June

Visitors are invited to a Colonial America celebration of **King George III's Birthday: Festival of Colonial Life** in mid-June at Tryon Palace. The palace grounds and gardens buzz with activity of 18th-century life including a regimental encampment, entertainment, craft demonstrations and activities for all ages. Interior and Drama Tours of the palace historic sites are offered at the regular fee. For information, call 514-4900 or (800) 767-1560.

July

As one of America's first towns to have a **Fourth of July celebration**, New Bern still enjoys a well-turned-out celebration full of traditional hot dogs and fireworks. Previously, fireworks were set off at the Ramada Inn, but live cinders fell on nearby sailboats, so the practice was quickly snuffed out. Now the fireworks display takes place

at Lawson Creek Park on First Street near downtown. Spectators can watch the sky light up at Lawson Creek, or from even better vantage points at either Union Point Park or Bicentennial Park. Military bands have traditionally performed patriotic music to complement the event. Additional holiday activities take place at Tryon Palace, where gardens are open free to the public and entertainment and activities occur throughout the historic site.

September

Sailors from all over the Southeast converge on New Bern for the annual **Rotary Cup Regatta** each Labor Day weekend. Formerly the Michelob Cup Regatta, the Rotary Regatta is a leisurely, fun sailing competition for cruising class boats beginning in Oriental and finishing in New Bern, a distance of about 12 miles on the Neuse River. Festivities begin on the eve of the race in Oriental and continue at the Sheraton Marina following the competition. The New Bern Rotary Club sponsors the event, and everyone can join the fun that usually involves dances, a road race and seafood feasts. For information, call 633-9463 or 444-2349.

The **Curtis Strange Shrine Classic** is a one-day golf exhibition occurring in mid-September at the Emerald Golf Club for the benefit of the Shriner's 22 hospitals. Celebrity golfers scheduled to play in the seventh annual exhibition classic in 1996 include Don January, Bruce Lietzke and Miller Barber. The event has raised more than $500,000 for the Shrine Hospitals during the six years it has been played.

October

Kicking off the festivities on New Bern's schedule in early October is **Oktoberfest**.

The early Saturday evening event gathers New Bernians with European roots to an oom-pah get-down at the Farmer's Market on Tryon Palace Drive in downtown New Bern where they polka the night away. For information call 636-1640.

Swiss Bear Downtown Revitalization group, in cooperation with Tryon Palace and the city of New Bern, hosts one of eastern North Carolina's major annual events, the **Chrysanthemum Festival**, in early October. The colorful three-day weekend festival is a celebration of gorgeous autumn weather, colorful flowers and an inviting downtown full of interesting activities. Spread along the downtown streets and waterfront area are booths of food, crafts, paintings and antiques, a classic car show and musical performances both in the street and on stages in various locations. Festival activities include sporting events and a bass fishing tournament, traditional and changing events for the entire family each year.

Tryon Palace grounds, highlighted with thousands of mums in bloom, are open without admission, and military encampments provide diversions on the wide back lawn. Craft demonstrations, entertainment and other activities attract a grand turnout year after year. For festival information call Swiss Bear at 638-5781. For palace activities, call 514-4900 or (800) 767-1560.

In late October, the New Bern Historical Society conducts its **New Bern at Night Ghost Walk**, complete with ghosts from New Bern's past. Walking tours take place from 5 to 9 PM on two weekend nights and feature historic homes and the Cedar Grove Cemetery. Ghost Walks focus on historic events particular to New Bern, and ghosts from historic occasions are present in homes and historic buildings on the tour to tell how the times affected them. Banners, T-shirts and books are available as souvenirs of a truly chilling experience. For information, call 638-8558.

Photo: Swiss Bear

There is fun for all ages at the Chrysanthemum Festival.

November

Residents and visitors from surrounding counties look forward to Tryon Palace's two-part **Decorating for the Holidays** workshop in mid-November. The workshops teach participants how to make innovative and natural holiday decorations. Subjects covered often include wreaths and wreath-making, garland-making, using Christmas greenery, kissing balls and spectacular centerpieces using fresh fruits and natural greenery. Admission to the workshops is by purchase of a $4 garden ticket or advance purchase of a Christmas Celebration Tour ticket. Workshop times and locations vary. For information call 638-1560.

December

It's traditional in New Bern that the city's **Coastal Christmas Celebration** begins the first weekend in December with a festive flotilla bringing Santa to Bicentennial Park. Now in its 11th year, the **Coastal Christmas Flotilla** is truly a water-land celebration bringing Santa to town aboard a Hatteras yacht. The flotilla proceeds down the Trent River and passes Union Point, giving spectators a long, lingering look at the boats festooned with sparkling lights, diving dolphins and red-nosed reindeer.

Staff and volunteers prepare for weeks for the **Tryon Palace Christmas Celebration**, and by early December the palace looks much as it did during the holidays in 1770, when Governor William Tryon hosted a "very grand and noble Entertainment and Ball" to celebrate the grand opening of his sumptuous home and the Royal capitol. The palace is lighted and adorned with fresh fruit and fragrant greenery. Cooks are busy in the kitchen, preparing confections and delicacies, and the air is filled with holiday aromas. **Christmas Insider Tours** take place through mid-December focusing on decorations and food in Tryon Palace and other historic sites from the 18th to 20th centuries. Through mid-December, palace horticulture staffers lead visitors on **Winter Garden Tours** focused on evergreens and exterior decorations. Two weekends are reserved for evening **Christmas Candlelight Tours** featuring 800 candles burning throughout the palace. Carolers, dancers and musical entertainment are continuous during the spectacular evening tours. For information, call 514-4900 or (800) 767-1560.

Other events in downtown New Bern's Coastal Christmas Celebration include a community and a North Carolina Symphony performance of **Handel's *Messiah*** at Centenary United Methodist Church. A living nativity, community caroling along the waterfront and lighting of the community Christmas tree in the yard of Christ Episcopal Church at Pollock and Middle streets each December will soften any Scrooge. You will definitely catch the spirit of the season in New Bern.

New Bern
Fishing, Watersports and Boating

Because of New Bern's location it's not surprising that New Bernians take to the water like, well, ducks. The weather is mild enough year round to entice the locals into sailing, skiing, fishing or relaxing on or around the rivers.

Fishing

Expect to hook bass, bream and flounder in local waters. Bass fishing tournaments are popular competitions often scheduled during the year as fund-raising events by area organizations. Swiss Bear Inc., usually schedules a bass-fishing competition during the Chrysanthemum Festival each October. The Neuse River is also home to many crabs, the catching of which provides tasty and profitable rewards for many locals.

Nearby **Croatan National Forest** permits fresh and saltwater fishing; however, fishing in the forest's freshwater lakes is poor because of the acidity of the water. But along its river shoreline, oystering, crabbing and flounder gigging can be worthwhile efforts. For the best spots, talk to a ranger at the headquarters office on Fisher Avenue, 9 miles south of New Bern just off U.S. Highway 70 E.

If you just like to cruise the backwoods, several forest locations have boat ramps or launch sites, including **Brices Creek**, **Cahooque Creek**, **Catfish Lake**, **Great Lake** and **Haywood Landing**. Some of these sites are deep in the forest, so it is best to check with a ranger for specific directions, or better yet, stop by headquarters and pick up a forest map.

For fresh bait, stop by **Neuse River Seafood**, 638-1891, or **Tripp's Seafood**, 637-7700.

Water-skiing

For skiing enthusiasts, the spot of choice is along the Trent River from Lawson Creek Park to Trent Woods. Smaller than the Neuse, the Trent is more protected from prevailing winds and usually has calm water. A number of area skiers enjoy the twists and curves of Brices Creek, although skiing there is becoming more and more limited with increased land development and the imposition of speed limits.

Boat Rentals and Charters

Boat rentals are offered by a few businesses around New Bern. One of the most popular is **Shorebird Boat Rentals**, 638-7075, (800) 948-3524, which offers rentals at the Comfort Suites and Marina on E. Front Street, at the Sheraton Hotel and Marina downtown and at Northwest Creek Marina in Fairfield Harbour. You can rent anything from a 17-foot power boat to a 24-foot pontoon. Shorebird offers canoes, Waverunners, sailboats and bikes as well as guided fishing charters, cruises and a tow service.

Nautical Adventures Sailing Charters, 633-1871, offers a variety of sailing options aboard the high-performance catamaran *Sea N' Double*. You can take a half- or full-day cruise, a sunset trip or extended charters to such places as Cape Lookout, Beaufort and Ocracoke. Captain Skipper Hill also offers sailing lessons.

On The Wind Sailing School and Charter Service, 633-0032, offers a variety of charters, including day and evening sails. All cruises depart from Northwest Creek Marina at Fairfield Harbor.

Sailing

For sailors, the premier events are the annual Rotary Cup and Coors Light-Ramada Regatta, both of which are detailed in our Annual Events chapter. Other sailing competitions take place throughout the year. For more information call **Blackbeard's Sailing Club**, 633-3990, or **On The Wind Sailing School and Charter Service** at Fairfield Harbour, 633-0032.

Several yacht clubs are active in the New Bern area including **Eastern Carolina Yacht Club**, which meets in Trent Woods at 4005 Trent Pines Drive and the **New Bern Yacht Club**, which meets at the Sheraton Grand Hotel and Marina downtown.

Waterways

Boaters in the New Bern area have two waterways to explore: the expansive Neuse River that flows into the Pamlico Sound; or the slow, meandering Trent River that flows into the Neuse.

The Neuse River is ideal for cruising by sail or power, with miles of sandy beaches, clearly marked channels, easy access via the **Intracoastal Waterway** (ICW) and Pamlico Sound and many marinas and protected anchorages. The Trent River is deep, has a marked channel and is navigable by small boat. Its lower reaches are fine for uncrowded water-skiing. Brices Creek, a tributary of the Trent, winds far into the forest and offers excellent fishing and wildlife observation.

Rotating bridges at New Bern open on demand daily except from 6:30 to 7:30 AM and 4:30 to 5:30 PM. On weekends and holidays between May 24 and September 8, the bridges are closed between 2 and 7 PM, with openings at 4 and 6 PM. The remainder of the year, the daily schedule is in effect seven days a week. The bridge tender monitors channel 13 VHF. The railroad bridges upriver from New Bern are always open except when in use. National Oceanic and Atmospheric Administration (NOAA) stations in the area are New Bern and Beaufort, WX-2 (162.475 MHz) and Hatteras, WX-3 (162.40 MHz).

A clearly marked channel up the Neuse from the ICW will bring you into historic New Bern. The natural channel depths generally run between 8 and 12 feet, with little noticeable tidal effect. A strong easterly or northerly wind will raise the level, while a sustained westerly breeze, say 25 knots, can lower this level by as much as 2 feet. Also noteworthy to boaters are sapling net stakes dotting the river, strung with nets in the early spring and late fall. The nets are usually buoyed by corks or plastic bottles or marked by white flags.

The Neuse is a very wide river, which invites day and night sailing in addition to motor-cruising and water-skiing. The many wandering tributaries promise scenic canoeing and exciting fishing.

Boats of all sizes can find berthing space in downtown New Bern and nearby marinas. Whether you're cruising the area or wish to launch your boat at one of the many local ramps, most locations have similar facilities. In the downtown area especially it is not unusual for leisure yachters or sailors to arrive for what they thought would be a short visit only to find themselves living aboard their vessels, staying weeks, sometimes months, even years.

Much of the Neuse River's shoreline south of New Bern forms a boundary of the vast 157,000-acre Croatan National Forest. Here locals and visitors enjoy public recreation areas, with swimming and picnic facilities near the Minnesott ferry terminal and at Flanner's Beach south of New Bern.

Marinas

If you're traveling to New Bern from some distance, it is wise to call ahead to assure docking space availability, especially during the warmer months.

The **Comfort Suites and Marina**, 218 E. Front Street, 636-0022, is in the historic district at the Riverfront Park on the Neuse River. Offering year-round services, the 24-slip marina has six transient slips and accommodates power or sailing vessels up to 120 feet. Its marked entry channel has a controlling depth of 20 feet; dockside depth is 10 feet. The marina offers some groceries, ice, laundry facilities and other amenities of the Comfort Suites including an outdoor heated whirlpool and swimming pool.

The **Sheraton Marina**, 1 Bicentennial Park, 638-3585, is part of the Sheraton Hotel complex. It is on the Trent River and has a floating breakwater/dock that can serve larger yachts. The marina is open year round, and it docks sail and power vessels up to 300 feet in its 200 slips, 25 of which are transient berths. The marina also has a marked entry channel and approach, a dockside depth of 12 feet, gas and diesel fuel, a pump-out station, ice, electricity, showers and a restaurant. All floating docks and finger piers were recently rebuilt. Telephone service is available, and cable TV is free.

Ramada Marina, 101 Howell Road, 636-2888, is across the Trent River from the Sheraton Marina. It is open year round and serves sail and power vessels up to 110 feet. It has 144 concrete floating slips, 10 of which are transient berths, a marked entry channel with 12-foot approach depth, dockside depth of 16 feet, pump-out station, ice, electricity, showers, laundry facilities, a restaurant and a snack bar. The marina has a patio and grills. Phone and cable TV hookups are also available.

The **River Bend Yacht Club**, 1 Ma-

The Sheraton Grand Hotel's marina berths Michelob Cup competitors.

Photo: NC Travel & Tourism

rina Drive, 633-2006, is reached by boat via an entry channel south of the Trent River bridge. It is about 5 miles upstream from downtown New Bern. A private club, the marina is open year round and serves sail and power vessels up to 40 feet. It has 75 slips, six of which are transient berths, a marked entry channel, launching ramp, gas, electricity and an approach and dockside depth of 6 feet. It offers propeller and hull repair services and stocks marine supplies, groceries and ice. In addition to dock space, which can be rented short- or long-term, guest memberships to the town's golf course, tennis courts and swimming pool can also be purchased. The Oar House Restaurant and Lounge is on site for food and libations.

Northwest Creek Marina, 104 Marina Drive in Fairfield Harbour, 638-4133, has become the center of action for this resort development. It is on the north side of the Neuse River, is open year round and serves sail and power vessels up to 60 feet. Larger boats are accommodated by special arrangements. It has 235 slips, 15 of which are transient berths, a marked entry channel with 7 feet of water depth, dockside depth of 12 feet, gas and diesel fuel, a pump-out station, a launching ramp, electricity, showers, a weight and sauna room and laundry facilities. The Harbour Breeze General Store can help provision your boat for the day or an extended cruise with groceries, supplies, clothing and fishing gear. Marina patrons have full use of all the resort's amenities including two 18-hole golf courses, indoor and outdoor pools and

lighted tennis courts. For dining, Captain Bordeaux Bar & Grill at dockside features an upstairs bar and lounge and casual fine dining in the downstairs restaurant. Transportation will be needed to visit New Bern's attractions.

Duck Creek Marina, Sandy Point Road, Bridgeton, 638-1702, is at the head of Duck Creek on the north side of the Neuse across from the Ramada Marina. It is open year round and serves sail and power vessels up to 46 feet. It has 55 slips, a marked entry channel with approach depth of 6 feet, dockside depth of 8 feet, railway and 35-ton lift, storage yard for repair work, marine supplies, electricity and showers. Because the marina is across the river from New Bern, you will need transportation for shopping or to visit the city's attractions.

Union Point Park, Tryon and E. Front streets, 636-4060, serves as a city park and public docks. Boaters often anchor here to orient themselves to the area and locate more permanent mooring. The park features a boat ramp and public facilities; however, a city ordinance prohibits overnight dockage. Work on new bulkheading and construction of a promenade in 1996 will not interrupt parking and boat-ramp access.

Tidewater Marina Co. Inc., 300 Madame Moore Lane, 637-3347, is on the Trent River. It is open year round and serves sail and power vessels up to 40 feet. It has 16 slips, three transient slips, a marked entry channel with controlling depth of 21 feet, 15 feet at dockside, railway and lift, a launching ramp, gas and diesel fuel, supplies and electricity. It also offers repairs on propellers and hulls. Because it is away from New Bern's hub, you will need transportation to see the sights.

Nearby Marinas

Nearby marinas at Clubfoot Creek, Minnesott Beach and Oriental, all on the Neuse River, are destinations for enjoyable day sails or cruising trips from New Bern. In addition, there are many marinas along the Crystal Coast, which is easily accessible from New Bern via the Neuse River and the ICW. See our Crystal Coast Marinas chapter for listings. For the convenience of boaters, we are including an alphabetical list of some of the marinas near New Bern that you can call on as you make your way up and down the Neuse River or toward Pamlico Sound.

Clubfoot Creek on the south side of the river near Havelock provides anchorage for water traffic, and the riverside community of Minnesott Beach on the north side of the Neuse also offers safe mooring. The quaint village of Oriental, on the ICW on the north bank of the Neuse, is called "the sailing capital of North Carolina," but many power and pleasure vessels find safe harbor at area docks as well.

Matthews Point Marina, RFD 1, Havelock, 444-1805, is off the beaten track on Clubfoot Creek on the south side of the Neuse River, 10 miles east of Cherry Point. Nestled comfortably in a safe harbor, the marina is open year round and serves sail and power vessels up to 45 feet. It has 106 slips, six of which are transient berths, a marked entry channel, approach depth of 7 feet, dockside depth of 6 feet, gas and diesel fuel, a launching ramp, electricity, a pump-out station, showers and ice. A clubhouse, cookout area and upper deck lounge are also available to boaters.

Minnesott Beach Yacht Basin, Bennett Road, Arapahoe, 249-1424, is on the north side of the Neuse River. It is open year round and serves sail and power vessels up to 50 feet. It has 150 slips, five of which are transient berths, a marked entry channel, approach depth of 8.5 feet, dockside depth of 10 feet, gas and diesel fuel, a 60-ton lift, electricity, a pump-out station, supplies, ice, limited groceries, showers, laundry facilities and a pool. Propeller and hull repairs are available for both gas and diesel vessels. The marina has a lounge with a TV and fireplace and is close to the country club golf course. Transportation to a nearby restaurant can also be arranged.

Oriental Marina, Hodges Street, Oriental, 249-1818, is just off the ICW. It is open year round and serves sail and power vessels of up to 80 feet. It has 15 slips, 10 of which are transient, an 8-foot entry channel, dockside depth of 6 feet, gas and diesel fuel, electricity, groceries, ice, showers, laundry facilities, a restaurant and an 18-room motel. Gas and diesel fuel are available as are some repairs.

Sea Harbour Marina, Harbour Way, Oriental, 249-0808, is on Pierce Creek about a mile from town. It is open year round, has 90 slips, serves sail and power vessels up to 45 feet, has gas and diesel fuel, a pump-out station, electricity, water hookups, a pool and restrooms.

Whittaker Creek Yacht Harbor, Whittaker Point Road, Oriental, 249-0666 or 249-1020, is about a half-mile from town on Whittaker Creek. It is open year round, has 160 slips including 20 transient slips, serves power and sailing vessels of up to 120 feet and has a marked entry channel with 8 feet of water on approach and at dockside. Gas and diesel fuel are available as are a pump-out station, electricity, supplies, a ship's store, ice, laundry facilities and restrooms. The marina offers repairs and a courtesy car. A pool and restaurant are on-site.

Off Pembroke Road and fronting the Trent River, Lawson Creek Park is the major boat-launching area for water enthusiasts.

New Bern
Sports, Recreation and Parks

New Bern is surrounded by water and great open spaces, making it an excellent location for sporting and recreational activities. There are numerous places for adults and children to exercise and take part in sporting programs. Walking is one favorite form of exercise in New Bern. Some call it strolling and use that time to check on the progress of neighbors, their children or area businesses.

For those who are seeking a more tiring pursuit, New Bern and Craven County both offer active recreation programs and public areas for tennis, power walking, running, baseball/softball and soccer. Both the city and county also maintain public boat ramps.

Golf is a year-round activity in this climate and is one of the most popular forms of recreation in the area. We have listed New Bern's public and private golf courses in this chapter.

Recreation

NEW BERN
RECREATION DEPARTMENT
636-4060

The New Bern Recreation Department operates the bulk of its programs from two centers — the **Stanley White Center** on Chapman Street, 636-4061, and the **West New Bern Recreation** Center, 1225 Pine Tree Drive, 636-4061. The programs vary at each center and with each season. Programming includes youth lessons in swimming and tennis, summer day camps, youth ceramic classes and football. T-ball and baseball is offered to youth between the ages of 6 and 12. Babe Ruth baseball is played by youths 13 through 18.

CRAVEN COUNTY
RECREATION AND PARKS
636-6606

Craven County's recreation facilities are connected to schools. Facilities offered to the public include tennis courts and ballfields. Youth programs include karate, gymnastics, T-ball, soccer leagues and camps, baseball, swimming and a six-week summer day camp. Adults can take part in numerous programs including softball, basketball, exercise and line-dance classes. The county recreation department also sponsors the area's Senior Games and Special Olympics. Craven Community College has a number of lighted tennis courts available for public use.

TWIN RIVERS YMCA
100 YMCA Ln.   *638-8799*

At the intersection of Fifth and Sixth streets is a 45,000-square-foot athletic facility that houses a 25-yard, six-lane heated indoor swimming pool, a regulation-size gymnasium with an upstairs track, a gym, a youth activity center, racquetball courts, a free weight room and a wellness center with step machines, a treadmill and bicycles. The staff will analyze patrons' fitness levels and help develop a personalized activity program, if needed. There is a CAM II Center with Nautilus equipment and a fitness center with a sauna and a whirlpool. Classes are taught regularly in swimming, gymnastics, aqua aerobics, arthritis aquatics, water safety instructor training, junior lifesaving, basic lifeguard training, scuba and cardiopulmonary resuscitation. There are programs in aerobics, fitness for people older than 40, racquetball, volleyball and weights. Competitions are conducted in a variety of activities. Youth programs are offered in gymnastics, basketball, volleyball, softball and T-ball, and transportation is provided from several schools for after-school programs. The Y sponsors day camps during Easter and Christmas vacations. Babysitting services are available, and the Y can host children's birthday parties.

COURTS PLUS

2911 Brunswick Ave.   *633-2221*

Courts Plus of New Bern is a membership racquetball facility with four indoor courts. The facility also offers swimming and aqua aerobics in its indoor and outdoor pools. The facility offers Nautilus workout equipment, karate, basketball, volleyball and aerobics. There are saunas, a steamroom and a whirlpool for soothing relaxation. Lockers, towel facilities and a tanning booth are also available. The pro shop offers apparel, equipment and accessories for your fitness needs. Courts Plus has several racquetball leagues and serves as site host for a number of regional racquetball tournaments. The lounge offers refreshments and light snacks. Child care and special programs for children are also offered.

Golf

Golf courses seem to fill the New Bern area. Many have won acclaim from amateurs and professionals alike and host a number of large golf tournaments. Golfing residents and visitors are fortunate: Popular courses are easily accessible, and the normally mild climate allows for year-round play.

Here is a list of the courses in the immediate vicinity. For information about nearby golf courses, see our Crystal Coast Golf chapter, which includes information on the Morehead City Golf and Country Club; Bogue Banks Country Club in Pine Knoll Shores; Star Hill Golf and Country Club in Cape Carteret; Brandywine Bay Golf Club near Morehead City; and Silver Creek Golf Club on Highway 58 near Cape Carteret.

THE EMERALD

6001 Clubhouse Dr.   *633-4440*

Rees Jones designed The Emerald, creating the 7,000-yard course to be a challenge to golfers at all levels of skill. Jones used various grasses to give each hole a totally different feel and appearance, and

Insiders' Tips

Check with area hotels about packages available that include rooms, greens fees, meals and more.

sculptured the 18-hole course to create variety. Most holes have four or five pin locations. The fourth tee, for example, features four locations that hit across the water and one high land route. Carts are available. While only residents of The Emerald community can be permanent members of the golf club, there are social memberships that entitle members to tennis, swimming pool and club facilities as well as golfing privileges. The Emerald is home to the Curtis Strange Golf Classic, played annually to raise money for the Shriners' Hospitals. Golfers can take advantage of a fully stocked pro shop, a driving range and lessons by pro Jerry Briele.

FAIRFIELD HARBOR
750 Broad Creek Rd., Bridgeton   638-5338

Fairfield Harbour is a resort community, with timeshare accommodations plus several large residential developments. To get there, cross the Neuse River on Highway 17. Turn right on Highway 55, and continue about a mile to Broad Creek Road. Signs will direct you from there. Fairfield Harbour has two 18-hole golf courses. Fairfield Harbour Country Club is a private links-style course with 18 holes and a par of 72. This enjoyable, almost 6,000-yard course affords lovely views of Broad Creek. The course is open to property owners, including those who own a week or more in the timeshare facilities. Sam Maraffi is Fairfield's PGA pro.

RIVER BEND
GOLF AND COUNTRY CLUB
94 Shoreline Dr., River Bend   638-2819

River Bend Golf and Country Club, an 18-hole course with a 71 par, is a semiprivate course allowing greens fee play. The course is open everyday. All you need to do is call and set your tee time. Ron Anderson

Windsurfing is great fun on any windy day.

is the club's PGA professional. River Bend offers a well-stocked pro shop, tennis courts and an Olympic-size swimming pool. This is truly one of the area's nicest courses.

NEW BERN
GOLF AND COUNTRY CLUB

4200 Country Club Rd.
Trent Woods   *637-2413*

This golf course is open to members and their guests. If you are new to the area and are interested in belonging to the country club, don't delay because there is generally a waiting list. Tennis courts are adjacent to the lovely clubhouse, which overlooks the Trent River with overhanging hardwood trees laced with Spanish moss. Members and guests will also find a swimming pool, tennis shop and pro shop.

Insiders' Tips

Union Point Park is a great place to take a break from an afternoon of exploring the New Bern waterfront.

CAROLINA PINES
GOLF AND COUNTRY CLUB

Carolina Pines Blvd.   *444-1000*

On the Neuse River just west of Havelock, this is a challenging 18-hole, par 72 course with a pro shop, driving range and target greens. Tim Dupre is the club pro. Golfers will also find tennis courts, a pool, and a club house with a lounge and patio overlooking freshwater lakes and golf links.

Parks

Several of New Bern's public parks and their offerings are listed below.

GLENBURNIE PARK

In the Glenburnie Gardens residential area off Oaks Road, this park has a boat landing and picnic and recreation areas, all shaded by a grove of old pine trees. There are several picnic shelters with tables and grills at the park.

GEORGE STREET BALLFIELD

Next to the United Senior Services building, this area includes basketball courts and other play areas.

KAFER PARK

Adjoining the George Street area, this ballpark was once home to New Bern's professional baseball team.

LAWSON CREEK PARK

Off Pembroke Road and fronting the Trent River, this is the major boat-launching area for water enthusiasts. The park also has two soccer fields, a nature trail and Jack's Island, a picnic area. The nature walk meanders through the marsh land that makes up much of the park area.

UNION POINT PARK

Another boat launching and picnic area, this park is downtown where the Trent River joins the Neuse. It is a great place to sit and watch the river traffic. The park includes a stage, where Sunday summer afternoon concerts are often performed.

FORT TOTTEN PARK

At the intersection of Trent Road and Fort Totten Drive, this small park has a ballfield and children's play area.

New Bern
Real Estate and Neighborhoods

Just a few years ago Craven County was listed as the fifth fastest-growing county in the state, and North Carolina was proclaimed as the fifth fastest-growing state in the nation. That growth continues as Craven County and New Bern attract new residents from across the state and country. Many factors are impacting the area's growth. These include the tide of retirees flowing into New Bern and the surrounding area, and the growing personnel demands from nearby Cherry Point military base. It's not surprising then that New Bern's housing market has expanded substantially to meet the increasing demands of homeowners.

The city appears to be in the midst of a vibrant community renaissance. In downtown's historic neighborhoods, it is still not unusual to find a structure in need of repair in the midst of beautifully restored buildings, but this will be short lived. Any unrestored Georgian, Federal and Victorian edifices are quickly being purchased and restored, adding to the enhancement of the city's Colonial charm. Visitors are charmed by the restaurants, bed and breakfast inns and shops that now exist in restored structures in the downtown historic district.

Another big plus for the city is its location near water. Positioned at the joining waters of the Neuse and Trent rivers, New Bern is less than an hour's drive from the ocean. Its moderate climate, nearby recreational waterways and challenging and well-maintained golf courses offer added pluses in making it a popular vacation, relocation and retirement spot for people from all walks of life.

With this in mind, New Bern's expanding homes market offers newcomers a wide range of neighborhoods and housing choices in styles and prices that are sure to appeal to any taste or income bracket. The range includes historic homes, contemporary structures, bungalows, ranch-style residences, riverfront condominiums, townhouses and building lots in ever-increasing new developments.

Because both waterfront and nonwaterfront homes and lots are often within the same district, real estate values can vary widely within the same neighborhood. Prices for lots and houses quoted here are approximations and, of course, are subject to change. The following descriptions of neighborhoods will help orient you to the personality, price range and availability of New Bern housing.

Neighborhoods

Downtown Historic District

This is the mecca for those who desire to live in New Bern's oldest and most distinguished homes. The downtown historic district encompasses the point of land jutting into the confluence of the Neuse and Trent rivers and extends west to Queen Street.

The New Bern Preservation Foundation, in the years since its organization in 1972, has bought and restored approximately 40 structures of historic or architectural significance. This has stimulated private interests in the community that has resulted in the restoration of more than 150 private homes. A few of these homes date from the mid-1700s, built shortly after New Bern was founded in 1710 by Swiss nobleman Christoph deGraffenried.

The focal point of the downtown historic district is Tryon Palace on Pollock Street. The former home of the Carolinas' British governor, William Tryon, its gardens and associated buildings have been beautifully reconstructed or restored. The state historic site draws thousands of visitors each year. In the surrounding neighborhood, professional offices, businesses and bed and breakfast inns occupy tastefully renovated old homes. The city has an astonishing total of 140 landmarks listed in the National Register of Historic Places, and most of these are found in the downtown district.

Facing the Neuse River north of the U.S. Highway 17 bridge are approximately a dozen square blocks of pedigreed houses dating from the 18th, 19th and 20th centuries. Most are two- and three-story elegant restorations, and occasionally one is available for sale at a dear price. Smaller restored homes away from the river in this neighborhood are available in the $100,000 range. The farther away you get from the river, blocks become more transitional and prices get lower.

The cost of homes throughout the entire downtown district varies enormously, depending upon location and the degree of restoration. Sometimes, homes along the fringes are offered in the $40,000 to $60,000 range, but you can bet they require a tremendous amount of work and TLC. Fully restored historic houses are offered for $160,000 to more than $300,000.

Riverside Historic District

This area includes National Avenue and the section east of it to the Neuse River. Noted as a historic district, this section unfortunately has fallen into disrepair over the years. Many of the larger homes were built between 1896 and World War II. The neighborhood built up around the lumber industry, which once flourished along the Neuse River. Measures are being taken to rejuvenate this once-handsome neighborhood that is characterized by high-peaked, two-story Victorian structures, with wrap-around porches and plenty of shade trees set well back from the road. Some of the homes have been beautifully renovated, while others are still a trifle run down. A few appear to have been abandoned and virtually cry out for restoration. On the cross streets running perpendicular to National Avenue and the Neuse are tidy rows of bungalows.

Homes along the River Drive waterfront are of an entirely different character. Here, you will find pretty brick ranch dwellings on small lots with plenty of trees and meticulous landscaping. Real estate values vary widely, with some of the older bungalows offered in the $30,000 to $50,000 range. Renovated historic dwellings here start at about $125,000, with ranch-style houses along the shore selling for a bit more.

Ghent Historic District

This is the newest of New Bern's three historic districts, with homes dat-

Photo: Benner's Studio

The Blades House is one of New Bern's fine old homes.

ing from between 1913 and World War II. It includes the area encompassing Spencer, Rhem and parts of Park avenues. It was developed as a trolley car suburb in the days when working folks wanted homes away from the hustle and bustle of downtown New Bern. Today, Spencer Avenue is considered to be one of the prettiest streets in New Bern, with old-fashioned street lamps along a landscaped median separating two lanes of traffic.

Ghent has the appearance of an energetic, blue-collar neighborhood with a distinctly lived-in look. In recent years, it has become a highly desirable section for homeowners and has undergone a lot of sprucing up. Bungalows and cottage-style homes with neat lawns make up a large part of the neighborhood.

Some residences feature antebellum column fronts, and many have open or screened porches for those warm summer evenings. One of the area's nicest amenities is a new, modern YMCA, which includes a Jr. Olympic-size swimming pool, a gymnasium, weight rooms and a racquetball court. It also offers day care and exercise classes. The Ghent neighborhood lies between Fort Totten Park, which has a baseball field and bleachers, and the larger Lawson Creek Park, a popular fishing spot. This park also has playing fields, nature trails, boat launches and picnic tables.

Homes here are larger than in many of the new housing developments surrounding New Bern, but many still require remodeling and renovation. Prices range from $65,000 to $120,000.

Taberna

Taberna is the newest community in the area. Under development by Weyerhaeuser, this community is about 5 miles east of downtown New Bern on Highway 70 east. Taberna means hospitality and actually was the first name of Bern, Switzerland, New Bern's sister city. Residences at the planned 1,100-acre golfing community will include single-family homes, patio homes and townhouses, with golf villas scattered throughout. Approximately 750 to 800 homesites will be available when all phases are complete. The focal point will be the championship 18-hole golf course. Features of the community include rolling hills, dense foliage, lakes, streams and wetlands, along with pedestrian trails, a canoe dock and a canoe trail system.

DeGraffenried Park

This distinguished neighborhood lies between Trent and Neuse boulevards, directly north of the Ghent Historical District. Homes here are generally large and well-placed on spacious, beautifully landscaped lots. Sidewalks invite neighborhood walks, and streets carry names such as Queen Ann Lane and Lucerne Way.

Many of the more notable residences are stately, two-story brick dwellings with dignified Federal features. Brick walls and wrought-iron fences embellish many of the houses in the district. You can expect to pay between $100,000 to $200,000 for these homes.

Trent Woods

This large, mature development lies between New Bern and the Trent River. Over the years it has spread out from the central New Bern Golf and Country Club. Now its winding lanes contain some of the ritziest neighborhoods and poshest dwellings in the area. It also embraces many large, ranch-style homes. It has been incorporated into a town to give residents better control over their neighborhoods, and there is virtually no commercial development within its borders. It is a neighborhood well-suited to young families with children.

Most of the structures here tend toward conservative rather than contemporary architectural styles and are constructed of wood, brick or stucco. Homes are large, with two and three stories, and usually have attached or separate two-car garages. Some homes have private docks along the Trent River waterfront. The lots are spacious, wooded and impeccably landscaped, often with Spanish moss draped in towering trees. If you take a drive through Trent Woods in the spring, you'll be greeted by a stunning display of flowering trees and shrubs.

In addition to the country club, the area boasts other amenities such as the Eastern Carolina Yacht Club. The average price for a home in this area starts around $100,000; building lots are priced from the mid-$30,000s; and waterfront houses begin in the $300,000 range.

Olde Towne Harbour

This is one of the nicest subdivisions in New Bern, just east of Trent Woods and south of Highway 70. Though just minutes from the downtown district and the shopping malls on Highway 17, the area offers quiet seclusion in a lovely, natural setting. Here, you can find some of the most lavish, custom-built contemporary homes and condominiums in New Bern. The largest of these sprawl along

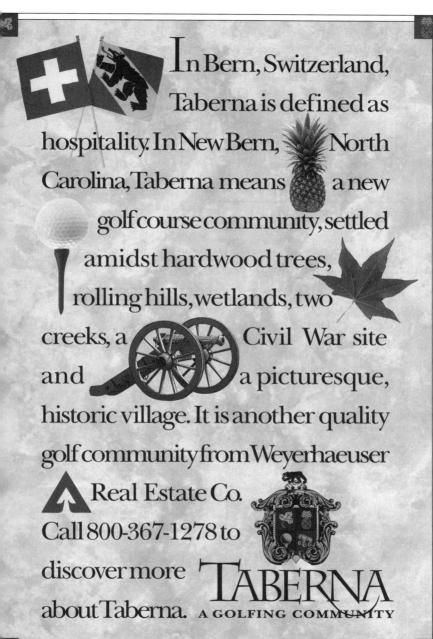

In Bern, Switzerland, Taberna is defined as hospitality. In New Bern, North Carolina, Taberna means a new golf course community, settled amidst hardwood trees, rolling hills, wetlands, two creeks, a Civil War site and a picturesque, historic village. It is another quality golf community from Weyerhaeuser Real Estate Co. Call 800-367-1278 to discover more about Taberna.

TABERNA A GOLFING COMMUNITY

the shores of the Trent River and Olde Towne Lake, (actually a river inlet). This is a strictly residential, built-in development, and it appears no expense has been spared by those who have recently purchased and built on these choice, waterfront lots. Lots here begin at about $45,000, condos at $175,000 and homes at $150,000. Waterfront homes, again, are another story, ranging upward into the $500,000 category.

River Bend

The 1,200-acre town of River Bend lies along a winding inlet on the north shore of the Trent River, about 5 miles south of New Bern. This location allows many of the homesites to have water frontage and private boat slips. The land was originally owned by the Odd Fellows, a fraternal group of black tenant farmers raising tobacco. During the recession of 1914, they were forced to sell their land to the "company store" for supplies and debts. During the first half of the century, a wealthy family owned the land and continued to have it farmed for tobacco. In 1965, real estate speculator J. Frank Efird recognized the area's potential as a retirement development for people moving south from the northeast. He organized The Efird Company to acquire and develop the old Odd Fellows farm.

True to Efird's vision, large numbers of retirees now live in River Bend, although there are also a number of young families. The community has its own country club to service its 18-hole golf course. The club includes a well-stocked pro shop, a small sandwich shop, an outdoor swimming pool and four lighted tennis courts.

River Bend, which today has a population of approximately 3,000, incorporated into a town in 1980 in order to maintain roads and provide other services. The municipal building, finished in 1986, has a 99-seat meeting hall and is adjacent to a small park with a children's play area, baseball field and small dock. The development consists mainly of single-family dwellings, all with attached or detached one- and two-car garages. In recent years, clusters of townhouses and duplexes have been added to the community. Houses here begin at just more than $100,000 for a nonwaterfront location. Townhouse prices depend on the development, but the average range is between $60,000 and $150,000. The neighborhood is near New Bern Quinn Elementary and New Bern High School.

Fairfield Harbour

This expansive community is across the Neuse River off Highway 55 and 6 miles down Broad Creek Road. It is a 3,000-acre resort development featuring a large canal system that gives many homes water access at their back doors.

The development is unique in that it is a combination of mostly single-family homes, with some condominiums, townhouses and timeshare condos added for good measure. In general, you can expect homes to start in the $80,000 range and continue on up into many thousands of dollars, depending upon proximity to the water.

Lots may be wooded, fronting one of two 18-hole golf courses, or on a canal where a private boat can be docked. Several hundred lots are available, with prices ranging from approximately $8,000 for an interior lot, $15,000 for a golf course lot, and from $44,000 to more than $100,000 for waterfront lots. Some waterfront sites have natural frontage, while others have bulkheads.

Condominiums and townhouses at Fairfield Harbour are arranged around small man-made lakes. Winding paths and roads connect all locations, and the combination of layout and landscaping gives a feeling of privacy, even with neighbors only a few feet away. The condos were built at different times in different styles, and they have varying levels of modern amenities. Jacuzzis and Jenn-Aire ranges are common in most, as are balconies, decks and screened porches. Most have two or three bedrooms. Developers have shown careful respect for the trees that were on the lots first. It is not unusual to see decks cut to accommodate a tree. Prices start in the $60,000 range for these maintenance-free homes.

The Harbour's combination of year-round residents and vacationers requires that a wide variety of activities be readily available. Established community activities are too numerous to list but include such interests as men's and women's golf associations, a chorus, quilting, weaving, swimnastics and garden, drama, book, bridge, RV, tennis and yacht clubs. The community features two 18-hole golf courses, one indoor and two outdoor pools, nine tennis courts, four of which are lighted, a country club with a restaurant, two pro shops and two marinas on the premises. Boat rentals and cruises are available year round.

Brice's Creek

A number of subdivisions exist in this area southwest of New Bern, including the Lake Clermont subdivision, Snug Harbor, Oakview, Deer Run and River Trace. Some of these are fully built up, while

What New Bern Owes John Lawson

A great deal has been written about Baron deGraffenried, the founder of New Bern, but only by delving into the annals of history do we learn of the important part John Lawson played in the establishment of the town.

John Lawson came to the Carolinas from England in 1700 when Native Americans ruled the land. Much of the territory was uncharted and thick vegetation and insects made traveling difficult.

It is believed that Lawson was educated at either Oxford or Cambridge. His extensive education is demonstrated in his approach to botanical collections and well-written texts. His book of 1709, *A New Voyage To Carolina*, is a fascinating chronicle of the terrain, wildlife, vegetation and Indians in eastern North Carolina from 1700 to 1711.

Lawson's wanderings through the eastern part of the state took him as far west as High Point, and his writings indicate that he explored more than 1,000 miles of territory in North and South Carolina. His travels brought him in contact with many of the Indian tribes of the day, and at one point he built a house in New Bern on "a pretty high piece of land by creekside" that today is known as Lawson's Creek. Lawson was eventually named Surveyor General of the province and played an important part in the founding of Bath and New Bern. In 1710, when deGraffenried established a colony in New Bern, Lawson helped lay out the town.

Throughout his book, Lawson reported that "the Indians are really better to us than we have been to them," and added, as though forecasting his fate, "but the Indians are revengeful and never forget an injury done until they have reached satisfaction." Another entry states, "We have abandoned our own Native Soil to drive them out, and possess theirs."

By 1711, the Indians being pushed out were the fierce Tuscaroras. Lawson describes them as "well-shaped, clean-made" people, inclined to be tall and straight. "Their gate is sedate and majestic and they are dexterous and steady." Their eyes "are black or dark hazel" and "no people see better in the Night or Day." Their skin color, "is of a tawney, which would not be so dark did they not dawb themselves with Bear's Oil and a Colour like burnt Cork. This is begun in their Infancy and Continued for a long time, which fills the Pores and enables them better to endure the Extremity of the Weather. They are never bald on their Heads, which I believe proceeds from their Heads being always uncovered, and the greasing their Hair so often as they do with Bear's Fat which is a great Nourisher of the Hair, and causes it to grow very fast."

John Lawson met his fate at the hands of these people that he so admired on September 22, 1711, during a fact-finding trip up the Neuse River. Lawson, two slaves and Baron deGraffenried headed out by boat to investigate the navigability of the upper Neuse and explore the surrounding land.

Unknown to the exploration party was the Indians' plan to raid the white settlers. Lawson's excursion took place only a few days before the massacre occurred.

The first night, Lawson and his party arrived at the Indian village of Corutra and were immediately surrounded by armed Indians. They were forced to march all night to another village inland. The following morning the Assembly of the Great met, and after questioning Lawson and deGraffenried, decided to free them. The next morning, however, Lawson got into an argument with village Chief Cor Tom and both Lawson and deGraffenried were sentenced to death. deGraffenried pled for his life, and King Taylor, from whom the Baron had purchased the lands of New Bern, spoke in his favor. The Baron's life was spared but Lawson's was not. The Indians told the Baron of the planned massacre, but said New Bern would be spared.

It was six weeks before deGraffenried, "quite lame, shivering with cold, nearly dead — my legs so stiff and swollen that I could not walk a step, but supported myself on two sticks," reached his New Bern home. He found the town partially destroyed and citizens frightened. While the Baron had been held captive, the Tuscarora Indians and their allies had carried out their plan of vengeance against the white settlers.

As for John Lawson, it is said that "his body was riddled with lightwood splinters to increase his agony. He knew these splinters contained enough pitch to guarantee them to burn profusely. His horror mounted as he watched the painted faces of his captors dance wildly about him."

others are in the beginning stages. The Brice's Creek region is just southwest of James City and south of the Trent River. Many homes are on interior lots, but the more elegant residences face the waterfront and are set well away from the road on large, wooded lots. They tend to be brick or stucco in contemporary styles. Homes on the waterfront generally sell in the $200,000 to $400,000 range depending on their water frontage. Houses away from the creek sell in the $90,000 to $175,000 range. The Craven County Airport, which only serves small aircraft, is just east of Brice's Creek.

Green Springs

Huge, contemporary dwellings on large, wooded lots grace the western banks of the Neuse River on Greensprings Road

just off Highway 70 E. between New Bern and Havelock. Waterfront homes start around $350,000, with lots in the price range of $125,000.

Farther east along Rivershore Drive, you can find older frame houses and large cottages tucked into the river bluffs. Prices here vary greatly because of age, size and lot space. Just across the street and facing the water, though not on it, is a small development of brand-new, one-story contemporary homes on half-acre lots. Prices of these homes start at about $85,000, but the value is increasing rapidly.

River Bluffs

This is a new subdivision just off Highway 70 E. outside of New Bern. It has half-acre interior lots and wooded waterfront lots on the Neuse River. It also has an inland lake. Lot prices range from $19,000 to $150,000. This developing neighborhood is well-suited for retirees and young families with children.

Carolina Pines

About 11 miles south of New Bern off Highway 70 on Carolina Pines Boulevard, Carolina Pines is a large, well-established residential resort golf community along the Neuse River. It offers a unique blend of quiet countryside living combined with country club flair and neighborly charm. Housing varies and includes modest patio homes, ranch styles and elegant two-story showplaces. Lot prices range from $125,000 to $160,000. A challenging golf course, a golf pro, a pro shop, tennis courts, a pool, a clubhouse with a restaurant and lounge and a patio overlooking freshwater lakes and the links are some of the extras residents enjoy. Homes and home sites are marketed by the Carolina Pines Real Estate Company, which is in the development.

West New Bern

This area is bounded by Neuse Boulevard on the northeast, Clarendon Boulevard on the southeast, Highway 70 on the southwest and Glenburnie Road on the northwest. Homes in this attractive neighborhood are large, brick ranch and two-story dwellings on generous lots. This part of New Bern is wooded, and there is plenty of undeveloped pine forest bordering many lots. Most of the homes have numerous large trees in the yards. Prices here begin at about $80,000 and go up to $100,000. These homes are very convenient to the West New Bern Recreation Center that offers tennis courts, baseball fields, a basketball court and a supervised game room with pool tables. The center also offers reasonably priced craft classes and senior citizen discounts. The Trent Park Elementary School and Fields Middle School are also here.

Colony Estates

Homes in this completed development are approximately 10 to 20 years old. They are one-story brick and wood houses, with many attractive, contemporary features. The lots are about a quarter-acre. Yards are nicely landscaped, and the neighborhood is very neat and clean. There is some variety in architectural design of homes here, although they tend to be three-bedroom ranch dwellings with attached garages.

Derby Park

Farther west, the newer Derby Park subdivision has one-story homes with three or four different floor plans. The builders here varied the exterior designs with combinations of wood, brick and vinyl siding in light pastels. Houses have nice-size backyards but are squeezed closely together. Most have at least three bedrooms, and all have attached garages. Homes in

both developments range in price between $65,000 and $85,000.

Greenbrier

Greenbrier is a distinguished 700-acre subdivision right in the middle of New Bern. It is off S. Glenburnie Road and is a neighborhood well-suited for families with young children and for retirees. Lots range from an eighth of an acre to more than a full acre, and excellent architectural planning has effectively blended a variety of home styles into a delightful community. Many homes are of contemporary brick designs, and all utilities are underground. Lot prices begin in the low $30,000s and go up to the high $80,000s. Homes on spacious lots begin at about $135,000. The entire development surrounds an 18-hole championship golf course managed by The Emerald Golf Club and designed by Rees Jones.

The clubhouse at The Emerald Golf Club at Greenbrier is often the chosen location for major local charity events. It contains an Olympic-size, Z-shaped pool and four lighted tennis courts. Golf club members can sharpen their skills on one of the finest new practice complexes in the state. A chipping green, fairway bunker and greenside bunker in association with the driving range are as popular as the nearby 11,000-square-foot practice putting green.

From Greenbrier's front gate, you are within 2 minutes of major shopping, 5 minutes from the local schools, hospital and adjacent to the campus of Craven Community College. The development phase at Greenbrier is nearly completed, and resales are handled by area real estate companies.

Real Estate Companies

There are many good real estate agencies in New Bern, and we have listed in alphabetical order some of those that come recommended. Likewise, there are a number of reliable building contractors in the area, and we have listed some of them for you. Also included is a list of building supply stores for the do-it-yourself homeowner. If you have questions about area real estate companies, consult the **New Bern Board of Realtors**, 636-5364. For questions about building contractors, contact Jean Overby of the

New Bern-Craven County Home Builders Association at 633-1889.

CAROLINA PINES
REAL ESTATE COMPANY INC.
390 Carolina Pines Blvd.   *447-2000*
(800) 654-5610

This 10-agent company specializes in new construction, resales, lots and acreage throughout Havelock and New Bern, particularly in the Carolina Pines subdivision south of New Bern off Highway 70 E. It is a member of the Multiple Listing Service.

CENTURY 21 ACTION ASSOCIATES
1916 S. Glenburnie Rd.   *633-0075*
(800) 521-2780

This company is the oldest Century 21 franchise in New Bern and has more than 1,000 listings throughout the area. In addition to working with sellers, the company also offers a buyer's service, meaning it negotiates price and terms in the best interest of the buyer. Its agents pride themselves in providing good follow-up and personal care for their clients. The firm also offers property management and rental services.

CENTURY 21 ZAYTOUN-RAINES
1307 S. Glenburnie Rd.   *633-3069*
(800) 548-3122
302 Tryon Palace Dr.   *636-1184*
(800) 635-6454

George Zaytoun began building homes in 1964, and Marvin Raines began a real estate career in 1971. In 1986, they combined their expertise to create what has become one of the area's most successful real estate companies. The firm has been awarded Century 21's most distinguished award, the Centurion Award, presented to only eight of Century 21's 176 offices throughout North and South Carolina. It is impossible to drive through New Bern and not see Zaytoun-Raines "For Sale" or "For Rent" signs. The services of about 20 agents are available to handle residential, commercial and investment properties as well as acreage and property management services.

COLDWELL BANKER
WILLIS-SMITH COMPANY
115 Middle St.   *638-3500*
(800) 334-0792

With more than 20 agents and a good reputation, this reliable firm's offices are downtown near the New Bern waterfront. The company operates as a seller's and buyer's agency, offering a full range of services that includes residential brokerage and development and referrals to and from its national network. Its well-trained and experienced agents are knowledgeable about available housing in all of New Bern's long-established neighborhoods and about homes on the market in many of the area's new developments and subdivisions. Coldwell Banker also handles some rental properties in the New Bern area.

D. SEIPLE LAND MARKETING
48 Shoreline Dr.   *633-4520*

Farms, acreage, building lots and commercial properties are the specialties of

Insiders' Tips

In 1894, New Bern adopted the armorial bearings and colors including the red and black bears of its namesake city, Bern, Switzerland. New Bern's athletic teams, since, have been "Bears" or "Bruins."

this company. Clients in pursuit of business or industry locations often rely on Dick Seiple to provide currently marketed property appropriate to their purposes.

EASTERN SHORE REALTY INC.

3317-E Hwy. 70 E.   *636-3050*

Eastern Shore Realty is the agent for the Eastern Shore townhouses in Bridgeton, which include both a garage and a boat slip for each condominium. It also can help you find acreage or homes in other areas of the county. Call Sandra Haddock with your residential or commercial real estate needs.

FAIRFIELD HARBOUR REALTY

750 Broad Creek Rd.   *638-8011*

Fairfield Harbour Realty operates in the Fairfield Harbour planned community. Its staff handles the sales of building lots, single-family homes, condominiums and timeshare condominiums. They also offer property management services.

HERITAGE REAL ESTATE

309 Metcalf St.   *638-4663*
(800) 728-4670

Heritage Real Estate is a growing and diversified agent-owned firm with offices in the historic district, just around the corner from Tryon Palace. The agency handles residential and commercial sales and rentals, and offers property management services. Its agents specialize in relocation and work extensively with retirees. Call ahead or stop by for an informative relocation packet, a brief orientation tour or an opportunity to have your questions answered. Heritage Real Estate's experienced agents are an excellent source of local knowledge about neighborhoods and home throughout the New Bern area.

KELSO-WHEELER BETTER HOMES AND GARDENS

1404 Neuse Blvd. 633-3043, (800) 638-1962
48 Shoreline Dr. 633-2434, (800) 846-0740

In business since 1962, the company's staff of more than 20 handles this nationally connected firm. It is a full-service real estate and insurance agency, and New Bern natives Chris Kelso and Gray Wheeler have an in-depth knowledge of homes and properties available throughout the area. The company handles both residential and commercial sales and has an in-house appraiser and builder.

LUPTON ASSOCIATES INC.

2002 S. Glenburnie Rd.   *637-6120*
(800) 833-5671

Lupton Associates Inc. is a full-service real estate agency and a well-known construction company that handles properties throughout New Bern, Craven County and surrounding areas. It is a family-run business that has been doing well for more than 10 years. One of its specialties is the handling of lots in Deerfield near River Bend.

NANCY HOLLOWS REAL ESTATE

624 Hancock St.   *636-3177*

A one-woman dynamo, Nancy Hollows specializes in knowing everything there is to know about New Bern's historic homes. She has a good understanding of ordinances that govern historic district properties; however, she handles sales of all types of property throughout New Bern. Her forte is one-of-a-kind purchases, and she enjoys helping customers who are looking for unique waterfront locations. In addition, she has assisted buyers in acquiring bed and breakfast inns and marinas. Her office is housed in a historic building next to her antique shop, The Antique Depot.

Older, stately homes are a mainstay in many New Bern neighborhoods.

NEUSE REALTY

601 Broad Creek Rd.	*633-4888*
	(800) 343-0186

Serving New Bern since 1977, this second-generation, family-owned firm focuses on relocation and total service, from the initial information-gathering process through site purchase, construction planning or resale services. Upscale and waterfront locations and Fairfield Harbor properties are their specialties. The firm is nationally affiliated with RELO, the largest intercity relocation service and is a member of the New Bern and Havelock Board of Realtors, the Employee Relocation Council and the Craven County Committee of 100. Neuse handles a broad selection of rental properties.

NEW BEGINNINGS REALTY INC.

50 Shoreline Drive	*636-5858,*
	(800) 331-8982

In business for 11 years, this company specializes in waterfront and golf areas for newcomers looking for retirement and relocation sites. It handles new residential homes, lots and resale of established homes. The firm has three agents who are happy to provide "no pressure," re-laxed tours of available homesites in the area. A free cassette tape that describes New Bern properties is available to those interested in relocating.

NEW BERN REAL ESTATE INC.

3601 Trent Rd., Ste. 5	*636-2200*
Village Sq.	*(800) 636-2992*

This independently owned-and-operated full-service agency opened in 1985 and specializes in locating homes for retirees and local residents. Free brochures and newcomer packages are available to inquiring home seekers. Six knowledgeable and experienced agents conduct between two and five comprehensive home-finding tours per week, covering 48 miles in about 3½ hours. Clients are provided with a free map and video tape, and the tour includes a complimentary lunch.

RESORT HOMES
OF THE CAROLINAS INC.

530 Hwy. 55 E. 637-8080, (800) 892-8901

Resort Homes of the Carolinas is a full-service real estate company with a construction division as part of its operation. It handles sales of building lots, homes, condominiums, timeshare properties and rental property management. The company specializes in Fairfield Harbour resales and also offers new homes in River Bend and Lakemere. A home model is erected in Fairfield Harbour on Pelican Drive.

TRYON REALTY
233 Middle St.   *637-3115*

In business for more than 32 years, Tryon is a small company that specializes in building and development. It is the main developer of Olde Towne subdivision on the Trent River. Contact Tryon Realty with your residential and commercial real estate needs, or for property management information.

TYSON AND HOOKS REALTY
2402 Clarendon Blvd.   *633-5766*
(800) 284-6844

This firm has been in business since 1972. It offers general real estate services including commercial and residential lots

and acreage, along with property management services and rental properties. There are five agents associated with the firm.

WEYERHAEUSER
REAL ESTATE COMPANY
119 Middle St.   *633-6100, (800) 622-6297*

Weyerhaeuser Real Estate Company is a subsidiary of Weyerhaeuser Company, the international wood and pulp giant. It offers an extensive inventory of home sites in New Bern and elsewhere in eastern North Carolina. Taberna is the latest Weyerhaeuser community and is advertised as a planned golfing community. A description of Taberna is offered in the neighborhood section above. In New Bern, the company established Greenbrier community development, a 700-acre, upscale residential neighborhood surrounding the championship golf course, The Emerald. Weyerhaeuser also handles waterfront

Photo: Benners Studio Collection

Fundraising efforts by the New Bern Preservation Foundation are being used to restore New Bern's Union Station.

properties in nearby developments of Creek Pointe, Dawson Bluff, Sandy Point and several other locations. Individual deep-water homesites vary greatly in size, ranging from a single acre to 50 acres and in clusters of eight to 54 homesites. The majority of Weyerhaeuser-developed properties offer homes directly on the water or on the golf course.

Builders/Contractors

JENNINGS OUTLAW CONSTRUCTION COMPANY
612 Madam Moore Ln.   633-4499

This is a family-operated contracting firm with a solid reputation for excellence in custom home building. Its services are organized into several categories, including design assistance and professional consultation before, during and after construction. The firm also does light construction work.

HOLLYBILLT INC.
3303 Clarendon Blvd.   637-4173

Bill Willis has operated Hollybillt since 1982. The company specializes in construction of upscale homes and also builds speculation houses and handles old-home restorations.

LUPTON ASSOCIATES INC.
2002 S. Glenburnie Rd.   637-6120

Lupton Associates Inc. began building in 1984 and specializes in low-maintenance, energy-efficient residential homes. It has a good reputation for well-built structures and constructs homes throughout Craven County.

NORTHWOOD BUILDERS
1315 Glenburnie Rd.   637-3011

Northwood Builders has been in business 17 years and specializes in the construction of new homes throughout the county. Company representatives can provide house plans or erect a customized home from plans chosen by the homeowner.

REGIONAL HOMES OF NEW BERN INC.
1702-D Hwy. 70 E.   633-6377

Owner Dale Gupton has been in the building business 15 years. His company specializes in new residential construction, custom building, remodeling and old-home restoration.

RICHARD HOFF BUILDERS
210 Hancock St.   633-4841

Richard Hoff Builders specializes in custom homes and can handle those complex designs and unusual floor plans. This company does not build in volume, instead Richard and his crew work one-on-one with clients to provide a quality finished product. The company also does remodeling and light commercial construction.

SCHEPER CONSTRUCTION INC.
4183 Hwy. 17 S.   637-9770

Scheper Construction Inc. is noted for its single-family homes at Lakemere and townhouses at Pier Pointe. The company specializes in custom-built homes, additions and renovations throughout New Bern and Craven County.

TARHEEL ASSOCIATES
1911-A S. Glenburnie Rd.   633-6452

Tarheel Associates is a design-and-build company operated by Lucien Vaughn, Lewis Stowe and Bud Stilley. The firm works primarily on contract to construct custom-built homes and has a combination of 50 years of experience in the construction business.

ZAYTOUN & RAINES CONSTRUCTION

1307 S. Glenburnie Rd.   *633-0106*

Zaytoun & Raines Construction is a branch of Century 21 Zaytoun & Raines. The construction company handles residential construction, remodeling and restoration work.

Building Supplies

The following is a list of building supply businesses that carry the most complete line of building materials. They also make deliveries.

Askew's Inc., 3600 Clarendon Boulevard, 633-5125

Lowe's of New Bern, 3310 Clarendon Boulevard, 633-2030

New Bern Building Supply, 3321 Neuse Boulevard, 638-5861

New Bern
Education and Child Care

New Bern residents have many excellent education opportunities. Adults have access to a state-supported university, college-level classes and a first-rate community college. Parents have the option of sending their children to the Craven County public schools or one of the many private schools in New Bern. There are also several trustworthy child-care options available for children who are too young for school.

Colleges and Universities

Those interested in furthering their education have a few options in the New Bern and Craven County area.

Whether you are pursuing an associate's degree, gaining credits to transfer to a four-year college or university, or taking continuing education courses, there are opportunities in New Bern.

CRAVEN COMMUNITY COLLEGE
S. Glenburnie Rd., New Bern   *638-4131*

Craven Community College offers two-year degrees and adult continuing education. Students are served in two-year associate's degree programs in the arts and sciences and more than 30 technical and vocational programs. The college offers basic adult education programs, two-year technical and transfer programs, one-year vocational programs and extension programs in occupational, practical and vocational courses of study. Craven Community College is part of North Carolina's 59-campus community college system.

EAST CAROLINA UNIVERSITY
Greenville   *328-6099*

A little more than an hour's drive from New Bern, East Carolina University in Greenville is a state-supported university that offers a wide range of study areas for bachelor's, master's and doctoral degrees. The university has an enrollment of about 17,000 students. Two popular curriculum areas are education and health sciences. Many working adult students pursue degrees by commuting to the Greenville campus. Craven Medical Center in New Bern is a clinical site for students enrolled in the ECU School of Nursing.

NORTH CAROLINA WESLEYAN COLLEGE ADULT DEGREE PROGRAM
New Bern Campus   *638-7209*

North Carolina Wesleyan College offers extension courses at its New Bern satellite campus that is on the campus of

Craven Community College. Students are offered three four-year degree programs — criminal justice, business administration and computer information. Wesleyan College's main campus is in nearby Rocky Mount. Call N.C. Wesleyan for a catalog to find out what courses are currently being offered.

Schools

Public

"Through commitment, teamwork and excellence, Craven County Schools, united with families and communities, will provide a quality education based on continuous improvement of student performance and educational services that will meet or exceed customer expectations." This is the mission of the Craven County School System.

The Craven County School System is a consolidated countywide system serving more than 14,600 city and county students. The county's public schools are fully accredited by the Southern Association of Colleges and Schools and the N.C. Department of Public Instruction.

The public school system employs about 1,050 teaching professionals and about 675 support personnel. The system's average teacher-student ratio is 1 to 26.

The school system offers a comprehensive curriculum based on the North Carolina Standard Course of Study. The education program includes music, foreign languages, art, dance, theater, athletics, computer classes and advance placement courses, in addition to the traditional academic offerings.

The high schools are involved in the comprehensive high school concept, which focuses on positive school climate, individual attention to vocational/career awareness needs and the identification and prevention of problems that may lead to students being unsuccessful in school. All high schools are on block scheduling which is a reorganization of school time. It allows students to take four courses each semester in 90 minute class periods. Each student completes four courses in December and four courses in May.

To prepare students for the workplace, Craven County Schools have implemented a developmental program designed to help students focus on career paths as they pursue more rigorous courses of study. Career guidance is designed to ensure graduates a smooth transition into the work force, associate degree programs at technical/community colleges, or bachelor's degree programs at four-year colleges or universities. Specific areas within the courses of study pair high-level math, science, English and social studies courses with technically-oriented vocational courses. Students entering high school choose a course of study based on their career choice. The career choice is addressed through the development of four year educational plans. The four major course areas of preparation in-

Many New Bern residents working on graduate and undergraduate degrees attend night school at East Carolina University. Post a note around town or at the local community college and chances are you can join a car pool for the 1¼-hour ride.

clude engineering/industrial/manufacturing technology, business/marketing and health/human services.

Middle schools are involved in the middle school concept, which provides educational experiences that bridge learning between elementary school and high school for students in 6th, 7th and 8th grades. Along with the core curriculum, team teaching, advisor/advisee, critical thinking and problem solving, health and fitness, cooperative learning and exploratory courses such as foreign language, vocational education, arts education and accelerated courses are offered.

Elementary education in Craven County allows students to meet academic objectives through developmentally appropriate activities. The use of hands-on experiences and problem-solving strategies are designed to be in harmony with the natural characteristics of the developmental stages of children. In addition to the core curriculum, students and teachers are involved with enrichment programs, communication skills, clustering, early intervention, thinking skills, integration of learning, hands-on science and math, cooperative teaching and learning, computers and learning styles.

The Craven County School System offers many support services including comprehensive testing, exceptional and academically gifted programs, student counseling services, dropout prevention and drug education programs, library/media skills programs and the services of school psychologists, social workers and nurses. Services are provided for students with visual, hearing, speech, orthopedic and other health impairments as well as for mentally handicapped, learning disabled and homebound students.

For more information about the Craven County School System, call the Board of Education at 514-6300.

Private

New Bern offers a number of private schools, and another is about 40 miles west in Kinston. Additionally, the Yellow Pages section of the phone book lists a number of day camps and day schools for young children.

RUTH'S CHAPEL CHRISTIAN SCHOOL
2709 Oaks Rd. 638-1297

Affiliated with Ruth's Chapel Free Will Baptist Church, this school serves about 250 students in kindergarten through 12th grade and an additional 35 students in day care and before- and after-school programs. A structured program is also offered to 3 and 4 year olds.

ST. PAUL'S SCHOOL
3007 Country Club Rd. 633-0100

St. Paul's has about 300 students from preschool through 8th grade. The school provides after-school care for its students and is affiliated with St. Paul's Catholic Church.

ARENDELL PARROTT ACADEMY
Kinston 522-4222

Arendell Parrott offers nonsectarian instruction for students in prekindergarten through 12th grade and has a total enrollment of 600 students. The school offers transportation to out-of-town students.

Child Care

As is the case across the nation, the need for quality day care has grown in New Bern with the emergence of two-income and single-parent families. Here are just a few

CRAVEN COMMUNITY COLLEGE

With more than 30 technical and vocational programs and freshman/sophomore level transfer courses accepted by colleges across the United States.

638-4131
800 College Court
New Bern, NC 28562

444-6000
Bldg. 4335
Cherry Point MCAS

of the many day-care facilities in and around New Bern.

ALL ABOUT CHILDREN
2610 Neuse Blvd.   *633-2505*

This day care accepts children from 6 weeks to 12 years old and offers before- and after-school care. Transportation to and from school is also provided.

COBB'S CHILD CARE CENTER
603 Gaston Blvd.   *638-8175*

Cobb's takes care of children from 6 weeks to 12 years old. The facility separates children into age groups and has its own kindergarten classes. Before- and after-school care and transportation to and from local schools are also available.

COLONY DAY CARE AND KINDERGARTEN
1108 Colony Dr.   *633-2787*

Colony cares for children from ages 1 year to 12 years and has a van service to and from local schools. Before- and after-school care is also available.

KID'S KORNER
403 Ninth St.   *638-2957*
3705 Old Cherry Point Rd.   *636-3791*

Kid's Korner accepts children from 6 weeks to 12 years. These two facilities offer before- and after-school care. The Ninth Street Kid's Korner also provides transportation to and from area schools.

New Bern
Commerce and Industry

Commerce and industry in New Bern are broad-based and receive strong support from the presence of Cherry Point Marine Corps Air Station and its affiliated Naval Aviation Depot (NADEP) in Havelock.

NADEP is one of the largest aeronautical maintenance, engineering and logistics support facilities in the Navy and is one of the largest civilian employers in eastern North Carolina. Managed by Marine officers, the facility has a work force of about 4,000 employees, most of which are civilian. That number continues to grow.

The depot refurbishes a variety of military aircraft and provides emergency repair and field modification teams to do repair work on aircraft unable to return to the depot. For more information about NADEP, see the Havelock chapter of this book.

Industries with large work forces in New Bern include Weyerhaeuser, Hatteras Yachts, Bosch Power Tool Company, Pepsi Cola, Maola Milk and Moen.

Weyerhaeuser grows and harvests timber and processes it in a huge pulp mill just outside New Bern. The company employs about 700 people and owns more than 500,000 acres in eastern North Carolina.

Hatteras Yachts builds luxury watercraft in its New Bern plant and employs about 750 people. **Bosch Power Tool**

Company has about 350 workers. A producer of plumbing fixtures, **Moen** has about 600 employees. **Maola Milk and Ice Cream** has about 390 workers, and **Chatsworth Products** produces computer stands and employs about 50 people.

Large non-industry employers include **New Bern-Craven County Schools, county government, Craven Regional Medical Center** and the **City of New Bern**.

The **New Bern Area Chamber of Commerce**, the **Committee of 100, Swiss Bear Inc.**, the **Craven County Economic Development Commission** and the **Tourism Development Authority** all help to guide and encourage growth of area businesses and industries.

The Committee of 100 is a private group formed by area business leaders to stimulate business growth. The Committee owns the 519-acre **Craven County Industrial Park** that straddles Highway 70 about 5 miles west of New Bern. The group owns two incubator facilities that offer free office and manufacturing space to new manufacturers. The Committee of 100 and the Economic Development Commission are constantly looking for new businesses to move into the industrial park or into the county.

Bosch-Siemens Dishwasher Products made a big announcement in 1995 that they are bringing a factory to New Bern.

New Bern
Retirement and Senior Services

New Bern's popularity as a delightful retirement location is evident in its relocation statistics. In 1995 nearly 2,000 retired couples moved to New Bern, an average of nearly six per day. New Bern's combination of mild climate, relatively low-cost living, beautiful surroundings and friendly people seems too good to pass up. Activities such as fishing, golfing, sailing, hiking and boating are possible within a stone's throw of river city living. The colonial setting of the city itself is inviting, and a wide range of social, cultural and recreational activities enhances the attractiveness of living along the Carolina coast.

New residents find the city's excellent regional hospital, doctors' offices, shopping centers, golfing and sports facilities, quality restaurants and numerous religious denominations important factors in making a decision about changing their location. Those who decide to take the plunge and move to New Bern are seldom disappointed.

As more retirees settle in the area, a growing number of services and programs are being developed and tailored to meet their needs and interests. Agencies and public service organizations are expanding their offerings, and retirement communities are being designed to create stress-free environments. Housing options vary according to the needs of individuals, and agencies offer a variety of services aimed at assisting new and retired residents.

Housing Options and Facilities

BERNE VILLAGE
RETIREMENT COMMUNITY
2701 Amhurst Blvd.   633-1779
(800) 634-7318

This 15-acre retirement and assisted living complex is near Highway 70 off Glenburnie Road. The village is a series of single-story apartment and service buildings set in a parklike environment.

The central building houses 60 rest home beds and is also the site of the community dining room, recreation facilities, library, barber and beauty shops. Facilities are available for the memory impaired, respite care and adult day-care services. In addition, the village has one- and two-bedroom, unfurnished apartments for independent living. Three financial arrangements are available: a rental plan, a year's lease or a buy-in deposit. All three arrangements cover utilities, weekly cleaning, insurance, maintenance, transportation, 24-hour security, one meal a day in the dining room and a personal emergency alert system in each bedroom and bathroom. Apartment residents are required to pay for their own cable TV and telephone services.

CHRISTIAN CARE
CENTER RETIREMENT HOME

104 Efird Blvd.   *633-3455*

This facility is just off Highway 17 S. at the entrance to River Bend. Each of the facility's one- and two-bedroom apartments has a stove, refrigerator and hookups for washers and dryers. Independent living apartments are available, and a rest home is on site. A residents' council works with staff to plan activities, and the center staff maintains the apartments and grounds. One month's rent plus a month's rent in advance is required for admission. Residents are responsible for their own electricity and phone charges, but water, sewer and garbage fees are included in the rent.

Nursing and Rest Homes

TWIN RIVERS NURSING CENTER

1303 Health Dr.   *633-8000*

Owned and operated by Craven Regional Medical Center, this new facility offers the advantage of being next door to the hospital should an emergency arise.

BRITTHAVEN OF NEW
BERN NURSING HOME

2600 Old Cherry Point Rd.   *637-4730*

Britthaven is equipped with rest home beds and nursing home beds. Additional nursing home beds have been added to a recently completed skilled Medicare unit. A unique feature of the facility is its specially designed wing that accommodates Alzheimer's patients. The new wing has a well-equipped activities room and dining room, as well as two enclosed patios and a large hallway to allow patients to walk about without the dangers of becoming lost or injuring themselves. Requirements for persons entering the Alzheimer's program are that they be at least partially ambulatory, able to control their bladders and bowels and able to feed themselves.

GUARDIAN CARE OF NEW BERN

836 Hospital Dr.   *638-6001*

This nursing bed facility is adjacent to Craven Regional Medical Center. Permanent staff includes a full-time dietician, social worker and activities director. Physical, speech and occupational therapies are available. Activity programs for residents include daily scheduled events, holiday parties and seasonal entertainment. Community groups often visit to provide entertainment and social interaction with residents.

CHARLES MCDANIEL REST HOME

2915 Brunswick Ave.   *638-4680*

With both private and semiprivate rooms, the facility provides basic rest home or custodial care. They also provide transportation to the doctor and community events. A full-time activities director is on staff.

Agencies and Services

A number of agencies and organizations in New Bern are equipped to deal specifically with problems that may confront older people or their relatives. These agencies employ skilled staff members to handle delicate situations with empathy.

Insiders' Tips

The New Bern Garden Club meets the second Thursday of each month at noon at the New Bern Woman's Club on Red Fox Road.

UNITED SENIOR SERVICES INC.

811 George St.   *638-3800*

Handling most of the city's services geared toward senior citizens, this agency offers a variety of programs and activities and serves a daily meal at its Senior Citizens Center on George Street. United Senior Services also operates centers in the communities of Havelock, Harlowe, Vanceboro, Dover and Trenton. Popular center pastimes include quilting, crafts, exercise programs, self-help and supportive services, health screenings and a wide variety of enrichment classes in cooperation with Craven Community College. The center operates a variety of programs: the Senior Companion Program through which seniors help seniors; the Silver Crime Advocacy Program for persons older than 60 who are victims of crime; the Silver Friends, an inter-generational program involving youths and seniors; the Elder Employment Program, which provides employment for eligible persons older than 60; the Hastings Security Program, an in-home security service for seniors and the disabled; the Elder Care Program, which meets special needs of seniors; the N.C. Tar Heel Discount Program, which provides shopping discounts at cooperating merchants; and the city's Meals-on-Wheels program.

United Senior Services also operates the **Craven County Information Line**, 636-6614, an informational service that covers a wide variety of topics and requests of interest to seniors and the public at large, including phone numbers and referrals.

The service conducts annual events such as Senior Awareness Day, Founder's Day, Volunteer Recognition Day and activities and celebrations on all major holidays. Tours, picnics, a grandparents' celebration, holiday dinners and birthday parties are also part of the regular activity schedule.

CRAVEN COUNTY DEPARTMENT OF SOCIAL SERVICES

2818 Neuse Blvd.   *636-4900*

The Department of Social Services offers information and assistance to seniors concerning health, Medicare and rest home and nursing home facilities. The department operates an in-home aide program, a transportation program and an Adult Home Specialist Service. It also refers clients to other agencies and organizations for help with special situations.

SOCIAL SECURITY OFFICE

2822 Neuse Blvd.   *637-1703*

Administering the Social Security and Supplemental Security programs, this office is open weekdays to provide information concerning Social Security guidelines and requirements and to answer other consumer questions. Clients are seen by appointment, and for those in Jacksonville or Morehead City, appointments can be made by calling (800) 772-1213.

HOME HEALTH HOSPICE SERVICES

Craven County Health Dept.
2818 Neuse Blvd.   *636-4930*

Serving homebound clients and those authorized for care by physicians, this or-

---

With just one volunteered hour per month, each Meals On Wheels volunteer assists 10 people in maintaining their independence at home.

Insiders' Tips

Photo: Frances A. Eubanks

Watching the sunrise on coastal waters is a magical way to start the day.

ganization provides in-home services, nursing, home health aid, nutritional care and physical, occupational and speech therapy. It also offers hospice care for the terminally ill and their families.

AREA AGENCY ON AGING (AAA)
Neuse River Council of Governments
O'Marks Sq., 233 Middle St. 638-3185
This agency was designated by the state of North Carolina to address the concerns and needs of the elder segment of the local population (estimated at 15 percent) as mandated through the Older Americans Act. The AAA is integrally tied to local governments in the area whose representatives make up the regional council policy board. The agency is responsible for direct contracting with local providers for priority services such as transportation, nutrition, in-home care, case management, housing, legal and other services. It also provides technical assistance involving training, grant preparation, community coordination efforts, needs assessments and resource inventories. It additionally carries out regional ombudsman assistance to county-appointed nursing home and domiciliary home community advisory committees. The agency oversees development and implementation of aging programs, assists in the development of multipurpose senior centers and designates community focal point facilities for delivering services to the older population.

HOME CARE SERVICES
1918 Clarendon Blvd., 633-8182
A division of Craven Regional Medical Center, the facility offers care for clients who have been authorized for services by their physicians. Home Care can provide skilled nurses, physical and speech therapy and home health aides. The organization is certified for Medicare.

GOLD CARE
Craven Regional Medical Ctr. 633-8902
This program, developed by Craven Regional Medical Center, is for adults 55 and older. Membership offers monthly healthcare seminars, a physician referral service, consultation to arrange home healthcare services, support groups, a Medicare hotline to assist with insurance and benefit matters, a quarterly newsletter and other activities. Annual membership is $15 for a couple or $10 for singles.

PROFESSIONAL NURSING SERVICE
1425 S. Glenburnie Rd. 636-2388
This service has licensed LPNs and RNs to assist with healthcare. The service can provide sitter companions, certified nursing assistance, private duty nurses and supplementary staffing.

New Bern
Hospitals and Medical Care

The availability of quality medical care is a primary consideration for newcomers and residents of any area, and New Bern is particularly fortunate to have a wide range of topnotch professional services. The quality of life and the presence of an excellent medical center have attracted many physicians and specialized health professionals to the area.

With the influx of retirees in recent years, additional healthcare services, such as home care professionals, cardiac rehabilitation services and geriatric care, are now provided in New Bern — services not often available in a town of similar size. The Craven Regional Medical Center recently developed an open-heart surgery unit that makes it the nearest hospital in North Carolina's central coastal region to offer the procedure. In addition, the medical center offers state-of-the-art diagnostic equipment and services at its New Bern Diagnostic Center, same-day surgery at New Bern Outpatient Surgery Center, a comprehensive medical rehabilitation center and a mental health unit.

CRAVEN REGIONAL MEDICAL CENTER
2000 Neuse Blvd. 633-8111

Since it opened in 1962, Craven Regional Medical Center has worked to keep up to date with equipment and services. Community leaders boast that the center is widely recognized as a leading medical facility serving eastern North Carolina and was the first in this part of the state to perform radiation therapy. The center is acutely attuned to quality medical care and implements a total quality management program.

The 314-bed facility offers a comprehensive range of services not often found outside larger urban areas. At least partly because of that, it has been named a primary health provider for a number of area counties and, most recently, for Defense Department beneficiaries in eastern North Carolina. An outstanding medical staff of more than 120 physicians, a dedicated professional and support staff of more than 1,100 and a progressive administration and board strive to combine the best of medical care with empathy for its patients.

All the major specialties are represented by the medical center's physicians and staff. Cardiac care is a focal point, with the area's most advanced services for diagnosing and treating heart disease including interventional cardiology and cardiac surgery. It was the first eastern North Carolina hospital to offer cardiac rehabilitation on an outpatient basis. Its modern cardiac surgery suite includes surgical, recovery and intensive care rooms. Likewise, the medical center's oncology services lead the area in chemotherapy and radiation therapy on an inpatient or outpatient basis including support services.

The medical center's outpatient services include the New Bern Diagnostic Center, offering state-of-the-art diagnostic imaging equipment, mammography, ultrasound, nuclear medicine, X-ray and EKGs in a comfortable private setting. You can arrange same-day surgery at the New Bern Outpatient Surgery Center, which includes procedures for cataracts, hernias and an ever-expanding list of surgical treatments. The Women's Center offers comprehensive gynecological care including outpatient procedures and laser surgical techniques, and the Family Birth Place stresses family involvement in childbirth.

Specialty units include Crossroads, a 24-bed facility specializing in group-based care of adult mental health disorders, and the Coastal Rehabilitation Center, a 20-bed unit designed to help victims of stroke, orthopedic and neurological disorders return to independent living and health as soon as possible.

Extended patient support services of Craven Regional Medical Center include home care and referral services, assuring that medical needs are met and services are provided.

EASTERN CAROLINA INTERNAL MEDICINE URGENT MEDICAL CARE
South Market Sq., Stes. 9 and 10
Glenburnie Ave. and Trent Rd. 636-1001

This new urgent care center opened in fall 1995 to provide treatment for minor emergencies and family medical needs after usual office hours. Hours of operation are from noon until 8 PM Monday through Saturday and 1 until 5 PM Sunday. No appointment is necessary. General practice and internal medicine physicians of the Eastern Carolina Internal Medicine group staff this urgent care facility and others located in Havelock and Pollocksville.

EASTERN CAROLINA INTERNAL MEDICINE
New Bern Medical Arts Ctr. 638-4023
1917 Trent Blvd. (800) 676-8221

Eastern Carolina Internal Medicine is a large group practice with offices also in Havelock and Pollocksville. A team of 16 physicians specializing in general and subspecialty internal medicine provides care for infectious diseases, cardiology disorders, lung diseases, arthritis, digestive disorders, cancer diagnosis and treatment, and hematology. The practice also specializes in aviation medicine. Its radiology department

Photo: Scott Taylor

A youngster trots along the sunlit beach.

includes diagnosis and treatments involving ultrasound, CT and nuclear medicine.

NEW BERN INTERNAL MEDICINE AND CARDIOLOGY

702 Newman Rd.   *633-5333*

Eight physicians with internal medi- cine specialties provide a complete range of diagnostic and therapeutic medical care for nonsurgical adult health problems involving cardiac and pulmonary medicine, respiratory allergies, digestive disorders and cancer diagnosis and treatment. All physicians are certified by the

American Board of Internal Medicine. Patients are seen by appointment, and office hours are 8:30 AM to 5 PM, Monday through Friday.

NEW BERN SURGICAL ASSOCIATES

701 Newman Rd.   *633-2081*
                    (800) 682-0276 ext. 8419

The New Bern Surgical Associates practice involves five physicians specializing in laparoscopic procedures, general, vascular and pediatric surgery. Patients are seen by referral and by appointment during office hours — 9 AM to 5 PM Monday through Friday. Emergency calls are received at 633-3557 at all other times.

COASTAL EYE CLINIC

802 McCarthy Blvd.   *633-4183*
                    (800) 252-6763

The Coastal Eye Clinic provides comprehensive medical, surgical and neuro-opthalmology services for patients with vision disorders. Five physicians and surgeons specialize in cataract surgery with lens implants, laser surgical techniques, glaucoma surgery and treatment, vitreous, retina and macular diseases, cosmetic surgery, pediatric ophthalmology and general eye examinations. Optical services allow for on-site selection of eyeglasses and contact lenses. The Coastal Eye Clinic also has offices in Morehead City.

New Bern
Surgical Associates, P.A.

❖ ❖ ❖

701 Newman Road - New Bern, NC

O. Drew Grice, M.D., F.A.C.S.
Richard E. Morgan, M.D., F.A.C.S.
Harry H. Ballard, M.D., F.A.C.S.
Henry Curtis Mostellar, III, M.D., F.A.C.S.
David L. Harshman, M.D., F.A.C.S.

General & Vascular Surgery

❖ ❖ ❖

Office Hours by Appointment
Monday through Friday 9-5

Telephone (919) 633-2081
Toll Free
1-800-682-0276 Ext. 8419

CRAVEN COUNTY
HEALTH DEPARTMENT

2818 Neuse Blvd.   *636-4920*

Housed with other county services including the Department of Social Services in the Human Services Complex on Neuse Boulevard, the health department provides assistance and referrals in family planning, maternity care, child inoculation, adult and child healthcare, dental care, home health and health education.

New Bern
Volunteer Opportunities

Many of New Bern's public service agencies and nonprofit organizations rely heavily on the services and talents of volunteers. Some simply could not operate without reliable volunteer assistance. New Bern has a number of spare-time opportunities, and new ones are popping up all the time. We've included several here, and you will find that volunteering with one organization often leads to developing interests in others. All organizations and agencies listed provide volunteer training.

NEW BERN HISTORICAL SOCIETY
510 Pollock St. 638-8558

The historical society relies on volunteers for most of its vital functions. Volunteers make up the society's membership, education, marketing and program committees, serve as tour guides, staff the gift shop, organize and carry out fund-raisers, put together the *Historical Society Journal* and a newsletter, help maintain historical buildings and grounds and coordinate special projects. Volunteers are in great demand during the city's Spring Homes and Gardens Tour and the New Bern at Night Ghost Walk. If you enjoy history and its preservation, you will find a niche here.

NEW BERN PRESERVATION FOUNDATION
510 Pollock St. 633-6448

Like the historical society, the preservation foundation counts on volunteers and uses their skills to operate its organization. Most volunteers are young retirees, and the foundation could not function without them. Docents serve as hosts or hostesses for home tours, help in the office, work to produce the foundation's newsletter, help with the foundation's annual Antique Show and Sale in February, cater meals and assist with property cleanup and maintenance of historical buildings and grounds. They are also called upon to do archival work and help with special events.

TRYON PALACE
610 Pollock St. 514-4900

The paid staff manages most of the year-round palace duties; however, during the Christmas season, when thousands of visitors and residents descend on the Colonial capital for day and candlelight tours, volunteer forces are called into action. Decking the palace halls with natural, handmade decorations requires the help of many, as does the making of confections and beverages in the palace kitchen. It is a very festive time, and volunteers seem to thoroughly enjoy their work.

CRAVEN COUNTY ARTS COUNCIL AND GALLERY
317 Middle St. 638-2577

Like any county-based arts organization, the Craven County Arts Council relies on volunteers to keep its wheels moving. Council volunteers serve as hosts in the main gallery, help in the office, assist with mass mailings, conduct programs such as the popular Jazz Sunday Showcase in February and Arts in the Schools, work on a variety of committees and assist with city-wide art projects, programs and fund-raising events throughout the year. If you have an affinity for art and organization, this is your kind of place.

CRAVEN COUNTY CONVENTION & VISITORS BUREAU
219 Pollock St.   *637-9400*
(relocating in October 1996 to Middle St. and Tryon Palace Dr.)

This is a wonderful place to contribute some time and help acquaint visitors with the places they should see in New Bern. Volunteers are warm, enthusiastic and truly seem to love sharing the city of New Bern. It's also a great place to learn about New Bern if you are newly relocated and have volunteer time to offer.

AMERICAN NATIONAL RED CROSS
1916 S. Glenburnie Rd.   *637-3405*

This well-known organization uses volunteers to assist with bloodmobile clinics, serve as instructors for first aid and CPR, aid in disaster situations and help out in the office. When necessary, the Red Cross provides training for specific volunteer positions.

CRAVEN REGIONAL MEDICAL CENTER
2000 Neuse Blvd.   *633-8111*

Officials here will tell you that the hospital would not run as well or as smoothly without its faithful volunteers. The center uses its 470-strong volunteer corps for everything from delivering mail to running the gift shop and snack bar. There is a junior volunteer group especially for 14- to 18-year-olds and a volunteer chaplaincy program for ordained ministers. Volunteers also help in the library, newborn nursery, emergency department and critical care waiting area. They operate the book cart and humor cart in the hospital, work in the office, assist in the nursing center and help with physical therapy and lifeline programs. The Gray Ladies and Gray Lads are perhaps the most active group, assisting with a variety of hospital-related duties. There's also an auxiliary group that coordinates activities in 25 different areas. If you have time and energy to spare, the center can put them to good use.

CRAVEN COUNTY SCHOOL SYSTEM
3600 Trent Rd.   *514-6300*

The school system welcomes volunteers to aid teachers and students in a variety of ways. Perhaps most in demand is assistance for children having problems in particular subjects, such as reading, English or math. Volunteers are also needed on field trips and in the library. Fund-raising is always going on, and the parent-teacher organization is pleased to have volunteers help with special programs and projects to benefit the schools and students.

CRAVEN COUNTY EMERGENCY SERVICES
406 Craven St.   *636-6608*

The right arm of the county government, this agency relies on an all-volunteer staff to oversee and operate 15 fire-fighting units and seven rescue squads. The service responds to emergency and non-emergency calls, hazardous materials cleanup standby, search and rescue, fire and many other immediate-action situations.

MEALS ON WHEELS
811 George St.   *638-3800*

This program, administered by United Senior Services, serves 66 meals a day with the help of its volunteers who deliver the meals and check on the recipients. The program requires eight volunteers five days a week for delivery and to help with day-to-day operations.

NEW BERN-CRAVEN COUNTY PUBLIC LIBRARY
400 Johnson St.   *638-7800*

The library seeks volunteers to provide library services to hospitals by circulating books and magazines to patients. Its Friends of the Library group helps with fund-raising and programs, and area artists volunteer to exhibit work in the library's Artist of the Month display. If you enjoy books and literature, you may find this organization worth exploring.

GUARDIAN AD LITEM
406 Craven St.   *633-0023*

This organization trains volunteers to advocate for children involved in neglect or abuse court cases. The volunteer is assigned to investigate the home situation, meet with the child and adults involved and report to the court. The information gathered is of particular assistance to the caseworker and can speed up the disposition of the case.

New Bern
Places of Worship

New Bern has a number of historic churches that are open to residents and visitors who would like to tour or attend services. In addition to the distinctive architectural styles seen in many of the downtown churches, several churches have features that stand out above the rest, such as the pipe organ at First Presbyterian Church on New Street, the stained-glass windows in Centenary United Methodist Church at Middle and New streets, the gifts from King George II displayed at Christ Episcopal Church on Pollock Street and the graceful white arches in First Baptist Church on Middle Street. All these churches are within three blocks of one another.

In New Bern, church-sponsored events attract community-wide interest. During the Christmas celebration in New Bern, many churches conduct special concerts. Another staple of the town's Christmas celebration is a full performance of Handel's *Messiah* by a combined church choir of hundreds of voices and soloists at Centenary United Methodist Church. Musicians for the performance are members of the North Carolina Symphony.

All major Protestant religions as well as Catholics and Jews have long-established churches in New Bern. We have highlighted a few of the downtown historic churches and listed just a few of the many others. This list is by no means inclusive of the places of worship in New Bern. You might want to look in the Yellow Pages for a complete list of other options.

CHRIST EPISCOPAL CHURCH
320 Pollock St.   *633-2109*

Having celebrated its 250th anniversary in 1991, the parish of Christ Episcopal Church is the oldest in New Bern and one of the oldest in North Carolina. This is actually the third church building to stand in this area. The first was completed in 1750 and was later destroyed by fire. The foundation of that first church is on the current church grounds. The second church was completed in 1824 and destroyed by fire in 1871. The current Gothic Revival building incorporates surviving walls of that second church and was completed in 1875. The church steeple, with its four-faced clock, is one

New Bern's oldest churches are wonderful places to learn about the area's history, and you can explore most of them while walking in the downtown area.

The National Cemetery in New Bern is a quiet place to explore history.

of the identifying marks of the downtown skyline. Among the treasures on display are a 1752 Book of Common Prayer, a huge 1717 Bible and a five-piece silver communion service given to Christ Church by King George II. Each bear the royal coat-of-arms. Today, the church has about 900 members. Those interested in touring the building should enter the side door weekdays between 9 AM and 5 PM.

CENTENARY UNITED METHODIST CHURCH

309 New St. 637-4181

First organized as a congregation in 1772, the current Centenary church was designed by Herbert Woodley Simpson and completed in 1904. Its rounded walls and turrets have an almost Moorish look. Standing at the corner of New and Middle streets, Centenary has about 800 members. Visitors can tour the building between 9 AM and 4 PM weekdays.

FIRST BAPTIST CHURCH

239 Middle St. 638-5691

Organized in 1809, the narrow Gothic Revival church was built in 1847. The church property adjoins McClellans and O. Mark Square. The main sanctuary is strikingly simple and peaceful in its design. The Sunday service is televised by WCTI-TV 12.

FIRST PRESBYTERIAN CHURCH

418 New St. 637-3270

The oldest continually used church building in New Bern, First Presbyterian was built in 1819-22 by local architect and builder Uriah Sandy. The congregation was established in 1817. The Federal-style church is similar to many built about the same time in New England but it is unusual in North Carolina. Like that of Christ Church, the steeple on First Presbyterian is a point of reference on the skyline. The church was used as a Union hospital and lookout post during the Civil War, and the initials of soldiers on duty in the belfry can still be seen carved in the walls. The church has about 1,200 members today. Visitors are welcome to tour the church between 9 AM and 2 PM weekdays.

St. Paul's Catholic Church
3005 Country Club Rd.　　　　*638-1984*

With its new church constructed about 10 years ago, St. Paul's is the oldest Catholic parish in North Carolina. Members built their first New Bern church on Middle Street in 1840. That building is open to the public during daylight hours. The new church features strikingly modern architecture and is in a large, park-like setting. Sharing the land is St. Paul's School, a private school.

Temple B'Nai Sholem Synagogue
505 Middle St.　　　　*638-4228*

The stucco, Neoclassical Revival synagogue is a beautiful, uncommon specimen of architecture in the area. A Herbert Woodley Simpson-designed structure, the synagogue was built in 1908 by the congregation organized about 1824.

New Bern
Service Directory

This section offers useful information about New Bern services and businesses. We suggest you consult the local phone directory for additional service providers or ask locals for references. In all cases, it is best to call ahead to verify services offered and prices. All the phone numbers are in the 919 area code.

Information Numbers

Emergency: Police, Sheriff, Fire and Rescue Service, 911
New Bern Police Department, 633-4010
New Bern Fire Department, 636-4066
Craven County Sheriff's Office, 636-6620
Crisis Line, 638-5995

Animal Services

Need a place for Spot to spend the night? Does Fifi need her nails clipped or fur coiffed? Let's hope it's not anything more serious. Should your pet need grooming or medical care, a number of local businesses and veterinarians can handle your needs.

Craven Animal Hospital, 637-4541
Pampered Pooch, 633-5822
The Pet Spa, 633-3933
Neuse Veterinary Clinic, 637-7128
Ridgeway Animal Clinic, 633-1204

Automotive Services

Whether your vehicle needs routine maintenance or something more intensive, a number of New Bern dealers, service stations and specialized shops can help you out. There are many domestic and foreign automobile manufacturers' representatives in the area, so check the Yellow Pages for listings.

A few automotive service outlets that can handle most anything are listed below.

70 East Foreign Auto Service, 1000 U.S. Highway 70 E., 633-0960
Baldree's, 2200 Trent Boulevard, 637-5552
Darnell's Gulf Service Center, 502 Broad Street, 633-3177
Lester Gaskins Auto Service, 2206 Neuse Boulevard, 637-4461
Neuse Starter and Generator Service, 2503 Alabama Avenue, 633-0719
White's Tire Service, 2813 Neuse Boulevard, 633-1170

Bus and Taxi Service

Carolina Trailways serves New Bern and has a station at 504 Guion Street. Call 633-3100 for schedule and fare information. The bus station is open limited hours.

Taxis are franchise operations in New Bern and operate 24 hours a day from the dispatcher at **Safeway Taxi Co.**, 633-2828.

Car Rental

You will need a car if you plan to see more of the area than downtown New Bern. A few car rental businesses are based at the airport.

Avis Rent A Car, Craven Regional Airport, 637-2130

Hertz Rent A Car, Craven Regional Airport, 637-3021

National Car Rental, Craven Regional Airport, 637-5241

Local Government Offices

New Bern City Hall, 300 Pollock Street, 636-4000

New Bern City Water and Sewer Department, 2825 Neuse Boulevard, 636-4056

Craven County Board of Commissioners, 406 Craven Street, 636-6601

Craven County Manager, 406 Craven Street, 636-6600

Craven County Water and Sewer Department, 412 Craven Street, 636-6615

Libraries

The **New Bern-Craven County Public Library**, 400 Johnson Street, 638-7800, has more than 87,000 books, numerous periodicals, magazines and newspapers, a children's library and theater, audiovisual equipment and an auditorium. A contribution for an expansion came from the Kellenberger Foundation, begun by the same family that spearheaded the restoration of Tryon Palace. The library's extensive North Carolina Collection is among the finest in the state, bringing many out-of-towners to this public library for genealogical searches.

Media Information

Newspapers/Magazines

The *Sun Journal*, 638-8101, provides coverage of the tri-county area. This daily newspaper includes state, national and local news from Craven, Pamlico and Jones counties.

New Bern Magazine, 637-8188, is a monthly freebie that includes calendars of events and articles about coming events and matters of local interest. Art, music, performances, exhibits and festivals are all detailed in the magazine.

Television

New Bern is home to ABC affiliate **WCTI-TV 12**, 638-1212. The station covers New Bern and the surrounding area with news and weather reports. Other television stations close by include **WNCT-TV 9**, 355-8500, the local CBS affiliate; and **WITN-TV 7**, 636-2337, the local NBC affiliate.

Cable television service is available through **Multi-Media Cable Vision of New Bern**, 638-3121.

If you arrive in New Bern by boat or plane, it is a good idea to get a rental car to explore the area.

Insiders' Tips

Radio

Besides a good selection of rock 'n' roll, nostalgia and easy-listening stations, New Bern is home to **WTEB**, 89.3 FM, 638-3434, a Public Broadcasting Service station at Craven Community College.

Other radio stations based in the area include **WNBR**, Bear 94.1 FM, 633-9401; and **WSFL**, 106.5 FM, 633-1065 or 633-2406.

Post Offices

There are numerous post offices throughout the area and in the surrounding towns and communities. The main New Bern Post Office is at 1815 S. Glenburnie Road, 638-6111.

Zip Codes

New Bern is assigned five zip codes. Zip codes used within the city are **28560**, **28561**, **28562**, **28563** and **28564**. Other zip codes that might come in handy when requesting information include:

Bayboro	28515
Bridgeton	28519
Cherry Point	28533
Havelock	28532
Oriental	28571

Storm and Hurricane Information

Craven County Emergency Services Office, 636-6608, is charged with the responsibility of assessing storms and damage. Hurricanes are not frequent along the

Photo: Scott Taylor

Wildlife such as this great white heron will always be a valued attraction on the NC Coast.

coast but should be taken seriously when predicted. For more detailed information about hurricanes and ways to prepare, check this book's Crystal Coast Service Directory chapter.

Tax Rates

The Craven County 1995-96 tax rate is 58¢ per $100 valuation and the New Bern tax rate is 47¢ per $100 valuation. These rates are subject to change July 1, 1996. North Carolina assesses a state income tax.

Utility Services

Water and Sewer

The City of New Bern provides water service to customers living within the city limits. The city **Public Works Department** is at 300 Pollock Street, 636-4025. **First Cra-** ven **Sanitary District**, 633-6500, and **Craven County Water and Sewer**, 636-6615, provide water and sewer services for those residents and business customers living outside the New Bern city limits.

Electricity

Carolina Power & Light, 1433 S. Glenburnie Road, 633-5688, serves residential and business customers in the areas surrounding New Bern. The **City of New Bern**, 249 Craven Street, 636-4000, provides electrical service to customers living within the city limits of New Bern and in Trent Woods.

Telephone

Carolina Telephone and 360° Communications, 633-9011, serves the entire area.

Inside
Havelock

Welcome to the city of Havelock. Best known as the home to Marine Corps Air Station Cherry Point, the largest Marine Corps Air Station in the world, Havelock is a diverse city with much to offer visitors and residents.

Havelock and the base have a population of about 20,500, making it the largest city in Craven County and the 23rd largest in North Carolina. This is a far cry from the 100 residents recorded in 1950. Admittedly, Havelock gained a few residents when the base was annexed, but it is still one of the fastest-growing urban areas in the state. More and more people are choosing to locate in the city because of its good climate and proximity to the coast.

Havelock was named for Gen. Henry Havelock, a British general best remembered for his courageous rescues of hostages during a bloody uprising in India in the mid-1800s. A marble bust of Gen. Havelock stands in the Havelock City Hall.

First called Havelock Station, the community saw action during the Civil War when troops from the Rhode Island Heavy Artillery came ashore in 1862 near what is now the base Officer's Club. From that point, Union troops captured New Bern and Fort Macon on Bogue Banks.

At one time, the production of tar and turpentine had more economic impact on Havelock than farming, but once steam engines began replacing wooden ships as transporters of goods, the market for tar and turpentine fell.

Because of its proximity to local waters and forests, Havelock gained notoriety in the late 1800s and early 1930s for its fishing and hunting opportunities. Area historians and artifact collectors value pictures of baseball great Babe Ruth, who often spent time in the area pursuing outdoor sports.

Today's residents and visitors to the Havelock area can enjoy being outdoors in the Croatan National Forest. This 157,000-acre forest spreads in a triangle between Morehead City, Cape Carteret and New Bern, and borders Havelock on three sides. The Croatan features many ecosystems, endangered animals, plant species and wildflowers. For more information about the Croatan National Forest, see the Crystal Coast Attractions chapter of this book.

Because of its continued growth, Havelock is experiencing more and more traffic, and the city has responded to its increased traffic needs. Streets were widened, turn lanes created and traffic lights synchronized. Additionally, a new back gate to the base was created a few years ago.

A bypass is also planned to guide traffic off the existing U.S. Highway 70 just west of Havelock to take that traffic south of Havelock and reconnect it to Highway 70 at the Craven County-Carteret County line on the east side of Havelock. This bypass will be connected to the city in several areas as it loops the city. Construction of small portions of the thoroughfare plan will begin in 1996 and continue over the next several years.

It will come as no surprise that the community shares in the pride and traditions of the Marine Corps. The most striking example of that pride is the Harrier monument in the center of town. Visitors and residents are reminded of their dependency on the military when a Harrier or an Intruder flies overhead. A sign in front of the base says it best: Pardon Our Noise — It's The Sound Of Freedom.

Havelock is often referred to as the "Gateway to Cherry Point." With more than 12,000 sailors and marines housed at the air station, Cherry Point is the largest Marine Corps Air Station in the world, and it ranks as the No. 1 industry for many of the surrounding counties.

The air station was first authorized by Congress in 1941. The arduous task of clearing the original 8,000 acres of swamp, farm and timberland began in August 1941, with actual construction beginning just 17 days before the attack on Pearl Harbor.

The air station was commissioned on May 20, 1942, as Cunningham Field, in honor of the Marine Corps' first aviator, Lt. Alfred A. Cunningham. In August 1942, the first troops arrived at the air station, and the Marine Aircraft Wing was officially formed in November 1942.

Although rumors abound on how the base took the name Cherry Point, it is believed to have been adopted from an old post office established in the area years before. The post office, used by the Blades Lumber workers, was closed in 1935. The original "point" was just east of Hancock Creek, and "Cherry" came from the cherry trees that once grew there. The airfield itself, consisting of the runways and tower, is still technically named Cunningham Field.

In April 1946, the 2nd Marine Air Wing found a home at Cherry Point and was integral in training thousands of Marines for the Korean Conflict, Vietnam and the Persian Gulf War. Now, the 2nd Marine Air Wing has elements permanently stationed at MCAS Cherry Point, MCAS New River, North Carolina, and MCAS Beaufort, South Carolina. It is equipped with helicopters, fighters and attack and refueler/transport aircraft.

Over the years, Cherry Point has grown from a small airfield to one of the Marine Corps' most important air stations. The original 8,000-acre area has been expanded continuously and now encompasses more than 11,000 acres at Cherry Point and an additional 15,000 acres in assorted support locations. Built in 1941 at a cost of $14.9 million, the plant value of the base is now more than a staggering $1.6 billion.

The economic impact on the surrounding communities is enormous. An estimated $602 million is pumped into the local economy each year, including expenditures for materials, supplies and military payroll. The 10,000 military personnel draw in excess of $283 million in pay. Add to that the estimated 6,300 civilian jobs at Cherry Point, and the payroll approaches $500 million.

One stop at the **Havelock Chamber of Commerce**, 494 Westbrooke Shopping Center, 447-1101, will certainly help visitors or new residents. The friendly staff provides maps and lots of information. The Havelock Chamber serves as a visitors center in addition to providing services for its more than 400 member-businesses. Chamber officials sponsor numerous events such as educational seminars, community services, social and business meetings, ribbon cuttings and workshops.

Havelock has a lot to offer, but don't just view the city from Highway 70. Take a turn here or there. Stop at a few businesses — you might be surprised at what you find.

Here we offer a quick look at the city of Havelock. One note about the addresses: Main Street is actually Highway 70. So, if an address is on E. Main Street, it would be on the town's eastern end of Highway 70. West Main Street is on the New Bern side of the intersection of N.C. Highway 101 and Highway 70.

Below, we have listed some general information about Havelock businesses, events and services. You'll find a listing of restaurants, accommodations, shopping, attractions, annual events, golf courses and real estate agencies. These sections are by no means comprehensive. A service directory is offered with information about automotive services and tax rates. Information about area industry and military services follows.

Restaurants

From fast-food to family dining, Havelock eateries are sure to satisfy whatever yen you may experience.

The restaurants listed alphabetically below represent only a small portion of the establishments in town. Ask locals for other recommendations or stop by the Havelock Chamber of Commerce. The price code noted below the restaurant name will give you a general idea of the cost of dinner for two, including appetizers, entrees, desserts and coffee. Because entrees generally come in a wide range of prices, the code reflects an average meal — not the most or least expensive items. Of course, lunch would cost less. The price code used in the reviews is as follows:

Less than $20 $
$21 to $35 $$

CHOP STICKS
500 Miller Blvd.   447-1521
$

Chop Sticks serves wonderful Japanese cuisine and draws diners from all around. In a small building beside a Jim Dandy Food Store, Chop Sticks could easily be missed. But if you skip over this restaurant, you'll be sorry. Open for lunch and dinner, Chop Sticks serves a variety of Japanese dishes featuring seafood, beef, chicken and pork.

MAMA ANGELA'S CREATIVE CAFE
424 W. Main St.   447-4669
$

Mama Angela's prides itself on homemade items, and the restaurant is quickly becoming popular. Lunch guests might enjoy fresh chicken salad or a meatball and mozzarella sub. Dinner guests select from a number of homemade pastas with a variety of sauces, stuffed shells, shrimp scampi and more. The restaurant takes pre-orders and reservations in order to serve you within your allotted time.

EL CERRO GRANDE
405 W. Main St.   444-5701
$

El Cerro Grande offers Mexican food at its best and is a popular lunch and dinner spot. Appetizers include guacamole salad and dip, chile with cheese or nacho chicken. Entrees vary from combination plates with a choice of chicken, cheese, beef, potato or spinach fillings to special dinner platters that offer tostadas, burritos, steak ranchero and fajitas. The vegetarian menu features a wonderful potato burrito and spinach enchilada. Desserts turn to such favorites as sopapillas and fried ice cream. The restaurant serves several Mexican beers, wine and mixed drinks — including fabulous Margaritas.

You "otter" see how much wildlife there is along North Carolina's coast.

Photo: NC Aquarium

WINSTEAD'S FAMILY RESTAURANT
1222 E. Main St.   447-2036
$-$$

Winstead's is a family dining establishment with a casual atmosphere. This restaurant is very popular with locals as well as visitors. Opened in 1987 by the Winstead family, the restaurant offers a fabulous lunch and dinner buffet. The buffet features a multitude of seafood entrees and chicken, beef and pork entrees along with fresh hot vegetables, a salad bar, a number of extras and dessert. The all-you-can-eat crab legs and the prime rib dinner are favorites. Winstead's recently expanded and is available for parties and banquets with seating for 175. The restaurant is open for lunch and dinner every day except Saturday, when only dinner is served.

Accommodations

Visitors to Havelock will be pleasantly surprised by the diverse accommodations offered. For years, only two motels served Havelock, with the majority of their clientele limited to traveling members of the armed services. With the increased popularity of nearby beaches and a local effort to attract industry to the area, new establishments have sprung up in recent years. We have only described a few in the section below.

For the purpose of comparing prices, we have placed each accommodation in a price category based on the summer rate for a double occupancy room. Please note that amenities and rates are subject to change, so it is best to verify the information when making inquiries. The rate code is as follows:

$25 to $52 $
$53 to $75 $$

BEST WESTERN HAVELOCK INN
310 E. Main St.   444-1414
$

Best Western has completed an expansion and now has 63 rooms offering a selection of sleeping arrangements. From a standard double to the Presidential and Honeymoon suites, there is a size and style to fit any traveler. The inn offers rooms with kitchenettes, balconies and Jacuzzis. A restaurant, lounge and outdoor pool are on site.

COMFORT INN

1013 U.S. Hwy. 70 E.   444-8444
$$ *(800) 228-5151*

Comfort Inn opened last summer and offers a total of 58 rooms. Rooms are designed in various configurations including standard king-bed and double-bed rooms and presidential and executive suites. Some suites offer microwaves, refrigerators and whirlpool tubs. Guests can enjoy an outdoor pool during the summer and an indoor exercise room year round. A free deluxe continental breakfast is served, and the inn is within walking distance of restaurants. A conference room is offered that can accommodate 40 people.

DAYS INN

U.S. Hwy. 70 E.   447-1122
$

Beside Winstead's Family Restaurant, Days Inn offers 73 rooms that open to an interior hallway. The hotel offers the comfortable and clean rooms people have come to expect from the Days Inn chain. The inn also has an outdoor swimming pool, and special rooms are available for those traveling with pets.

HOLIDAY INN

400 U.S. Hwy. 70 W.   444-1111
$$ *(800) HOLIDAY*

This 103-room establishment offers room service during restaurant hours. Rooms vary in size and furnishings from a standard room to the executive suite, which features a small conference room and two adjacent bedrooms. Conference and banquet facilities for up to 350 people are available. A restaurant and lounge are accessible from the inn's main lobby, and an outside pool is open during the summer months.

HOSTESS HOUSE

449 McCotter Blvd.   447-3689
$

This unique motel might just revolutionize the way travelers think of hotels. Hostess House offers 85 units in several configurations, and most include kitchenettes for longer-staying guests. An on-site laundry facility is an added feature. Hostess House is behind Food Lion grocery store at the east end of town. A Hostess House is also in Newport (see the Crystal Coast Accommodations chapter).

SHERWOOD MOTEL

U.S. Hwy. 70 W.   447-3184
$

The Sherwood Motel is well-established, having been in business for many years. Guests will find a clean, quiet motel offering 89 rooms complete with cable TV, HBO and all the expected comforts. Kitchenettes are available, and an outdoor swimming pool is open in the summer.

Shopping

Shopping opportunities continue to grow in Havelock. There are no shopping malls or major retail chain stores, but there is plenty of variety. Additionally, many Havelock residents shop in nearby Morehead City and New Bern, and military families have the opportunity to shop at the base exchange. Many of the shops in Havelock are service oriented — video outlets, hair-styling salons and laundry facilities. You'll also find a number of furniture stores, pawn shops and military surplus outlets. Below, we have chosen to highlight a few of our favorite shops. Antiques shops and flea markets are listed at the end of this section.

BOB CLARK'S PHARMACY

233 W. Main St. 447-8102

This pharmacy offers the usual items you would expect plus a wide selection of gift items. The store also has North Carolina souvenir items such as mugs, thimbles, spoons, bells etc., which are perfect for gifts for out-of-state or out-of-country friends.

BIKE DEPOT

Century Plaza, U.S. Hwy. 70 W. 447-0834

The Bike Depot offers Cannondale, Trek and Giant bicycles and makes repairs on all types. The store carries clothing, accessories, helmets and used bicycles. It's in the Century Plaza at the west end of town.

DOLLS GALORE

314 U.S. Hwy. 70 W. 447-4147

This shop offers all kinds of collector and better play dolls. Shoppers will find lovely Madame Alexander dolls and collector Barbies.

MICHAEL'S FRAME & ART & COUNTRY STORE

Westbrooke Plz. 447-3582

Michael's offers a variety of arts and crafts materials, along with a large selection of cross-stitch supplies. Custom framing and prints are also available.

PALATE PLEASERS

U.S. 70 W.
Maxway Shopping Ctr. 447-2577

This gourmet shop is a tempting place to browse. You'll find a good selection of gourmet foods, wines, cheeses, coffees and teas. Palate Pleasers also offers wonderful gift items or can prepare a gift basket for you.

Antiques/Flea Markets

HEIRLOOM SHOP

100 Jaycee St.
Commercial Shopping Ctr. 447-3154

Lamps, lamps and more lamps. The Heirloom Shop can make a lamp from just about anything — a decoy, bottle, carving — then fit it with a lampshade made of silk, cotton, muslin, linen or other materials. This shop also sells antique furniture and table linens.

PLAZA TRADE CENTER FLEA MARKET

U.S. Hwy. 70 E.
Cherry Plz. 447-0314

This place offers a new concept in flea-market retailing. With about 85 dealers and room for more, the Flea Market offers rental booths. Each item is marked with the vendor's number. When a sale is made, whether the vendor is there or not, the market's cashier handles the transaction and credits the vendor's account.

Annual Events

Havelock hosts a number of events each year that are enjoyed by both residents of the city and visitors. We have listed a few of the larger and most popular events.

CHERRY POINT AIR SHOW

MCAS Cherry Point 466-4241

This is one of the largest events in the area, with more than 60,000 people attending when the air station opens its gates to the public. The free air show features a variety of aerial displays from military and civilian aircraft. The numerous static displays allow visitors to get an up-close look at many of the military's high-tech aircraft. Cars are parked on the runways, so wear comfortable shoes — you may have to walk a slight distance. The show is conducted

each April and alternates location from one year to the next between Cherry Point and New River Air Station in Jacksonville.

EASTER EGG HUNT
U.S. Hwy. 70 E.
Walter B. Jones Park   444-6429

All children younger than 9 are invited to the park to hunt for eggs stuffed with gift certificates, money and toys. The day of the event changes each year, depending on when Easter falls, so call ahead. Children need to bring a basket.

TWO-MAN CLASSIC
INVITATIONAL GOLF TOURNAMENT
Area courses   447-1101

The Two-Man Golf Tournament is sponsored by the Havelock and New Bern chambers of commerce and draws a field of about 300 players. Held in mid-April, the tournament course varies from year to year.

FLOUNDER JUBILEE
GOLF TOURNAMENT
Carolina Pines Blvd.
Carolina Pines Golf and Country Club   444-1000

The competition is sponsored by the Men's Golf Association of Carolina Pines each June. There is no deadline for entering, but early entrants are given first consideration. The event is a two-person superball competition.

OLD FASHIONED FOURTH OF JULY
U.S. Hwy. 70 E.
Havelock City Park   447-3212

As the name says, this is the city's Fourth of July celebration and is the prelude to the fireworks display later that evening. In prior years, crowds have enjoyed a variety of entertainment including musical groups, clowns and games. Food is available.

NORTH CAROLINA
CHILI COOK-OFF CHAMPIONSHIP
U.S. Hwy. 70 E.
Walter B. Jones Park   447-1101

Havelock hosts the state Chili Cook-Off Championships, and it really is a big deal. Folks come from all over to compete for prizes and to eat some of the best chili around. So, if you like chili, Havelock is where you need to be each October. Havelock plays host to 50 of the state's premier chili chefs, each vying for the title of state champion and the right to compete in the national cook-off contest. The festival also attracts cooking teams that travel the region. This is one event not to be missed, whether you like chili hot, mild or not at all. In addition to chili, music, crafts and other displays keep everyone busy. A number of local charities benefit from the profits.

CHRISTMAS PARADE
U.S. Hwy. 70   447-1101

Like most area towns, Havelock hosts a Christmas parade each December. What makes this parade different is the fact that the featured performers are the members of the Marine Corps 2nd Marine Air Wing Band.

CHRISTMAS IN THE PARK
U.S. Hwy. 70 E.
Havelock City Park   447-1101

This is one of the area's favorite Christmas celebrations. It is usually held each year on the Thursday before Christmas. The event consists of a Christmas carol sing-along and a live nativity scene.

Attractions

Although there are few bona fide attractions in and around Havelock other than Croatan National Forest, the ones listed here are must-sees for anyone traveling in the area.

CHERRY POINT BASE TOURS

It is possible to tour Marine Corps Air Station Cherry Point and see unclassified points of interest. The tours were first started in 1984 as a way to promote understanding between the air station and the surrounding community, and they continue today. Tours are offered every Thursday of the month from April through September. During the winter months, tours are offered on the first and third Thursday of each month. Those interested in taking a tour must go to the station's main gate early in order to obtain a visitor pass, (a driver's license and vehicle registration are required, and this takes a few minutes) and meet the tour guide no later than 8:45 AM. Reservations are needed for groups of 10 or more, and school groups are welcome. Tours vary depending on activities but could include a look at the weather and radar facilities, the military working dogs, the tower or a squadron and last about two hours. For exact times and details, call the Joint Public Affairs Office, 466-4241.

HARRIER MONUMENT

An AV-8A Harrier jump jet looms at the intersection of Highway 70 and Cunningham Boulevard. Mounted on a pedestal and encircled by flags, the AV-8A is a symbol of the past. Although Cherry Point is home to the largest number of Harriers in the world, the jet was taken out of service during the mid-1980s and replaced by the new AV-8B. The most noticeable difference between the two jets is that the landing gear on the A was located on the wing tips, while the B landing gear is closer to the center of the wings. This mounted jet was the second AV-8A

military officials gave to civilians for display purposes. The first is on display at the Smithsonian in Washington, D.C.

AIRCRAFT VIEWING

The sound and sight of aircraft in flight is a regular occurrence for locals. However, it is often the very thing a visitor wants to experience. Although there is no designated or best spot for prime viewing, a good vantage point is along Highway 101 near the main gate. Runway 5 ends here and, if the winds are right, it is often used by Harriers, Intruders and C-130 cargo planes. The sound can be deafening, so a few words of caution: Brace yourself, warn your children and protect infants' ears from the noise.

CROATAN NATIONAL FOREST

This 157,000-acre national forest borders Havelock on three sides and offers visitors and residents a wide range of activities. Outdoor recreational activities include camping, picnicking, boating, hiking, hunting and salt- or freshwater fishing. For more information about the Croatan National Forest, see the Crystal Coast Attractions section, or contact the Ranger's Office, 141 E. Fisher Avenue, New Bern, 638-5628.

Golf

Unless you have access to the golf course on the air station, you will end up traveling out of town to play. Numerous courses are on the Crystal Coast and in New Bern. The closest course to Havelock is described below.

CAROLINA PINES
GOLF AND COUNTRY CLUB

Carolina Pines Blvd.   *444-1000*

Between Havelock and New Bern, this 18-hole, par 72 course is open year round. Carolina Pines is a residential resort development, and unlike most courses that get you in touch with nature, this course also gets you in touch with the neighbors. Residential homes dot the areas along the beautifully designed and challenging course.

Marinas

Those boaters with access to the air station also have access to a number of launching facilities. Two boat ramps will get you into either Slocum or Hancock creeks. Two other marinas, one on the Neuse River and the other on Slocum Creek, provide boat rentals and docking facilities. Without base access, your choices of marinas and ramps near Havelock are limited. Check the marina listings in the Crystal Coast and New Bern sections for nearby facilities. Below are a few of the closest choices.

MATTHEWS POINT MARINA
Temples Point Rd.   *444-1805*

At the mouth of Clubfoot Creek, this is a private membership marina, but often boaters are able to use an available wetslip overnight. A clearly marked entry channel is provided with facilities to accommodate both sail and power boats. The approach depth is between 7 and 8 feet. Open year round, the marina has ice, gas and diesel fuel available. Finding the marina by land is more difficult than by water. Seekers should follow Highway 101 toward Beaufort. Just a few miles out of Havelock, a church marks the corner of the highway and Temples Point Road. The marina is at the very end of Temples Point Road.

CAHOOGUE CREEK

The National Forest Service offers a boat ramp at Cahoogue Creek, which ac-

tually allows boats to access Hancock Creek and the Neuse River. In addition to the ramp, the facility provides grills, picnic tables and a small dock designed primarily to aid boarding. There are no bathroom facilities. Hancock Creek is great for water-skiing because it is sheltered, and the surface of the creek can be as smooth as glass. This boat ramp is found at the end of Cahoogue Creek Road, a dirt road off Highway 101. There aren't really any landmarks to look for, so slow down and look for the road sign.

Real Estate

Residential housing is abundant, with prices ranging from around $35,000 to $250,000. The majority of homes in Havelock and surrounding areas are less than 10 years old. Many planned communities have popped up in the surrounding areas and appeal to a wide range of individuals. Lured by the mild climate, low tax rate and relatively low cost of living, many retirees, both military and civilian, are finding a home in the Havelock area. Some of today's primary growth areas are the waterfront developments along the Neuse River and large creeks.

Because of the number of military entering and exiting the Havelock area, renting a place here for a period of time is a lot easier than in most areas. Rentals are abundant and come in many forms, including houses, apartments or mobile homes. Rental prices vary according to the type of accommodation and could range from $225 to $750 per month. Many storage units are also available and vary in size.

Century 21 Home Realty of Havelock is in Westbrooke Shopping Center and is one of two Century 21 offices in Havelock. Home Realty, 447-2100 or (800) 858-4663, offers sales in residential and commercial property and handles resi-

dential rentals. This is the place to find someone with extensive knowledge of the area and access to property in the surrounding four counties with multiple listing.

Century 21 Town & Country, 406 W. Main Street, 447-8188 or (800) 334-0320, is a good place to start looking for a home in or around Havelock. This is the oldest franchise real estate company in the city. Town & Country is an independently owned, full-service agency with a large market share of new and existing homes, residential and commercial rentals and investment properties for sale.

Carolina Pines Real Estate Com-pany, 447-2000 or (800) 654-5610, markets new homes, resales, lots and acreage throughout Havelock and New Bern. Carolina Pines handles the Carolina Pines subdivision.

Coldwell Banker First Realty, 102 Roosevelt Boulevard, 444-3333 or (800) 396-7772, is a good place to start your search for that special house or commercial property. Let owner-broker Gwen Schultz show you properties in Craven and Carteret counties. The Company also has a full property management department.

First Carolina Realtors - Better Homes & Gardens, 447-7900 or (800) 336-

5610, is easy to spot. The office is in an attractive two-story, homelike structure at the junction of highways 70 and 101. Stop by First Carolina Realtors for information about residential and commercial property for sale in the area.

The Property Shoppe, 957 E. Main Street, 447-1031, offers a wide range of services. Carol DeGennaro is the owner-broker and has been in the real estate business since 1977. The Property Shoppe is a well-established firm that handles sales of residential and commercial property in both Carteret and Craven counties, as well as rental property management.

Service Directory

Automobile Services

Serving the needs of the military is one of the prime objectives of all local businesses. As a result, and to no one's surprise, several new and used car dealerships and service centers dots the city.

AAA Tire Service, 174 Highway 70 W., 447-2121, carries Uniroyal and Michelin along with other tire lines and used tires. The business offers four-wheel alignment, brake work and computerized precision wheel and alignment balancing.

For quality tires and service, stop by **Super Tire Store of Havelock**, 447-1084. At 610 E. Main Street (Highway 70), the shop is owned by Allen Norris. Super Tire offers clients a full line of Michelin, Bridgestone and Kelly tires for any make or model automobile. Also offered are mag wheels at wholesale prices and complete exhaust work. Super Tire is celebrating its 28th year in business in 1996.

Media Information

HAVELOCK TIMES
13 Park Ln., Havelock   *444-8210*

Published each Wednesday, the *Havelock Times* covers news and features in the Havelock and Newport areas. The paper is owned by Carteret Publishing Company of Morehead City, and it is based in Havelock.

WINDSOCK
MCAS Cherry Point   *466-4241*

The *Windsock* is published weekly and distributed on Marine Corps Air Station Cherry Point. The newspaper features messages from the Commanding General, Marine news, Squadron spotlights and information from the Naval Aviation Depot. The paper also includes Socksports, a sports section, recreation listings and classified advertisements.

Tax Rates

The Craven County 1995-96 tax rate and the municipal tax rates are based on $100 valuation and are subject to change at the end of the fiscal year. Craven County's rate is 58¢ and Havelock's rate is 39¢. New Bern's tax rate is 47¢. For information about Carteret County's tax rate or the rates of nearby cities, check the Service Directory in the Crystal Coast section of this guide.

Utilities

Utility service is provided by a number of companies. Here we have listed a few of the larger providers.

CABLE TELEVISION
Time Warner Cable (for MCAS Cherry Point)
447-7101
Time Warner Cable (for service in Havelock)
447-7902

ELECTRIC COMPANIES

Carteret-Craven Electric
   Membership Corporation   247-3107
Carolina Power & Light   633-5688

TELEPHONE SERVICES

Carolina Telephone   633-9011

WATER DEPARTMENT

Havelock City Water and Sewer   444-6404

TRASH COLLECTION

American Refuse Systems   633-6330

Commerce and Industry

The number of manufacturing companies in Havelock continues to grow. Through the years, a number of private firms have popped up and are helping to diversify the economic base of the city. This growth is in part thanks to the efforts of the Craven County Economic Development Commission (EDC) and Craven County's Committee of 100, 633-5300. The county has two incubator facilities and an industrial park. Here, we have highlighted a few of the largest industrial/manufacturing influences on Havelock's economy. Although it is not a private company, we have listed first the Naval Aviation Depot (NADEP) at Cherry Point because of its tremendous economic impact on the area.

NAVAL AVIATION DEPOT

MCAS Cherry Point   466-7999

NADEP is one of the largest civilian employers in eastern North Carolina. Managed by Marine officers, the facility currently has a work force of about 4,000, but this number is growing as other military bases are closed and employees are transferred to Havelock.

NADEP was originally established in 1943 as the Assembly and Repair Department at the air station. Since then, the facility has grown into one of the finest aeronautical maintenance, engineering and logistics support facilities in the Navy. Its depot refurbishes a variety of military aircraft including the AV-8 Harrier, C-130 Hercules, H-46 Sea Knight helicopter, F-4 Phantom, A-4 Skyhawk, CH-53E Super Stallion and MH-53E Sea Dragon. NADEP also has extensive facilities designed to test and repair a number of different engine types, including the T58-400, which is used in the VH-3 presidential-executive helicopters. The depot also provides emergency repair and field modification teams to do repair work on aircraft unable to return to the depot. At a moment's notice, these field teams can be sent to any location around the world. Depot personnel were sent to various locations in the United States and overseas during the Persian Gulf War to perform such services.

JASPER TEXTILES INC.

103 Outer Banks Dr.   444-3400

Jasper Textiles was the charter member of the Havelock Industrial Park off Highway 101. The company manufactures men's knit sweaters under the "Outer Banks" label. Jasper Textiles opened the Havelock plant in 1991 and employs about 170 people.

UPS offers express letter and parcel delivery, and the Havelock facility is a regional terminal. Opened in 1986, this facility currently employs about 50 people. Call (800) 742-5877.

Military

The military plays a large part in the lives of all Havelock residents. More than 12,000 sailors and marines work aboard the air station.

Military Organizations

Cherry Point is home to two Marine Aircraft Groups, as well as a Marine Wing Support Group and a Marine Air Control Group.

MAG-14 consists of three All-Weather Attack Squadrons, currently flying the A-6E Intruder. These aircraft are expected to be phased out and replaced with the state-of-the-art F/A-18D. Cherry Point recently gained three full F/A-18 squadrons. In addition to the three A-6 squadrons, there is also one Tactical Electron Warfare Squadron of EA-6B, Prowlers, one Aerial Refueler and Transport Squadron with KC-130 aircraft and one Aerial Refueler and Transport Training Squadron.

MAG-32 came to Cherry Point in 1976, utilizing both the AV-8 Harrier and the A-4 Skyhawk. Since then, the Skyhawk has been totally phased out, and the original AV-8 aircraft has been replaced with the improved AV-8B. Cherry Point is home to five Harrier squadrons, including a squadron that trains all Harrier pi-

lots for the Marine Corps. In addition to the AV-8B, the training squadron also utilizes the two-seat TAV-8B.

Two other groups also support operations for the 2nd Marine Air Wing. Some of their duties include air traffic control, weather, runway operations and air defense.

Services

A number of services are available to the military and their dependents ranging from housing to recreational facilities. All military personnel are entitled to live in base housing if they desire and if space is available. Often there is a wait to get housing. More than 2,700 housing units are available for married personnel, ranging from apartments to houses. Three housing areas for noncommissioned officers are along the perimeter of the base and are accessible from Havelock. Thousands of barrack rooms are available for single personnel.

Military personnel are also able to utilize the new three-story **Naval Hospital Cherry Point**, which was dedicated in memory of Pharmacist Mate Second Class William D. Halyburton, a North Carolina native. The new $34 million, 201,806-square-foot hospital houses the most modern technology to support its 23 medical/surgery beds, two operating rooms, three birthing rooms and two labor and delivery rooms. Additionally, the hospital provides for the primary medical needs of our community.

Other facilities aboard the base are designed to afford military personnel a wide variety of conveniences and recreation. The **Marine Corps Exchange** offers a department store, grocery store, flower shop, liquor store and a number of small shops. There are also a child development center, a bank, dry cleaning and laundry facilities and a service center with a convenience store.

Recreational activities are also available and are geared to Marines and their dependents. These include a large gymnasium, fitness center, three pools, an 18-hole golf course, a bowling center and a number of marinas.

Although the base offers many services for convenience and fun, the Marine Corps stresses the importance of improving one's education. The **Joint Education Center** provides a wide range of educational services. Offices are operated by Craven Community College, Southern Illinois University, Boston College and Park College. The center provides services such as admissions testing, independent study course catalogs, counseling and a basic skills education program. The base has one of the most comprehensive libraries in the area with everything from reference materials to children's books.

Many more services and facilities are on base. MCAS Cherry Point is a community in itself. For more information, call **Base Information**, 466-2811, or the **Joint Public Affairs Office**, 466-2536.

Inside
Oriental

Sitting beside the Intracoastal Waterway, Oriental is known as the Sailing Capital of North Carolina. It is not a big harbor city with fancy marinas and plush businesses, rather it is a town that has managed to retain its small-village atmosphere despite the record number of sailors who visit the town each year or call Oriental home port. And that small-village feeling is just the way locals like it.

Oriental is in Pamlico County and is only a 20-minute ferry ride from the Crystal Coast or a short drive in the car via New Bern. The free Cherry Branch-Minnesott Beach Ferry leaves from outside Havelock (see our Ferry chapter), crosses the Neuse River and docks in Minnesott Beach. From there, it is only about 10 miles to Oriental.

The inspiration for the town's name came from the federal transport ship *Oriental* that sank off Bodie Island during a storm in May 1882. In 1896 when the community needed a post office, a vote for a name was held, and the townspeople chose Oriental.

Oriental is unlike many coastal communities. While most are dealing with new-found popularity and increased demands for housing and services, Oriental is enjoying a relaxed time. In 1910 the town's population was 2,500. Today, there are about 1,000 year-round resi-

dents. At the center of the older section of town is Raccoon Creek. Seafood plants with their rugged commercial trawlers line the docks alongside sleek yachts and sailboats. In recent years, new neighborhoods and marinas have sprung up around the town, offering waterfront lots, boat ramps and recreational areas.

Oriental's popularity soars on the Fourth of July weekend as thousands of visitors attend the annual Croaker Festival in celebration of that most vocal of fish. If you've never heard a croaker's croak, you need to spend more time on the water. Oriental's New Year's Eve community dragon run is very unique. Organized by community members, this Chinese New Year celebration attracts many visitors. There is an 8 PM dragon run for the children and an 11 PM run for the late-night revelers.

Oriental has a surprising number of businesses, and the fact that it is a haven for sailors is apparent by the number of sail makers and by the number of stores offering marine supplies, equipment and repairs. In the last few years many art studios and craft shops have opened. Oriental is the perfect getaway for relaxing, browsing, dining and enjoying the water, and the tree-lined streets of downtown are perfect for strolling or biking. Oriental is in the 919 area code.

For those interested in getting on the

water, several businesses offer charters for half-day or full-day trips. There are sailing schools, creek cruises aboard a small trawler and boats and bicycles to rent. If you are interested in learning to sail, Oriental is home to a number of sailing schools. Try the Oriental School of Sailing, 249-0960, or Carolina Sailing, 249-0850.

Pelican Players is the community's performance company, and the group regularly has productions. For more information about coming plays, times and dates, call 249-1003.

Town maps are available outside beside the Oriental Motel and Restaurant and at most real estate offices. Once you get the map, it is time to explore. Here are a few suggestions for places to go in Oriental.

Restaurants

The **Trawl Door Restaurant**, New Street, 249-1232, is the best-known restaurant and nightspot in town. The restaurant's dinner menu features seafood and beef with excellent prime rib, the featured entree on weekends. There is often live entertainment in the lounge, which has a special menu. The Trawl Door has all ABC permits and offers banquet rooms for private parties.

Village Restaurant, Broad Street/Highway 55, 249-1700, is a popular spot for breakfast, lunch or dinner. Breakfast is from the menu and includes homemade favorites. The lunch salad bar and clam chowder are local favorites, along with the fresh-made hamburgers, trout and chicken sandwiches and shrimp burgers. Dinner favorites include rib eyes and fried or broiled seafood platters. The Saturday night seafood buffet a favorite among locals.

Oriental Marina Restaurant, Hodges Street, 249-1818, serves lunch and dinner inside a lovely dining area. The restaurant is very popular and offers seafood, steaks, sandwiches, soups, salads and creative pasta dishes.

Accommodations

Accommodations can be found in motels or bed and breakfast inns. **Ori-**

Photo: Scott Taylor

The Coast is a great place to slow down and take it easy.

Photo: Scott Taylor

What could be better than fresh oysters steamed on the grill?

ental Marina and Restaurant, Hodges Street, 249-1818, is on the downtown harbor. Guests of this motel are right on the water and in the heart of the downtown area.

River Neuse Motel at the corner of S. Neuse Drive and Mildred Street, 249-1404, is a two-story motel in a quiet residential area beside the Neuse River. This motel offers 16 rooms.

The Cartwright House, 301 Free Mason Street, 249-1337, is a Victorian bed and breakfast inn with private baths in each of the five rooms. A favorite room is the cozy one on the third floor. Guests can make themselves at home on the wraparound porch, in the library or near the fireplace. The hosts serve a hearty breakfast and can arrange sailboat trips of any length.

The Tar Heel Inn Bed and Breakfast, 205 Church Street, 249-1078, offers eight bedrooms with private baths. Three rooms are on the first floor, five rooms are on the second floor and all rooms are nonsmoking. A brick patio, a courtyard and gardens are delightful, and

guests will be treated to a wonderful breakfast.

Shopping

Some people might call the Ol' Store on S. Water Street a curiosity shop, while others might call it a junk shop. Regardless of what it is, it is the best of its kind. The shop is jam-packed and filled to the brim with stuff. This place is really worth a look — you never know what you'll find, inside or out.

Inland Waterway Treasure Company, Hodges Street, carries marine hardware, charts, foul-weather gear, books, gifts, T-shirts and nautical clothing. The company also rents bikes.

Croakertown Shop, 807 Broad Street, offers a unique collection of gifts, books, gourmet foods and coffees. The shop also is known as a fireplace shop.

Across the street is Circle 10 Art Gallery, a cooperative that features acrylics, oils, watercolors, basketry, fiber art, jewelry and much more.

The old hotel at the corner of Broad and Hodges streets was bought last year and is now filled with shops. The **Old Hotel Gallery**, offers unique ceramics and sculpture. Many pieces have a nautical theme. **White Heron Gallery**, is a wildlife and marine art shop that is filled with carvings, paintings and replicas.

Realty Companies

If you are interested in real estate in Oriental, either to buy or rent, there are several firms that can help.

Sail/Loft Realty Inc., Broad Street, 249-1787 or (800) 327-4189, handles sales of residential and commercial property, vacation and long-term rentals along with property management services, appraisals and storage units.

Coldwell Banker Harbor Realty, Hodges Street, 249-1000 or (800) 326-3748, can help you locate a residential or commercial property to suit your needs and offers a limited number of rentals. **Village Realty**, Broad Street, 249-0509 or (800) 326-3317, offers patrons sales of residential homes and lots and commercial property. Village also handles vacation and long-term rentals. **Mariner Realty Inc.**, Broad Street, 249-1014, offers residential and commercial property sales and vacation and long-term rentals. Mariner also offers appraisals and property management services.

For more information about Oriental, contact the town hall, 249-0555.

Belhaven has been celebrating the Fourth of July for the past 80 years with a parade, fish fry, ski show, art show, dances and concerts. The day of excitement ends with fireworks over the Pungo River.

Inside
Daytrips

Daytrips are the ideal way to see and enjoy more of North Carolina's coast, so we've provided this quick guide to some of our favorite getaway spots. These places are close by and are Insiders' favorites for various reasons — the relaxed atmosphere, scenic beauty, rich history, delicious restaurant fare or quiet evenings. After getting a taste of and learning more about these places, you might want to plan a longer visit.

The North Carolina Travel and Tourism Division of the Department of Commerce, Raleigh 27611, (800) VISIT NC or 733-4171, offers information about sights throughout the state. And the North Carolina Department of Transportation, P.O. Box 25201, Raleigh, 27611, can provide the latest state maps, featuring travel information and details about state bicycle paths. Also, you should check out other books in the Insiders' Guide® series about cities and regions close by, such as *The Insiders' Guide® to North Carolina's Outer Banks* and *The Insiders' Guide® to Wilmington and North Carolina's Southern Coast.* Descriptions of these publications and an order form are provided at the back of this book.

Outer Banks

Ocracoke Island

Visitors to Ocracoke love the leisurely, easy pace of this tiny island. From the time you arrive on the island until the time you leave, you will be on Ocracoke Time — slow down and enjoy the relaxed life.

The fact that you can get to Ocracoke only by water or air has something to do with the carefree pace. Most visitors and residents travel to and from the island via state operated ferries, so there is no need to hurry — you can only come and go when the ferry does. The island's airstrip is about 1 mile from the village.

From the Crystal Coast, daytrippers take the Cedar Island-Ocracoke Ferry. This 2-hour and 15-minute ride ends in the heart of Ocracoke Village. Many people bring their cars to the island, but some passen-

Insiders' Tips

gers prefer to leave their cars on Cedar Island and walk or bike onto the ferry since there is no parking fee at the ferry terminal. Once in Ocracoke, visitors can walk or bike to just about any location on the island. Bike rentals are available on the island, as are rentals of fishing equipment, sailboats and boards, beach umbrellas and chairs, and camping and hunting supplies.

Ocracoke was established as a port by the colony of North Carolina in 1715. Early maps refer to the settlement as Pilot Town, because it was home to the men who were responsible for piloting ships safely into the harbor. About that same time, Edward "Blackbeard" Teach discovered the Outer Banks. The pirate and his crew robbed ships, murdered crews and terrorized island residents until 1718, when Lt. Robert Maynard of the Royal Navy and his crew ended Blackbeard's reign. Blackbeard was killed at a spot off Ocracoke now known as Teach's Hole. Legend has it that the pirate's head was mounted on Maynard's ship's bowsprit. Blackbeard's body was thrown overboard, where it reportedly swam around the ship seven times before it sank.

The island's solid white lighthouse was built in 1823 to replace the 1798 lighthouse that was just inside Ocracoke Inlet and remained in operation until 1818 when it was damaged in a storm. This is the oldest and shortest of the Outer Banks' lighthouses, measuring only 65 feet in height, or 75 feet with the lantern included. The light was manned by a keeper until 1929 when it was given electrical power. It is now operated by the Coast Guard.

Ocracoke Village is nestled on the edge of Silver Lake on the southern end and the broadest part of the small island. There are docks for pleasure and commercial fishing boats, inns, gift shops, private homes, historic graveyards, seafood wholesale and retail businesses, restaurants and marsh lands surrounding the water. Some homes date to the late 1800s, and many were built with timber from shipwrecks. As more visitors discover the island hideaway, more homes and lodgings are being built, and the face of the village is changing.

N.C. Highway 12, the island's main road, stretches the entire 16 miles of the island, from the Hatteras-Ocracoke ferry terminal on one end to the Cedar Island-Ocracoke ferry terminal at the other end. But much of the beauty of Ocracoke lies on the side streets. Howard Street is the most noted of the village's side streets. It was probably named for William Howard, who supposedly purchased Ocracoke Island in 1759 and is said to have served as Blackbeard's quartermaster.

Thirteen miles of undisturbed area stretch between Ocracoke Village and the Hatteras-Ocracoke Ferry terminal. On one side of the road is marsh leading to the sound and on the other is the Atlantic Ocean. This is the southern tip of Cape Hatteras National Seashore. This quiet area is the perfect spot for shelling, fishing, sunbathing and ocean sports.

Because of the town's small size, many of Ocracoke's businesses do double duty. Restaurants are also nightspots, inns feature restaurants and restaurants offer gifts. Ocracoke has a surprising number of businesses. The more you explore the village, the more places you will find tucked away.

Restaurant specialties vary from place to place, but you can rest assured that there is plenty of seafood. Hyde County does not allow mixed drinks, but you can order beer and wine.

There are all types of accommodation choices on the island, including inns, motels, bed and breakfasts and rental cottages. While not all the places stay open year

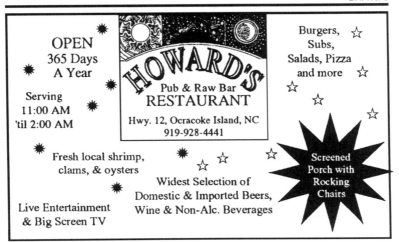

round, those that do offer some inviting winter rates. Here is a small sampling of the shops, restaurants and accommodations you will find on Ocracoke.

The village is dotted with arts, crafts, gift and apparel shops. **Island Ragpicker**, Highway 12, 928-7571, and **Village Craftsmen** on Howard Street, 928-5541, are two favorites which sell handmade crafts.

The Back Porch, 928-6401, offers relaxed dining on its screened porch or in its dining room. The restaurant is an island favorite with such offerings as smoked bluefish, crab beignets, pastas, salads, seafood prepared in creative ways, prime meats, secret sauces and freshly ground coffees. Unfortunately, it is closed in the winter.

Island Inn and Dining Room, Highway 12, 928-7821, is the oldest inn and restaurant on the Outer Banks. Guests are offered 16 traditional rooms in the 1901 country inn and 19 more modern rooms in another wing that fronts the island's only heated pool. The dining room is generally open for breakfast and dinner.

Howard's Pub & Raw Bar, Highway 12, 928-4441, is the home of the Ocracoke Oyster Shooter — a raw oyster covered with Texas Pete or Tabasco, a shot of beer and black pepper. Try it! Howard's is also the best place to go on Ocracoke for good food and a good time. Enjoy local seafood, burgers, subs, salads, soup or any of the many menu choices and appetizers inside or on the large screened porch. Howard's doesn't close for hurricanes, holidays or winter, so chances are you'll find the place open from 11 AM until 2 AM.

Silver Lake Motel, Highway 12, 928-5721, overlooks Silver Lake and offers one wing with 20 rooms facing a shared porch. A newer wing has 12 suites with private balconies and some extras, such as huge whirlpools. The rustic inn is open all year, and dock space is available for guests with boats.

Anchorage Inn, Highway 12, 928-1101, offers accommodations fronting Silver Lake Harbor. Chairs are scattered around the porches. The five-story inn stands high above the traditional island structures, and its brick exterior is atypical of the local architecture. Guests are offered a pool, a boat ramp and docks, and rental sports equipment.

Pony Island Motel & Restaurant, Highway 12, 928-4411, offers rooms, efficiency units and cottages. This well-established motel has offered inexpensive accommodations for nearly 20 years, and remodeling has just been completed. The adjoining restaurant is open for a hearty breakfast and for dinner.

For more information about Ocracoke, stop by the Ocracoke Museum and Visitors Center, which is in the two-story yellow house across from the ferry terminal, or call the Ocracoke Civic Club, 928-6711.

Outer Banks Attractions

If you venture a little farther north than Ocracoke, you will discover all of North Carolina's Outer Banks. Of course, once you leave Ocracoke on the Ocracoke-Hatteras Inlet Ferry, you really aren't daytripping anymore — you're traveling.

The Hatteras Inlet Ferry, a 30-minute trip, actually puts passengers off at Hatteras Village. From there, Highway 12 strings along the narrow islands all the way up to Corolla at the northern tip of North Carolina's Outer Banks.

An overview of the Outer Banks would take a whole book and, luckily, there is one. You can learn more about the Outer Banks by reading *The Insiders' Guide® to North Carolina's Outer Banks*. As one of our sister books, it is laid out like this book and it begins at Corolla, taking you south through Ocracoke with history, descriptions of restaurants, accommodations, shopping and much more. We are not going to attempt to duplicate that information here. Instead, we'll just whet your appetite with a description of a few of the larger attractions on the Outer Banks. So go on, pack the car and explore North Carolina's dynamic Outer Banks.

For additional information about North Carolina's Outer Banks, contact the Outer Banks Chamber of Commerce, P.O. Box 1757, Kill Devil Hills 27949, 441-8144, or the Dare County Tourist Bureau, Box 399, Manteo 27954, 473-2138.

The **Elizabeth II State Historic Site** in Manteo, 473-1144, features the *Elizabeth II*, a 69-foot, square-rigged replica of a 16th-century English sailing ship. The ship is moored in Shallowbag Bay in downtown Manteo and is open for touring. The visitors center at Manteo offers educational programs and colorful exhibits describing the motives for exploration, shipboard life and the lives of the Native Americans encountered by the English colonists more than 400 years ago. Admission fees are $3 for adults, $2 for senior citizens and $1.50 for children 6 and older. Group discounts are available. Also at the site is the Outer Banks History Center.

Since 1937, more than 3 million people have experienced the rousing spectacle of song, dance, drama, fireworks and special effects of the outdoor drama *The Lost Colony* at Fort Raleigh on Roanoke Island, 473-3414 or (800) 488-5012. Written by Pulitzer Prize-winning playwright Paul Green, *The Lost Colony* is the nation's premiere symphonic outdoor drama, staged where most say the real-life events took place more than 400 years ago. The drama describes the circumstances of 120 men, women and children who set sail from Plymouth, England, in the winter of 1586 to begin a new life in the New World and later vanished, leaving no trace of their whereabouts. Reservations are needed for this summer production. Performances are held Sunday through Friday nights. Tickets cost $12 for adults, $11 for seniors and $6 for children younger than 12. On Mondays children 6 and younger get in for $3. On Fridays, senior citizens receive a $1 discount.

The **N.C. Aquarium At Roanoke Island**, Airport Road, Roanoke Island, 473-3493, is a marine-oriented education and research facility. Tanks of fish, lots of exhibits, films, a touch tank and innovative displays are housed at the aquarium. Guided tours and field trips can be arranged. The aquarium is one of three in the state — others are in Pine Knoll Shores on the Crystal Coast and at Fort Fisher, near Wilmington. There is a small admission charge.

The Outer Banks lighthouses at Corolla, Bodie Island and Cape Hatteras are very popular attractions. The 150-foot, red-brick **Currituck Beach Lighthouse** at Corolla was put into commission in 1875 and is still active. The lighthouse at Corolla is open to the public, and the long climb up to see the view is well worth the effort.

The 162-foot **Bodie Island Lighthouse** was built in 1872 and is the third to stand at or near Oregon Inlet. It features black and white horizontal stripes. The visitors center is in what used to be the keeper's quarters.

Cape Hatteras Lighthouse was built in 1872 and its black and white spiral design is probably the most recognizable of the Outer Banks structures. This landmark is 208 feet in height, making it the tallest brick lighthouse on an American coast. The former keeper's quarters serves as a visitors center.

Cape Lookout Lighthouse and **Ocracoke Lighthouse** are the other North Carolina Outer Banks lighthouses. For more information about Cape Lookout see the Crystal Coast Attractions chapter of this book, and for information about Ocracoke Lighthouse see the Ocracoke section of this chapter.

At the **Wright Brothers National Memorial**, Highway 158 Bypass, MP 8, Kill Devil Hills, 441-7430, visitors can learn all about Orville and Wilbur Wright's first flight and other aviation pioneers. The visitors center contains full-scale reproductions of the Wrights' 1902 glider and their 1903 flyer, as well as documentation of their adventures. On Kill Devil Hill, a 91-foot hill, sits a 60-foot monument to the Wright brothers. The cost per entry at the guard gate is $2 per person or $4 per car.

Bath

The small, historic hamlet of Bath is North Carolina's oldest town. Located in Beaufort County, this coastal village is about 2 hours by car from the Crystal Coast. It can be reached by taking U.S. Highway 70 to New Bern to U.S. Highway 17, which will lead you to Washington, where you take N.C. Highway 92 to Bath. Another option is to take the more leisurely and scenic ferry route. Board the Cherry Branch-Minnesott Branch Ferry outside Havelock (see our Ferries chapter), which will take you to the other side of the Neuse River on N.C. Highway 306. Drive along Highway 306 to the Aurora-Bayview Ferry, which will deposit you

Visiting the Outer Banks in the fall and winter is a good way to avoid the flock of summer vacationers.

Insiders' Tips

on the other side of the Pamlico River. You will soon reach Highway 92, which you follow for a few short miles into Bath.

Incorporated in 1705, Bath has remained a small town, and seeing its historic sites can easily be done on foot. Today's residents take pride in their heritage, and the restoration of the town's significant 18th- and early 19th-century buildings began around 1970. Before heading out on your own, stop by the visitors center on Carteret Street and view the orientation film *A Town Called Bath* as background for your walking tour. Although Bath is a small village, it has a number of historic sites well worth exploring.

Out the back door of the visitors center is a path leading to the **Van Der Veer House** (c. 1790). The structure was relocated from the waterfront on the north edge of town. Continuing along the oyster-shell walkway, you will come to the **Palmer-Marsh House** (c. 1740), with its large double chimney. The building is an excellent example of a large house from the Colonial period and its architecture and history were the basis for its being designated a National Historic Landmark. The house opens for tours in April, and admission is by ticket obtained at the visitors center.

Crossing Water Street to Harding's Landing you will find a public boat dock that offers a picturesque view of the town shoreline. Heading south on Main Street to the corner at Craven Street leads you to the **Glebe House**. This c. 1835 structure was the residence of several notable 19th-century Bath citizens. It has been restored and is property of the Episcopal Diocese of East Carolina. It is not open to the public.

Behind the Glebe House is probably the town's greatest landmark, the **St. Thomas Church**. The church was built between 1734-62 and remains the oldest church in the state. It has been restored, and services are conducted each Sunday. Visitors are welcome for self-guided tours. Continuing one block on Main Street will lead you to the **Bonner House** (c. 1830). The house was the home of the Bonner family, one of the distinguished families in Beaufort County history. It is an excellent example of North Carolina coastal architecture, which is characterized by large porches at the front and rear. Main Street in Bath is characterized by late 19th- and early 20th-century homes and commercial structures. The ballast stones used for walls and building foundations are reminders of Bath's maritime heritage.

Admission and guided tours of historic homes and buildings are by ticket that can be obtained at the visitors center. The historic town's visitors center hours are Monday through Saturday from 9 AM to 5 PM and on Sundays from 1 to 5 PM. For information before you go, call the visitors center at 923-3971.

Belhaven

If you've ventured as far as Bath, you'll be doing yourself a great disservice if you don't drive the few extra miles to scenic Belhaven. The riverside village is on the shores of the Pungo River and has a population of about 2,500. The river provides many advantages — swimming, sailing, and skiing — and is a favorite fishing spot because of crabs and a wide variety of fish. The area is well-known among hunters of white tail deer, geese and ducks.

Located on the Intracoastal Waterway, the town is accessible by boat or car. From the Crystal Coast, you can get to Belhaven on four wheels by taking the Cherry Branch-Minnesott Beach Ferry and the Aurora-Bayview Ferry. By boat, simply follow the Intracoastal Waterway.

The main industries in Belhaven are

fishing, farming, phosphates, forestry and garment manufacturing. The county is the state's largest crab meat processing center and soybean and pulpwood producer.

Belhaven has been celebrating the Fourth of July for the past 80 years with a parade, fish fry, ski show, art show, dances and concerts. The day of excitement ends with a fireworks display over the Pungo River.

Belhaven's **Memorial Museum** is one of the 14 sites on the Historic Albemarle Tour. The **City Hall**, which houses the museum, is included in the National Register of Historic Places. The museum, open seven days a week from 1 to 5 PM, has a unique collection of items depicting the area's past. The town also has an art gallery that displays a wide range of paintings, sculpture and artwork. A re-created **Indian village** and a **Chamber of Commerce Welcome Center** are nearby.

One of the most popular places in Belhaven is **River Forest Manor**, 600 East Main Street, 943-2151 or (800) 346-2151, a rambling riverfront home that offers guest accommodations. Rooms are filled with antiques, and guest amenities include a hot tub, a swimming pool and a full-service marina. The inn is famous for its wonderful Southern cuisine and lavish smorgasbord. The original owner, John Aaron Wilkinson, president of a lumber company and vice president of Norfolk and Southern Railroad Construction, be-

Photo: Dare County Tourist Bureau

The Ocracoke Lighthouse dates from 1823 and is the oldest and shortest of the Outer Banks' Lighthouses.

• **455**

gan construction of the Victorian mansion in 1899. Italian craftsmen were called in to carve the ornate ceilings, and by 1904 the mansion was completed. Carved oak mantels surround each of the 11 fireplaces, cut glass is leaded into windows, and crystal chandeliers and mahogany features garnish the house. Two of the baths include oversize tubs for two. In 1947, the house was purchased by Axson Smith of Belhaven and the inn was opened. Mr. Smith's family continues to offer Southern hospitality.

For more information about Belhaven, contact the Belhaven Community Chamber of Commerce, P.O. Box 147, Belhaven 27810, 943-3770.

Lake Mattamuskeet Wildlife Refuge

OK, so a trip to Lake Mattamuskeet might require a bit more than a day. We have included it in the Daytrips chapter because it seems like an appropriate side journey if you make the jaunt to Oriental, Bath or Belhaven. The expansive wildlife refuge is on U.S. Highway 264. Well-placed road signs make it easy to find.

Mattamuskeet National Wildlife Refuge stretches from Englehard on the east to Swan Quarter on the west. The refuge's 50,000 acres of water, marsh, timber and croplands is managed by the U.S. Fish and Wildlife Service. This beautiful area lies in the middle of the Atlantic Flyway and from October to March, the shallow 40,000-acre lake, which is said to be no deeper than a swan's neck, is a winter refuge for many migrating birds. Waterfowl populations are at their peak from December through February, and so are bird watchers. According to refuge information, 35,000 tundra swan winter at Mattamuskeet, and more than 150,000 birds gather at the lake between October

and March. Thousands of snow and Canada geese and 22 species of ducks are seasonal inhabitants. The refuge provides habitat for osprey, red-tailed hawks, coots, blue herons, green-winged teals, black and ruddy ducks, cormorants, widgeons, mergansers, loons and many other birds. The refuge is also home to otters, bobcats, deer and black bears. Several endangered bird species, such as the peregrine falcon and the bald eagle, seek refuge around the lake. The refuge provides public hunting of swans, ducks and coots in season. For current information on hunting dates and procedures, contact the refuge manager.

The 18-mile long and 5 to 6-mile wide lake is the state's largest natural lake, making it and its adjacent canals a popular spot for boating and sport fishing. Largemouth bass, striped bass, catfish, bream and other species can be taken from March 1 to November 1. Fishing is excellent in the canals and along the lake shore in spring and fall.

Herring dipping and blue crab fishing at the water control structures are very popular sports enjoyed by all ages. Herring dipping is permitted from March 1 to May 15, and crabbing is permitted year round from the water control structures. All fishing activities must be conducted in accordance with state regulations. Bow fishing for carp and other rough-fish is permitted during the fishing season.

Prohibited activities in the refuge include camping, littering, swimming, molesting wildlife and collecting plants, flowers, nuts or berries. Fires and firearms are also prohibited without special authorization. The speed limit on refuge roads is 25 miles per hour, and no vehicles, such as overland vehicles or trail bikes, are allowed outside regularly used roads and trails. Boats may not be left on the refuge overnight without a special use permit.

Exploring the nature trails on Ocracoke Island is a great year-round activity.

Photo: Tabbie Nance

Nearby accommodations can be found in Englehard, Fairfield, Swan Quarter and Belhaven. For additional information about area accommodations and restaurants, write or call Hyde County Chamber of Commerce, P.O. Box 178, Swan Quarter 27885, 925-5201.

For information about Mattamuskeet National Wildlife Refuge, contact the refuge headquarters, Route 1, Box N-2, Swan Quarter 27855, 926-4021.

Wilmington

A visit to Wilmington will probably require more than a day if you want to do more than drive into town, walk the waterfront and return to the Crystal Coast. This upscale but laid-back river city is about 45 miles south of Jacksonville on Highway 17, about a 2-hour drive from the Crystal Coast area, and is a good jumping off point to explore several nearby beaches and attractions.

There is much to discover about this delightful city and its nearby attractions. For a complete guide to accommodations, restaurants, shopping, sightseeing and beaches, pick up a copy of *The Insiders' Guide® to Wilmington and North Carolina's Southern Coast*. The tele-

phone area code for all numbers in the Wilmington area is 910.

There are two plantations that make for interesting sidetrips while in the Wilmington area. **Poplar Grove Historic Plantation**, 686-9989, is an estate at Scotts Hill, 9 miles north of Wilmington on Highway 17. The 628-acre plantation is open to the public February through December and is listed on the National Register of Historic Places.

Orton Plantation and Gardens, just south of the city and a few miles off Highway 17, features a tour of the outbuildings; gardens of brilliant azaleas; Luola's Chapel, built in 1915; and an exterior view of Orton House, built in 1735. The house is one of the region's oldest historically significant residences in continuous use. The plantation is open March through November. For information, call 371-6851.

Several nearby beaches and attractions are a few minutes drive from downtown Wilmington. Fifteen minutes from the town hub lies **Wrightsville Beach**, which is primarily a family beach and small island community that features a number of quality hotels, motels, apartments, cottages, condominium developments and many marvelous seafood restaurants.

Down U.S. Highway 421 is **Carolina Beach**, best known for its wide, uncrowded shore, swimming, surfing, pier fishing and deep-water charter boat fishing. Its shops, water slides, boardwalk and family amusement park offer something for everyone. Carolina Beach State Park, on the Intracoastal Waterway at Carolina Beach, is known for its collection of diverse plants, including the endangered Venus's flytrap. The state park has 1,773 acres with a marina, picnicking spots, hiking areas and a camping area. Call 458-8206 for general information or 458-7770 for the marina.

Continuing down U.S. Highway 421 is **Kure Beach**, a site convenient to several attractions. It is adjacent to Historic Fort Fisher and is less than 2 miles from the N.C. Aquarium. The Fort Fisher Historic Site on U.S. Highway 421 is near the mouth of the Cape Fear River and includes the remains of the old fort, a visitors center, a museum with items salvaged from blockade runners and a reconstructed gun battery. Guided tours of the old earthwork fortifications are available, and the site's 287 acres offer 4 miles of recreational beach, fishing and swimming areas, nature trails, boat ramps, picnic areas and refreshment facilities.

Nearby, the **N. C. Aquarium at Fort Fisher** houses display tanks, the largest shark tank in the state, a hands-on touch tank and changing displays and exhibits. One of the state's three aquariums, it is open year round and activities include films, talks, lectures, field trips, workshops and educational programs. For information call 458-8257.

Back to the river city of Wilmington. This historic town is home to one of the East Coast's fastest-growing deep-water ports. During the Revolutionary War, Wilmington gained importance as a point of entry, and its port was the last one on the Atlantic coast open to blockade runners during the Civil War. Continuous restoration and preservation make the town a history buff's delight. Its fast-growing population includes many students who attend the state university, UNC-Wilmington.

Almost everyone who visits Wilmington includes a tour of the Battleship *North Carolina*, 350-1817, on the Wilmington waterfront.

Another "must see" in Wilmington is **St. John's Museum of Art**, 763-0281, at 114 Orange Street in the historic district. Housed in three restored buildings dating from 1804, the museum exhibits one of the world's major collections of romantic color prints by renowned 19th-century American artist Mary Cassatt.

The **Bellamy Mansion Museum of Design Arts**, 503 Market Street, 251-3700, is a classic Victorian example of Greek Revival and Italianate architecture. The mansion currently houses a museum of the design arts, embracing regional architecture completed in 1861, landscape architecture, preservation and decorative arts.

Another point of interest is **Brunswick Town** on N.C. Highway 133 just off Highway 17, the site of the first successful European colony in the region. There are excavated ruins of the Colonial port town founded in 1726 and burned by the British in 1776. Displays include St. Philip's Church; Russellborough, the home of two royal governors; and the earthen mounds of the Confederate Fort Anderson.

Cape Fear Museum, 814 Market Street, (910) 341-4350, is a must for history buffs. The long-term exhibition "Waves and Currents: The Lower Cape Fear Story," follows the progress of the Lower Cape Fear from settlement to the

20th century and presents an expansive picture of southeastern North Carolina's heritage. Scenes come alive with life-size figures and miniature re-creations of Wilmington's waterfront, c. 1863, and the Fort Fisher Battle paints a picture of antebellum and Civil War times. Interactive children's activities, videos, changing exhibitions and special events add vitality to this learning experience.

Thalian Hall, 310 Chestnut Street, (910) 343-3664 or (800) 523-2820, is a historic center for performing arts. The hall regularly hosts dramatic and musical performances, many featuring national stars.

For shopping, Wilmington's downtown streets are lined with unique stores and restaurants. Be sure to check out the **Cotton Exchange**, 321 N. Front Street, 343-9896. Housed in eight restored 19th-century buildings on the waterfront, it features distinctive shops and several good restaurants. **Independence Mall** at Oleander Drive and Independence Boulevard, 392-1776, is home to more than 90 stores.

For an overnight stay, Wilmington has a number of fine chain hotels, and delightful bed and breakfasts are bountiful in the downtown historic district. The **Inn at St. Thomas Court**, 101 S. Second Street, 343-1800; the **Worth House**, 412 S. Third Street, 762-8562; the **Graystone Inn**, 100 S. Third Street, 763-2000, and **The Curran House**, 312 S. Third St., 763-6603, are several noteworthy examples.

The river city abounds with fine restaurants offering delectable food. Some that come highly recommended are **Cafe Atlantique**, Market Street at Water Street, 763-8100; **Elijah's** in Chandler's Wharf, 343-1448; **The Pilot House** in Chandler's Wharf, 343-0200; **Caffe Phoenix**, 9 S. Front St., 343-1395; **Szechuan 132**, 419 College Road, 799-1426; **Crooks By The River**, 138 S. Front Street, 762-8898. But these are just a few of the many wonderful eateries available.

In spring, Wilmington's annual **Azalea Festival** draws visitors from miles around. Hundreds of lovely, old Southern homes on lots filled with huge trees draped with Spanish moss are surrounded by blooming azaleas. The entire community gets in on the act, with parades, contests and citywide celebrations. For information about the festival, call (910) 763-0905.

Index of Advertisers

Index

ORDER FORM
Fast and Simple!

Mail to:
Insiders Guides Inc.
P.O. Drawer 2057
Manteo, NC 27954

Or:
for VISA or
MasterCard orders call
(800) 765-BOOK

Name _____

Address _____

City/State/Zip _____

Qty.	Title/Price	Shipping	Amount
	Insiders' Guide to Richmond/$14.95	$3.00	
	Insiders' Guide to Williamsburg/$14.95	$3.00	
	Insiders' Guide to Virginia's Blue Ridge/$14.95	$3.00	
	Insiders' Guide to Virginia's Chesapeake Bay/$14.95	$3.00	
	Insiders' Guide to Washington, DC/$14.95	$3.00	
	Insiders' Guide to North Carolina's Outer Banks/$14.95	$3.00	
	Insiders' Guide to Wilmington, NC/$14.95	$3.00	
	Insiders' Guide to North Carolina's Crystal Coast/$12.95	$3.00	
	Insiders' Guide to North Carolina's Mountains/$14.95	$3.00	
	Insiders' Guide to Myrtle Beach/$14.95	$3.00	
	Insiders' Guide to Atlanta/$14.95	$3.00	
	Insiders' Guide to Boca Raton & the Palm Beaches/$14.95	$3.00	
	Insiders' Guide to Sarasota/Bradenton/$14.95	$3.00	
	Insiders' Guide to Northwest Florida/$14.95	$3.00	
	Insiders' Guide to Tampa Bay/$14.95	$3.00	
	Insiders' Guide to Mississippi/$14.95	$3.00	
	Insiders' Guide to Lexington, KY/$14.95	$3.00	
	Insiders' Guide to Louisville/$14.95	$3.00	
	Insiders' Guide to Cincinnati/$14.95	$3.00	
	Insiders' Guide to the Twin Cities/$14.95	$3.00	
	Insiders' Guide to Boulder/$14.95	$3.00	
	Insiders' Guide to Denver/$14.95	$3.00	
	Insiders' Guide to Branson/$14.95	$3.00	
	Insiders' Guide to Civil War in the Eastern Theater/$14.95	$3.00	

Payment in full (check or money order) must
accompany this order form.
Please allow 2 weeks for delivery.

N.C. residents add 6% sales tax _____

Total _____